M000169224

INFORMATION
AND COORDINATION

Library of
1881

INFORMATION AND COORDINATION

Essays in Macroeconomic Theory

AXEL LEIJONHUFVUD

New York   Oxford
OXFORD UNIVERSITY PRESS
1981

Copyright © 1981 by Oxford University Press, Inc.

Library of Congress Cataloging in Publication Data

Leijonhufvud, Axel.
Information and coordination.

Bibliography: p.
Includes index.
1. Macroeconomics—Addresses, essays, lectures.
2. Money—Addresses, essays, lectures.   I. Title.
HB171.L616   339.3   80-15166
ISBN 0-19-502814-7
ISBN 0-19-502815-5 (pbk.)

Printing (last digit): 9 8 7 6 5 4 3 2 1

Printed in the United States of America

Preface

Coordination because macroeconomics, in this book at least, is the study of the coordination of activities in large, complex, economic systems. *Information* because that is the perspective from which macroeconomics is approached in these essays. Thus my title.

When the earliest of these essays were written, the altogether dominant approach to macroeconomics explained coordination failures—and most importantly, of course, large scale unemployment—as the consequence of rigidities in the economic system which prevent it from adjusting appropriately to changing conditions. Within this approach, it is generally not an interesting question whether individual agents do or do not correctly perceive the potential gains from trade that the existing rigidities in any case will prevent them from exploiting. Hence, one may as well assume that they have full information about their opportunities since this assumption will justify reliance on the standard conceptual apparatus of static equilibrium theory. Economists of this persuasion, consequently, have little reason to question the adequacy of standard neo-Walrasian theory as a microfoundation for macroeconomics; they are likely to accept the characterization of Keynes as a Classic laying uncommon stress on the rigidity of money wages; and they are also apt to be content with IS-LM as the general framework for macroeconomic analysis.

In the incomplete information approach followed here, coordination failures are explained as the consequence of the failure of agents to perceive correctly and completely the opportunities present in the system. Thus, stickiness of certain prices, for example, are interpreted not as due to constraints on price setters, but as due to their ignorance of changes in relevant market conditions. Economists who try to follow this approach make trouble for themselves: since all the constructs of static theory tend to be fashioned on the assumption that agents do know market conditions (i.e., the demand and supply curves they face), this tool-kit becomes treacherous to use; the relationship between microeconomics and macroeconomics becomes problematical; and even the simplest IS-LM construction appears productive of obscure little riddles.

Whether these disadvantages are worth suffering for such promises as the information approach may offer is ultimately for the reader to decide. This book brings together my attempts to reexamine the main questions of macroeconomic theory, and the answers that have been given to them, from this angle. My own commitment to this approach starts from the conviction that what was, some fifteen or twenty years ago, the commonly accepted conclusion to the Keynes and the Classics debate was essentially an impossible one. Preoccupation with the Keynes and the Classics issues stemmed in turn from dissatisfaction, developed during student days, with the unclear relationship between the (neo-Walrasian) microeconomics and the (Keynesian) macroeconomics that were standard fare around 1960. These concerns are the most often recurring ones in this collection—to the point, I am afraid, of a good deal of repetition that could not be eliminated without editing some of the papers out of their original shape.

The first four chapters are essentially attempts to summarize parts of my 1968 book, *On Keynesian Economics and the Economics of Keynes,* and to emphasize certain themes in it. The previously unpublished No. 8 also dates from this time. Chapter 5 originated as classnotes with the pedagogical objective of teaching students to recognize nonsense about Say's Law when they see it—which is bound to be often.

There is not much of what T. S. Kuhn would call "normal science" in this collection, that is, not much in the way of puzzle-solving within the confines of given "paradigms." Instead, these papers are mainly attempts to understand the ill-defined relationships between different types of economic theory or between contending theories. One does not study the relationships between theories so much for its own sake as to try to perceive what a viable synthesis might look like—and what must be discarded and what constructed in order to move in the direction of such a synthesis.

I do not have a synthesis but I have two proposals in that direction. The first is the "corridor-hypothesis" of Chapter 6 which seeks to reconcile Keynesian and neoclassical economics in a different manner from the so-called neoclassical synthesis. The second is the suggestion, in Chapter 7, that the Liquidity Preference hypothesis of interest rate determination—that is, the hypothesis that the excess demand for money governs the price of bonds—be rejected, and the propositions derived from it weeded out of Keynesian macrotheory, so as to achieve, among other things, an understandable relation between what then remains of Keynesianism and Monetarism.

Chapters 8 through 10 deal with monetary matters. Chapter 8 quibbles diffidently with the economist from whom I have learned the most over the outlines of the history of monetary theory. The two following chapters on inflation show all too plainly that they were written (in the winter of 1974–75) in haste and ill-temper. But Chapter 9 is roughly right, whereas the monetary theory that implies that inflation has trivial consequences is precisely wrong. And Chapter 10 points out what should be self-evident but has not been: that the notion of a social welfare function with inflation and unemployment as its arguments is utter nonsense and, in the nature of nonsense, dangerous when taken seriously. So they are reprinted here without any attempt to edit into them more coherence and balance than they originally possessed.

Chapters 10 through 12 have been put at the end of the book because they are neither about the economy, nor about economics, but mostly about how economists do economics. This is a sometimes fascinating but seldom edifying subject which, as a diversion from real economics, should be put in its place. The 1975 Conference on Growth of Knowledge theories that the Latsis Foundation arranged in Napflion, Greece, with participation of philosophers, physicists, and economists was the intellectually most rewarding conference I have ever attended. Chapter 11 is on the whole a product of that conference—it does not much resemble my contribution to the actual proceedings. Chapter 12 had for some years such a successful *zamidsat* circulation that I am almost sorry I let it get into print. Once done, twice won't hurt.

I have been a member of the UCLA faculty since 1964, and am grateful to my colleagues and students there for the stimulating and congenial environment in which these papers were written. No one will be surprised if I single out Robert Clower in this connection. In the UCLA spirit, responsibility for remaining errors will be allocated to the highest bidder.

I wish to thank Lorraine Grams, Jere Kim, Kevin Quinn, and David Blair for their assistance in putting the collection together.

My gratitude to Earlene and to my daughters, Gabriella and Christina, extends far beyond the making of this book.

Strasbourg   A. L.
June 1980

Acknowledgments

I wish to express my appreciation to the below-mentioned parties for their permissions to reprint the works indicated.

To the American Economic Association for "Keynes and the Keynesians: A Suggested Interpretation," *American Economic Review*, May 1967.

To the Western Economic Association and the editor of *Economic Inquiry* for "Keynes and the Effectiveness of Monetary Policy," *Western Economic Journal*, March 1968; and for "Life Among the Econ," *Western Economic Journal*, September 1973.

To the Institute of Economic Affairs, London, for *Keynes and the Classics: Two Lectures*, Institute of Economic Affairs, London 1969.

To the editor of the *Intermountain Economic Review* and to my co-author, Robert W. Clower, for "Say's Principle, What It Means and Doesn't Mean," *Intermountain Economic Review*, Fall 1973.

To the editor of the *Scandinavian Economic Journal* for "Effective Demand Failures," *Swedish Economic Journal*, March 1973.

To the International Economic Association and to Macmillan, London and Basingstoke, for "Costs and Consequences of Inflation," in G. C. Harcourt, ed., *The Microeconomic Foundations of Macroeconomics*, Proceedings of a 1975 International Economic Association Conference in S'Agaro, Spain, Macmillan, London 1977; and for "Inflation and the Economists: Critique," published as an Appendix to the previous paper.

To the Cambridge University Press and Spiro Latsis for

ACKNOWLEDGMENTS

"Schools, 'Revolutions,' and Research Programmes in Economic Theory," in Spiro Latsis, ed., *Method and Appraisal in Economics,* Cambridge University Press, Cambridge 1976.

An earlier version of "The Wicksell Connection: Variations on a Theme," was circulated as a Report of the Institute of Advanced Studies in Jerusalem. A later version appeared in the UCLA Working Paper series.

The review article, "Monetary Theory in Hicksian Perspective," printed here as written in 1968, has not been previously published.

Contents

INFORMATION
AND COORDINATION

CHAPTER ONE

Keynes and the Keynesians: A Suggested Interpretation

I

One must be careful in applying the epithet "Keynesian" nowadays. I propose to use it in the broadest possible sense and let "Keynesian economics" be synonymous with the "majority school" macroeconomics which has evolved out of the debates triggered by Keynes's *General Theory*. Keynesian economics, in this popular sense, is far from being a homogenous doctrine. The common denominator, which lends some justification to the identification of a majority school, is the class of models generally used. The prototype of these models dates back to the famous paper by Hicks[1] the title of which I have taken the liberty of paraphrasing. This standard model appears to me a singularly inadequate vehicle for the interpretation of Keynes's ideas. The juxtaposition of Keynes and the Keynesians in my title is based on this contention.

Within the majority school, at least two major factions live in recently peaceful but nonetheless uneasy coexistence. With more brevity than accuracy, they may be labeled the "Revolutionary Orthodoxy" and the "Neoclassical Resurgence." Both employ the standard model but with different specifications of the various elasticities and adjustment velocities. In its more extreme orthodox form, the model is supplied with wage rigidity, liquidity trap, and constant capital-output ratio, and manifests a more or less universal "elasticity pessimism," particularly with regard to the interest-elasticities of "real" variables. The ortho-

1. Hicks (1937).

3

doxy tends to slight monetary in favor of fiscal stabilization policies. The neoclassical faction may be sufficiently character- ized by negating these statements. As described, the orthodoxy is hardly a very reputable position at the present time. Its influ- ence in the currently most fashionable fields has been steadily diminishing, but it seems to have found a refuge in business cycle theory—and, of course, in the teaching of undergraduate macroeconomics.

The terms of the truce between the two factions comprise two propositions: (1) the model which Keynes called his "gen- eral theory" is but a special case of the classical theory, obtained by imposing certain restrictive assumptions on the latter; and (2) the Keynesian special case is nonetheless important because, as it happens, it is more relevant to the real world than the gen- eral (equilibrium) theory. Together the two propositions make a compromise acceptable to both parties, permitting a decent burial of the major issues which almost everyone has grown tired of debating—namely, the roles of relative values and of money—and, between them, the role of the interest rate—in the "Keynesian system." Keynes thought he had made a major contribution towards a synthesis of the theory of money and "our fundamental theory of value".[2] But the truce between the orthodox and the neoclassicists is based on the common under- standing that his system was *sui generis*—a theory in which nei- ther relative values nor monetary phenomena are "important."

This compromise defines, as briefly as seems possible, the result of what Clower aptly calls the "Keynesian Counterrevolu- tion."[3]

II

That a model with wage rigidity as its main distinguishing fea- ture should become widely accepted as crystallizing the experi- ence of the unprecedented wage deflation of the Great Depres- sion is one of the more curious aspects of the development of Keynesianism, comparable in this regard to the orthodox view that "money is unimportant"—a conclusion presumably

2. Keynes (1936), pp. vi–vii.
3. Clower (1965).

prompted by the worst banking debacle in U.S. history. The emphasis on the "rigidity" of wages, which one finds in the New Economics, reveals the judgment that wages did not fall enough in the early 1930's. Keynes, in contrast, judged that they declined too much by far. It has been noted before that, to Keynes, wage rigidity was a policy recommendation and not a behavioral assumption.[4]

Keynes's theory was dynamic. His model was static. The method of trying to analyze dynamic processes with comparative static apparatus Keynes borrowed from Marshall. The crucial difference lies in Keynes's inversion of the ranking of price- and quantity-adjustment velocities underlying Marshall's distinction between the "market day" and the "short run." The initial response to a decline in demand is a quantity adjustment. Clower's investigation of a system, which responds to deflationary disturbances in the first instance by quantity adjustments, shows that the characteristic Keynesian income-constrained, or "multiplier," process can be explicated in terms of a general equilibrium framework.[5] Such a model departs from the traditional Walrasian full employment model only in one, eminently reasonable, respect: trading at "false prices"—i.e., prices which do not allow the realization of all desired transactions—may take place. Transactors who fail to realize their desired sales, e.g., in the labor market, will curtail their effective demands in other markets. This implies the amplification of the initial disturbance typical of Keynes's multiplier analysis.

The strong assumption of "rigid" wages is not necessary to the explanation of such system behavior. It is sufficient only to give up the equally strong assumption of instantaneous price adjustments. Systems with finite price velocities will show Keynesian multiplier responses to initial changes in the rate of money expenditures. It is not necessary, moreover, to rely on "monopolies," labor unions, minimum wage laws, or other institutional constraints on the utility maximizing behavior of individual transactors in order to explain finite price velocities. Keynes, in contrast to many New Economists, was adamantly opposed to theories which "blamed" depressions on such obstacles to

4. Patinkin (1948).
5. Clower, *op. cit.*

5

price adjustments. The implied proposition that, if "competition" could only be restored, "automatic forces" would take care of the employment problem was one of his pet hates. Atomistic markets do not mean instantaneous price adjustments. A system of atomistic markets would also show Keynesian adjustment behavior.

In Walrasian general equilibrium theory, all transactors are regarded as price takers. As noted by Arrow, "there is no one left over whose job it is to make a decision on price."[6] The job, in fact, is entrusted to a *deus ex machina:* Walras' auctioneer is assumed to inform all traders of the prices at which all markets are going to clear. This always trustworthy information is supplied at zero cost. Traders never have to wrestle with situations in which demands and supplies do not mesh; all can plan on facing perfectly elastic demand and supply schedules without fear of ever having their trading plans disappointed. All goods are perfectly "liquid," their full market values being at any time instantaneously realizable. Money can be added to such models only by artifice.

Alchian has shown that the emergence of unemployed resources is a predictable consequence of a decline in demand when traders do not have perfect information on what the new market clearing price would be.[7] The price obtainable for the services of a resource which has become "unemployed" will depend upon the costs expended in searching for the highest bidder. In this sense, the resource is "illiquid." The seller's reservation price will be conditioned by past experiences as well as by observation of the prices at which comparable services are currently traded.[8] Reservation price will be adjusted gradually as search continues. Meanwhile the resource remains unemployed. To this analysis one need only add that the loss of receipts from its services will constrain the owner's effective demand for other products—a feedback effect which provides the rationale for the multiplier-analysis of a system of atomistic ("competitive") markets.

To make the transition from Walras' world to Keynes's

6. Arrow (1959), p. 43.
7. Alchian and Allen (1964), Chapter 31.
8. Compare Keynes (1937), p. 264.

world, it is thus sufficient to dispense with the assumed tatonnement mechanism. The removal of the auctioneer simply means that the generation of the information needed to coordinate economic activities in a large system where decision making is decentralized will take time and will involve economic costs. No other "classical" assumptions need be relinquished. Apart from the absence of the auctioneer, the system remains as before: (1) individual traders still "maximize utility" (or profit)—one need not assume that they are constrained from bargaining on their own, nor that they are "money illusioned" or otherwise irrational; (2) price incentives are still effective— there is no inconsistency between Keynes's general "elasticity optimism" and his theory of unemployment. When price elasticities are assumed to be generally significant, one admits the potentiality of controlling the activities of individual traders by means of prices so as to coordinate them in an efficient manner. It is not necessary to deny the existence of a vector of nonnegative prices and interest rates consistent with the full utilization of resources. To be a Keynesian, one need only realize the difficulties of finding the market-clearing vector.

III

It is a widely held view that the main weaknesses of Keynesian theory derive from Keynes's neglect of the influence of capital and real asset values on behavior.[9] It is above all on this crucial point that the standard model has proved to be a most seriously misleading framework for the interpretation of Keynes's theory. This is readily perceived if we compare the "aggregative structures" of the standard model and the *General Theory* model. In either case, we are usually dealing with but three price relations, so that the relevant level of aggregation is that of four-good models:

Standard Model	*General Theory*
Commodities	Consumer goods
Bonds	Nonmoney assets
Money	Money
Labor services	Labor services

9. For example, H. G. Johnson (1961), pp. 9, 11 and 17, or Patinkin (1965), p. 636.

7

The aggregate production function makes the standard model a "one-commodity model." The price of capital goods in terms of consumer goods is fixed. The money wage is "rigid," and the current value of physical assets is tied down within the presumably narrow range of short-run fluctuations in the "real" wage rate. Relative prices are, indeed, allowed little play in this construction. "Money" includes only means of payment, while all claims to cash come under the heading of "bonds."

The four-good structure of the *General Theory* is a condensed version of the model of the *Treatise on Money*[10] with its richer menu of short-term assets. All titles to prospective income streams are lumped together in "nonmoney assets." Bond streams and equity streams are treated as perfect substitutes, a simplification which Keynes achieved through some quite mechanical manipulations of risk and liquidity premia.[11] The fundamental property which distinguishes nonmoney assets both from consumables and from money is that the former are "long" while the latter two are "short"—"fixed" (or "illiquid") and "liquid," respectively.[12] The typical nonmoney assets are bonds with long term to maturity and titles to physical assets with a very long "duration of use or consumption." Basically, Keynes's method of aggregation differentiates between goods with a relatively high and a relatively low interest elasticity of present value. Thus the two distinctions are questions of degree. As a matter of course, the definition of money includes all types of deposits, since their interest elasticity of present value is zero, but "such instruments as treasury bills" can also be included when convenient.[13]

Keynes's alleged neglect of capital is attributed to his preoccupation with the short run in which the stock of physical capital is fixed. The critique presumes that Keynes worked with the standard model in which the value of such assets in terms of consumables is a constant. But in Keynes's two-commodity model, this price is, in principle, a short-run variable and, as a consequence, so is the potential command over current con-

10. Keynes (1930).
11. Keynes (1936), Chapter 17.
12. Cf. Keynes (1930), Vol. I, p. 248.
13. Keynes (1936), p. 167 n.

sumables which the existing stock of assets represents. The current price of nonmoney assets is determined by expectations with regard to the "stream of annuities" in prospect and by the rate at which these anticipated future receipts are discounted. The relevant rate is always the long rate of interest. In the analysis of short-run "equilibrium," the state of expectation (alias the marginal efficiency of capital) is assumed to be given, and the price of assets then varies with "the" interest rate.

In Keynes's short run, "a decline in the interest rate" and "a rise in the market prices of capital goods, equities, and bonds" are interchangeable descriptions of the same event. Since the representative nonmoney asset is very long-lived, its interest elasticity of present value is quite high. The price elasticity of the output of augmentable income sources is very high. The aggregative structure of this model leaves no room for elasticity pessimism with regard to the relationship between investment and the (long) rate of interest. It does not even seem to have occurred to Keynes that investment might be exceedingly interest inelastic, as later Keynesians would have it. Instead, he was concerned to convince the reader that it is reasonable to assume that "a moderate change in the prospective yield of capital-assets or in the rate of interest will not involve an indefinitely great change in the rate of investment."[14]

The relationship between saving and the interest rate is of less quantitative significance, but Keynes's ideas on the subject are of considerable interest and give some clues to his theory of liquidity preference. The criticisms of his supposed neglect of wealth as a variable influencing behavior have been directed in particular against the *ad hoc* "psychological law" on which he based the consumption-income relation. This line of criticism ignores the "windfall effect" which "should be classified amongst the major factors capable of causing short-period changes in the propensity to consume."[15] This second psychological law of consumption states simply that the propensity to consume out of current income will be higher the higher the value of household net worth in terms of consumer goods. A decline in the propensity to consume may, therefore, be caused

14. Keynes (1936), p. 252.
15. *Op. cit.*, pp. 92–94.

either by a decline in the marginal efficiency of capital[16] or by a rise in the long rate.[17] In the short run the marginal efficiency is taken as given and, so, it is the interest rate which concerns us.

The usual interpretation focuses on the passages in which Keynes argued that "changes in the rate of time-discount" will not significantly influence saving. In my opinion, these well-known passages express the assumption that household preferences exhibit a high degree of intertemporal complementarity, so that the intertemporal substitution effects of interest movements may be ignored. Consequently, the windfall effect of such changes must be interpreted as a wealth effect.

Hicks has shown that the wealth effect of a decline in interest will be positive if the average period of the income-stream anticipated by the representative household exceeds the average period of its planned "standard stream."[18] Households who anticipate the receipt of streams which are, roughly speaking, "longer" than their planned consumption streams are made wealthier by a decline in the interest rate. The present value of net worth increases in greater proportion than the present cost of the old consumption plan, and the consumption plan can thus be raised throughout.

This brings our discussion of the *General Theory* into pretty unfamiliar territory. But Keynes's "vision" was of a world in which the indicated conditions generally hold. In this world, currently active households must, directly or indirectly, hold their net worth in the form of titles to streams which run beyond their consumption horizon. The duration of the relevant consumption plan is sadly constrained by the fact that "in the long run, we are all dead." But the great bulk of the "fixed capital of the modern world" is of a very long-term nature,[19] and is thus destined to survive the generation which now owns it. This is the basis for the wealth effect of changes in asset values.

Keynes's *Gestalt*-conception of the world resembles Cassel's.

16. *Op. cit.*, p. 319.
17. *Op. cit.*, p. 94; also Keynes (1930), Vol. I, pp. 196–97.
18. Hicks (1946), especially pp. 184–88.
19. For example, Keynes (1930), Vol. II, pp. 98, 364.

Cassel used the wealth effect to argue the "necessity of interest,"[20] an argument which Keynes paraphrased.[21] The same conception underlies Keynes's liquidity preference theory of the term structure of interest. Mortal beings cannot hold land, buildings, corporate equities, British consols, or other permanent income sources "to maturity." Induced by the productivity of roundabout processes to invest his savings in such income sources, the representative, risk-averting transactor must suffer "capital uncertainty." Forward markets, therefore, will generally show a "constitutional weakness" on the demand side.[22] The relevance of the duration structure of the system's physical capital has been missed by the modern critics of the Keynes-Hicks theory of the term structure of interest rates.[23]

The recent discussion has dealt with the term structure problem as if financial markets existed in a vacuum. But the "real forces of productivity and thrift" should be brought in. The above references to the productivity of roundabout processes[24] and the wealth effect indicates that they are not totally ignored in Keynes's general theory of liquidity preference. The question why short streams should command a premium over long streams is, after all, not so different from the old question why present goods should command a premium over future goods. Keynes is on classical ground when he argues that the essential problem with which a theory of asset prices must deal derives from the postponement of the option to consume, and that other factors influencing asset prices are subsidiary: "we do not devise a productivity theory of smelly or risky processes as such."[25]

IV

Having sketched Keynes's treatment of intertemporal prices and intertemporal choices, we can now consider how "changing

20. Cassel (1903).
21. Keynes (1936), p. 94.
22. Hicks (1946), p. 146.
23. Meiselman (1962), pp. 14–16. H. G. Johnson (1962), pp. 347–48.
24. Keynes, *op. cit.*, Chapter 16.
25. *Op. cit.*, p. 215.

views about the future are capable of influencing the quantity of employment."[26] This was Keynes's central theme.

"It is by reason of the existence of durable equipment that the economic future is linked to the present."[27] The price of augmentable nonmoney assets in terms of the wage unit determines the rate of investment. The same price in terms of consumables determines the propensity to consume. This price is the focal point of Keynes's analysis of changes in employment.

If the "right" level of asset prices can be maintained, investment will be maintained and employment at the going money wage stabilized. If a decline in the marginal efficiency of capital occurs, maintenance of the prices of long-lived physical assets and equities requires a corresponding drop in the long rate and thus a rise in bond prices. To Keynes, "the sole intelligible explanation"[28] of why this will normally not occur is that bear speculators will shift into savings deposits. If financial intermediaries do not "operate in the opposite direction."[29] bond prices will not rise to the full extent required and demand prices for capital goods and equities will fall. This lag of market rate behind the natural or "neutral" rate[30] will be associated with the emergence of excess demand for money—which always spells contraction. "The importance of money essentially flows from its being a link between the present and the future."[31]

Contraction ensues because nonmoney asset prices are "wrong." As before, "false prices" reveal an information failure. There are two parts to this information failure: (1) Mechanisms are lacking which would ensure that the entrepreneurial expectations guiding current investment mesh with savers' plans for future consumption: "If saving consisted not merely in abstaining from present consumption but in placing simultaneously a specific order for future consumption, the effect might indeed be quite different."[32] (2) There is an alternative "circuit" by

26. *Op. cit.*, p. vii.
27. *Op. cit.*, p. 146.
28. *Op. cit.*, p. 201.
29. Keynes (1930), Vol. I, pp. 142–43.
30. Keynes (1936), p. 243.
31. *Op. cit.*, p. 293.
32. *Op. cit.*, p. 210.

which the appropriate information could be transmitted, since savers must demand stores of value in the present. But the financial markets cannot be relied upon to perform the information function without fail. Keynes spent an entire chapter in a mournful diatribe on the Casino-activities of the organized exchanges and on the failure of investors, who are not obliged to hold assets to maturity, to even attempt "forecasting the prospective yield of assets over their whole life."[33]

Whereas Keynes had an exceedingly broad conception of "liquidity preference," in the Keynesian literature the term has acquired the narrow meaning of "demand for money," and this demand is usually discussed in terms of the choice between means of payment and one of the close substitutes which Keynes included in his own definition of money. Modern monetary theorists have come to take an increasingly dim view of his speculative demand, primarily on the grounds that the underlying assumption of inelastic explanations represents a "special case" which is unseemly in a model aspiring to the status of a "general theory."[34] But it is only in the hypothetical world of Walrasian tatonnements that all the information required to coordinate the economic activities of a myriad traders is produced *de novo* on each market day. In any other construction, traders must rely heavily on "memory" rather than fresh information. In the orthodox model, with its interest inelasticity of both saving and investment, there is admittedly no "real" reason why traders' past experiences should be of a narrow normal range of long rates. In Keynes's model, there are reasons. In imperfect information models, inelastic expectations are not confined to the bond market. The explanation of the emergence of unemployed resources in atomistic markets also relies on inelastic expectations. To stress "speculative behavior" of this sort does not mean that one reverts to the old notion of a Walrasian system adjusting slowly because of "frictions." The multiplier feedbacks mean that the system tends to respond to parametric disturbances in a "deviation-amplifying" manner—behavior which cannot be analyzed with the pre-Keynesian apparatus.

33. *Op. cit.*, Chapter 12.
34. Cf. Fellner (1946), pp. 145–51; Tobin (1958); Johnson (1961), p. 10, and (1962), p. 344.

A truly vast literature has grown out of the Pigou-effect idea, despite almost universal agreement on its "practical" irrelevance. The original reason for this strange development was dissatisfaction with Keynes's assertion that the only hope from deflation lies "in the effect of the abundance of money in terms of the wage-unit on the rate of interest."[35] This was perceived as a denial of the logic of classical theory. Viewing Keynes's position through the glasses of the standard one-commodity model, it was concluded that it could only be explained on the assumption that he had overlooked the direct effect of an increase in real net worth on the demand for commodities.[36] The one-commodity interpretation entirely misses Keynes's point: that the trouble arises from inappropriately low prices of augmentable nonmoney assets relative to both wages and consumer goods prices. Relative values are wrong. Absolute prices will "rush violently between zero and infinity,"[37] if price-level movements do not lead to a "correction" of relative prices through either a fall in long rates or an induced rise in the marginal efficiency of capital.[38] It is hard to see a denial of "our fundamental theory of value" in this argument.

V

We can now come back to the "terms of the truce" between the neoclassicists and the Keynesian orthodox. I have argued that, in Keynes's theory: (1) transactors do maximize utility and profit in the manner assumed in classical analysis, also in making decisions on saving and investment; (2) price incentives are effective and this includes intertemporal price incentives— changes in interest rates or expected future spot prices[39] will significantly affect present behavior; (3) the existence of a hypothetical vector of nonnegative prices and interest rates which, if once established, would bring full resource utilization is not denied.

35. Keynes (1936), p. 253.
36. For example, Patinkin (1948), pp. 269–70, and *idem*, (1965), Note K:1.
37. Keynes, *op. cit.*, pp. 239, 269–70.
38. Keynes, *op. cit.*, p. 263.
39. Keynes, *loc. cit.*

The only thing which Keynes "removed" from the foundations of classical theory was the *deux ex machina*—the auctioneer which is assumed to furnish, without charge, all the information needed to obtain the perfect coordination of the activities of all traders in the present and through the future.

Which, then, is the more "general theory" and which the "special case"? Must one not grant Keynes his claim to having tackled the more general problem?

Walras' model, it has often been noted, was patterned on Newtonian mechanics. On the latter, Norbert Wiener once commented: "Here there emerges a very interesting distinction between the physics of our grandfathers and that of the present day. In nineteenth century physics, it seemed to cost nothing to get information."[40] In context, the statement refers to Maxwell's Demon—not, of course, to Walras' auctioneer. But, *mutatis mutandis*, it would have served admirably as a motto for Keynes's work. It has not been the main theme of Keynesian economics.[41]

40. Wiener (1964), p. 29.

41. The paper is an attempt to summarize some of the conclusions of a lengthy manuscript, "On Keynesian Economics and the Economics of Keynes: A Study in Monetary Theory," to be submitted as a doctoral dissertation to Northwestern University.

CHAPTER TWO

Keynes and the Effectiveness of Monetary Policy*

The Keynesian tradition in macroeconomics, particularly in the United States, has been associated with a decided preference for fiscal over monetary stabilization policies. In the development of this school of thought, certain arguments to the effect that monetary policy is generally ineffective have historically played a large role. By no means all the major contributors to the Keynesian tradition can be tarred with this brush. But, of those who have been outspokenly pessimistic about the usefulness of monetary policy, the vast majority would certainly be popularly identified as "Keynesians." Since the proposition that monetary policy is ineffective has in this way become associated with his name, it is of some interest to examine the case originally made by Keynes.

Since abounding faith in fiscal measures and a withering away of interest in monetary policy was one of the most dramatic aspects of the so-called "Keynesian Revolution," there is, I believe, a tendency to impute these views, as well as the analytical tools with which they were propounded, to the *General Theory*. It is of course true that this work, on the one hand, expressed doubts about the efficacy of banking policy and, on the other, argued for public works programs and for "a somewhat comprehensive socialization of investment."[1] But Keynes'

*The material of this paper, as well as that of an earlier paper [Leijonhufvud (1967)] has been drawn from a lengthier manuscript, *On Keynesian Economics and the Economics of Keynes,* published by Oxford Univeristy Press. I am deeply indebted to the Relm Foundation for making possible my work on this article.
1. Keynes (1936), p. 378.

position on the issue was a good deal less clearcut than one would gather from standard textbook expositions of the "Keynesian system." The position on these policy-issues advocated in the *General Theory,* moreover, was not at all "revolutionary" in the sense of making a distinct break with Keynes' own past ideas. On the scales of his personal judgment, there had been only a subtle shift away from reliance on monetary policy and in favor of direct government measures. The extent of this shift has been much exaggerated.

The exaggerated popular view of the extent to which Keynes' *magnum opus* downgraded the usefulness of monetary policy reflects an over-simplified and mechanical interpretation of his contribution which is deeply embedded in the "Keynesian" tradition. This paper seeks to restore some perspective on the issue. The motive for this attempt is the one common to most doctrine-historical essays: Misconceptions of where one has been and of the path followed to the present most often mean ignorance of where one is, and whither one is going.

Sections I and II below are of a purely doctrine-historical nature. The continuity of Keynes' thought on matters of "Applied Theory" is emphasized, and some of the reasons why this continuity has not been more apparent to his readers are discussed. Sections III and IV continue the doctrine-historical documentation of the assertions made about Keynes' views but deal mainly with some theoretical issues that, while neglected in the Keynesian literature, should still be of interest for their own sake. Section III considers Keynes' diagnosis of the disequilibrium characterizing a persistent unemployment state. Section IV relates the alternative cures of monetary expansion and fiscal deficit to his diagnosis of the unemployment problem.

I

Today, the *General Theory* is remembered chiefly as signaling a revolution in professional thinking and popular attitudes on stabilization policy. Among modern economists, Keynes' reputation derives chiefly from the book's impact on practical affairs, for the outcome of the "Keynes and the Classics" debate represents the rejection of his claims to being a major theoretical innovator. The fact is however that, while Keynes' earlier *Treatise on Money* gave equal space to "Applied Theory" and "Pure Theory," the *General Theory* was written as a treatise on pure theory. Its sundry reflections on policy-matters appear in passages scattered as the progression of the theoretical argument dictates. There are no separate chapters on stabilization policy, corresponding to the systematic treatment of the subject given by modern textbooks on "Keynesian macroeconomics."

One must recall, therefore, that the main corpus of fiscal policy theory identified with the "New Economics" was constructed by later Keynesians. "Balanced Budget Multipliers," for example, belong to a later period. The once-popular idea that the maintenance of full employment requires ever-increasing government expenditures also came into fashion first with the later incorporation of the accelerator in Keynesian models. Similarly, the standard "Keynesian" argument *against* monetary policy is simply not to be found in the *General Theory* but was a later development about which Keynes expressed the deepest reservations.[2]

In an earlier paper,[3] I have argued that, contrary to the conclusions embodied in the so-called Neoclassical "synthesis," Keynes was indeed justified in claiming that his 1936 work presented a more "general" theory than that of the Classics.[4] That, however, applies to the *General Theory* as "Pure" theory. When we turn to Keynes' comments on alternative stabilization policies, we have to deal with his "Applied Theory," and here such a sweeping claim for generality cannot be upheld.

This observation is particularly pertinent to the issue of the effectiveness of monetary policy. The usual textbook discussion of the issue proceeds in terms of the properties of a static simultaneous equation model. It makes no reference to past states of the system, nor to a specific historical and political real world context. Consequently, the conclusions tend to emerge as if they were universally valid: "The interest-elasticity of invest-

2. Cf. the letter of Keynes quoted by L. R. Klein (1947), pp. 66–67.

3. Leijonhufvud (1967).

4. Put briefly, Classical general equilibrium theory assumes that transactors have perfect information on market opportunities. The characteristic implications of Keynes' theory flow from its rejection of the Classical treatment of the information-problem.

ment is for various reasons quite low. Hence, monetary policy is not a very useful stabilization instrument." This familiar type of argument does not rely on specific conditions obtaining at a particular time and place.

Keynes' judgment on the issue as it gradually developed to the position voiced in the *General Theory* was based on a number of considerations. These were, on the one hand, assumptions about how unemployment disequilibria generally develop and about the nature of the monetary transmission mechanism. The empirical status of these hypotheses was certainly not settled by his casual empiricism and some of them, at least, must still be regarded as in doubt at this late date. On the other hand, his discussion of monetary policy drew on his personal diagnosis of the nature of the problems facing Britain in the interwar period and also on his judgments with regard to the kinds of policy that were politically feasible in that context. These time- and place-bound considerations naturally cannot without further ado be invoked in judging the effectiveness of monetary policy, say, in the United States of the sixties. Finally, the interest-inelasticity of investment—the pivotal argument in the New Economics position of the issue—was not involved in Keynes' analysis at all.

To Keynes' American readers, in particular, the doubts as to the efficacy of monetary policy expressed in the *General Theory* must nonetheless have been one of the book's most dramatic features. His two previous major works (the *Tract on Monetary Reform* and the *Treatise*) had both dealt almost exclusively with monetary issues, and it was on these books that his theoretical reputation outside Britain chiefly rested. Not only had the *Treatise* been devoted wholly to explaining how monetary policies worked and should be used; its most controversial feature had been the theory that income disequilibria generally had monetary "causes"[5]—for which, consequently, monetary remedies were appropriate.

5. Its neglect of "real" causes had been severely criticized, especially by F. A. von Hayek (1931b–1932).
   The sense in which "cause" is used here will become fully clear only in the context of Sections III and IV. Briefly, the present usage is designed to emphasize that a movement in the natural rate (regarded in the *Treatise* as due to "real" factors) is not a sufficient condition for the emergence of an income disequilibrium. Instead, the strategic

Comparisons between the *Treatise* and the *General Theory* will easily give an exaggerated impression of the change in Keynes' policy-views also for another reason. The *Treatise* had next to nothing to say about fiscal measures. But in his efforts as a financial journalist, Keynes had consistently argued for public works ever since 1924.[6] There were two parts to this advocacy. On the one hand, the government was urged to subsidize or directly to undertake investment in certain sectors as a matter of longer-run growth policy. Underlying this recommendation was Keynes' judgment that capital outflow from Britain would otherwise lead to too little domestic long-term investment. In the *Treatise,* this theme received but brief mention—it is significant that it was put under the heading of "International Complications."[7] Following Britain's return to gold at the old parity, maintenance of employment under conditions of an overvalued currency became the main ground on which Keynes advocated this policy. On the other hand, he also argued for public works as a supplement to monetary policy in combatting the short-run "Credit Cycle." His testimony before the Macmillan Committee makes it clear that, in this context, he saw public works as a "pump-priming" device[8]—i.e., as a method of jolting a disorganized economy back towards equilibrium, not as a continuing measure needed to close an otherwise inexorable "deflationary gap."[9] On both counts, then, he differed from the policy-prescriptions later propounded on the basis of closed-system, comparative static models.

The *General Theory* added very little to this. What mainly made his position more radical in that work was the fact that the "socialization of investment" was there argued with little explicit reference to the International Complications that had ini-

---

factor lies in the failure of market rate to adjust, and it is on this inadequacy of the endogenous adjustment-mechanisms that Keynes focused in both the *Treatise* and the *General Theory.*

6. Cf. Harrod (1951), pp. 345–51 and 411–24. Again, these efforts were of course less known in the United States than in Britain.

7. Keynes (1930), Vol. II, p. 376.

8. Harrod, *op. cit.,* p. 417. For a fuller background on the development of Keynes' views prior to the *General Theory,* on his work on and testimony before the Macmillan Committee, Harrod's biography is indispensable.

9. Compare Section IV below.

tially prompted him to advance this recommendation. It is hard to judge to what extent this represents merely the omission of part of the supporting argument. But there can be little doubt that his increasing pessimism with regard to the efficacy of the monetary policies that Central Banks could be persuaded to pursue made him state the case for fiscal policies in a more uncompromising fashion.

II

A superficial comparison of the analytical frameworks utilized in the *Treatise* and in the *General Theory* respectively may easily reinforce the impression that, in the later work, Keynes suddenly scuttled monetary policy. These eye-catching differences in analytical approach therefore deserve some comments.

What are the major differences between the two works? Many economists are likely to think first of the changed definition of saving. Because of the trouble caused readers, much space in the early discussion was devoted to unraveling the implications of this. But such definitional changes were made as a matter of analytical expediency and do not reflect changes in the substance of the underlying theory.

The switch from the "Fundamental Equations" of the *Treatise* to the investment-multiplier of the *General Theory* as the expository device, whereby Keynes sought to compress a complicated and sophisticated theory in a nutshell, is more significant. Yet, it must not be misinterpreted. The "Multiplier" does indeed summarize the two major changes in his model, i.e., (*i*) the idea that the system responds to disturbances by quantity-adjustments and not simply by price-level adjustments (while remaining at full employment), and (*ii*) the idea that initial disturbances are amplified through the consumption-income relation.[10]

In another respect, however, this switch of expository devices can very easily be misleading. The Fundamental Equations were recognizable descendants of the traditional Equation of

10. Cf., Leijonhufvud (1967), pp. 402–3.

Exchange.[11] In the *Treatise*, the Quantity Theory lineage is still very evident—the various factors affecting income are still analyzed in terms of their impact on the excess demands for the assets and liabilities of the banking system.[12] The multiplier-analysis, in contrast, focuses directly on the demand for and supply of commodities. This switch in the immediate focus of the analysis from the excess demand (supply) of "money" to the excess supply (demand) of commodities has probably contributed heavily to the widespread impression that the *General Theory* represented a clean break with Keynes' "monetary" past and an attempt to approach macroeconomics practically from scratch—and from the "real" side. But it does *not* reflect any basic change in Keynes' views of the processes generating changes in money income and of the role of financial markets in such processes. This cannot be too strongly emphasized. If the further discussion of the *General Theory*'s appraisal of monetary policy is to make any sense at all, one must first be free of the notion that it was based on some newfound conviction that "money is unimportant."

The development of Keynes' views relevant here did not take place between the *Treatise* and the *General Theory* but between the *Tract* and the *Treatise*. By and large, the *Tract* respected the traditional boundary between monetary theory and value theory, whereby the former field deals with the demand for output in general and the value of money, and the latter with relative prices. In the interval between the two books, Keynes—very much under the influence of D. H. Robertson—had come to the conviction that it was necessary to relinquish this traditional compartmentalization in order to explain the disequilibrium processes producing changes in money income and price-levels and, in particular, to explain the *modus operandi* of monetary policy. The disaggregation of total output into consumer-goods and investment-goods was a *sine qua non* of the

11. Keynes (1930), Vol. I, Chapter 10:iv, and Chapter 14. The Fundamental Equations sought to marry Keynes' saving-investment analysis to the Equation of Exchange by incorporating the difference between saving and investment as a determinant of changes in velocity in the latter. For present-day appraisals of this apparatus, cf. Burstein (1963), Chapter 12, Appendix A. and Hicks (1967), Chapter 11.

12. Keynes, *op. cit.*, Vol. I, pp. 142–44, 182–84.

process-analysis presented in the *Treatise,* which invoked systematic changes in the relative price and in relative rates of output of the two in explaining how money income moves from one short-run "equilibrium" level to another.[13] The trouble with the Fundamental Equations was that they still incorporated a variable purporting to represent the total physical volume of output, in the way of the traditional Equation of Exchange, and thus were inconsistent with the verbal explanation of the processes studied.

In the *General Theory,* the Fundamental Equations—and mathematical ambitions generally—were given up. All a bit ironic, for Keynes' successors immediately reverted to an algebraic model devoid of relative prices and with only a single commodity-aggregate. Through the glasses of this standard model, Keynes' claim to having brought "the theory of prices as a whole back to close contact with the theory of value"[14] looks incomprehensible. In fact, it has not been widely comprehended. In any case, the *General Theory* retained all the essentials of the theory of the *Treatise,* although its dramatic extension to account for sustained unemployment drew attention away from its older elements.

It is important to understand clearly the nature of the two commodity aggregates with which Keynes worked. The consumption-good is "Liquid"—when looking for an illustration in the *Treatise,* he hit on bananas: "ripe bananas will not keep for more than a week or two."[15] Investment, on the other hand, is

13. The basic contention here is that a monetary injection, for example, will not impinge with the same force on all markets and all prices and that an understanding of the *modus operandi* of monetary policy therefore requires an analysis of the disequilibrium process which descends at least one step from the ultimate level of aggregation of both the Cambridge-Equation and the Equation of Exchange. (This idea was later all but buried in the avalanche of static, one-commodity models produced first by the Keynesian Revolution and then by the Neo-Classical Resurgence.) When all is serene once more, of course, only the new level of nominal values remains as an "unreal" monument to past Central Bank efforts. Keynes' repeated acknowledgments of the validity of the Quantity Theory in the long run show that he understood quite clearly that this traditional tool was sufficient in order to obtain comparative static results, just as his criticisms of Quantity Theories reveal his understanding of what witnesses to the later Neutrality debate know only too well, namely that comparative static analysis can tell us nothing about the "real" powers of a Central Bank or of how they should be used in different circumstances.

14. Keynes (1936), p. 293.

15. Keynes (1930), Vol. I, p. 178.

in very durable "Fixed Capital," illustrated by "Land, Buildings, Roads and Railways." These are the types of capital-assets for which he advocated some "socialization of investment"—not a very radical recommendation from today's standpoint. Two notes on this definition of the investment-variable need be made.

First, the "short run" for Keynes' theoretical model of fluctuations in investment is not so short in terms of calendar time as we are likely to think. We are exceedingly familiar with "Keynesian" models of inventory-cycles à la Metzler. The *Treatise* did contain a good discussion of variations in stocks of Liquid Capital but explicitly argued that they were of interest as an amplifying and not as an initiating factor in business fluctuations. In the *General Theory,* the "minor miscalculations" underlying inventory cycles rate only a bare mention.[16] The modern ambition is to stabilize employment on a year-by-year or even quarter-by-quarter basis. Keynes' perspective, however, was not that of the Kitchin-cycle but rather that of the Juglar or, perhaps, the "Long Swing," to use the not entirely appropriate terminology of Business Cycle Theory. Mere questions of short-run "business conditions" held little interest for him. He dealt with problems in which he saw a threat to the civilization of his time.

Secondly, "the sensitiveness of these activities even to small changes in the long-term rate of interest, though with an appreciable time-lag, is surely considerable."[17] The determination of the price of the representative "Fixed Capital" asset, Keynes handled as an ordinary present value problem. On the one side, the price depends upon entrepreneurial expectations of the earnings stream in prospect. These expectations were discussed in terms of certainty-equivalents, and such certainty-equivalent streams he treated as perfect substitutes for bond-streams of comparable time-profile. On the other side, the rate of interest for the appropriate maturity-class of bonds is the discount rate by which the present value of prospective earnings is to be evaluated.[18]

16. Keynes (1936), p. 322.
17. Keynes (1930), Vol. I, p. 364.
18. Cf., e.g., *op. cit.,* Vol. I, p. 180.

Within this framework, *if* the price of long-term bonds can be raised by the monetary authority, there will be a proportional rise in the demand-price for Fixed Capital. In Keynes' language, "a decline in the interest rate" *means* "a rise in the market prices of capital goods, equities, and bonds." Thus control over long rate means control over investment and, thereby, money income and employment. The later dogma of interest-inelasticity of investment as the bane of monetary policy originated, not in Cambridge, but in Oxford. The problem with monetary policy, in Keynes' view, is that the required changes in the rate of interest may not be "practicable."[19]

III

In the previously cited paper, I argued that Keynes never departed from the "Classical" presumption that a hypothetical vector of nonnegative prices will exist which, if once established, would permit all traders to carry out their corresponding transactions-plans, including the desired sales of labor services. Price-incentives are effective so that it is possible, in principle, to control individual activities so as to make them mesh. When coordination fails, it is because the requisite information is not generated and transmitted, a state of affairs reflected in the persistence of a price-vector different from the one conducive to full employment.

When dealing with Keynes' views, one cannot very well divorce the question of the appropriateness and efficacy of monetary measures from the perceived problem that they are designed to correct. Keynes' diagnosis of the social malady, for which monetary policy was one of the cures to be considered, is best discussed in terms of the relationship between the actual and the "equilibrium" price-vector. It is not necessarily true that only one vector of spot prices is consistent with full employment in the current period, but for simplicity of exposition we shall assume this to be the case in what follows.

Spot-prices: Wages versus Asset-prices

It is tempting to start with the sweeping assertion that in Keynes' eyes wages were "always right." For this aspect of his

19. Keynes (1936), p. 164.

position has been utterly lost sight of in the interminable literature on the Pigou-effect which seems generally to presume that,
if there is unemployment, wages are *ipso facto* above the level
consistent with equilibrium. Whereas Keynes obviously recognized unemployment as the most serious of the symptoms of
deflationary disequilibrium, his diagnosis of the malady blamed
too low asset-prices. But the generalization is somewhat too
broad. There was, as Wright has noted "another Mr. Keynes
. . . though admittedly a junior partner. *He* is the man who
points out that money wages can be too high."[20]

Three notes on this will suffice: (1) the possibility that the
monetary authority will have to deal with a disequilibrium
caused by "spontaneous" wage-push is indeed recognized in the
Treatise.[21] But the discussion is fairly perfunctory and the problem soon fades from view. (2) There was one period in which
Keynes found himself forced to grapple with a situation in
which "too high wages" were the crux of the problem, namely
the years of Britain's ill-starred relapse to gold at the old
parity.[22] Even so, he would have prescribed a low interest policy
if not deterred by the prospect of increased capital outflow, and
the partial socialization of long-term investment was not his
only scheme for avoiding the pains of wage-deflation.[23] Here,
however, "too high wages" translate simply into "overvaluation
of currency" and this case is therefore of limited relevance in
the usual closed system context. (3) His attitude toward the gold
standard incident was an instance of a more general value-judgment on which he differed profoundly from Wicksell. For, if a
Wicksellian inflation had once been permitted, he argued, the
monetary authority should live with its past mistakes and try to
stabilize prices (or employment) at the prevailing level of
wages.[24] In effect, the Central Bank ought to act *as if* the actual
wage-level were the "proper" one.

This, then, leaves "too low" demand prices for augmentable
assets as the problem to be dealt with in a situation of deflation

20. Wright (1961), p. 19.
21. Keynes (1930), Vol. I, pp. 166ff.
22. Harrod (1951), esp. p. 411.
23. The present interest-equalization scheme is just the sort of thing Keynes would
come up with—as long as he could not see any prospect of flexible rates being adopted.
24. Wicksell, of course, spent much of the 1920's trying to persuade the Swedish authorities to reverse the World War I inflation.

and/or unemployment. The issue provides a fair illustration of the characteristic mix of "Pure" theory, casual but shrewd empiricism, and personal value-judgments of which Keynes' "Applied Theory" is composed.

Intertemporal Values:
Entrepreneurial Expectations versus Market Rate

There are two, broad reasons why asset prices may be wrong: (*i*) entrepreneurial expectations may be unduly pessimistic or optimistic in relation to the returns in prospect, were the system to follow a hypothetical equilibrium path. Since savers do not place forward orders for consumption goods, the market mechanisms are lacking that would provide entrepreneurs with adequate information on the future demand conditions presently to be reckoned with. (*ii*) Long-term market rates may be too high or too low. Only in the very long run need they conform to the underlying intertemporal transformation possibilities and saving propensity. In the "short-run"—which in terms of calendar time may be measured in years—speculation in securities markets will make them diverge from the levels that would obtain under conditions of full information.

This distinction, I believe, provides the key to the considerations that led Keynes to take a dimmer view of the prospects for effective monetary policy in the *General Theory* than he had done in the *Treatise*.

By the time that Keynes was writing the *General Theory*, Britain was again off gold, and the constraints due to "International Complications" discussed at length in the *Treatise* were no longer of current relevance. Consequently, we may now disregard these complications in appraising the *Treatise*. Looking only at the closed-system arguments, the bulk of the work presumes that *entrepreneurial expectations are roughly right*. But it is also assumed that entrepreneurs generally tend to over-react. "The real prospects do not suffer such large and quick changes as does the spirit of enterprise."[25] This characteristic Keynesian assumption is not generally accepted.[26] It means, however, that

25. Keynes, *op. cit.*, Vol. II, p. 362.
26. Cf., e.g., Arthur F. Burns' criticism of this assumption (1954), pp. 231–35.

implicitly, the *Treatise*'s analysis of how monetary policy should be conducted in the current short period presumes that the system already has a history of appropriate monetary policies up to the present time. Otherwise, the expectations ruling at the outset of the period might just as well be wildly inaccurate as roughly right, since entrepreneurs would have over-reacted to past experiences of excessive or deficient aggregate demand.

The normative force of the main prescription of the *Treatise* derives from this assumption.[27] If expectations are not approximately right, there is nothing "natural" about the natural rate. The recommendation that the monetary authority cause market rate to move in such a manner as to maintain the demand-prices for augmentable assets inherited from last period, presumes that this long rate will generally be an "equilibrium" rate. Whenever investment starts to rise or fall, thereby threatening inflation or deflation, the *Treatise* treats this as evidence of an inappropriate level of market rate. Consequently, the appropriate cure consists of a monetary policy designed to correct market rate. It is this presumption that Hayek attacked in criticizing Keynes' neglect of "real" causes of business fluctuations. Keynes' views, of course, flew in the face of the widespread contemporary opinion that the causes of depression were often to be found in the "excesses" of the preceding boom.[28] In Keynes' position that one should never resign oneself to a depressed but supposedly salutary period in which past mistakes were to be "weeded out," one again perceives his characteristic mixture of empirical hypothesis and personal value-judgment.

On this issue, I believe that the relinquishing of the Wicksellian apparatus in the *General Theory* reflects a further development of Keynes' theoretical views, although with no change in his value-judgments towards the "purgatory" views indicated above. The reason for relinquishing the natural rate-market

27. At the same time its practical relevance is thereby circumscribed. The task set for the Applied Theory of the *Treatise* is for the most part too easy: when the curtain goes up for Keynes' usual One-Act Morality Play, the Laborers are fully employed and the Entrepreneurs regard the future with firm and sober realism. The Moral of that tale is simple and is preached in no uncertain terms. But what if unemployment is rampant and entrepreneurial expectations have become seriously distorted?

28. For example, *op. cit.*, Vol. I, pp. 178–79. For a recent reappraisal of Hayek's position, cf. Hicks, "The Hayek Story," in his (1967).

rate apparatus are but perfunctorily sketched in the *General Theory* however.[29] The crux of the matter one finds implicit already in the important penultimate chapter of the *Treatise* in which the assumption that entrepreneurs are right was finally dispensed with. But before turning to that pivotal case, we should consider the difficulties which Keynes saw in the way of conducting an appropriate monetary policy under the simpler conditions when, save for minor miscalculations, the entrepreneurs are right.

Keynes' views of the "normal" difficulties facing Central Bankers must be seen in relation to his diagnosis of the objective situation to be dealt with in the interwar period. He ascribed the prosperity of the early twenties primarily to a Schumpeterian concatenation of war-induced innovations promising quick and high profits. The consequent investment boom had pulled long rate up to a level that, in historical perspective, was exceptionally high.[30] As the new industries caught up with demand, and war damage and investment backlogs from the war were made good, the abnormal levels of interest rates would no longer be "natural." Over the longer term, the problem facing the monetary authority was that of ensuring that market rate kept pace with the downward trend of natural rate.

In the *Treatise*, there is no question but that the monetary authority can do it—if it only keeps at it continuously. A steady chastisement of bearish speculators might be needed, but the banking system "can by the terms of credit influence *to any required extent* the volume of investment."[31]

There is still a major problem in the execution of the proper policy: "we have *not* claimed that the banking system can pro-

---

29. Keynes (1936), pp. 242–44.

30. Keynes (1930), Vol. II, esp. pp. 378ff.

31. *Op. cit.*, Vol. II, p. 346, italics added. In practice, as Keynes sternly pointed out, the Federal Reserve System did exactly the opposite of what was required. Predictably, the decline of long rates was associated with a drastic upward revaluation of the shares of public utilities and similar "semi-monopolistic" enterprises (*op. cit.*, Vol. II, p. 381). The speculation on the trend, which this required change in the level of equity-values set off, caused the System to adopt a contractionary policy at the time when its proper objective was still that of helping to nudge down the market rate. This could only restrict the "Industrial Circulation" with little direct effect on the "Financial Circulation" and thus served to trigger the decline in output and prices.

duce any of these effects instantaneously; or that it can be expected always to foresee the operation of non-monetary factors
in time. . . ."[32] We have already quoted Keynes on the "appreciable time-lag" between changes in long rates and changes in
the rate of output of capital goods. But the lag that mainly concerned him was that inherent in the traditional Bank Rate *cum*
Bills Only mode of operation to which Central Banks were addicted—unfortunately and unnecessarily so, in Keynes' opinion.
One of the reforms most emphatically urged in the *Treatise,* and
echoed in the *General Theory,* was that the monetary authority
should operate directly in the long end and not "leave the price
of long-term debts to be influenced by belated and imperfect
reactions from the price of short-term debts."[33] The dangers inherent in this lag were forcefully, if not altogether tastefully, illustrated by his bismuth-castor oil analogy.[34]

By the time of the *General Theory,* Keynes had reason to be
less sanguine about this lag-problem. The Macmillan Committee had given him the best possible platform from which to
press this reform on the authorities—but he had found them
unwilling to listen.[35] This experience must be taken into account in judging his reasons for being "now somewhat sceptical
of the success of a merely monetary policy directed towards
influencing the rate of interest."[36] But his own views on the
long-term problem had also darkened, quite apart from what
the Bank of England could be made to do. He seemed to be
looking forward to an indefinite period of deflationary pressure
from which "socialization of investment" was well-nigh the only
salvation. These were the passages that the Stagnationists fas-
tened upon and enlarged into an elaborate doctrine. Keynes'
position at this time was based on two assumptions. Against one
of them one must surely object[37]—the idea that a state of capital saturation and zero marginal efficiency of capital would be

32. *Op. cit.,* Vol. II, p. 346.
33. Keynes (1936), p. 206.
34. Keynes (1930), Vol. II, pp. 223–24.
35. Harrod (1951), pp. 413ff.
36. Keynes (1936), p. 164.
37. For the objections, cf., e.g., Samuelson (1963), p. 584, or Bailey (1962), pp. 107–14,
123–30. The classical statement is that of Cassel (1903).

reached within a generation if full employment was maintained.[38] Against the other most economists would hold grave
reservations—Keynes' conviction that the long rate will only
come down at a most excruciatingly slow pace. There are arguments in favor of his pessimism with regard to manipulating
the long rate deftly enough over the "Credit Cycle,"[39] but
surely the *General Theory* drew an exaggerated picture of both
the obstinacy and the power of the Bear army. When he states
that the long rate "may fluctuate *for decades* about a level which
is chronically too high,"[40] one should take into account the historical background of "obstinate maintenance of misguided
monetary policies"[41] that he painted. But his position on the
inflexibility of long rates still seems extreme.

While the Liquidity Trap "might become important in the future," Keynes in 1936 knew "no example of it hitherto."[42] The
future envisaged in this passage is one in which capital saturation is so near that the "objective" marginal efficiency of capital
would have crept below the margin necessary to cover lender's
risk and the cost of intermediation. The diagnosis of the American thirties as an illustration of the static Liquidity Trap came
into Keynesian economics with Alvin Hansen and others.
Keynes' own stagnationist fears were based on propositions that
must be stated in terms of time-derivatives. Modern economies,
he believed, were such that, at a full employment rate of investment, the marginal efficiency of capital would always tend to
fall *more rapidly* than the long rate of interest.[43] As an inherent
tendency of capitalistic civilization, this chronic disparity between the two time-derivatives seems a doubtful proposition.
But it sums up a considerable proportion of the passages in
which Keynes vented his later doubts on the efficacy of monetary policy.

38. Keynes, *op. cit.*, pp. 420, 375ff.
39. Cf. Section IV below.
40. Keynes, *op. cit.*, p. 204 (italics added).
41. Keynes (1930), Vol. II, p. 384.
42. Keynes (1936), p. 207.
43. *Op. cit.*, pp. 219, 228.

IV

Through the better part of the *Treatise,* the technical prescriptions for the conduct of monetary policy presume, explicitly, an inherited situation of full employment, and implicitly, the prevalence of enterpreneurial expectations of future demand such as will be by and large fulfilled if only the market rate is brought into correspondence with the natural rate. These beneficial bequests of the past imply, in effect, that past monetary policy has successfully followed the guidelines that Keynes proceeded to prescribe. The conduct of monetary policy in such circumstances poses a relatively easy task, even if we admit that Keynes made light of the practical target-indicator problems involved in keeping track of the unobservable, and supposedly volatile, natural rate with the help of instruments afflicted with seriously lagged effects. In all fairness, he repeatedly acknowledged that the preservation of good health cannot be the end-all of medical practice: "It is much easier to preserve stability than to restore it quickly, after a serious state of disequilibrium has been allowed to set in."[44] But in the *Treatise,* Chapter 37 was the only one wholly devoted to the cure of the already ill, thereby foreshadowing the main concerns of the *General Theory.*

Consider then, a depressed situation in which entrepreneurial expectations are attuned to a continuing slump. This is reflected in the current market-values of Fixed Capital assets. Again, asset demand-prices can be raised if only long rates can be brought down—there is no problem of interest-inelasticity of investment. As always with Keynes, the interest-elasticity of the demand for savings-deposits associated with the Speculative Supply of long-term securities is the Central Bank's main problem. To restore a full employment rate of investment, market rate has to be brought down much further than would be needed if entrepreneurial expectations had not already been adversely affected. But, the Keynes of the *Treatise* concluded, this makes no difference in principle. The prescription indicated will not be so much a different policy as more of the

44. Keynes (1930), Vol. II, pp. 351, 352.

same—an "extraordinary" dosage of open-market purchases "to the point of satisfying to saturation the desire of the public to hold savings-deposits."[45]

To demand the execution of this "monetary policy *à outrance*" means to *"impose on the Central Bank the duty of purchasing bonds up to a price far beyond what it considers to be the long-period norm."*[46] This is made clearer if we explicitly assume that the initial under-valuation of assets is due entirely to the pessimism of entrepreneurs and that the actually prevailing long rate is exactly the one that would enter into a hypothetical full information state equilibrium vector. The holders of securities are right and entrepreneurs wrong, instead of *vice versa* as in the previous case. The policy recommended is thus one of dragging the righteous through purgatory for the salvation of the unbeliever. For, if the Central Bank succeeds in raising asset demand-prices and making a full employment rate of output of augmentable assets profitable, entrepreneurs will find their pessimistic forecasts falsified by reviving aggregate demand. With the consequent revival of the "spirit of enterprise," the demand prices of capital goods and equities will shortly shoot up *above* the level consistent with continuing stability, if market rate is maintained at the level reached. Having bought high, the Central Bank will therefore be obliged to sell low and thus to "show a serious financial loss."[47]

At this point, obviously, Keynes has arrived on the verge of a "Keynesian" policy. For, surely, the step is not long from recommending Central Bank losses to advocating government deficits. If, in fact, orthodox prudence is to be defied, the most promising tack to take may well be to insult the fiscal prudence of elected politicians rather than the financial prudence of self-sufficient central bankers. Keynes, of course, had no success at all in selling this idea to the Bank of England; but, then, the *Treatise*'s scarcely veiled intimations that the Central Bank's losses would be its Just Desert for letting the contraction get under way were presumably of little help.

The Central Bank would not be the only loser. Although

45. *Op. cit.*, Vol. II, p. 370.
46. *Op. cit.*, Vol. II, p. 373.
47. *Loc cit.*

Keynes makes no mention of it, speculators content to go along with the Central Bank will also have their fingers burned—to the elbow, if they collaborated vigorously. Keynesian bond-holders are notable for long memory; this learning-experience would swell the Bear army and make the Central Bank's task harder the next time a monetary policy *à outrance* is tried. Thus, if the actual market rate is already at the level that would obtain in a hypothetical full employment state, the case for a massive assault on securities markets to drive yields down is not self-evidently a strong one.

The alternative would be a policy of government deficit spending designed to "correct" entrepreneurial demand-forecasts. Direct expenditures on commodities will prevent the self-fulfillment of pessimistic prophecies. By falsifying the forecasts, a rise of asset-values should be obtained at the going market rate of interest. This is a "pump-priming" case, for as full employment is approached the government spending-program may be phased out without throwing the system back into depression.

In the *General Theory,* the whole context of the discussion of short-run problems was one in which entrepreneurial expectations were "depressed," as in Chapter 37, and not objectively right, as in the bulk of the *Treatise.* Keynes recommended continuing government intervention to deal with the long-term threat of stagnation and with the long-term consequences of being committed to maintaining an over-valued currency, as we have seen in previous sections. This should be carefully distinguished from the fiscal measures that he found appropriate for dealing with the short-term problem of internal business fluctuations. His Macmillan Committee testimony was explicit on the transitory nature of the injections he deemed needed: "Government investment will break the vicious circle. . . . I believe you have first of all to do something to restore profits and then rely on private enterprise to carry the thing along."[48]

Further reflection on the case of Chapter 37 may well have contributed significantly to Keynes' new-found favor for fiscal "pump-priming" over the monetary stabilization measures he

48. Quoted by Harrod, *op. cit.,* p. 417.

had previously advocated. In the *Treatise* and the *General Theory*, evidence bearing directly on this point is sparse, however, and this suggestion must therefore be a matter more of speculation than of straight-forward exegesis. Somewhere, one would think, in Keynes' oral testimonies before official bodies, letters, memoranda, and vast printed output, there should be further evidence bearing on the question. Quite possibly, however, he never did carry the explicit analysis of this particular issue beyond the point reached at the end of the *Treatise*.[49] On points of technique, Keynes, after all, was hardly the contemporary master of process-analysis. But questions concerning the extent to which Keynes successfully developed his mode of analysis will today only excite doctrine-historians. His basic approach, however, is still of more than historical interest. The Keynesian tradition, with its biases towards static analysis, against price-theory, and against monetary policy, has not preserved all the worthwhile elements in Keynes' thought, nor has it discarded only his analytical errors and most ill-considered empirical hunches. The standard simultaneous equation model generally accepted as embodying "the Keynesian System" does not represent the successful realization of Keynes' theoretical aims. It is not even a promising point of departure for the development of a rigorous body of analysis which could cope systematically with the type of disequilibrium problems informally sketched in Sections III and IV.

V

All Keynes' arguments, of course, dissolve entirely under the eyes of anyone convinced that, when everything is said and done, the fact remains that the improvement or augmentation of "Land, Buildings, Roads and Railroads" are *not* activities

49. It should be recalled that the whole of *General Theory*, Chapter 12, is devoted to painting a lurid picture of the Games that People Play on the Stock Exchanges ("Snap, Old Maid, Musical Chairs"), i.e., of the kind of speculative activity which in Keynes' opinion was principally responsible for preventing the adjustment of "the" rate of interest to its "natural" level. The language is in fact even stronger than in the corresponding passages of the *Treatise*. This would seem to indicate that Keynes still regarded a "too high" rate of interest as the main cause of persistent deflationary pressures. Then, however, the case for attacking the rate of interest with a monetary policy "to the point of saturation" would remain unimpaired.

highly sensitive to changes in the rate of interest. If the major components of aggregate expenditures are in fact highly interest-inelastic, that would pretty well settle the matter and one's interest in the more complicated case made by Keynes would then be merely "academic." Among the "elasticity-optimists," furthermore, some may well feel that his theoretical framework is not the most appropriate one for organizing the empirical questions bearing on the substantive issue, or even that it tends to be positively misleading for such purposes. Those, finally, who both tend to agree with Keynes on the interest-elasticities and find his theoretical framework useful, will presumably disagree with his empirical or political judgment on several of the points discussed above. The substantive issues, of course, remain untouched by the clarification of Keynes' views on them attempted here.

We may conclude that Keynes weighed fiscal versus monetary policies on the basis of a more complex set of considerations than is apparent from the standard "Keynesian" textbook discussion and also that his views were quite different. It is especially important to consider carefully the nature of the case for government spending and against Central Bank action that emerges from the analysis of Section IV. It is a case against reliance on monetary policy for the pursuit of certain objectives under certain conditions, i.e., in this instance, for the reversal of a "cumulative" process triggered by a disequilibrium diagnosed as being of a particular type. It is *not* a case for the general uselessness of monetary policy. On the contrary, the analysis makes very clear the great power for good or evil that monetary policy is seen to retain within Keynes' theoretical framework. For it is still as vital as ever that the Central Bank acts vigorously so as to hold market rate continuously in the near neighbourhood of an appropriately defined natural rate. The main prescription of the *Treatise* is not affected by the finding that there are conditions to the correction of which fiscal measures are better fitted than monetary measures. In the context of Keynes' theory, the diagnosis of disequilibria, on the lines sketched in sections III and IV, is thus seen as a prerequisite for the choice of an appropriate mix of fiscal and monetary policies in a particular situation.

CHAPTER THREE

Keynes and the Classics:
First Lecture

I. INTRODUCTION

The full title of my recent book is *On Keynesian Economics and the Economics of Keynes—A Study in Monetary Theory*. It may indicate to you that I am not a man of few words. Accordingly, I have been invited to summarise it. The invitation, I hope, means that it is felt that the book "hits a few nails on the head." The invitation specifically to summarise, I fear, means that it is also felt that it contains a distressing lot of fumbling about for the hammer. So, in the time available to me here, I will have to wield my hammer with more abandon. If this leads me to overstating my case on some points, I must refer you to my book for a better documented and, hopefully, more well-balanced treatment.

I have come here directly from Sweden, where one of the favourite topics of gossip among economists concerns the award of the first Nobel Prize in Economics. So, I will begin by asking you to consider this question: if John Maynard Keynes were alive today, whom would you nominate for the Prize?

The question is, of course, merely a cheap attempt on my part to make you consider the topic of my two talks as fresh and alive in some measure, and not just as a mouldly, doctrine-historical subject. Rhetorical tricks are, perhaps, not required today in order to make economists consider Keynes' role in twentieth-century economics. When I made the decision, some years ago, to write my doctoral dissertation on Keynes, all had been quiet on the Keynesian front for quite some time. *Ex ante*—to be terribly Swedish about it—I had to worry about whether anyone would care to read it. *Ex post,* I have experienced the curious feeling of having been part of a rather sudden and mysterious (since altogether unco-ordinated) outpouring of ink on a subject where it seemed, not so long-ago, that the wells had finally run dry.

In recent years, we have had Hutt's *Keynesianism: Retrospect and Prospect;* Lekachman's *The Age of Keynes;* Stewart's *Keynes and After.* Roll's *The World After Keynes* and Hutchison's *Economics and Economic Policy in Britain, 1946–1966* also devote considerable space to Keynes' influence on the formulation and execution of stabilisation policies in the post-war world. Shackle's *The Years of High Theory* and Hicks' *Critical Essays on Monetary Theory* are in large measure concerned with Keynes' contribution to economic theory.[1]

Time magazine in the United States and *Encounter* in the United Kingdom have both discussed "whether we are all Keynesians now"—and, if so, in what sense. Not a very useful query, perhaps; that it is asked at all is, at any rate, testimony in Keynes' favour that seems relevant to my initial—and equally specious—question. Consider also some of the titles above: *The Age of Keynes, Keynes and After, The World After Keynes.* Try substituting the name of some other twentieth-century economist for that of Keynes . . .

There can be no doubt, I think, that Keynes is generally recognised as the predominant figure among economists of this century. Yet I submit that there is still, more than two decades after his death and more than three decades after his *General Theory,* considerable uncertainty about exactly why he occupies this position. Wherein lies his greatness—not as a man of many achievements in diverse fields—but specifically as an economist, and preferably as an economist's economist? If we are quite clear on what our subject is all about, where it has been, and where it is going, this is a question to which we should have a clear answer. Yet, to return to my hypothetical question: if you had to write the harangue motivating the posthumous award of the Nobel Prize to Keynes, what exactly would you say?

"Keynesianism" is a rather amorphous "movement" or

---

1. W. H. Hutt (1963); Robert Lekachman (1967); Michael Stewart (1967); Sir Eric Roll (1968); T. W. Hutchison (1968); G. L. S. Shackle (1967); Sir John Hicks (1967).

"school." The significance of its influence may be considered under at least three different headings : (i) economic theory, (ii) economic policy, and (iii) socio-political ideology. In my book I concentrate almost exclusively on the first topic—Keynes' contribution to theory. I have nothing to say on the third. (Indeed, I doubt that anything very sensible can be said about it.) But it is not just under this heading, but under the other two as well, that matters are complicated because the propositions, prescriptions, and opinions frequently advanced as "Keynesian" bear little relation to Keynes' views.

II. ECONOMIC STABILISATION

Let us first consider the significance of Keynes' contribution to economic stabilisation. The plea in his behalf is well-known. One finds it developed, for example, in the books by Lekachman and Stewart; I need not paraphrase it here.

All along, however, there have been some demurrers. If, indeed, we grant weight to all such reservations, the case for Keynes is not clear-cut.

A sampling of the debates on policy in the thirties shows that Keynes, although certainly a most prominent participant, was very far from alone, either in opposing general wage-cuts and budget balancing or in pressing for budget deficits and public works. As the valuable Appendix to Professor Hutchison's recent book amply documents, Keynes had the vast majority of influential academic economists actively with him on all these issues. Professor Pigou was a particularly important ally. (It was, of course, at the London School of Economics that Keynes' opponents were concentrated.) Professor J. R. Schlesinger has emphasised that opposition to a policy of general wage-cuts was quite widespread in the United States at the time, both among policy-makers and economists.[2] Policies that we have later come to label "Keynesian" were actively advocated by Swedish economists from the very beginning of the depression and, in the United States, by Professor Jacob Viner and his colleagues at Chicago.[3] It is understandable that the infamous "Treasury

2. J. R. Schlesinger (1968).
3. J. R. Davis (1968).

View" looms large in British accounts of Keynes' efforts in this period, but it may at least be questioned whether it was held anywhere outside London. The *General Theory* has been given much credit for disposing of it. Yet it was not an orthodoxy among economists. As Professor Hutchison points out, Pigou had attacked it before the First World War.

It is not my intention to minimise Keynes' contribution. But if one is to be historically accurate (and fair to his contemporaries) one must note that in these debates on policy he did not loom head and shoulders over them in the way that we have become used to thinking of him.

It is a far step, furthermore, from Keynes' advocacy of public works to the full-blown fiscal policy theory of the New Economics. One cannot deny Keynes the role of patron saint to those who have built this corpus of theory, but neither can he be given full credit—or responsibility—for it. Sir Roy Harrod is, in my opinion, quite right in pointing out that there are important elements in "modern" thinking on stabilisation policy that are anti-Keynesian—in the strict sense of the term.[4]

The final questions under this heading are the most difficult of all and concern the benefits that society has derived from "Keynesian" economic policies. On this topic, one still hears echoes of the stagnationist Keynesian view of the 'forties. From the perspective of the stagnationists there was but one way to save the world—and Keynes invented it. Today, however, we have a very different understanding of the economic events of the two inter-war decades from that of the early "Keynesians." We do not view the Great Depression as due to an "exhaustion of investment opportunities" or other inexorable "real" forces.

Following the work of Friedman and Schwartz and other American neo-quantity theorists, we no longer regard the worst banking panic of all time as just incidental to the worst depression.[5] We have known all along, of course; that it was not "Keynesian" fiscal policies that brought us out of the depression. Sad to record, Schickelgruber did it. But the "monetarist" re-examination of the historical period out of which Keynesian

4. Sir Roy Harrod (1964).

5. Cf., e.g., Milton Friedman and Anna Schwartz (1963), Chapter 7; Karl Brunner and Allan Meltzer (1968).

economics emerged all-triumphant also raises the question of what it would have been like had not first the domestic monetary system of the United States (in particular) and then the international monetary system broken down.

It is a terribly hypothetical question, of course. But it is a serious and important question nonetheless which, once raised, suggests another one that strikes closer to home. To what extent is the relatively favourable unemployment record of the post-war years due to the use of the ever-growing armoury of fiscal instruments? It is part and parcel of the conduct of economic policy that one takes credit for whatever goes well, while what does not go well (a) was inevitable, and (b) would have been still worse but for one's brave efforts against impossible odds. Nor are we economists, as a profession, loath to have the public feel thankful for modern macro-economics. But it is really not at all easy to come to a well-founded judgement on how much the industrious manipulation of fiscal instruments has contributed. Here one does not need to turn to the neo-quantity theorists in order to be cautioned against exaggerated claims—although they certainly stand ready to supply abundant material for the purpose. The question has recently been considered by Professor Matthews.[6] His paper was originally delivered before this audience so that I need not dwell on his argument here.

At the very end of my second lecture, I will have a comment or two of my own that I consider of some relevance to this question, since they pertain to the concept of the "government expenditure multiplier." But, that apart, I will leave this line of inquiry in abeyance. I have given what is, at best, only a cursory sketch of the kind of critical arguments that could be marshalled against Keynes. No amount of elaboration would make one deny that he is a major figure in the development of methods of economic stabilisation. My only intention with this sketch has been to indicate that, were we to judge him on these grounds *alone,* he would not loom larger than life-size—as we are wont, perhaps, to regard him.

That stature we accord him, of course, because of his *General*

6. R. C. O. Matthews (1968).

Theory. But, then, the *General Theory* was not at all a treatise on stabilisation policy. There is very little on that topic in it. It is a theoretical work. So, if we grant Keynes a greatness of a different order from that of other economists of his or our time because of this work, we should do so on the basis of his contribution to economic theory.

III. ECONOMIC THEORY

We come then to the real question—Keynes' contribution to theory. The truth is, however, that he is no longer universally acclaimed as a major theoretical innovator. We cannot award our hypothetical Nobel Prize to a man just because of the "sound and fury" his works have generated. So the basis of the modern negative evaluation of Keynes' theoretical contribution needs to be examined. This is my objective from here on.

The negative conclusion is embodied in what has become known as the "neo-classical synthesis." The term "synthesis" indicates the main contention, namely, that Keynes' theory is in the end quite consistent with inherited theory—with the theory that he labelled, and attacked as, "classical." Consequently, it is regarded as containing no major innovation.

The neo-classical synthesis was the result of a long and exceptionally voluminous debate. That it was long is no cause for surprise, even if one agrees with the result, for Keynes' theory was couched in terms of an analytical apparatus quite different from the traditional one. The "Keynes and the Classics" debate may be regarded as spanning at least some 20 years—from Hicks' 1937 paper with that title (and more or less simultaneously appearing papers by Reddaway and Meade) to the first edition of Patinkin's *Money, Interest, and Prices* (1956) or, perhaps, to the Hicks-Patinkin exchange in the *Economic Journal* that followed.[7] Things have been pretty quiet since then.

We have to hop, skip, and jump in a fairly arbitrary way through these years of literature. In the contributions that concern me fairly definite ground-rules for the debate have been

7. J. R. Hicks (1959); W. B. Reddaway (1936); J. E. Meade (1937); Don Patinkin (1956), (1965); Hicks (1957); Patinkin (1959).

observed. Basically these comprise use of a static, simultaneous equation model of the type proposed by Hicks in 1937. Each discussant is equipped with

1. a consumption- (or savings-) function,
2. an investment function,
3. a saving-equals-investment condition,
4. a money demand function,
5. an exogenous money supply,
6. an equilibrium condition for money,
7. an aggregate production function, from which is derived
8. a labour demand function,
9. a labour supply function, and—depending upon whether Keynes or the "Classics" is the immediate concern—
10a. a given money wage level or
10b. an equilibrium condition for labour.

Optional equipment includes equations for government expenditures and receipts, exports, and imports, etc. It is understood that the system contains a "securities," "credit," or "bond" market, although equations for that market need not be represented.

The ground rules also comprise the formulation of the problem to which the apparatus is to be applied: Keynes' model will settle down to an unemployment situation—which Keynes chose to call an "unemployment equilibrium"—and the Classic model cannot. Whatever exactly "Classics" is agreed to mean, the "Classic" model cannot. So this is taken to be *the* difference between Keynes and the Classics that needs to be explained.

Keynes criticised the "Classics"—among whom he insisted on giving a prominent place to his most valuable ally in the policy debates of the immediate past, Professor Pigou—on numerous points and he also made several assumptions that were not the "standard" classical ones.

Consequently, the question of the debate was: Which assumption is, or what assumptions are, *critical*—in the sense of being both necessary and sufficient—in accounting for the "fundamental difference" between Keynes and the Classics.

Consider first how the issue looks from the perspective of

Professor Franco Modigliani's famous 1944 paper, "Liquidity Preference and the Theory of Interest and Money."[8] Modigliani used the basic model to resolve numerous issues, but here we are only interested in two of his exercises with it. We can call these two the "basic" and the "special" case, respectively.

A. The Basic Case

Consider two sets of equations side-by-side, both representing systems with four goods—commodities, bonds, money, and labour. One—the "classical"—has demand and supply equations for commodities, money, and labour, *and* equilibrium conditions for each of the three, including labour. The other one—the "Keynesian"—should have the restriction (10a) $w = \bar{w}$, in place of the condition (10b) $N^s(w/p) = N^d(w/p)$.

The classical equation system we can solve, getting full employment, a corresponding equilibrium real wage, w/p, and also the equilibrium interest rate, $\hat{r}$. Given the specified value for the money supply, $M^s = \overline{M}$, we also find the money values for the price level and wage rate, $\hat{p}$ and $\hat{w}$, the ratio of which is the full employment real wage.

Assuming that this solution is unique, it follows that, if we add the restriction $w = \bar{w}$, where w is chosen so that $\bar{w} > \hat{w}$—say, for simplicity, $\bar{w} = 2\hat{w}$—the system will not have a full employment solution. Indeed, it will not have any solution, but that we can take care of by changing the equations for the labour market. We specify that, for $(\bar{w}/p) > (w/p)$, the short side of the market (i.e., the amount of labour demanded) determines the amount actually exchanged (employed). The only use left for the labour supply function is then that it enables us to find out the amount of unemployment. We have then arrived at the "Keynesian" model.

Comparison of the two systems immediately indicates that, if money wages were only "free" to fall—in response to the excess supply of labour—from $\bar{w}$ to $\hat{w}$, all would be well. Hence the

---

8. *Econometrica*, 1944. The page reference below is to the reprint in F. A. Lutz and L. W. Mints, eds., *Readings in Monetary Theory*.

conclusion is that the critical assumption in Keynes' "basic case" is that *wages are rigid.*

The conclusion may be somewhat amplified. The initial "classical" set of equations exhibits "neutrality of money," i.e., the solution values for all "real" variables would be the same no matter what value is given to the nominal supply of money, M. Consequently, had we had twice the amount of money, when first solving the system, we would have had the same values for employment (namely "full" employment), output, consumption, investment, "real" money holdings, and real wage, but with $p = 2\hat{p}$ and $w = 2\hat{w}$. If, then, the trouble with the "Keynesian" set was that, with $M = \overline{M}$, $w = 2\hat{w}$ "caused unemployment," setting $M = 2\overline{M}$ will give us full employment for the equation system containing this "Keynesian" restriction on the value of the money wage.

Hence, we get the conclusion in the form that Modigliani put it:

> The low level of investment and employment are both the effect of the same cause, namely a basic maladjustment between the quantity of money and the wage rate.[9]

In our little example, this maladjustment can be removed, so as to get a full employment solution, either by cutting the money wage in half, or by doubling the money stock.

B. The Special Case

Consider once more the solution to the "Classical" set of equations. In "Keynes' special case" we again look at the consequences of adding a restriction to the system. This time, however, instead of specifying a money wage higher than the equilibrium wage of the "Classical" solution, we focus on the possibility of having to make do with a rate of interest higher than its "Classical" solution value, $\hat{r}$.

It is allowable here to write the consumption, investment, and money demand functions in "real" terms. From the consumption function we obtain directly a function for real saving, $S = S(X,r)$, which we juxtapose against the simple investment

9. *Op. cit.*, pp. 224–25.

function, $I = I(r)$. Let $X = X^f$ be the rate of real output required for full employment, and focus on the savings-interest rate schedule, $S(X^f, r)$, that corresponds to it. In the original "Classical" solution, the condition that $S(X^f, r) = I(r)$ defines the equilibrium interest rate, $\hat{r}$.[10]

If we now add the restriction that $\bar{r} > \hat{r}$, we will again have no full employment solution. Indeed, if we just added an equation specifying this restriction, the system would have no solution at all. (We have assumed that the "Classical" solution was unique.) Before, in the "basic case," we took care of that by eliminating the equilibrium condition for the labour market. Here, we do not eliminate the equilibrium condition for the "hidden" securities market. Instead, we do two things. First, the restriction is introduced, not by adding a separate equation, but by specifying the form of the money demand equation such that, at $\bar{r} > \hat{r}$, we have a so-called "Liquidity Trap." This gets us rid of the possibility of having an "unremovable" excess demand for bonds at the above-equilibrium interest rate, since the import of the "trap" is that current owners of outstanding bonds stand ready to supply from their inexhaustible holdings—in order to hold money instead. Secondly, in order to assure ourselves of a solution, the labour market equilibrium condition has to go again. This time, however, the money wage can be left a "free" variable—there will still be no full employment solution.

We find that here it is no longer true that changing the relation that the money wage rate holds to the nominal money supply will get us out of trouble. Changing M^s will, by assumption, neither depress $\bar{r}$ to $\hat{r}$, nor will it cause either the investment function or the saving function to shift in such a way that the saving people would like to undertake at full employment income becomes equal to planned investment at $r = \bar{r}$. Falling money wages will allow money prices to fall in the same proportion, but this has no other effect than increasing the real value

10. Parenthetically, we should not forget that "a special case of the special case" has figured rather prominently in the discussion. It is the case which Pigou called "Keynes' Day of Judgement." In it, it is assumed that the "Classical" solution—and, again, it is unique—gives a negative value for the interest rate. Thus, the only algebraic solution is not an economically meaningful one. The possibility explored is one of the non-existence of equilibrium.

of the money stock—and we have already checked that that does nothing.

C. The Real Balance Effect and the Elimination of the Special Case

The next step is to add to the analysis the "effect," named after Pigou, but for which Haberler and Scitovsky also share honours. The argument which concerns us here is found already in a famous paper by Patinkin from 1948.[11]

Put briefly, the argument is the following: In systems where (a) changes in the general level of money-prices and -wages affect the real value of some component of consolidated net worth, and (b) the propensity to save out of any given rate of income depends inversely on real net worth, a large enough all-round deflation will restore full employment even in a system that has fallen into a "liquidity trap." The first property, (a), will be exhibited *inter alia* by all systems where some component of the money stock is made up of so-called "outside" money. The second property, (b), we should accept on general choice-theoretical grounds.

Consequently, the "special case" is, for all purposes, eliminated. Since it is shown that a sufficient reduction of wages (and thus prices) will result in full employment, we are left with only the "basic case." The *critical* assumption in Keynes' theory, it is concluded, is that wages are *rigid downwards*.[12]

D. The Last Skirmish

Any pre-Keynesian economist, asked to explain the phenomenon of persistent unemployment, would automatically have

---

11. Don Patinkin (1948) reprinted in Lutz and Mints, eds., *op. cit.* The full integration of this effect into systems of the kind we are discussing was achieved in Patinkin's 1956 book.

12. It has been argued from certain passages of *The General Theory* that Keynes himself based the wage-rigidity property of his model on the assumption that workers were money-illusioned. I do not agree with that interpretation. In any case, most later Keynesians have emphasised the "monopolistic" behaviour of unions and the "administered pricing" practices of large firms instead.

started with the assertion that its proximate cause must lie in too high wages that refuse to come down. If, then, we are left with the "basic case," we are forced to conclude that Keynes added absolutely nothing new to the "pure" theory on this problem. It is an astounding conclusion. But we must be quite clear on one thing—the logic behind it is remorseless; the conclusion is mathematically *inescapable*—given the ground-rules of the analysis.

The Hicks-Patinkin exchange of 1957–59 may have been the last straw in convincing "Keynesians" of this. In reviewing Patinkin's book, Hicks started by noting that the idea of something going wrong with the adjustment of the long-term rate of interest seemed quite fundamental to Keynes' conception of the causes of unemployment. He went on to complain that Patinkin's exegesis did not at all give prominence to this idea. Now, Hicks' intuitive understanding of Keynes' theory was eminently sound on this point—but, in working the argument out, he followed the same static equation-system ground-rules that we have followed here. This meant that, in effect, he ended up restating the "special case" in a somewhat more elaborate way. Patinkin was then able simply to point out that he had overlooked the real-balance effect in the saving function.

Hicks' failure to overturn the argument that reduces Keynes' theory to the trivial special case of Classical theory where money wages are rigid seems to have been virtually the last rear-guard action of those Keynesians who have tried to maintain a place for Keynes on this lofty plane of abstraction.

IV. KEYNES: A THEORETICAL CHARLATAN?

I have, of course, picked somewhat arbitrarily from the welter of arguments that make up the "Keynes and the Classics" debate. The appraisal is more complicated than this—especially because of the accommodation that has been reached between the theoretical neo-classicists and the practical, policy-oriented Keynesians. They agree that wages *are* rigid "in the real world," and that the Pigou-effect, therefore, remains a theoretical gadget that one could not lean on to solve real unemployment problems. In discussion of "practical issues," consequently, the "special case" has acquired a second life. Removed from the lofty level of theoretical abstraction, the "pragmatic" version of the "special case" has become less precise in its propositions, less definite in outline—just enough so, one would say, that the "pure" theorists can be expected to leave its practitioners alone and not come poking about again. The liquidity trap is not spoken about as absolute—it is just that the interest-elasticity of money demand is likely to be very high just when you wish it was not. A negative rate is not spoken of as required for making investment equal saving at full employment income—it is just that saving and investment are likely to be very interest-inelastic, so that "practicable" reductions of interest rates will not be of much help. Thus, "for practical purposes," we have the same conclusions that, "in theory," apply only to the original "special case"—for example, that increasing the supply of money will not help you. (Well, in principle, it will—it is just that you had better not trust it.)

This seems to be the kind of shadow-life that Keynes' theory leads. Properly speaking, there is no such theory. Not one that could serve for your advanced graduate theory courses, at any rate. But there is this "apparatus" (of which you do not speak to your theorist friends for fear of being sneered at), which serves so admirably in the proper care and feeding of undergraduates.

So, having descended to greet Keynes' shadow in the Hades of undergraduate instruction, we should return to the Light that is our preferred habitat as proper theorists. The purely theoretical appraisal of Keynes can stand some further reflection.

It is, after all, not just that the interpretation I have sketched makes Keynes' theory trivial. Although those who hold to it have been much too polite to say so, this interpretation—if we do, indeed, take it quite seriously—makes of Keynes himself a charlatan who hid his trivial manipulations in fogs of words on irrelevant topics. Consider a few of the things to which Keynes devoted pages and whole chapters in (apparently) trying to divert his readers' attention:

a. The "basic case" makes no use of Liquidity Preference. It is irrelevant to the analysis whether the interest rate enters into the money demand function or not. It follows, of course, that the bulls and the bears and the games "of Snap, of Old Maid, of Musical Chairs" that they play on the exchanges, as well as the troublesome "Essential Properties of Money"—all these favourite themes on which Keynes spent some of his best literary effort—do not matter either.

b. The beloved "Multiplier" does not figure in the "basic case," either. We do not need it to explain unemployment. Keynes' all-out attack on Say's Law of Markets turns out to have been as irrelevant as the rest of his critique of "Classical" theory.[13] The Pigou-effect literature sheds a most unfavourable light on the early chapters of the *General Theory* where Keynes' main assault on the "Classics" is launched. As Professor Samuelson has said:

> Had Keynes begun his first few chapters with the simple statement that he found it realistic to assume that modern capitalistic societies had money wage rates that were sticky and resistant to downward movements, most of his insights would have remained just as valid. . . .[14]

(Again, Samuelson is also too polite to point it out—but we have just found out—that for all "purely theoretical" purposes, Keynes would, apparently, have been well advised to *end* right at that point too. On matters of theory, what did he have to add?)

c. If the consumption function is not needed for the "Multiplier," it is not needed at all. It, the investment function, and the saving-investment equality are just a funny way of writing the equations for commodity demand and equilibrium in the commodity market. They are better dispensed with, as in Patinkin's book, so that one is not distracted by Keynes' "talk" about saving-investment "problems" or by poetic images of "the dark forces of time and ignorance that envelop our future."

---

13. The one, utterly trivial, exception would be his rejection of what he called the "second classical postulate," i.e., the proposition that the marginal disutility of the existing amount of employment will equal the real wage. This proposition must naturally be relinquished in order to analyse unemployment situations.

14. Paul A. Samuelson (1969b), p. 332.

From the theoretical point of view, then, the consumption function and the Multiplier, Liquidity Preference and the Speculative Demand for Money, the saving-investment problem, and all the criticism of the Classics *are* just so much "sound and fury signifying nothing." So there!

We have given a partial list of the propositions that loom large in the *General Theory* but that seem irrelevant from the standpoint of the neo-classical appraisal of Keynes' contribution. We should also turn this around and consider a partial list of the propositions that have played a significant role in the "Keynes and the Classics" debate, and check what role they play in *The General Theory*:

1. Labour suffers from money illusion.
   —It is *not* in the *General Theory*.

2. The labour market is dominated by unions that refuse to see money wages reduced.
   —It is *not* in *GT*.

These were the two alternative explanations for why wages are rigid found in the Keynesian literature. And, indeed, when we check:

3. Wages are rigid.
   —It is *not* in *GT*.

4. The trouble is that wages are too high.
   —It is *not* in *GT*.

5. The trouble is that the interest rate is too high.
   —It *is* in *GT*.

6. The Liquidity Trap.
   —It is *not* in *GT*.

7. Investment is interest-inelastic.
   —It is *not* in *GT*.

8. Saving is interest-inelastic.
   —It is *not* in *GT*.

9. The trouble is that at no positive interest rate would saving equal investment.
   —It is *not* in *GT*.

10. Effects of falling wages and prices on real balances.
     —It *is* in *GT*.

11. Effect on consumption demand of changes in real net worth.
     —It *is* in *GT*.

12. Effect on aggregate demand of changes in the real value of the money component of net worth.
     —It *is* in *GT*.

Strange story, isn't it? What do we make of it?

CHAPTER FOUR

Keynes and the Classics: Second Lecture

My first lecture was purely polemical in intent and, perhaps, even overly so in execution. It was necessary, for my purposes, to impress upon you, as vividly as I might, how *anomalous* is this whole business about our appraisal of Keynes' role in the development of "modern" economics. If that is not excuse enough, perhaps I should claim that outrageous polemics is but an act of piety towards Keynes. Today, at any rate, I should try to be more constructive.

What I ought to attempt now, of course, is to resolve all the contradictions that I pointed out yesterday. But, obviously, that puzzle is too large for one lecture. I will have to concentrate on some parts of it, while trying to give you a "feel" for how the whole thing would look. I propose to deal primarily with three issues:

1. Keynes' theory of Liquidity Preference;
2. his Multiplier; and
3. his "persistent unemployment state."[1]

I will start with some rather simplistic notes about Liquidity Preference, then deal with the Multiplier and the unemployment state, and finally, come back to some further observations relevant to Keynes' conception of Liquidity Preference. This

---

1. Keynes, of course, used the term "unemployment equilibrium." Even cursory examination will reveal, however, that it is not an "equilibrium" in the strict sense at all. It is preferable, therefore, to use some more neutral term which does not carry the connotation that no equilibrating forces at all are at work. The real question is why, in the Keynesian unemployment state, the forces tending to bring the system back to full employment are so weak.

seems an appropriate procedure, since it is possible—as emphasised, in particular, by Professor George Horwich[2]—to go some
way towards a more adequate understanding of the role of
Liquidity Preference in Keynes' theory while staying pretty
much within the ground-rules of the usual approach. In discussing the other two issues, on the other hand, we will have to try
to escape from the traditional way of looking at Keynesian
theory. If we succeed, it will then pay to take a second look at
Liquidity Preference.

V. LIQUIDITY PREFERENCE

The point about Liquidity Preference can be made very simply
if we only go from the pure statics of the so-called "basic case"
to a simple comparative static exercise. The conclusion drawn
from the static argument, you will remember, was that unemployment is due to a "basic maladjustment" between the money
wage rate ($\bar{w}$) and the money supply ($\bar{M}$). Investment and
Liquidity Preference at no point entered into the reasoning.

In comparative statics, the convention is that the initial state
is assumed to be an equilibrium state. So we start from full
employment. The next thing to do is to specify the parametric
disturbance that produces the terminal unemployment state.
All sorts of disturbances can have this consequence, of course.
If the initial disturbance is *either* a "wage-push" *or* a reduction in
the money supply, the previous conclusion that the trouble lies
in a "wrong" relation between $\bar{w}$ and $\bar{M}$ can call for no amend-
ment. Investment plays no causal role, and Liquidity Preference plays no part since the result we are after—
unemployment—follows also if we have, e.g., a constant velocity
money demand function.[3]

The disturbance standard with Keynes, however, is a "decline
in the marginal efficiency of capital." The impact effect of this
is to create an excess supply of commodities and an excess
demand for "bonds" at the initial values of income and interest

2. Horwich (1964).

3. I.e., a function which specifies that the amount of money demanded equals a given
fraction (usually the "Cambridge k") of a year's income and that the value of this fraction does not depend on other endogenous variables, in particular the level of interest
rates.

rate. The excess demand for bonds drives their prices up. With a Keynesian Liquidity Preference function this will cause an excess demand for money at the initial level of income. The decline of the rate of interest will in this way be halted before it reaches $\hat{r}$—the value required for full employment. We now have an excess demand for money and a corresponding excess supply of commodities. With wages and prices inflexible, this disequilibrium will force a decline in output and income.

We have thus arrived at an unemployment state, although $\bar{w}$ and $\overline{M}$ are still the same as in the initial full employment situation. We could not have done so, starting from a disturbance impinging on investment, without invoking Liquidity Preference. Liquidity Preference is a *sine qua non* in explaining fluctuations in money income that are associated with a "variable velocity" of money.

VI. A GENERAL SYSTEMS PERSPECTIVE

Keynesian economics has been immersed in controversy from the start. If we adopt a General Systems Theory perspective for a while, we can remove ourselves a bit from what is specifically "economic" about the problem at hand—so that, if I succeed in striking some sparks of controversy, they will not fall in the heaps of ideological tinder that surround Keynesian economics.

Consider how a distinguished microbiologist formulates the general question that has animated the tremendous surge of new research in recent years in that field:

> An organism is an integrated unit of structure and functions. In an organism, all molecules have to work in harmony. Each molecule has to know what the other molecules are doing. Each molecule must be able to receive messages and must be disciplined enough to obey orders. How has the organism solved the problem of intermolecular communication?[4]

This is consciously put as a General Systems type of question—there is nothing specifically biological about the problem being posed. We see this immediately if we just translate two of the nouns:

> An *economy* is an integrated unit of structure and functions. In an economy, all *transactors* have to work in harmony. Each transactor has to know

4. Andrew Lwoff (1965), p. 8.

what the other transactors are doing. Each transactor must be able to receive messages and must be disciplined enough to obey orders. How has the economic system solved the problem of inter-transactor communication?

Now, to be really comfortable with this formulation, we would probably want to change the bit about "harmony" to "equilibrium" and the phrase about "obeying orders" to something like "responding in a predictable fashion to market signals." But, otherwise, the passage might be Hayek or, perhaps, even Menger. (At any rate, the soundest guess would be a member of the Austrian School.) Its spirit, naturally, is straight from that Good Old Bottle of Adam Smith's, since the answer to the query is the time-honoured answer to Mercantilism. But it definitely could *not* be Walras, and it is very unlikely that it could have come from one of the modern Walrasians—*because of the last sentence.*

One disturbing note before we pass on: we find it natural to expect that successful efforts by a team of biophysicists and biochemists, in explaining how it is possible for the molecules in a particular organism to "work in harmony," would result in a theory that a biomedical team would find directly applicable to its questions—of what happens when the thing malfunctions and of what to do about it. Not so in economics. We use "Walrasian" models for the first type of question, and "macromodels" for the second: and we act as if this schizophrenic State of the Arts was something that we are willing to live with indefinitely. The theory of value and resource allocation deals with how economic activities are co-ordinated. Macro-theory deals with co-ordination failures—at least, that was the original problem. But the structure of the two types of models is so dissimilar that the price-theoretical content of "Keynesian" macromodels is often difficult to distil.

I find this particularly anomalous since economists should be well trained to appreciate—in a general sort of way—how the answer to Lwoff's query about biological organisms would go. We have a longer acquaintance than other sciences with theories of the self-regulation of complex systems, and with the basic concepts of homeostatic control and negative feedback mechanisms.[5] The seminal idea could not be put more convincingly than in Adam Smith's exposition of the "Invisible Hand." We had it first—but we seem to have lost our "feel" for it. Perhaps we have repeated the "answer" to the problem for so long that, knowing it by heart, we have forgotten that there ever was a serious question.

In the "answer" to a Walrasian set of excess demand equations we have a still picture—a *nature morte*—of the state in which the "harmony of the molecules" is perfect. How can the system fail to get there? The assumptions of the Classical theory of how individual activities are *controlled,* so as to make their co-ordination feasible, direct our attention to certain specific possibilities. Broadly, the assumptions are:

1. that price-incentives are effective; that transactors do respond to changes in relative prices by changing the quantities produced and consumed in a qualitatively predictable manner;
2. that prices tend to move, and are "free" to do so, in response to excess demands or supplies and in such a manner as to induce transactors to alter their behaviour in the directions required for all activities to 'mesh'.

Negate one of these broad assumptions and you negate the economic theory that Keynes inherited. The efforts at isolating the essential departures of Keynes from the Classics have generally presupposed that this is what he must have done. As we have seen the discussion has focused attention on the following possibilities:

1. that inter-temporal price-incentives are almost completely ineffective; specifically that neither savers nor investors are "disciplined enough" to obey the "orders" implicit in interest rate movements;

5. The familiar illustration of a homeostat is that of a heating system controlled by a thermostat. This automatic control system is equipped to observe discrepancies ("errors") between desired and actual temperatures and to respond to them by changing the actual temperature. When the response *reduces* the size of the error, the "feedback" is said to be "negative."

2. that wages or the "trapped" interest rate are rigid—the "orders" are simply not disseminated.

But neither one of these easy routes was the one taken by Keynes in making good his escape from the Classics. In my first paper on this subject[6] I tried to document his acceptance of the traditional conception of how individual activities are controlled. My conclusions were that, in Keynes' theory:

a. Transactors do maximise utility and profit as assumed in classical analysis. They are not assumed to be constrained from bargaining on their own (e.g., by unions or minimum-wage laws) nor are they money-illusioned or otherwise irrational. The analysis of saving and investment decisions is, in the same way, founded on quite standard choice-theoretical premises.
b. Price incentives are effective and this includes intertemporal price incentives. Present behaviour will be significantly affected by changes in interest rates or expected future spot prices.
c. Prices do move in response to excess demands and excess supplies in the corresponding markets.[7]

I will not repeat the analysis supporting these contentions. Instead, I will ask you to accept them for the sake of the argument.

If Keynes did not use any variant of these obvious ways of overturning classical analysis that we have just considered, there must be something that we miss in looking at the system in the way employed hitherto. We have focused on what is required in order to *control* the behaviour of individuals so as to make them fit into the puzzle of demands and supplies. I suggest that we should look more systematically and explicitly at the generation and dissemination of the *information* needed to achieve this co-ordination of activities.

Now, distinguishing between the problems of communication

6. Leijonhufvud (1967).

7. Markets are, in fact, treated on the assumption of their being "competitive" (in the sense of "atomistic"). Keynes had not shown much interest in the theory of "imperfect competition"—which otherwise was such a prominent development of the 'thirties—and it has left no mark on *The General Theory*.

and control in this way comes close to hairsplitting. It is perfectly possible to argue, for example, that the two concepts cannot be separated since meaningful communication must always entail producing a controlled response. We have, for example, already talked about price-"rigidity" in terms of a failure to disseminate the information that a certain reallocation of resources is required. Nonetheless, the notion of control applied so far is too "mechanical" and misses much of the point.

The system consists of a set of markets. Each of the product markets, in turn, has two variables—price and the rate of output—that are to be controlled. Corresponding to these two, the market has two homeostatic devices. Each of the two can be shown, very simply, to produce "deviation-counteracting" (negative) feedback when the value of the respective controlled variable deviates from the equilibrium value—*as long as* (at any rate) the demand curve has a negative and the supply curve a positive slope.

The first device is the "Walrasian homeostat" which we can regard, in the manner of R. M. Goodwin,[8] as a servomechanism designed to regulate price. It adjusts the actual price in response to the observed excess demand "error" and obeys the built-in rule of search for the equilibrium price of raising price when excess demand is positive and lowering price when excess demand is negative.

Correspondingly, the "Marshallian homeostat" is the one that regulates the rate of output. It adjusts actual output in response to the discrepancy between supply price and actual market price and obeys the rule of raising the rate of output when the excess supply price "error" is negative and lowering it when the error is positive.

Each of the mechanisms studied separately shows negative feedback and convergence of the process on the "right" price, $\hat{p}$, and the "right" quantity, $\hat{q}$, respectively. But when we put the two interacting mechanisms together (as we should), it is immediately apparent that two interacting controls, each operating with negative feedback, may well produce a process that does *not* lead to $(\hat{p}, \hat{q})$—the most familiar single-market

8. R. M. Goodwin (1951).

illustration of a failure to do so, of course, is the so-called "explosive cobweb" or "hog-cycle" possibility.[9]

Now, the cobweb per se has nothing to do with Keynesian economics. I mention it only as an illustration of a well-known principle: that whether an adjustment process will or will not lead to a predesignated equilibrium depends upon its *lag-structure*. The point, of course, is that this is something that we get no information on at all from the kind of static inspection of a system that we engaged in yesterday (Lecture I).

So, what kind of a "lead" to Keynes' thought might we get from this?

Well—that we should look for descriptions of *processes*, rather than of states, in *The General Theory*. There are several reasons why Keynes' exposition of the *Multiplier* and attendant matters can be expected to get us on the trail of what he was really about:

1. First, the multiplier is conceived of as a process in the early literature and not as the kind of "fifth wheel" under the "wagon" of comparative static analysis that it has become in later macro-textbooks.

2. Secondly, there is an immediately obvious contrast between Keynes and Marshall with regard to the lag-structure presumed in the description of market adjustment processes. In Marshall, roughly speaking, prices are assumed to adjust "very fast" relative to the speed of output adjustments. Prices move to wipe out excess demand "errors" already within the "market day," while the rate of output is adjusted to remove the discrepancy between supply price and demand price only in the "short run." In Keynes, rates of output (and employment) are the first to "give" when a disturbance occurs, and prices (especially wages) lag behind.

3. Thirdly, the multiplier is described as a *deviation-amplifying*

---

9. The cobweb model assumes, *inter alia*, a lagged response of output to price and produces a sequence of alternating price- and output-responses. When (roughly speaking) both the price-response to a given change in output and the output-response to a given change in price are "large," the resulting oscillations of p and q around p̂, q̂ will diverge further and further from these equilibrium values—the process "explodes." Co-ordination of consumers' and producers' plans fails because information on the price that will result from present output decisions is fed back to producers "only when it is too late."

process,[10] whereas in Walrasian analysis there should be only *deviation-counteracting* forces at work following a disturbance that has reduced income and output below equilibrium levels.

4. Fourthly, the multiplier is intimately connected in Keynes' exposition with his attack on Say's Law of Markets and with his introduction of the concept of "effective demand."[11]

VII. THE MULTIPLIER

In order to get Keynes' contribution to theory into sharper focus, we need a more detailed picture of certain aspects of "Classical" theory than that provided by the kind of "Classical" models discussed in my first lecture. The Walrasian general equilibrium tradition, which since Keynes' time has gained so much in rigour through the contributions of Professors Hicks, Samuelson, Patinkin, Arrow, Debreu, and others, provides the best contrasting background for our further discussion.

In the world of Walrasian theory, all transactors are price-takers. They make decisions only on what *quantities* to buy and sell, consume and produce, but never have to worry about at what prices to do so. They are simple price-takers because "each morning," so to speak, they are supposedly handed the market-clearing vector of prices $[\hat{P}]$, on a platter. This list of prices—made up as a result of "last night's *tâtonnement*"[12] carries *all the information* that anyone needs to know.[13]

10. I.e., a reduction in government expenditure of a given magnitude will lead to successive rounds of further reductions in output and expenditures, with the total decline in spending equalling some multiple of the initial "shock."

11. From a general equilibrium, Walrasian, standpoint the notion of "effective demand"—presumably as opposed to some other kinds of demands—is a strange one. From the very beginning of their education in economics, students are exposed to the term a lot. Yet they will often give evidence of having trouble with the concept if pressed with questions: Are you sure you know how to define "ineffective demand" in a meaningful way? If you don't, why say "effective demand" instead of just "demand"? If you do know what "ineffective" means, why do you call it a "demand" at all?

12. *Tâtonnement* (literally "groping") was Walras' term for the hypothetical trial-and-error auction process which he sketched as a simulation suggesting how an actual economic system might arrive at the equilibrium vector of prices. His sketch assumed that actual economic activities were suspended during the "groping"-process and only resumed when the right solution was found.

13. . . . provided that each and all are "atomistic competitors." The reason for keeping to this assumption is that a central question of the debate has been whether or not Keynesian analysis applies to "competitive" systems.

It is not just any old price-list. The analysis presumes, for example, that it is distributed to transactors with the guarantee:

a. that it lists the *best* prices obtainable (whether you are a buyer or a seller of the goods in question);

b. that you can be *assured* of being able to buy and/or sell all you want to of each and every good involved.

From the standpoint of the individual transactor, (a) and (b) together mean that all goods are "perfectly liquid" in the sense of being instantly marketable at no loss. Models of this type provide no explicit rationale for the use of one of the goods as a means of payment. Exchange opportunities, as represented by the $[\hat{P}]$-vector, are such that the individual seeking, say, to obtain consumer goods for his labour does not stand to gain by exchanging, first, labour for "money" and then "money" for consumer goods. Indeed, the offer of any good constitutes an exercise of "effective purchasing power" over any other good that is demanded in exchange.[14]

In order to deal with Keynes' problem, one must begin by taking a more realistic view of the individual decision situation and of the information available to decision-makers. When "in the real world" the market situation is changing, it is not possible to have all transactors making decisions just on quantities but never on prices. They must decide what prices to charge *or to accept.* This applies also to transactors whom we do not normally think of as "setting" the prices at which exchanges actually take place. Thus, when excess supply develops in a market (to take the directly relevant case), sellers must decide on their *reservation-prices,* i.e., the minimum prices at which they will consent to sell.

A newly unemployed worker, for example, does not know where the best job at the best wage is to be found. He must *search* for it—which is to say, engage in a process of acquiring information that is costly, at least, in terms of immediate earnings foregone. In sampling available job opportunities, he must decide what offers at what wages he will turn down. This means setting himself a reservation-wage which, roughly speaking, will

14. Cf. Robert W. Clower (1967).

reflect the best terms that he *believes* he should be able to obtain for himself.

Initially, the information relevant to fixing this belief will consist primarily of the "memory" of his past wages and of his knowledge of the current wages of those still working at his past place of employment. As his sampling of job openings progresses, his knowledge of the current state of the market improves and his reservation-wage will be adjusted accordingly—downwards or upwards depending upon whether the market is found worse or better than initially anticipated. At some point, the rate at which the best offer known improves will appear no longer to warrant the costs of further search and he will accept a job.[15]

The analysis assumes so-called "inelastic expectations"—past experience largely determines what the individual expects he will now be able to obtain. The assumption of inelastic expectations we recognise from Keynes' analysis of behaviour in securities markets and of the speculative demand for money. In a falling market prospective sellers with inelastic expectations will regard their resources as "illiquid." Thus the newly unemployed worker will refuse immediate re-employment at a wage much below that previously earned since he would regard it as selling his services "at a loss."[16]

During the time that the individual searches for a new job, he is "unemployed" in the everyday sense of the word. Keynes' multiplier is based on the assumption that the loss of receipts from current sales of labour services during this period will make him reduce his spending on consumer goods. This se-

---

15. In my book, I cited Professors Armen Alchian and Kenneth Arrow in connection with the analysis here paraphrased. I would here like to make retribution for the worst sin of omission that I have so far found myself guilty of: Professor W. H. Hutt's *The Theory of Idle Resources* (1939), ought to have been my *locus classicus* in this connection.

16. If the individual considered the last wage offered him as the only piece of evidence relevant to the appraisal of present market prospects, and thus attached no information value to past experience, we would have the extreme case of "perfectly elastic" expectations. He would then regard the subjective value of his leisure (as unemployed)—rather than the expected remuneration of some yet-to-be-found job—as the relevant opportunity cost of accepting employment; hence, he would take the first job paying enough to recompense him for lost leisure. An individual with such expectations would behave as if his "wealth" underwent sudden large changes, and at the same time, as if his resources were, in effect, "perfectly liquid" at each turn. This is not the kind of behaviour we observe in the real world.

cond-round reduction in effective demand will cause additional unemployment, a consequent third-round reduction in demand, etc. Each successive increment to unemployment and decrement in aggregate demand will be smaller than the last, so there will be a limit to the total decline in income consequent upon an initial reduction in expenditures of given magnitude. But the process entails an *amplification* of the initial deflationary disturbance.

It also entails a distortion of the information disseminated through the system for individual agents to act upon. Following the disturbance of the initial equilibrium, there exists, conceptually, a new full-employment equilibrium—characterised by a new allocation of resources and a corresponding, new $[\hat{P}]$-vector—towards which the system "ought" to be moving. If the multiplier-process takes hold, however, some prices that "ought" to be rising may be falling, and some industries that "ought" to be expanding will then be induced to contract.[17]

VIII. UNEMPLOYMENT AND EFFECTIVE DEMAND

The deviation-amplifying, information-distorting process just described could never take place in a barter system. The Keynesian disequilibrium problem is peculiar to systems of markets in which goods are always exchanged for *money* and money for goods. The means-of-payment function of money is essential to this model in a way that it is not to monetary general equilibrium models.[18] This feature of his model is the key to Keynes' Effective Demand doctrine, on which the multiplier is based; it is one of the two main arguments in his attack on Say's Law of Markets and it is *the* theme of the critique of Pigou; it provides the explanation of why the forces tending to bring the system out of Keynes' unemployment state are so

17. Let, for example, the initial disturbance be a lowering of the prospective rate of return on investment. From a "Classical" point of view, the system "ought" to adjust to a lower (full employment) growth path, with a lower rate of interest, less investment and more output of consumer goods. In the Keynesian analysis of this case, not only investment, but the output of consumer goods as well, will decline. This particular illustration is pertinent because it is the peculiar feature of Keynesian models that they "have a terrible time" switching from one rate of growth to another whenever this also requires going to lower levels of interest rates.

18. Cf. Clower, *op. cit.*

weak and, consequently, of why this state tends to persist for prolonged periods of time.

These propositions may be illustrated in a simple fashion. Consider the state of the system at a point in time when the multiplier has ceased operating, unemployment has ceased growing, and saving and investment are equal *ex ante*. Keynes would describe the situation as one of "unemployment equilibrium." In the standard, highly aggregative, model the system has but four goods: labour services (N), commodities (X), securities (B), and money (M). The state of the system and the tendencies present towards changing that state would be differently characterised by a Walrasian general equilibrium theorist and by Keynes. With some over-simplification (not affecting the present argument) it would look like this:

	N	*X*	*B*	*M*	*Sum*
Walras	Excess supply	Excess demand	0	0	0
Keynes	Excess supply	0	0	0 (ED)	< 0 (0)

In the top row, we suppose that we have information on the transactions plans that individuals would draw up *if*, at the prices prevailing in this unemployment state, they were to presume (*a*) that these prices were the best obtainable, and (*b*) that they were to be able to sell and buy all they wanted to of each and every good at these prices. As presented, the Table assumes that planned purchases and sales of securities would "mesh" at the prevailing interest rate, and that there would be no tendency, in the aggregate, to attempt either to build up or to draw down money balances. At the given relation between commodity prices and money wages, however, offers of labour services exceed the demand. Corresponding to this excess supply there is an excess demand for commodities (of the same money value)—showing that the unemployed would, on finding their offers of labour services accepted, devote their *entire* wage proceeds to consumption.[19] The sum of the values of excess

19. This is the over-simplification admitted to earlier.

demands is shown as zero since each and every individual transactor draws up his plan so as to make sources and uses of funds equal—an analytical convention that we refer to as Say's Principle.

In this situation, Walras' hypothetical auctioneer should, in obeying his rules of search for finding the equilibrium vector of prices, *raise the money prices of commodities* and lower money wages. He would then try out the thus "amended" list of prices in the same manner. On inspecting the new excess demand distribution, having thus lowered the real wage, he would find that planned output and the amount of labour demanded to produce it are higher, while the supply of labour and the demand for commodities are lower. The trial-and-error process would be continued in this manner until the price vector is found at which all activities are perfectly co-ordinated.

Clearly, the conceptual experiment just described does not simulate the forces acting on a monetary exchange economy in depression. There is no upward pressure on commodity prices[20]—this, indeed, is the problem. In the Keynesian excess demand distribution (bottom row) this is recognised—when saving and investment are equal *ex ante,* there is no stimulus towards expanding production. The offer of labour services (by the unemployed) does not constitute exercise of purchasing power over commodities, i.e., it does not constitute *effective* demand.

If the unemployed demanded "payment" in the form of the products of the individual firms, producers would perceive this as demand for a larger volume of output than is being produced. As long as the unemployed did not demand more in exchange than their marginal physical product, competitive producers would have no reason to turn such barter-bargains down. But, just as workers find that their labour is not a source of direct purchasing power over output, producers find that their output is not a means of payment for the purchase of labour inputs. In offering their services to firms that do not

20. According to the "Walrasian" way of looking at things, moreover, the pressure of excess demand for commodities should be stronger the higher is unemployment. Thus an increase in unemployment—through, say, teenagers leaving school and joining the labour force—should result in an accelerated rise in commodity prices. (I have "borrowed" this illustration from Professor Clower.)

produce a balanced basket of consumer goods, workers ask for *money wages*. From the standpoint of prospective employers, therefore, the offer of labour services is not directly connected with a demand for additional output.[21] Not perceiving that more output is called for, individual firms will, consequently, turn such offers down (a) even if no more than labour's marginal value product (evaluated at going prices) is being asked for, and (b) even if no more than the money wage rate that the system would have in equilibrium is being asked for. Once the multiplier has done its dirty work, the system may remain in an unemployment state although the money wage is "right" from the standpoint of overall equilibrium—a point to which we return below.

In the last two columns of the bottom row of the Table, we recognise an ambiguity of usage. Nothing is ever offered without demanding something (of equal value) in exchange. Consequently, from the conventional standpoint of the Theory of Exchange, we should recognise an excess demand for money of equal value to the labour services going begging. If we do so (as is done within the parentheses), the values of excess demands sum to zero as usual—Say's Law of Markets is upheld. Alternatively, we may argue that the unemployed are not planning to accumulate money balances but are demanding money only in order to buy consumer goods with it. Even if they were planning to "hoard," moreover, their demand for money is "ineffective" as long as their offers to sell labour are not accepted. Effective attempts to hoard would mean an ongoing tendency for the "velocity of money" (and thus for money income) to decline, but the situation portrayed is one of Keynesian income-"equilibrium" where, by definition, no such tendency is present. If, on these grounds, we put the excess demand for money down as zero, we find that the values of the effective excess demands sum to less than zero. Which convention is followed is of little consequence. The point of Keynes' attack on Say's Law is clear—the excess demand distribution that it presupposed is *irrelevant* to the analysis of the dynamic motion of the system.

A comparison of the two rows of our little Table indicates the

---

21. Thus Keynes' critique of Pigou harped on one theme: Pigou insisted on analysing the labour market in "real" terms—as if the wage-bargain was struck in barter terms.

communication failure that prevents the system from just "bouncing back" from a Keynesian unemployment state. As the top row shows, the unemployed supply labour and demand bread. But, as the second row shows, the demand is an "ineffective" demand that does not constitute a stimulus to increased (and labour-demanding) production of bread. *The market signals* presupposed in general equilibrium analysis *are not transmitted.*

IX. THE SAVING-INVESTMENT PROBLEM

We have found that unemployment may persist even with the "right" level of money wages. Two questions remain: If wages are "right," what then has gone wrong? What to do about it?

Previously, we associated the equilibrium price-vector, [$\hat{P}$], of a Walrasian set of excess demand equations with a "perfect information" state of the system. Keynes' disequilibrium we have discussed as due to a "communication failure" that disrupts the coordination of economic activities. One way of studying "what has gone wrong," then, is to consider in what ways the vector of prices obtaining in a Keynesian unemployment state differs from the "perfect" [$\hat{P}$]-vector.

The clue is provided by the second of the two arguments used by Keynes in his attack on Say's Law. This argument concerns the saving-investment problem and it, also, centres around the concept of effective demand. "A fresh act of saving," Keynes argued, may mean a net reduction in effective demand, i.e., in the demands on current resource utilisation *as perceived by producers.* An individual decision to save more is a decision to consume less today in order to consume more at some future date. Ideally, the producing sector should respond to such household decisions by switching resources away from the production of current consumables and into the (current) provision for an augmented output of consumables in the future, i.e., into investment.

The trouble is that, while producers cannot fail to feel the direct impact of the reduction in demand for current consumables, they may fail to pick up any "signals" that could tell them where to re-employ the resources freed from the production of consumer goods. They "ought to" revise upwards their forecasts of future demands, but future markets are missing in which the increased demand for specific products could be communicated already now to the respective producers. The "circuits" for the transmission of the market signals presupposed by inter-temporal general equilibrium theory are missing. They are missing for a good reason, moreover—it does not pay to organise such markets because savers do not wish to place orders for the future delivery of specific products. Rather than committing themselves to some future consumption pattern now, and accumulating such contracts, they wish to command "wealth as such," that is the "potentiality of consuming an unspecified article at an unspecified time." At bottom, it is the Liquidity Preference (in this broad sense) of households that is the problem. One sector does not receive the appropriate signals simply because the other chooses not to emit.

Since the future demand implicit in the behaviour of savers is not an effective demand, producers' demand forecasts do not respond in an appropriate and reliable fashion to changes in saving behaviour. But the switch of resources into investment may still be accomplished. Increased saving will mean a downward pressure on the yields of securities and in Keynes' theory, as already remarked, investment responds to changes in interest rates. Here, however, Liquidity Preference will again come into play—rising securities prices and declining yields will induce speculators (with inelastic expectations) to sell and hold deposits instead, thereby preventing the decline in yields from becoming as large as required and necessitating a reduction in money income. As indicated at the very beginning of this lecture, Liquidity Preference will, in the same manner, come in the way of proper co-ordination of saving and investment decisions also when the initial disturbance is a change in entrepreneurial expectations (i.e., a "shift of the marginal efficiency schedule").

Having sketched how Keynes looked at the problem of co-ordinating the inter-temporal decisions of consumers and producers, we may now come back to the question of "what goes wrong" with the vector of prices.

Keynes' analysis of movements in income focuses on changes in the investment component of total income. Simplifying somewhat, we may formulate the problem thus: there exists a critical value for aggregate investment that would give full employment at the money wages inherited from the last period. Corresponding to it, a critical ratio of the demand price for productive assets to money wages may be defined such that, when faced with this price constellation, profit-maximising capital goods producers will be induced to undertake the required amount of production of new such assets. If the actual value of this relative price falls below the critical value, $p_a/\bar{w}$, money income will be too low to permit full employment.

If, then, this relative price is too low, and the economy consequently in recession, the first question becomes whether this is because p_a is too low or $\bar{w}$ too high. In both the *Treatise on Money* and the *General Theory*, Keynes' discussion generally presumes that money wages are "right" and that the trouble is too low a demand price for capital goods. The most serious consequence of this disequilibrium is the unemployment emerging in the labour market, but this does not mean that the cause is to be found in too high wages.[22]

The level of asset prices, p_a, may be too low for either of two reasons. Estimates of the income that will accrue to such assets may be too low (entrepreneurial demand forecasts may be "too pessimistic"), or the interest rate, at which these income streams are discounted in order to appraise their present value, may be too high.

In the bulk of his theoretical writings Keynes was concerned with the case where the interest rate is too high. He regarded the post-First World War period as one in which capital accumulation was steadily running ahead of innovation and population growth, etc., with the result of a persistent downward trend in the rate of return that could be earned on capital. The

---

22. Note that it is a *relative* price that is wrong. In discussing whether the system could get out of the unemployment state "on its own" Keynes consequently showed little interest in the case of *balanced* deflation (money prices falling, but relative values staying constant). The possibility of such a deflation being of help in the bitter end is the one elaborated in the Pigou-effect literature. Keynes concentrated instead on the possibility that deflation, by increasing the purchasing power of the given money stock, would become *unbalanced* in such a manner that relative values were "corrected" in the process. He gave a fully adequate analysis of this possibility, in spite of which his discussion has been given a failing grade in the Pigou-effect literature—where little understanding has been shown for the role of relative prices in Keynes' theory.

problem was that rates of interest *tended to lag behind*—in part because of Bank of England efforts to defend the exchange rate with the help of Bank rate—so that the level of asset prices was persistently threatening to sink below its "critical" value.

If the rate of interest is permitted to fall behind, recession and unemployment will result. In all this Keynes followed in the Wicksellian tradition: deflationary pressure on the system is due to a market rate of interest above the "natural rate."

This element of his theory is really a hypothesis about how the boom breaks. Keynes had a broad streak of rationalistic optimism in him and concentrated a good deal of his work on how to prevent a recession from developing. During the 'thirties he had to contend with the problem of getting out of a deep depression, of repairing a disaster that had already been allowed to develop. A sketch of this problem had appeared in the last chapter of the *Treatise* in 1930 and is there seen to involve the "other reason" for too low a level of asset demand prices. In the process of contraction, interest rates come down, while entrepreneurial expectations are, at the same time, undermined by the experience of declining aggregate demand. Although it is assumed that the process is triggered by the concatenation of roughly appropriate demand forecasts and inappropriately high interest rates, in the depths of the depression we have the opposite case—the "right" interest rate, but too pessimistic expectations.

X. FISCAL POLICY AND THE MULTIPLIER

Early in my first lecture, I promised to close with some observations concerning Keynesian fiscal policy and the concept of the "government expenditure multiplier." These will have to be quite brief and even sketchier than what has gone before. I hope they may suggest to you that the issues I have discussed are of more than doctrine-historical interest.

We have outlined two alternative diagnoses of a state of deficient aggregate demand. One is a hypothesis about how the system comes to depart from the neighbourhood of a full employment equilibrium with stable prices. That diagnosis points to a *"wrong" level of interest rates* as the source of the problem. The other is a hypothesis about the salient characteristics of a deep depression state. The diagnosis in this case points to *entrepreneurial expectations* as the root of the trouble. If entrepreneurial expectations were to approximate more closely to the demand that would actually be experienced at full employment, they would become self-fulfilling, for interest rates and money wages are not at levels that would stand in the way of a restoration of full employment equilibrium.

Naturally, these two diagnoses would not apply to the downturn and trough, respectively, of every cycle. If we assume situations to which they would apply, however, it is striking how they seem by themselves to suggest the policy remedies that should be appropriate. Faced with a diagnosis that pinpoints the "wrong" value of one variable as the source of the disequilibrium of the entire system, the natural impulse is to look around for some policy instrument that would impinge as directly as possible on this variable while, ideally, leaving alone those which are already "right." Much more would need to be said, to be sure, to provide the proper *caveats,* and the full context, for Keynes' policy recommendations but, by and large, this natural impulse points in the direction of his prescriptions. Thus, in the neighbourhood of *full employment equilibrium,* where the problem is to keep market rates of interest in the near neighbourhood of the "natural rate," Keynes would keep close to time-honoured British tradition in stabilisation policy and rely on monetary measures—Bank rate reinforced by open market operations.

It is the other case that concerns us here, for it is this case which caused the break with tradition and the innovation of "Keynesian" fiscal policies used for short-run stabilisation purposes. Entrepreneurial demand forecasts are attuned to a continuation of depression. The immediate objective is to change them while meddling as little as possible with interest rates that are already at (or below) the level they would have been in general equilibrium. Direct government expenditure would do the trick. The expenditures by themselves will belie the expectations that demand will continue unchanged at its depressed level and thus set in motion a process of upward revision of demand forecasts. This process will be powerfully reinforced by the "multiplier" which takes hold as previously unemployed workers are gradually re-employed and able to make their demand for consumption goods "effective." Consequently, the government's deficit spending can be gradually phased out as the system nears full employment; the effective demand stemming from those reabsorbed into the work force will prevent backsliding into renewed depression. Thus the original case for fiscal measures for stabilisation purposes was a so-called *"pump-priming"* case and the argument for it hinged on the multiplier effects that government spending could unleash.

What does this analysis have to suggest about the usefulness of "Keynesian" fiscal policies in dealing with cyclical fluctuations of the fairly "moderate" variety that have characterised the post-war period? Clearly, counter-cyclical variation of government spending and (whether automatic or discretionary) of its tax-take will help.[23] But it is clear also that, if one were not to be able to count on multiplier effects at all for help, such measures would have to be of a *very* large magnitude to be commensurate with the problem.

The Multiplier as an Illiquidity Phenomenon

The neo-quantity theorists have, of course, attacked the "multiplier optimism" which they see as in large measure the basis for the popularity among economists of fiscal stabilisation measures. More directly to the point, however, are the modern theories of the consumption function.[24] Professor Milton Friedman's permanent income hypothesis[25] and the Modigliani-Brumberg-Ando "life cycle hypothesis"[26] alike imply such a low value for the multiplier that it would not be worth bothering about. The modern theories have in common the emphasis on

23. At least they will help if monetary policy is simultaneously used to ensure that interest rates are not allowed to move in the "wrong" direction. The nearer one is to full employment equilibrium, the larger the element of truth that has to be accorded to the despised "Treasury view." The use of monetary policy in the manner indicated will, of course, also raise the issue of the extent to which the effects of the total policy package must be ascribed to its monetary policy component.

24. For a survey of the developments in this area since Keynes, cf. James Tobin (1968).

25. Milton Friedman (1957).

26. Albert Ando and Franco Modigliani (1963).

income prospects over the *long* run, or "wealth"—rather than *current* receipts—as the primary determinant of household consumption. "Wealth" in this context stands as proxy for what the households, taking the long view, subjectively perceive themselves as "being able to afford" in terms of current consumption. Changes in current income receipts that the household envisages as temporary (or "transitory") will have little or no impact on its wealth-position in this sense, and thus little effect on its consumption. In the limiting case, the wage-earner loses his job and thereby all labour income, but the household maintains its consumption at the accustomed level.

We are obliged, in conclusion, to consider this view of the determination of consumption for at least two reasons. First, the modern theories of the consumption function have yielded much better empirical results[27] than the simple consumption-income relation presupposed in our explanation of the multiplier. Secondly, the hypothesis that the household's view of its "wealth" is insensitive to short-run changes in income receipts "fits in," most naturally, with our description of individual behaviour in the labour market. To say that a worker shows "inelastic expectations" with regard to the wages that he thinks he will be able to obtain is, in effect, to say that he regards his *human capital* as more or less unimpaired by the loss of his previous job.

Is it possible to reconcile the explanation of Keynes' multiplier outlined above with the modern theories of the consumption function? We should conduct a second examination of the analysis of the unemployed worker's behaviour, this time while accepting the view that the individual regards his long-run income prospects as virtually unchanged. We emphasised that he cannot offer his labour services in direct market exchange for consumables. They can only be sold for money and he must offer money for goods. The option of selling his labour for money, at *some* price, is open to him, but he does not take it since, at the prices immediately obtainable, he would regard accepting a job as "taking a loss." In the given situation, his labour is an "illiquid" good, i.e., it cannot be turned into cash.

Now, if the same considerations were to apply to *all* other

27. Cf. Friedman, *op cit.;* Ando and Modigliani, *op. cit.*

components of his net worth as well, the sought-for reconciliation would be found. To borrow against future labour earnings, for example, can frequently be done only at terms which render it a very expensive way of turning human capital into ready purchasing power. Similarly, those components of his net worth that are in the form of physical capital are generally "illiquid" too—they cannot be turned into cash without incurring what the individual will regard as a "capital loss." Borrowing with such assets as collateral is also an expensive proposition.

We may thus envisage an individual who, while he regards his "wealth" as in itself justifying a maintenance of accustomed living standards, finds that no component of his net worth can be realised at a market price that meets the reservation price he puts on it. He finds himself "locked in," in effect, with the balance sheet he has. Only in this way can we rationalise the behaviour of consumers who let current income receipts be the operative constraint on their consumption. The multiplier emerges from this analysis as an *illiquidity* phenomenon.

By the same token, we should not expect the multiplier to take hold in a recession as long as unemployed households still have a "cushion" of liquid assets, such as savings deposits. Some pieces of evidence consistent with this view may be noted. Thus P. A. Klein has found that households do maintain their consumption standards for several months of unemployment until their liquid assets are run down quite low. S. H. Hymans has studied the American experience since the First World War and found that consumption held quite steady in the face of falling incomes in all recessions *except one*—the Great Depression of the 'thirties.[28]

A "Monetary" View of Great Depressions

To summarise: We started arguing a case for fiscal policy by considering a disequilibrium situation diagnosed as due to ex-

28. P. A. Klein (1965) and S. H. Hymans (1965). In connection with Hymans' exception, it is interesting to note that the controversial study by Friedman and Meiselman (1963) reports one sub-period for which the investment multiplier performed better than monetary velocity—the 'thirties. In similar experiments on British data, Professor Walters and associates found the inter-war period, 1921–38, to constitute an exceptional "Keynesian interlude." Cf. A. A. Walters (1969).

cessively pessimistic entrepreneurial expectations. An increase in government spending rather than central bank action was indicated because it would operate to "correct" these expectations. Further analysis showed this to be a case for fiscal "pump-priming," since multiplier effects would be triggered that would reinforce the movement back towards full employment. The two salient features of the situation were not accidentally juxtaposed. They are clearly logically related: producers' demand forecasts could not remain so far off target without any tendency towards self-correction *except* when the consumption demands of the unemployed are in large measure "ineffective," i.e., except when the feedback of the relevant market signals is interrupted. And it is only under such circumstances that there will be latent multiplier effects of sizeable magnitude for the policy-maker to exploit.

What the analysis of this section suggests is that communication failures of this serious a magnitude are not a normal occurrence in market systems where most economic agents keep "buffer stocks" of liquid assets. They emerge as products of "liquidity crises."

To the extent that preference for the use of fiscal measures for stabilisation purposes rests on the belief that they will have an amplified impact on aggregate demand, we do not find a case for them along the lines of analysis pursued here as far as states of the system "fairly close" to full employment equilibrium are concerned.

By pursuing Keynes' analysis we have ended up with an essentially "monetary" view of Great Depressions. In a very general sense, at least, quantity theorists and Keynesians should be able to agree on one thing—how great disasters are fashioned. On one view or the other, the system becomes prone to them only when it has first been squeezed dry of "liquidity."

CHAPTER FIVE

Say's Principle, What It Means and Doesn't Mean[*]

> The doctrine in question only appears a paradox, because it has usually been so expressed as apparently to contradict . . . well-known facts; which, however, were equally well known to the authors of the doctrine, who, therefore, can only have adopted from inadvertence any form of expression which could to a candid person appear inconsistent with it.
>
> J.S. Mill, *Some Unsettled Questions of Political Economy* (1844)

Students with some exposure to macroeconomics will recall that the standard verbal statement of "Say's Law" (SL) is "Supply creates its own demand." Students will also recall—at least if they have had the usual indoctrination in these matters—that the rejection of SL was associated with the development of Keynesian macroeconomics. Classical (pre-Keynesian) economists, so it is said, could not explain prolonged unemployment because they believed in SL, but Keynes denied the validity of SL and so was able to lay the foundations for a modern and reasonably adequate theory of income and employment . . . etc.[1]

Like most fairytales, this one contains an element of truth. Anyone who bothers to delve into the matter[2] will discover that textbook discussions of SL are seldom fair to pre-Keynesian writers; this is not surprising. Doubts about the meaning and significance of SL have been perplexing economists more or

---

*This pedagogical excursion originated in a set of mimeographed "Class Notes on Say's Principle" written by Leijonhufvud and distributed to students at the Economics Institute, University of Colorado in 1972. The original notes have been extensively rewritten and extended.

1. For example, McConnell (1972), pp. 203–7.

2. A good book to start with is Sowell (1972).

less continuously for nearly two centuries. The extensive literature since Keynes has done little to resolve these doubts, largely because it has failed to address squarely the main issues in dispute and so has got bogged down in a mire of conceptual and semantic confusions.

To avoid the same mistake, we shall ignore the previous literature for the time being and start by explaining and analyzing a simple but fundamental proposition that we shall call "Say's Principle" (SP). This principle, though elementary and outwardly trivial, is crucial for clear understanding of macro-theory. Indeed, there is hardly a single problem in macro-theory (or, for that matter, micro-theory) that can be consistently analyzed without it. The same principle permits us to resolve all issues of substance associated with earlier discussions of SL. It is essential, therefore, that students acquire a clear understanding not only of what SP means and does not mean, but also of what it implies and does not imply.

I. FUNDAMENTALS

In the following paper the term "commodity" will refer to any exchangeable object. Thus the usual macro-model, involving labor services, goods, bonds and money, has four commodities. Similarly, we shall use the term "transactor" (or individual) to refer to any economic agent or decision-making unit.[3] For reasons that will become clear later, we shall deal directly with just one type of economic activity, namely exchange. Occasional references to consumption, production and other non-trade activities are introduced only by way of illustration.

To lend direction to the argument, we begin by associating SP with a brief verbal statement that is easy to remember—not, however, with the phrase "Supply creates its own demand." A mnemonic much to be preferred is: *the net value of an individual's planned trades is identically zero.* (Notice, for reasons to be made clear later, we do not say net market value.) This is a restriction that we impose on the commodity trades that transactors are permitted to contemplate within the conceptual framework of economic theory, trades that we shall later refer to as theo-

3. We will not bother to distinguish among households, business firms, financial intermediaries, government agencies, and so on.

retically admissible. It is not an assertion about the income and expenditure plans of flesh-and-blood humans (the world is full of thieves and philanthropists as well as people who can't calculate the cost of their weekly groceries). Neither is it an assertion that applies to all commodity transfers that occur in the real world (the acquisition of cash by a pickpocket is a case in point). What the restriction does and does not entail, however, is better indicated by argument than example.

Starting from familiar ground, consider one of the first exercises encountered in microeconomics, namely, the household decision problem of determining how a given amount of money, $s_{m,0}$, will be allocated to purchase quantities d_x and d_y of two commodities that are available at given money prices p_x and p_y. In this problem, the set of all possible budgets may be associated with the set of all points $d^* = (d_x, d_y)$ in the nonnegative (northeast) quadrant of the diagram shown in Figure 5-1. However, if the head of the household is presumed to be honest—or merely risk-averse—the set of all theoretically admissible trades of money for commodities will consist of points that lie on a single budget line (shown as L in Figure 5-1). This line is defined by the equation:

$$p_x d_x^* + p_y d_y^* - s_{m,0} = O, \tag{1}$$

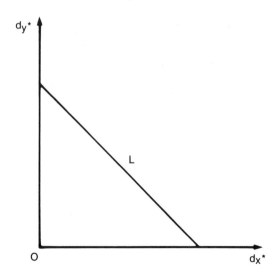

Figure 5-1.

where (by hypothesis) p_x, p_y and $s_{m,0}$ are given decision para-meters (i.e., constants, from the point of view of the individual). Points to the northeast of L represent budgets that have a value greater than $s_{m,0}$ dollars, while points to the southwest represent budgets that have a value less than $s_{m,0}$ dollars. Only those points that lie on the budget line represent budgets that have a value of precisely $s_{m,0}$ dollars. Let us denote budgets that satisfy equation (1) by $d = (d_x, d_y)$. The set of budgets d is, of course, a subset of the set of all possible budgets d^*. By definition it is literally true that

$$p_x d_x + p_y d_y - s_{m,0} \equiv O; \qquad (2)$$

that is to say, all theoretically admissible budgets d identically satisfy equation (1).[4] This zero-net-value identity, i.e., identity (2), is an exact rendition of SP as it appears in the context of the present discussion.

At first sight, the preceding argument might seem to suggest that SP is implied by the assumption that household purchases are constrained by the budget equation (1). On closer inspec-tion, however, it will be seen that the true relation between SP and the budget equation is precisely the reverse of this, for the validity of SP is tacitly presupposed in our initial definition of the budget equation. Thus SP appears in this instance as an in-dependent assumption rather than a derived conclusion. In fact, this instance illustrates the general rule rather than the ex-ceptional case; i.e., the restriction on individual trading behav-ior that we call SP is a fundamental postulate of economic theory that holds quite independently of other behavior as-sumptions.

---

4. It may help clarify the distinction between d and d*, and the related distinction be-tween the conditional equation (1) and the identical equation (2), if we consider a simple analog. Suppose that an algebraist is assigned the problem of choosing one value of the variable x^* that satisfies the equation $x^{*2} = 9$. Clearly, most values of x^* that might be considered won't do. However, two values of x^*, namely, $x^* = 3$ and $x^* = -3$, do satisfy the equation. The set of theoretically admissible solutions to the original problem thus consists of two numbers. The original problem, which involves choosing some element x^* of the set of all real numbers is thus transformed into the more re-stricted problem of choosing some element x of the set of just two real numbers, [3,–3]. Since the latter set is defined in such a way that all of its elements satisfy the conditional equation $x^{*2} = 9$, it follows trivially that any element x of the set $\{3, -3\}$ satisfies the same equation *identically*; i.e., $x^2 \equiv 9$. The algebraist, like the household, still has a choice to make, but the choice is narrowed down considerably by the require-ment that $x^2 \equiv 9$ as compared with the weaker requirement that $x^{*2} = 9$.

The full significance of the last observation will become clear later. Meanwhile, the following comments may be helpful:

> The budget equation (and so the budget line) is a special case of a class of behavioral restrictions that occur over and over again in economic analysis, restrictions that follow from a completely general proposition that we shall call *Say's Principle*. This proposition asserts, broadly speaking, that trade is a two-way street; i.e., individuals can expect to acquire commodities from other individuals only by giving commodities (or money) of equal market value in exchange. Say's Principle might seem almost too obvious to be worth stating, but it is as well to take nothing for granted at this point. It should be remarked, for example, that Say's Principle (and the budget equation) refers not to quantities actually purchased or to prices actually paid, but rather to expected purchase prices and planned quantities purchased. It is evident that if one pays, say, $10 for all groceries that he *actually* acquires in a supermarket, the total value of the separate items purchased must add up to $10—or else the supermarket checkout clerk has made a mistake. But it is neither obvious nor always true that a shopper who *plans* to spend $10 on groceries in a supermarket also plans to walk out of the store with a collection of goods that is valued at just $10; the shopper may be a shoplifter as well as a customer! In effect, Say's Principle constitutes an implicit definition of the concept of a transactor as distinguished from the concept of a thief or a philanthropist. Thus it restricts our vision as economists to just one aspect of individual behavior, for it excludes (by assumption) facets of behavior which, although they involve the acquisition and disposal of commodities—and so are of economic interest in some sense—fall outside the purview of formal economic analysis.[5]

II. EXTENSIONS

In keeping with the logical primacy of SP, let us now reverse direction and consider the consequences of applying SP to situations that are more general (and less obviously contrived) than the problem of household choice outlined in the previous section. Let us start by considering a simple generalization of the household choice model in which we permit some of the money available for expenditure to be retained by the household for future disposal. Applying SP to this case, we may suppose that the set of theoretically admissible budgets, $d = (d_x, d_y, d_m)$, is defined by the zero-net-value identity:

$$p_x d_x + p_y d_y + (d_m - s_{m,0}) \equiv O, \qquad (3)$$

5. Quoted from Clower and Due (1972), pp. 64–65.

where d_m denotes the quantity of money that the household plans to hold for future disposal (other variables are defined just as before).

Another easy extension of our model is accomplished by admitting the possibility that the household may be a supplier of non-money commodities as well as a supplier of money. In this case, application of SP yields the zero-net-value identity:

$$p_x(d_x - s_{x,0}) + p_y(d_y - s_{y,0}) + (d_m - s_{m,0}) \equiv O,^6 \qquad (4)$$

where the symbols $s_{x,0}$ and $s_{y,0}$, like the symbol $s_{m,0}$, represent decision parameters and denote (non-negative) stocks of non-money commodities currently available for possible sale (the values of $s_{x,0}$ and $s_{y,0}$ may be zero, of course, for one or both commodities).

Yet another extension of our model is obtained by supposing that the individual is a potential trader of a large but finite number of commodities. Using numerical subscripts, 1, 2, . . . , m to distinguish different commodities, and treating the m-th commodity as money, we obtain:

$$p_1(d_1 - s_{1,0}) + p_2(d_2 - s_{2,0}) + . . .$$
$$+ p_{m-1}(d_{m-1} - s_{m-1,0}) + (d_m - s_{m,0}) \equiv O, \qquad (5)$$

as the zero-net-value identity implied by SP. Notice that this condition—like analogous relations set out earlier—holds for all values of the price variables, p_i, and not just for one or a few specially chosen price lists. Further notice that the validity of identity (5) does not depend in any way on the assumption that the symbols $s_{i,0}$ represent (given) decision parameters rather than (unknown) decision variables whose values have to be determined by the individual decision maker. This being so, it is superfluous to work with gross demands and gross supplies when we are considering transactors as commodity traders, for only net demands and net supplies are relevant in this case. Ac-

6. More accurately, SP yields the set of budgets defined by identity (4) if, as is conventional, we assume that each of the non-money commodities (x) and (y) can be traded directly for each other as well as for money. We shall not elaborate on this theme here; for additional details see Clower (1967) and Veendorp (1970). However, in general, a single constraint such as identity (4) can be used to define the set of admissible budgets only in a world where individuals consider themselves able to trade any given collection of commodities directly for any other collection in a *single* exchange transaction.

cordingly, to simplify notation let us define the individual's excess demand (ED) for the i-th commodity by the relation:

$$x_i = d_i - s_i \ (i = 1, \ldots, m). \tag{6}$$

In general, x_i may be positive, zero or negative. In the last case, the individual would appear as a potential seller rather than buyer (or non-trader) of the i-th commodity, in which event we might call x_i the individual's excess supply (ES) of the i-th commodity. Using the notation of equation (6), identity (5) now takes the simpler but logically equivalent form:

$$p_1 x_1 + p_2 x_2 + \ldots + p_{m-1} x_{m-1} + x_m \equiv O.^7 \tag{7}$$

As a final generalization consider a large (but finite) collection of transactors; we distinguish among quantities associated with different transactors by adding a second numerical subscript, 1, 2, $\ldots$, k to relevant variables (e.g., the variable x_{ij} denotes the j-th transactor's ED for the i-th commodity). For simplicity, suppose that all transactors face the same money prices; this uniform price assumption is so conventional in general equilibrium theory that its presence is sometimes not even recognized.[8] We also assume (as usual) that the trading behavior of each and every transactor is constrained in accordance with SP. On these assumptions, we obtain not one, but rather a set of K zero-net-value identities to characterize the set of admissible net trades that transactors as a group are permitted to contemplate. These relations are displayed in matrix form in Table 1.

Each row in Table 1 shows the money value of the corresponding transactor's EDs—valued at some arbitrary set of money prices (the same set for all transactors). In accordance with SP, the sum of these money values is identically zero

---

7. The money price of a unit of money is necessarily unity, $p_m \equiv 1$; so identity (7) is equivalent to the more symmetrical identity:

$$p_1 x_1 + p_2 x_2 + \ldots + p_{m-1} \, x_{m-1} + p_m x_m \equiv 0 \tag{7'}$$

8. For future reference, we observe here that the assumption involves a drastic over-simplification; it means we ignore differences in price for the same good between different localities, bid-ask spreads for the same good in the same locality, discrepancies in prices charged for different sellers, etc. These omissions represent serious abstractions from reality. However, they do not affect the logic of our argument (which would merely become more complicated if the assumption of uniform prices were relaxed).

TABLE 1 Matrix of Admissible Trades

Transactors (I_j)	Commodities (C_i)			(Money)	Net value
	C_1	C_2	C_{m-1}	C_m	
I_1	$p_1 x_{1,1}$ +	$p_2 x_{2,1}$ +	$\cdots\cdots\cdots + p_{m-1} x_{m-1,1}$ +	$x_{m,1}$	$\equiv$ 0
I_2	$p_1 x_{1,2}$ +	$p_2 x_{2,2}$ +	$\cdots\cdots\cdots + p_{m-1} x_{m-1,2}$ +	$x_{m,2}$	$\equiv$ 0
.					
.					
.					
I_k	$p_1 x_{1,k}$ +	$p_2 x_{2,k}$ +	$\cdots\cdots\cdots + p_{m-1} x_{m-1,k}$ +	$x_{m,k}$	$\equiv$ 0
Aggregate excess demands	$p_1 X_1$ +	$p_2 X_2$ +	$\cdots\cdots\cdots + p_{m-1} X_{m-1}$ +	X_m	$\equiv$ 0

(right-hand column). Of course, some of the individual terms in each sum may also be zero, indicating that the transactor in question neither plans to buy nor sell units of those commodities. In particular, if the i-th commodity is assumed to be an imaginary object, or a commodity that has no concrete counterpart (e.g., the English monetary unit called the "Guinea"), then $x_{ij} \equiv 0$ for all transactors since, by its very definition, such a commodity cannot seriously be contemplated as an object of trade by any transactor.[9]

The first K terms in each of the first M columns of Table 1 indicate which transactors are net suppliers and which are net demanders of the corresponding commodity. We shall refer to the sum of the individual EDs in each column as the aggregate ED for the corresponding commodity. In symbols:

$$\sum_{j=1}^{j=k} x_{ij} \equiv X_i, \ (i = 1, \ldots, m) \tag{8}$$

On the assumption that a common price is relevant for valuing all individuals EDs, we may then write the money value of aggregate ED for the i-th commodity as:

9. The relevance of this outwardly trivial observation will become clear below.

$$\sum_{j=1}^{j=k} p_i x_{ij} \equiv p_i \sum_{j=1}^{j=k} x_{ij} \equiv p_i X_i, \ (i = 1, \ \ldots, \ m) \qquad (9)$$

Because the money value of individual EDs may be negative as well as positive or zero, the magnitude and sign of $p_i X_i$ may be positive, negative or zero. However, since the (row) sum of the money values of any single transactor's EDs is identically zero, and since the sum of K zeroes is zero, it follows that the money value of all individual EDs summed over all transactors and all commodities, is identically zero.[10] Even though we can place no restrictions on the size or sign of any of the first M terms in the bottom row of Table 1 we may assert unequivocally that the last term is zero; i.e., the money value of the sum of all aggregate EDs is identically equal to zero.[11] In symbols,

$$\sum_{i=1}^{i=m} p_i X_i \equiv 0, \ (i = 1, \ \ldots, \ m) \qquad (10)$$

This proposition effectively summarizes the whole of the preceding argument. In the final analysis it asserts much the same concept as the simple individual version of SP defined earlier; however, it applies to a group of transactors rather than a single individual. Where we specially wish to emphasize that we are referring to the group identity (10), we shall identify it henceforth as the aggregative version of SP (where the sense of our argument is not in doubt, however, we shall omit qualifying phrases and speak simply of SP).

10. Notice that this proposition is valid even if the prices used to value individual EDs are not the same for different transactors:

$$\sum_{j=1}^{j=k} \sum_{i=1}^{i=m} p_{ij} x_{ij} \equiv 0, \ (i = 1, \ \ldots, \ m) \ \text{and} \ (j = 1, \ \ldots, k) \qquad (9')$$

where p_{ij} represents the money price of the *ith* commodity as seen by the *jth* transactor. Hence, the proposition holds even more strongly if prices are uniform over all transactors (i.e., if $p_{ij} = p_i$ for all values of j).

11. For the record we can find no hints of any such aggregative proposition in J. B. Say's economic writings. In our view, however, it would be historically accurate to credit J. B. Say with the weaker (but still fairly powerful) proposition (9') where the sum of all individual notional EDs, valued at money prices as seen by individual transactors is identically zero. This, or some similar disaggregative version of SP is, we believe, what most pre-Keynesian writers had in mind when referring to "Say's Law of Markets."

Three features of the aggregative version of SP merit special emphasis before we proceed:

1. *The proposition is valid for any (uniform) set of prices and for every theoretically admissible set of aggregate EDs;*
2. *No general statement can be made about the sum of the money values of any proper subset of the aggregate EDs;* i.e., if one or more of the terms $p_i X_i$ is excluded from the summation in identity (10), we can place no restrictions whatever on the sign or magnitude of the sum of the remaining terms;
3. The aggregate ED for each commodity in identity (10) is defined by identity (8) as the sum over all transactors of *planned* (notional, intended, desired) purchases or sales of the same commodity. *If aggregate EDs were defined in terms of anything other than planned quantities, we should have no assurance that the aggregative version of SP would still hold.*

III. STANDARD THEMES AND DOCTRINES

We are now in a position to discuss certain interpretations of SP that appear frequently in the economic literature.

A. Old Familiar Phrases

1. "A general glut of commodities is impossible." This sounds archaic . . . which is natural, since it is a version of SP that was much in vogue among early nineteenth century economists. Glut means ES (negative ED). If general glut is interpreted to mean notional ES prevailing for all commodities simultaneously, then such a situation is flatly inconsistent with SP in any of its variants and, in that sense, the statement is true.

2. "Supply creates its own demand." This is perhaps the most ambiguous statement that students of economics are ever asked to ponder. Consider, for example, the following alternatives:

i. "Supply of a commodity at some price gives rise to an equal demand for the same commodity at that price." This version is, of course, false. But it illustrates one possible interpretation of a special case of the version of SL that the

Classical economists are often accused of believing (see Section C, below).

ii. "No one plans to supply anything of value without also planning some use for the proceeds from the sale, which may include simply planning to hold money until a later decision is made to purchase other commodities." This statement is correct and sensible.

iii. "Confronted with given prices, each transactor must plan to supply commodities of sufficient value to finance all his planned net demands." This statement is also correct.

iv. "If prices are given, each transactor's planned sales will create the means to finance his planned purchase." This statement resembles (ii) but it is quite different—false rather than true. Suppose that aggregate ES exists for all commodities that the transactor plans to sell; it is then likely that actual sales will be less than planned (perhaps nil). Hence, planned receipts will not serve to finance planned purchases. SP refers only to purchase and sale intentions; it asserts absolutely nothing about the possibility of their realization.

B. General Equilibrium

An economic system may be said to be in equilibrium when the values of all variables that are considered relevant for describing its observable behavior are equal over time to the values of a corresponding set of theoretical variables that define the virtual (notional) behavior of the system along a postulated equilibrium path. This very general concept is consistent with the existence of non-stationary equilibrium paths. In elementary accounts of general equilibrium theory, however, equilibrium paths are typically defined in terms of constancy over time in the values of a set of relative prices, $\bar{P} = (p_1, p_2, \ldots, p_m)$, where one commodity, say the m-th, serves as a unit of account or *numeraire* so that $\bar{p}_m = 1$. This simple definition of economic equilibrium is arrived at by conceptualizing the economic system as a collection of named, but otherwise nondescript, transactors whose trading activities are centrally coordinated by some kind of "trading authority" that acts as a bargaining agent and commodity distribution center for all transactors. At the beginning of any given bargaining period (implicitly defined as a time interval of sufficient length for everything we wish to talk about to occur), each transactor formulates a definite trading plan on the basis of a set of provisional prices, P_0, which are announced by the trading authority. These plans are communicated to the trading authority who first checks each plan to see that it satisfies SP (individual version), and then sums all plans to arrive at a set of provisional aggregate EDs, $X_0 = (X_{1,0}, X_{2,0}, \ldots, X_{m,0})$. If X_0 includes some elements that are non-zero (by SP—the aggregate version—at least *two* elements must be non-zero in this case), the trading authority knows that individual plans are not mutually consistent at the price vector P_0 (i.e., not all planned net trades can be executed as scheduled). It then selects and announces a new set of provisional prices, P_1, and requests the assembled mob of transactors to formulate new plans. This process continues until at some stage, say the t-th when the trading authority manages to announce a price vector P_t at which each and every aggregate ED is exactly equal to zero: i.e., $X_{i,t} = O$ $(i = 1, \ldots, m)$. In this case, all individual trades can be executed as planned (through the collection and distribution facilities conveniently—and costlessly—provided by the authority), and the prices, P_t, are called equilibrium prices for the current trading period. In the absence of changes in technology, preferences, or other data that might influence individual trading plans, the same prices should yield equilibrium in all subsequent periods.

Such, in brief, is the story that underlies the condition $P = \bar{P} = $ constant, as a comprehensive criterion for equilibrium in elementary general equilibrium theory. According to this story, constancy of prices over time implies corresponding constancy of trading plans. But neither of these conditions can prevail unless, in every period, $X_i = O$ for all commodities. Hence the condition $P = \bar{P} = $ constant, is logically equivalent to the economically more informative requirement:

$$X_i = O \quad (i = 1, \ldots, m). \tag{11}$$

We emphasize that this simple requirement is in no sense sufficient to characterize general equilibrium except in very simple models; however, it is usually (but not always) a necessary condition and, for the purposes of the present argument, it may be regarded as both necessary and sufficient. In what follows, therefore, we shall refer to equation (11) as the general equilibrium condition.

Whether or not we wish to regard equation (11) as the only condition for general equilibrium (as in fact we do here), we might treat it as a universally valid, necessary condition for what might be called full coordination of economic activities, that is, situations in which, for each and every commodity, purchase and sale intentions are consistent in the aggregate. In a world without a central trading authority, knowing that equation (11) is fulfilled does not assure us that all trading plans can in fact be executed. It is conceivable (just barely) that each and every transactor could actually carry out each of his intended purchases and sales and not end up in a situation where all the sellers known to him are out of stock and all the buyers he contacts are unwilling to buy. As a practical matter, however, even this weak requirement that all aggregate EDs be zero is unlikely ever to be realized in any real-world situation; hence, the probability that all transactors should ever simultaneously achieve full execution of their individual trading plans may be set at zero.

Having run through essential preliminaries, we turn now to the relation between SP and the concept of general equilibrium. Without being too formal let us suppose that we have to deal with an economy in which there exists one and only one price vector, $\bar{P}$, for which the general-equilibrium condition equation (11) is satisfied.[12] We know that SP is satisfied in the present model for *all* price vectors P; the rules imposed by the trading authority positively guarantee this. But not all price vectors are consistent with general equilibrium; indeed, under our present assumptions only one such vector exists. Hence we conclude: the satisfaction of SP implies nothing whatever about the satisfaction of the general equilibrium condition; neither has gen-

---

12. For any specified state of resource endowments, production technology, property and contract laws, and consumer tastes, there exists a unique price vector $\bar{P}$ for which $X_i = 0$ for all commodities.

eral equilibrium any bearing on SP. If the general equilibrium condition is satisfied, it is obvious that:

$$\sum_{i=1}^{i=m} X_i \equiv 0,$$

but this fatuous proposition should never be confused with Say's Principle.[13]

Suppose that the general equilibrium condition is not satisfied, so that aggregate ED for at least two commodities is non-zero. In this case, the economy may be said to be in a state of disequilibrium. It is impossible for all trades to be executed as planned, so prices and trading plans must be revised. Some of the commodities in aggregate ES may be labor services. It follows that SP is entirely consistent with the existence of large-scale unemployment.

SP is also consistent with indefinite persistence of unemployment on a large scale, for it involves no assumptions and yields no implications about the dynamic adjustment behavior of the economic system. Imagine observing the system in a state of serious disequilibrium. Knowing that SP holds true for the system will *not* permit us to predict whether or not this disequilibrium will tend automatically to disappear with the passage of time. (Hence, SP is totally irrelevant to any ideological discussion and in particular to discussion of the pros and cons of so-called *laissez-faire*). For example, SP would still hold in a system where *every* commodity was subject to effectively enforced price-control. (Shortages and surpluses would be felt everywhere, but aggregate EDs would still have a total zero money value.)

That a general glut is impossible is not an empty statement. SP refutes, for example, the recurrent, fearful popular notion that productivity increasing innovations (automation, nuclear power, or whatever) will create or increase aggregate ESs for some commodities without affecting the aggregate EDs for the others. But the reassurance that this knowledge entails is very limited. It is utter nonsense, for example, to maintain (as some students, unfortunately, have a tendency to do) that, although

13. Even great economists sometimes nod: ". . . Say's Law is valid only in a state of perfect equilibrium . . ." Schumpeter (1954), p. 619.

the Principle is consistent with each and every aggregate ED being non-zero and large, it still asserts that the economy will be in overall equilibrium in that total demand and total supply are equal in money value. It is nonsense, because the statement completely empties the term equilibrium of all meaning. This particular piece of nonsense is not always so easy to spot. Quite a few otherwise reputable economists have put in print the proposition that Classical economists were unable to provide a meaningful and useful theory of large-scale unemployment because they believed in SL. This is simply inane: SP, by itself, could not possibly pose a mental block to the development of unemployment theory. On the contrary, correct and systematic application of it is necessary for the construction of a consistent theory of any disequilibrium (or equilibrium) phenomenon.

Needless to say, it does not follow that all, or even most, Classical economists fully understood what the Principle means and does not mean. A doctrinal investigation might well show, for example, that some notable writers muddled the conceptual distinctions between SP and propositions relating to the existence and stability of general equilibrium. We do not lack, after all, latter-day examples of the confounding of these separate issues.[14] The existence problem concerns the question whether a price vector exists such that, if it were to be obtained, aggregate ED for each commodity would be zero. SP alone will not allow one to deduce an answer one way or another to this question. The stability problem concerns the question whether it can be deduced that prices will adjust so as to reduce the absolute magnitude of aggregate EDs until, eventually, all aggregate EDs are zero (presuming such an equilibrium solution exists). SP contains no laws of motion of prices, nor is it even helpful in deducing what these laws might be. A fairly large set of assumptions completely independent of the Principle, must be made in order to obtain answers to stability questions.

14. "However, the satisfaction of *all* the stability conditions . . . is not implied in Say's Law. Say's Law implies only that enough of the stability conditions of the system hold, to assure the existence of a stable equilibrium for two broad classes of commodities, namely, the class of products and the class of factors and direct services." Cf. O. Lange (1942), p. 59. A proposition that states that the money values of some or all aggregate EDs sum to a certain number implies nothing about the fulfillment of any stability condition. Moreover, the notion of equilibrium for broad classes of commodities is just as empty and misleading as that of overall equilibrium which we have just criticized.

Many pre-Keynesian writers, who simply believed in the existence of general equilibrium, assumed "flexible prices"; they also assumed or argued that flexible prices would tend to move in such a manner as to reduce aggregate EDs to zero. Some of them may have been unable to conceive of persistent mass unemployment as a realistic possibility; however, it was clearly these sundry beliefs and assumptions—*not* SP—that constituted mental blocks for them.

C. National Income Analysis

In macroeconomics texts, SP (aggregative version) is sometimes said to imply that aggregate demand always equals aggregate supply. If one's definitions of aggregate demand and aggregate supply are, respectively, the summed money value of all commodities in aggregate ED and the summed money value of all commodities in aggregate ES, then, naturally, this is what SP means. (It is not an implication of the Principle, but simply a restatement.) However, the accepted, conventional definitions of aggregate demand and aggregate supply are quite different. The coinage of both terms is associated with the development of Keynesian macroeconomics, and it is the usage within that body of doctrine that must be decisive. In macroeconomics, aggregate demand is defined as the summed value of the demands for all final goods and services; similarly, aggregate supply is defined as the summed value of supplies of all final goods and services.

Final goods and services are a subset of all currently-produced commodities. (Current production of intermediate goods and services is excluded.) Current output is, in turn, a subset of all commodities in the system that excludes not just money but also all existing assets and many inputs as well. Suppose, then, that of the commodities in Table 1, those indexed 4 through 17 are designated as final goods and services. It is immediately apparent that the sum of the values of the demands for these goods (aggregate demand) cannot be asserted to equal the sum of the values of the supplies of the same goods. To assert this we should have to know—in addition to SP—that the sum of the values of the EDs for goods 1 through 3, and 18 through *m* were zero, and the latter condition, of course, will not in general be fulfilled. This example suffices to disprove the general validity of the proposition that SP implies equality between aggregate demand and aggregate supply.

There is another point to be made in this connection. In national income analysis, the term aggregate demand has come to mean the total value of actual spending—not *planned spending*—on final goods and services. If actual prices differ from equilibrium prices, actual spending will almost certainly differ from planned purchases (since not all plans can be carried out). SP, to repeat, is a proposition about trading *plans* and carries with it no direct implications about the realization of plans. On this account, therefore, the assertion that SP implies equality between aggregate demand and supply is seen to be the product of muddled thinking.[15]

D. General Deflation

Of all the innumerable disequilibria that are consistent with SP, one subset is particularly worth singling out because of the potential practical seriousness of the conditions defining it; namely, disequilibria in which the sum of the values of EDs for all currently produced commodites is negative and equal in value to the positive ED for money. This means, on balance, that the entire business sector is under general deflationary pressure.[16] The typical industry will be laying off workers. If there are some industries hiring, they won't hire enough; unemployment will be widespread.

If the real money supply (i.e., the stock of money in relation to the general price level) could be increased in this situation, prevailing deflationary pressures could be relieved—though that alone would not necessarily permit the economy to snap into general equilibrium. The supply of money in real terms might be increased in two ways: 1) by letting excess supplies drive prices down so that the general price level is reduced in

---

15. Another version of the same muddle consists of the assertion that SP implies coincidence at every point between the aggregate demand function and the 45° line in standard "Keynesian Cross" diagrams.

16. General deflationary pressure means here a situation in which ESs cannot be eliminated by merely changing relative prices.

relation to an unchanged stock of nominal money balances; 2) by increasing the nominal money stock at prevailing prices. Alternative 1 is the automatic solution; but if prices and wages are rigid downward, this way out is simply not open to us. Even if prices and wages are not rigid, the process envisaged in this solution may be a long-drawn-out affair that entails heavy costs in terms of resource unemployment and human misery and which, therefore, might well be regarded as unacceptable. Alternative 2, the interventionist solution, might seem more promising than 1 as a procedure for accomplishing the same results more quickly and at less social cost. But its use raises other issues. To whom is "the engine of inflation" to be entrusted? What limits to that party's discretionary use of the throttle would it be advisable to impose?

The Classical economists were not unaware of this class of disequilibria or of their seriousness. John Stuart Mill, for example, diagnosed general depressions of trade in precisely these terms. It is also true, however, that many British Classical economists tended to discuss the problem as if the automatic alternative 1 offered the only way out. Some of them did not regard the nominal money supply as a policy instrument that the Bank of England of the time could control. Others were of the view that the central bank had or could be endowed with the powers to control the money stock, but believed very strongly that the central bank on the whole ought to let balance-of-payments deficits and surpluses determine variations over time in the monetary base and, hence, in the money stock.[17]

Reliance on the automatic solution, in this view, is argued to be the lesser of two evils. Naive *laissez-faire* notions do not figure at all in the theory of economic policy of the British Classical school. Nor was Classical thinking on this subject in any way inhibited by prevailing views about "Say's Law of Markets." SP is entirely consistent with confirmed disbelief in the possibility of general gluts and, simultaneously, with clear recognition

17. From the standpoint of domestic stabilization policy, this is a self-denying ordinance—the monetary authorities cannot at one and the same time be bound by such a rule and retain discretion to intervene in domestic economic affairs whenever they deem it advisable.

of the actuality of frequent and prolonged bouts of general deflation. John Stuart Mill's *Principles*, the "Bible of Economics" during the later Classical period, is the perfect illustration.

E. Lange's Laws: A Restatement and Criticism

The aggregative version of SP as we have defined it earlier, is formally equivalent to a proposition that is known more familiarly in the literature as Walras' Law, a label that was first attached to it by Oscar Lange (Lange [1942]). Two names for the same concept is, in general, a luxury that economics can well do without. But we have good reasons for making an exception in the present case. The central portions of Lange's argument are concerned with conceptual experiments that involve just two models, namely:

i. A model of a barter economy with $m-1$ commodities, all of which are either currently produced final goods and services or currently supplied factor services. Commodities not classified in this manner cannot be traded at all. In particular, nothing called money is included in the set of tradable commodities, which means that the system is "equivalent to a barter economy."[18]

ii. A model of a money economy that is identical with the first in all respects except that an m-th commodity called money is added to the set of tradable commodities—functioning as "medium of exchange as well as numeraire. . . ."

Since money does not exist in the first economy, it cannot be traded. However, it still can be regarded by us as a unit of account (*numeraire*) for expressing prices, so we may continue to speak of the money value of aggregate EDs even when referring to the barter system.[19]

The proposition that the sum of the money values of all EDs in system i is identically zero is called Say's Law by Lange.[20] The

18. Lange (1942), p. 64.

19. Individuals in system i would be concerned, of course, only with *ratios* of such money prices, i.e., with rates of exchange between pairs of tradable commodities.

20. Lange simply assumes that the proposition is true for the system described, but the proposition could be shown to hold as a consequence of standard assumptions underlying the definition of the demand and supply functions that Lange introduced at the outset of his analysis.

proposition that the sum of the money values of all EDs in system ii is identically zero Lange then called Walras' Law. Since the two propositions are identical, the reader may well wonder why Lange assigns them different names. The answer to this apparent mystery is that Lange, unlike us, starts by considering only a so-called "money economy" (system ii). He defines Walras' Law in relation to this kind of system, and then asks, in effect: In what circumstances will the total money value of ED for all commodities exclusive of money be zero? Not very surprisingly, he discovers that his condition will be satisfied if and only if the ED for money is zero, a state of affairs that he calls "monetary equilibrium." He then defines SL *not* as a proposition that holds only for situations of monetary equilibrium, but rather as a proposition that together with Walras' Law, holds identically for all possible states of system ii. These two stipulations effectively make system ii indistinguishable from system i.

From this point onward, Lange's argument is all downhill. In order to elaborate the implications of what he calls "Say's Law," he first asks: What conclusions follow if we suppose that aggregate EDs in a money economy such as ii simultaneously satisfy *both* Walras' Law and SL? The words in which the ensuing discussion are couched strongly suggest that the simultaneous assumption of Walras' Law and SL leads one to economically nonsensical results. Thus, he argues that money prices are indeterminate (obviously, since only ratios of money prices are relevant in system i). Lange argues further that people will never desire to change their money balances (obviously, since money in system i is like romantic love—you take what you can get, but it's not for sale!). He goes on to observe that money in such a system is merely a worthless medium of exchange and standard of value. (Here the nonsense is Lange's, for whatever else money may be in system i, it can't be a medium of exchange, worthless or otherwise). Clearly, if one focuses attention not on the words Lange uses but rather on the properties of the system he is talking about (namely, system i rather than system ii) all of his results appear to be either entirely sensible or to involve confusion or errors of logic on his part. An example of the latter is his assertion that, ". . . under Say's Law an excess supply of primary factors and direct services *always* implies an excess demand of equal amount for products, and vice versa.

This tends directly to restore equilibrium." As we have emphasized in earlier remarks, SP has no bearing whatever on the dynamic adjustment properties of any economic system.

Using the terms as he defines them, Lange concludes that Walras' Law is true in general and that SL is true for barter but not for money economies. Since Lange's distinction between the two types of economies is purely verbal, not analytical, this conclusion is fatuous. In Lange's article (and in the present paper) the word "money" serves only to name one commodity, specifically, that commodity (it might be any of them) that serves as a unit of account for expressing prices. At no stage in Lange's formal analysis is money endowed with any other special properties as compared with other commodities.[21]

Attributing a belief in SL (in his sense) to Classical economists, Lange also argues that pre-Keynesian theories of employment, interest and money are (a) logically false, and (b) economically nonsensical because they rest on the assumption that SL is valid for a monetary economy. In this part of his argument, Lange is guilty not only of repeated sins of verbal sophistry but also of gross historical inaccuracy. As argued earlier the statement that the summed values of aggregate EDs over a subset of tradable commodities is identically zero involves a most elementary error.[22]

So what remains of Lange's analysis when all is said and done? Our answer is, quite bluntly: nothing of value. Nonetheless, Lange's terminological innovations—including, in particular, the entirely superfluous term Walras' Law—somehow have taken root in macroeconomics; and his associated criticisms of Classical economics are now part of the mythology of the subject.

F. Say's Principle and Walras' Law

As we remarked at the outset of the preceding section, what we have called the aggregative version of SP is formally equivalent

21. This may be seen most easily by noticing that if what Lange calls money were a liquid asset that came in bottles marked "100 proof Scotch Whisky" rather than pieces of paper labelled "In God We Trust," no one would notice it.

22. As far as we know, no major Classical economist has ever been shown to commit this error outright; but even if such a sinner could be found by hunting around among lesser figures, we (the authors) should follow Mill's gracious example and attribute the blunder to inadvertence.

to what Lange called Walras' Law. Formally equivalent, they certainly are, but economically equivalent they sometimes are not. Two observations will suffice to make clear the sense and validity of this distinction.

1. Walras' Law is sometimes described as asserting that, if prices are such that all markets for non-money commodities satisfy the general-equilibrium condition (i.e., if $X_i = O$ for $i = 1,2, \ldots , m$-1), then the money market must also be in equilibrium (i.e., $X_m = O$ also);[23] or, more shortly, that if supply equals demand on M-1 markets then the same equality must also hold on the m-th.[24]

Now, our definition of SP (aggregative version) involves the concept of aggregate demand in an essential way, but it does not in any way depend upon or refer to the concept of a market. Our avoidance of any reference to the word market was quite deliberate. The term market, as used in ordinary discourse, carries with it a host of intuitive associations that have no counterpart in standard accounts of individual decision-making behavior. In common parlance, a market is (among other things) a place where one pays (receives) money to (from) another person in exchange for some other commodity at some date in time. To establish a theoretical analog to this conception, we should have to specify the logistics of commodity trade in fine detail—fine enough detail, indeed, to permit us to assert within the framework of formal theory precisely when and where each transactor trades what commodities with whom and in exchange for which other commodities. No such specification is even attempted in existing accounts of macro- or microeconomic theory.[25] Thus, to speak of markets for labor services, goods, bonds, money, etc. in connection with conventional theoretical models is, strictly speaking, meaningless. It is entirely sensible to speak of aggregate ED for these commodities but to link aggregate EDs with markets is to invite needless confusion and misunderstanding.[26]

23. Patinkin (1965), p. 25.

24. Arrow and Hahn (1971), p. 4.

25. An instructive example of just such a careful specification is provided by Ostroy (1973).

26. A common example of such confusion arises in macroeconomic theory in the mere listing of four markets, one for each distinct commodity. Since exchange necessarily

To insist on this terminological distinction between aggregate ED for a commodity and market ED (for the same commodity) may seem overly fastidious. And it is, in fact, not necessary in a discussion that does not go beyond SP. In more general contexts, however, the distinction is far from pointless. When one moves on to the task of constructing a theory that describes how the economic system adjusts when in disequilibrium, it is traditional to use the term "market excess demand" to denote the relevant forces governing price adjustment. It is a distinct and potentially dangerous jump in logic, however, to take it for granted that these forces are always measured by aggregate EDs (which is the custom in the existing literature). For example, in models where market ED cannot be obtained by aggregating over individual planned net demands and supplies, we have no assurance whatsoever that the sum of measured market EDs, valued at the prevailing market prices, is equal to zero or any other number (though SP, in the generalized form given by equation (9), above, holds as usual for the aggregate of individual planned EDs).

2. Most statements of Walras' Law in the existing literature, unlike our statement of SP, tacitly presuppose that the trading plans of individual transactors satisfy one or another of the optimality conditions (i.e., maximize some criterion function) in addition to relevant behavior constraints. This is certainly true for the statements of Lange, Patinkin, Debreu and Arrow and Hahn, all of whom assume that individual ED functions (or correspondences) are defined independently of Walras' Law. This corresponds to the point of view adopted in the first section of this paper, where we first illustrated the nature of SP. It differs sharply, however, from the view adopted later. While we have no logical objection to the approach of other writers, we should remark that such a procedure makes SP appear much more limited in application than it actually is. SP is also significantly diminished as a theoretical proposition by suggesting incorrectly that it is valid only if all individuals in the economic system are behaving optimally.

involves at least two commodities, the very phrase "market for commodity Z" presupposes that we know what commodity or commodities Z is traded for or else it must be regarded as a contradiction in terms.

CHAPTER SIX

Effective Demand Failures *

There is no reason why the *form* of a realistic model (the form of its equations) should be the same under all values of its variables. We must face the fact that the form of the model may have to be regarded as a function of the values of the variables involved. This will usually be the case if the values of some of the variables affect the basic conditions of choice under which the behavior equations in the model are derived.

Trygve Haavelmo [1]

INTRODUCTION

My primary concern over the past several years has been with certain theoretical problems embedded in the Keynesian literature that I believe (of course) to be important, unresolved, and difficult. The ramifications of these problems are such that a few of us cannot hope to deal effectively and satisfactorily with them all. In order to enlist others in the work, one has to convince them that the problems in question have not been satisfactorily solved and have a high claim on their attention relative to other matters currently in professional fashion. To do so in this case, I believed and believe, requires a revision of recent macro-doctrine history. Economists who accept without qualification the inherited image of the Keynesian past will not share my views about either the present or the directions for the future.

*This paper draws on work done together with my colleague, Robert W. Clower. Still, Clower's responsibility for any stupidities or errors is somewhat less than 50 percent. I am indebted also to Daniel Benjamin for numerous helpful discussions.
1. Cf. Haavelmo (1960), p. 205.

In this paper, I provide a sketch, free of doctrine-historical subplots, of a number of issues and problems that stand in need of fresh attempts at theoretical modelling and/or empirical testing. Space, time, and dull wits combine to prevent me from treating any of the problems in detail and with rigor; I have chosen instead to convey to the reader how part of the working agenda for theoretical macroeconomics is perceived by someone with a "revised" perspective of the historical development of the field.

The broad theme of the paper is the theory of Effective Demand. In Part II, the theory of effective demand failures is examined, in turn, from the following vantage-points: (A) The Theory of Markets and Money; (B) Theories of the Consumption Function; (C) Quantity Theories of Money Income Determination. Part I sketches the broader context within which I would presently view the theory, and is correspondingly informal and opinionated. Contrary to what seems to be current professional practice, I make my tentative opinions explicit. There are two reasons for doing so. First, one cannot today presume the kind of consensus in macroeconomics that makes it unnecessary to explain why one regards certain issues and approaches as more significant than others. Second, the reader may well want some hints as to the prejudices and biases that underlie what is to follow.

I

In my opinion, the central issue in macroeconomic theory is— once again—the extent to which the economy, or at least its market sectors, may properly be regarded as a self-regulating system. In what respects does it, or does it not, behave in such fashion? How well, or badly, do its "automatic" mechanisms perform? This issue, to illustrate, lies at the heart of two of the most prominent controversies in the field over the last decade: the Fiscalist versus Monetarist controversy over income determination and aggregate demand management, and the controversy over the long-run stability of the Phillips-curve. The volume of writings on each of these continues to mount steadily with no clear-cut resolution in sight—in large measure because this central issue is not being effectively addressed.

The social problem to which the issue of the system's self-regulatory capabilities pertains we may term "the coordination of economic activities." The reference is to coordination of desired sales and purchases at the market level; "full coordination" for our purposes means simply that existing markets clear; it does *not* mean "efficient allocation." Our central question is to be put in that frame. Does the market system (as presently instituted in the United States or in Sweden . . . etc.) tend to move "automatically" towards a state where all market excess demands and supplies are eliminated? How strong or weak are those tendencies?[2] The significance of these questions is not affected by the admission that one deems the probability of actually ever observing an economy in a perfectly coordinated state to be zero.

When the issue is put in this very general, diffuse way and with reference to real-world systems rather than particular classes of models, modern economic theory can as yet provide no answer.[3] And the message out of all the empirical work in macroeconomics of the past decades is very largely in the (casual) eye of the beholder. Yet, on almost all economic questions of major importance, systematic inquiry can only proceed on some presumption of what the answer is likely to be. Otherwise determinate results are unobtainable. Few, if any, major questions have the same answer independently of whether the en-

2. Note that if the conclusion from the proposed inquiry were to be that the system does tend towards establishing a state of "full coordination," no laissez-faire implications whatever follow. My conception of "full coordination" omits most of the criteria for Pareto-optimality—it allows markets to be monopolistic or monopsonistic, sales or income taxes to be present, non-existence of organized markets for certain goods and other causes of external effects, and so on. Quite apart from all that, the system's homeostatic mechanisms might be so slow in their operation that policy intervention would be deemed desirable simply to speed up the (in themselves) "automatic" self-regulatory tendencies of the system.

The reader will have observed that the term "equilibrating" is eschewed here in favor of "self-regulatory," "homeostatic" or other more or less cumbersome circumlocutions. The reason, of course, is that the discussion moves in a realm of discourse where the "unemployment equilibrium" notion of textbook Keynesianism unavoidably insinuates itself. Since that is not a "coordinated" state, the stability properties asserted for it are not of the kind to which our central question is addressed.

The term "stability" is also better avoided because of its firm associations with certain classes of models. What should concern us is the dynamic behavior of actual economics—and we do not want to prejudge how that behavior is most appropriately to be modelled.

3. The current boundary markers on this front are set out in K. J. Arrow and F. H. Hahn (1971), esp., Chapters 13 and 14.

tire system of markets "works" to coordinate activities or whether one or more markets fail to function as homeostatic mechanisms. This is most obviously true of macroeconomic issues,[4] but applies as well to a host of problems to which most economists would affix the "micro" label.[5]

The researcher or instructor must then proceed on some presumption or other with regard to the self-regulating capabilities of economic systems—or find that he has nothing to say. The assumptions made may be backed up to some extent by broad and casual empiricism and by reference to scraps of rigorous theoretical results obtained for a variety of special, simplified cases. But ammunition to compel the agreement of a disbelieving colleague will be lacking. At the same time, the validity of the work that an economist does will ultimately hinge on whether his presumptions on this matter do or do not in some sense approximate reality. If they do not, his work is likely to end up on the scrapheap of forgotten intellectual games. The emotional stakes are high, while solidly based knowledge is at best fragmentary.

Briefly put, then, our situation is one of emotionally charged ignorance with regard to a central issue of the science. In such situations one expects a high incidence of technically qualified men rejecting out of hand the work of other, equally qualified men—or, indeed, spurning entire branches of current inquiry. A's models are but "meretricious games" to B—and B's regression results only "meaningless numbers" to A. And one also expects, rather sadly, to hear charges flying that "the other's" work can only be understood by drawing the always tempting inference that it is the product of nonscientific, biased motives.

From a history of science point of view, none of this is novel,

---

4. A most familiar example concerns the consequences of an increased propensity to save as deduced (a) from a neoclassical growth model, or (b) from a simple Keynesian ("Paradox of Thrift") model. Most standard conceptual experiments in macroeconomics produce the same disturbing result—qualitative predictions for some of the important variables emerge with opposite signs from the two coexisting bodies of theory.

5. Consider a social benefit-cost calculation for a labor-saving government investment project under the alternative assumptions (a) that the displaced labor will be reabsorbed into other employments, and (b) that it will be permanently unemployed. More to the point, perhaps, consider the benefit-cost calculator's utter impotence if he were completely ignorant about which assumption (or combination of the two) is applicable.

nor is it by itself unhealthy. It could be said of many episodes in diverse fields that we now look back upon as the gestation period of major advances—but, one feels sure, also of many now forgotten controversies that produced only heat and no light in their time because the issues were never given a "soluble" formulation.

What seems to me unhealthy about the situation in macro-economics is that the central issue does not occupy center stage. In the unending controversies to which it is critical, it keeps bobbing to the surface only as conflicting declarations of faith. I do not think it has been given "soluble" formulation. It is being avoided, I would infer, because the diffuse nature of the question—itself a result of past neglect—makes it very difficult to address it except in terms that (as here) fall short of present-day standards of precision and rigor in theoretical debate. Still, how can the profession go on for decades with this issue remaining out of focus?

The settled, conventional acceptance of having general economic theory split down the middle is, I believe, very largely to blame. Despite the several alternative ways that we have developed to make the gulf between microtheory and macrotheory seem plausible to new generations of students, the micro-macro distinction remains basically that between models with "perfectly coordinated" solutions and models where one or more markets reach such solutions only by chance. Both sets of exercises are referred to as "theories," but there could be no real-world economy for which both theories are true at once.[6] One allows oneself the major convenience of static modelling by making one courageous decision (for each market). Either the market has demand-equals-supply equilibria *only,* or it has no tendency to eliminate excess demands *at all.*

A fully adequate characterization of the two alternative visions of what real-world market systems are like, to which neoclassical and Keynesian models give formal representation,

6. In theory teaching, the schizophrenic pressure on young minds can be kept within tolerable bounds by dwelling on self-regulating systems on, say, Mondays, Wednesdays, and Fridays—reserving Tuesdays and Thursdays for the economy that "doesn't work that way." In the applied fields, micro and macro have to co-exist. Example: the elasticity and absorption approaches to balance of payments theory.

would be space-consuming. A crude sketch of the two economic "cosmologies" might run as follows.

Assume that we can define a "fully-coordinated" time-path for the economy. The first cosmology then attributes the following properties to the system. It tends to home in on the ideal path and, in the absence of disturbances, to stay on it. Shocks that displace it from the path will trigger immediate deviation-counteracting feedback control mechanisms. The larger the displacement, generally speaking, the stronger will be the homeostatic tendencies working to bring the system back.[7]

According to the second cosmology, the system has no "automatic" tendency to home in on the ideal path, would reach it only by chance—or through deliberate policy-intervention— and will not maintain itself on it if the path were reached. This system may settle down anywhere "between zero and full employment"[8] with all servo-mechanisms idle. When displaced by shocks from a previous position, moreover, the system will exhibit endogenous ("Multiplier") tendencies that, instead of counteracting the displacement, amplify it.

These, then, are in brief summary the two opposed visions of how a market economy behaves that we are saddled with. Both are firmly entrenched in the literature. The first goes back, of course, to Adam Smith, and was *the* cosmology of economists for more than 150 years—if this was not your belief, you were almost by definition not an economist, but at best an amateur. Then, the Great Depression prepared the ground for a mass conversion of economists to the second. But the Keynesian Revolution did not quite succeed in making a clean sweep. The older view survived and has again grown in strength as the 1930's recede from memory and mass unemployment on that

---

7. I.e., price adjustment velocities will be monotonically increasing functions of discrepancies between demand and supply in respective markets—where, in Clower's terminology, it is "notional" demand and supply that are measured. Similarly, adjustment velocities for rates of output and factor employments increase monotonically as functions of discrepancies between supply price and demand price—with these schedules also defined in notional terms. Cf. A. Leijonhufvud (1970). The last statement in the text also assumes, roughly speaking, that excess demands and excess supply prices increase monotonically with the "displacement" from the equilibrium price- and output-vectors, respectively.

8. Cf., e.g., Robert Lekachman (1966), p. 90.

scale has failed to recur. The two are inconsistent images of the world but nonetheless manage to coexist—and in rather implausible comfort at that.

Clower's original venture into the uncomfortable no-man's land between Neoclassicism and Keynesianism[9] sought to provide a microtheoretical foundation for the core concept of Keynesian theory—Effective Demand. For the contesting cosmologies, the ramifications of his success appeared at first rather one-sidedly in favor of Keynesianism. Solid microtheoretical respectability for the most important Keynesian doctrines seemed suddenly within grasp. At the same time, "effective demand failures" had to be perceived as an hitherto unrealized, pervasive malfunction of price-systems, casting grave doubt on the entire neoclassical vision of the self-regulating capabilities and *modus operandi* of market systems.[10]

Time has by now allowed sundry second thoughts on the effective demand doctrine. The result is a less one-sided, more balanced perspective. Whether it is also a truer perspective remains to be seen. If I were to sum up my present views as a "cosmology"—neither more, nor less crude than the preceding ones—it would have the following outlines. The system is likely to behave differently for large than for moderate displacements from the "full coordination" time-path. Within some range from the path (referred to as "the corridor" for brevity), the system's homeostatic mechanisms work well, and deviation-counteracting tendencies increase in strength. Outside that range these tendencies become weaker as the system becomes

---

9. R. W. Clower (1965).

10. I should add the following: It *is*, I think, true that the ramifications of Clower's contribution were seen as "one-sided"—by those who focused intently on the purely theoretical implications: Keynesian theory now had to be taken seriously by general equilibrium theorists; *tâtonnement* stability theorems had to be quoted at drastically reduced empirical values, etc.

My own work in the same vineyard, however, confused the picture no end for many people. By my attempts to explain and document in some detail the departure of "Keynesian economics" from the "economics of Keynes," and the prominence that I gave to purely doctrine-historical themes, I was in effect launching an attack on the scholarly repute of (conventional) Keynesianism—albeit from a totally different quarter. (Cf. the review by Harry G. Johnson [1970].) Some readers, therefore, have found the book "anti-Keynesian" and see it, even, as "just another Chicago-school attack"—the emphasis on labor-market search behavior and on the significance of the structure of relative prices arouses, it seems, suspicion.

increasingly subject to "effective demand failures." If the system is displaced sufficiently "far out," the forces tending to bring it back may, on balance, be so weak and sluggish that—for all *practical* purposes—the Keynesian "unemployment equilibrium" model is as sensible a representation of its state as economic statics will allow. Inside the corridor, multiplier-repercussions are weak and dominated by neoclassical market adjustments; outside the corridor, they should be strong enough for effects of shocks to the prevailing state to be endogenously amplified. Up to a point, multiplier-coefficients are expected to increase with distance from the ideal path. Within the corridor, the presumption is in favor of "monetarist," outside in favor of "fiscalist," policy prescriptions. Finally, although within the corridor market forces will be acting in the direction of clearing markets, institutional obstacles of the type familiar from the conventional Keynesian literature may, of course, intervene to make them ineffective at some point. Thus, a combination of monopolistic wage-setting in unionized occupations and legal minimum-wage restrictions could obviously cut the automatic adjustment process short before "equilibrium employment" is reached.[11]

II

A. Theory of Markets and Money

Pre-Keynesian views of how activities are coordinated in market systems were based on two broad assumptions; (*a*) that price-incentives are effective in controlling the behavior of transactors (price-elasticities of excess demands are not zero throughout in any market and, in principle, market-clearing solutions at nonnegative prices exist for all markets); (*b*) prices are "free" to move in response to excess demands and supplies and will move towards their market-clearing values. The Keynesian model posed the spectre of a coordination failure of indefinite duration. How could that possibly be? Until relatively recently, the generally accepted answers interpreted Keynesian theory as

11. It is generally true of homeostatic mechanisms, studied in other fields than economics, that their self-regulating capacities are bounded. Displacements so large that the system cannot "cope" are always possible. Is it farfetched to hypothesize that this is true also of economic systems?

necessarily denying either one or the other of the two broad assumptions—or both.[12]

Arguments for denying the pre-Keynesian assumptions can be developed in a great number of ways, of course, and we cannot comment on all the versions. There are theoretical and/or empirical reasons for being at least "very uncomfortable" about all of the arguments I am familiar with. The inelasticity of saving and investment behavior with respect to intertemporal prices (interest rates) is an instance of denying (a). This denial has been argued, for example, on the grounds that theoretical reasons for assuming non-zero elasticities can only be derived from strong underlying assumptions of "rationality" and "foresight." But this argument won't hold water.[13] Similarly, the one-time belief that these strict inelasticities had solid empirical support has not stood up. With regards to denials of (b), it is enough to point out that the prime test-case of Keynesian theory must be the Great Depression. But "rigid wages" due to monopolistic unions could only apply to a relatively small (and shrinking) proportion of the U.S. labor force at the time. And in fact money wages were not "rigid"—there is no more dramatic wage-deflation on record than that of 1930–33. And so on. The long survival and endless repetition of sundry arguments denying (a) and (b) appears in retrospect a product of psychological necessity: On the one hand, economists could *not imagine* the persistence of coordination failures on a large scale if both (a) and (b) had to be accepted as "true." On the other hand, the horrors of the Great Depression were impossible to ignore.

Clower's explanation of effective demand failures offered a release from this dilemma. Price-incentives may be effective in all markets and all prices may be "flexible"[14] and a market sys-

---

12. For amplification of these remarks, cf. my (1969) pp. 24 ff.

13. Cf. Gary S. Becker (1962).

14. The main reasons for insisting on working out the theory of effective demand failures first while assuming atomistic markets and no institutional restrictions on price-adjustments are implicit in—but obvious from—the text. Another one is also of some importance. Even when the main results are more easily obtained by *ad hoc* "rigidity" assumptions, that procedure had better be shunned—since it carries the false suggestion, "Break up the unions and monopolies (if you dare!)—and all will be well with the world!" The insistence on working with atomistic markets, etc., has been misconstrued by some economists as revealing an "anti-Keynesian bias" and what not.

As pointed out at the very end of Part I, once the general outlines of the theory have been clarified, empirically verified "rigidities," etc., should, of course, be put back in.

tem may still go hay-wire in its groping for the coordinated solution. Conditions are possible, and are not far-fetched, under which some prices may show no tendency to change although desires to sell and to buy do not coincide in the respective markets. Not only that. Prices may be at their "right" (general equilibrium) levels, but amounts transacted differ persistently from the desired rates of sale and purchase in some markets.[15] And not only that. Prices that were at their GE values may tend ("automatically") to move *away* from those values so that the information disseminated by price changes is "false" and makes the coordination failure confusion worse.

It was surely inevitable that the early discussion of effective demand theory would focus almost exclusively on the newly discovered possibilities for system malfunction. The net result of this concentration on all the fascinating ways in which the system conceivably can go wrong, I now think, was to give a rather grossly exaggerated picture of the propensities of actual real-world economies to lose track and fail to home in towards a coordinated state. Second thoughts on effective demand theory suggest that the capabilities for self-regulating behavior of actual market systems are likely to be a good deal more "robust"[16]—even though the early models of this type were not robust at all, but instead extremely sensitive to changes in specification that explicitly incorporate the conceptual distinction between "notional" and "effective" excess demands.[17]

15. Cf., e.g., R. J. Barro and H. I Grossman (1971). Check the "B-solutions" to the various cases they consider.

16. I.e., suggest the notion of "the corridor" within which market forces, as they were traditionally conceived, are strong enough to override the disorganizing tendencies arising from "trading at false prices," etc. Perhaps I had better make it explicit that this is not in Keynes. Obviously, Keynes' theory envisages a world in which potential deviation-amplifying endogenous mechanisms are as strong (multiplier-coefficients as large) in the immediate neighborhood of the "perfectly coordinated" state as they are far away from it.

I have not changed my mind on the significance of Keynes' contribution to economic *analysis*. I think it of fundamental importance. I have long since parted company with Keynes on many aspects of his economic theory, in the sense of *beliefs* about how real-world systems function.

17. In this paper we will be dealing only with one branch of the effective demand doctrine, namely, that concerned with effective demand failures among current spot-markets. Issues that belong to this branch include: (a) the possibility of persistent states of large-scale unemployment; (b) the "original" multiplier based on the simple consumption-income relation; and (c) the independence of model solution-states of conditions determining the supply of labor.

The original modelling context for the discussion was that of a standard Walrasian model "without the auctioneer" (as I chose to put it). Two properties should be emphasized here; (i) all quantities appear as *flows* (albeit cumulated over the "period"), and (ii) *none* of the goods is explicitly given the singular attribute of being the only *means of payment*.[18] The discussion began, thus, with a *non-monetary* "pure flow" representation of an economy.[19] Within that setting, the consequences of letting individuals trade at disequilibrium prices ("false trading") were then examined. With the budget-constraints of a pure flow model, it is readily (albeit not immediately!) apparent that, if the transactor fails to realize his desired sales due to excess supply in those markets, he will not have the wherewithal to realize his desired purchases. If the actual price-vector at which trading takes place differs at all from the GE vector, furthermore, some markets must exhibit excess supply and, consequently, some transactors must necessarily fail to realize desired sales at prevailing prices. It follows that, as soon as you have a departure from the GE price-vector, the demands of some transactors must be sales-constrained—in the model stipulated.

Another point about the mental setting of these conceptual

Point (c) is more brief than accurate. Note that, in standard Keynesian models, shifts in the supply of labor function that increase or decrease the excess supply of labor (without, however, making it negative), *never* change the solution obtained. The changes in corresponding planned demands for other goods in the system are always treated as "ineffective."

The other branch of effective demand theory pertains to *intertemporal* effective demand failures. More than half of my 1968 book dealt with topics in this area (Saving-Investment coordination; Wicksellian cumulative processes; the Keynes-effect *versus* the Pigou-effect, etc.). Space will not allow second thoughts on this set of problems.

18. Clower's reasons for *not* considering a *stock-flow* system are given, *op. cit.*, pp. 114–15. The reader who chooses to check this statement will find that the reasons still hold true—for the *analytical* problem posed in that essay. He will also find, however, that the very same reasons would compel us to use stock-flow representations whenever the object is to derive theoretical inferences about the self-regulating capabilities of real-world systems.

When it has already been said that we deal with a pure flow model, it is naturally redundant to add that we do not have the stock-good, "money," in it. The reasons for nonetheless emphasizing the point will be apparent shortly.

19. Since the very simplest Keynesian models (the "45° Keynesian Cross," etc.) do not include the stock of "money," but deal simply in relationships among flows, and since these elemental models exhibit all the properties that one deems singularly and particularly "Keynesian," this seems "the way to go," all right. But . . . it turns out to be misleading.

experiments is relevant; the consumption-income relation (from which the "multiplier" is obtained, for instance) seems *the nexus* of all the "singularly Keynesian," "obviously anti-Classical" model-properties that concern us here.[20] It is natural, therefore, to concentrate on a particular case of the above conceptual experiment as the very archetype of it—namely, the case of a household failing to realize desired sales of labor and thus finding its consumption demand *income-constrained*.[21] (Note that unsold labor-services cannot be stored for sale in the next period—again the case analyzed tends to direct one's attention away from stocks.) The analytically crucial aspect of Keynesian theory seems thus to have been isolated: *realized transactions* appear as arguments in the excess demand functions of such systems, whereas they have no place in Classical models belonging to the Lausanne-school ("modern") tradition.[22] The troubles with effective demand failures follow immediately—in the archetype case, we will have no effective excess demand for wage-goods in an unemployment situation even though "notional" household consumption demand exceeds current output. Wage-goods output is too low . . . but the servo-mechanisms of the market system are idle.

In this setting, all we thought we knew about the stability of market system seems suddenly imperiled. Stability theorems

20. Two notes: I say (i) "seems the nexus" because Keynes' Employment Function (*General Theory*, Chapter 20) expressed the analogous sales-constraint on the demand for labor on the business sector side of the market. But Chapter 20 is pretty far into that book . . . and elemental Keynesian models do not make use of either the Employment function or its converse, the aggregate supply-price function; (ii) "all the . . . properties that concern us here," because intertemporal effective demand failures we have ruled out of order (see note 17 above).

21. Beyond concentrating on income-constrained consumption demand of labor-suppliers at the expense of the sales-constrained labor demand of commodity suppliers, the same considerations led me to focus on the search-behavior on the supply-side of labor markets at the expense of demand-side behavior. The latter deficiency I share with numerous authors (Stigler, Alchian, etc. . . . . good company!).

Barro and Grossman, *op. cit.*, have two virtues in this context: (a) they give equal attention to the sales-constrained demand behavior of producers, and (b) in considering explicitly also situations of purchase-constrained supply-behavior, they forcefully remind us that false trading in inflationary situations must also be encompassed by the theory.

E. S. Phelps (1968) models a system in which demanders of labor do the "groping." The not-so-easy task remains of constructing a model in which *both* sides of the market "grope."

22. Clower, *op. cit.*, pp. 111–12, 119–20.

proved for systems of notional excess demand equations apparently prove nothing, because notional and effective excess demands coincide only when the system is already in general equilibrium.[23] *Any* trade at false prices might upset the applecart. Trade at false prices will surely take place if prices do not move *instantly* to their GE values when a disturbance occurs, etc. For models of the type considered, all of this is true—but getting a balanced perspective on its "relevance" is another matter.[24] The income constraints derived from this type of model are "too tight."

Second thought, if not necessarily wisdom, starts from the observation that realized sales have been made to do heavy, in fact triple, duty in the above context. Realized sales appear (i) as a proxy for *expected income,*[25] (ii) as a constraint on current *purchases,* and (iii) as a constraint on the demand-*signals* that may be currently emitted. These three ideas need to be kept carefully distinct.

i. If *realized income is expected,* income expectations will be realized. One assumes that sellers know beforehand what sales they will succeed in making. But, strictly speaking, this assumption makes sense only for that subset of the possible states of the system that are Keynesian "income-equilibria." Most of these states are, of course, coordination failures—disequilibria from a neoclassical standpoint. The assumption *allows* the analysis of some of the properties of such states with the aid of essentially static model-constructions—a convenience that recommends it for certain expository purposes. But it also *precludes* analysis of the recursive interaction processes that propel the system from one Keynesian income-equilibrium to another.[26]

23. Clower, *op. cit.,* p. 123.
24. To take just one example, I committed the following: "Income-constrained processes result not only when price-level velocity is zero, but whenever it is short of infinite." Leijonhufvud (1968a), p. 67. A number of other authors have followed suit.
25. Following Keynes' procedure of collapsing, for convenience, short-term expectations with realized results. Cf., Keynes (1936), pp. 50–51. But, apart from the issue noted in the text below, following Keynes here risks fudging another distinction as well, namely, that between Friedman's concepts of measured and permanent income—an aspect of the issue that we save for the next section.
26. Cf., Leijonhufvud, *op. cit.,* pp. 74–75.
  The collapsing of realized and expected income was a feature (albeit not a necessary one) of Clower's original treatment of the "dual decision hypothesis." It remains in use, e.g., in H. I. Grossman (1971) as well as in Barro and Grossman, *op. cit.*

The inherent limitations on what we might learn about the dynamic behavior of such systems in this way are obvious. But there is also, I think, a not so obvious danger to the procedure. It rather invites making *ad hoc* assumptions about the information available to transactors in making the decisions that, in effect, the steady-state assumption dictates that they make.[27] Having put price-rigidities and price-inelasticities to one side, effective demand theory seeks to explain coordination failures that arise through faulty communication among transactors. Communication takes place through market interactions. Hence, ideally, all statements of the type: "Transactor A is expected to behave in such-and-such a manner at date t, because he has good information on x, no information about y, and false information about z . . ." etc., should be justifiable with reference to a history of market interactions that would reasonably produce such a state of knowledge. This means tracing the recursive process. In my, no doubt overly jaundiced view, therefore, steady-state constructions divert attention away from the fundamentals of the theory.[28]

ii. *Realized sales as constraint on purchases.* As long as Say's Principle is the well-enforced law of the land, the model obviously must have this property. Nonetheless, it is easy to get one's bearings on the real world wrong at this point, particularly when focusing narrowly on the labor-selling, wage-goods-

27. I.e., much the same kind of *ad-hoc*-ery that makes so much of neoclassical microtheory useless to the macrotheorist. For the purposes of the "new" macroeconomics, models with assumptions of the type "sellers just *know* the demand-schedules they face" can simply not be trusted. It is not that such assumptions do not make sense in context. For the steady-state they often do. It is that they avoid the question: *How* did they come to know? Since one does not know the process through which this knowledge was gained, one is hard put to start grappling with the questions that count (in macro). For example: In what circumstances would that process teach them some things "that ain't so"?

28. Note that "imperfect information" is a rather misleading label for the theories developing in the area under discussion, since it is likely to be understood as referring to "generalized probabilistic uncertainty." The rich literature on that topic from Knight through Arrow is not particularly relevant or helpful here. We are concerned with "incomplete information" in the sense of certain specific pieces of information missing—and missing for reasons inherent in the structure of the model. (The weakest postulate here might be: Nobody interacts directly with everybody.)

Situations for which we assume "good information about x, no information on z . . ." etc., will sometimes produce inferences of "asymmetric behavior" that are apparently peculiarly offensive to theorists used to steady-state frames of reference. For an example, cf. A. A. Alchian (1970), p. 44n.

purchasing household experiment. In the pure *flow* model, realized sales are interpreted as *current income* (from the sale of labor-services). But, whereas it is obviously true that the value of purchases has to be financed by the value of sales, it is not at all true that they must be financed out of current income. A supplier of *x* does not have "current *x*" as his only source of funds; he can (*a*) sell "stored *x*," and (*b*) other things.

The point here is as simple as it is important to our main theme. In pure flow models, realized sales have the interpretation of "income." Income constrains legal acquisition of goods directly. Any little "blip" in the realized income-flow must show up (100% at that) in purchases—the gearing between income receipts and expenditures being that tight. As soon as some market does not clear and false trading takes place, multiplier repercussions should necessarily be observed. This income constraint is too tight; it lures one to adopt an exaggerated view of the potential instability of real-world economies—*stock-flow* economies.

In stock-flow systems, the stocks act as "buffers" between physical inflows and outflows and between financial income and expenditure flows. Stocks of liquid assets—of *cash balances,* in particular—allow expenditures to be maintained when receipts fall off; indeed, they are maintained by traders exactly for the purpose of meeting such contingencies. Modern economies maintain, in normal times, an enormous, elaborate system of physical and financial buffer stocks.

Conclusions: (*a*) in such economies, we must expect the propagation of shocks impinging on flows to be heavily damped—*as long as* the shocks are not of greater magnitude than anticipated by transactors in making their decisions on the levels of buffer stocks to maintain; (*b*) such economies are, therefore, much more "robust" than pure flow models would suggest—within "the corridor"; (*c*) if disturbances are of unanticipatedly large magnitude, buffer stocks may be exhausted—at which point, the direct gearing of inflows and outflows of the "tight" income-constraint takes over. For such large displacements, effective demand theory in the version considered becomes a better guide to the behavior of the system than "Classical economics."

iii. *Realized sales as restriction on demand-signals.* Consider a system in which each good may be traded against every other good. Let us have this "barter economy" in the midst of a most un-Walrasian false trading debauch: quantities actually transacted (and produced) are far below what they would be in a coordinated state; exchange ratios differ from the GE vector of relative prices;[29] and resources are unemployed. For our archetypical case, we would explain: workers fail to sell their services, so their purchases of wage-goods are constrained; producers fail to sell wage-goods, so their purchases of labor services are constrained, etc. Realized sales of labor (wage-goods) in this setting are in themselves realized purchases of wage-goods (labor); there is no intermediate "money"-commodity to separate sale and purchase. Labor services constitute direct "purchasing power" over wage-goods and *vice versa*.

What are the *signals* that the market homeostat would respond to in such a case? If at the going rate of real wages,[30] the desired supply of labor exceeds employment, producers will *ipso facto* receive the signal that demand exceeds current sales and output; if the desired supply of wage-goods exceeds current sales and output, workers will *ipso facto* receive the message that demand for labor exceeds current employment. Note that, at a particular date, both statements could well apply at once[31]—indicating, simply, that the ongoing rate of transactions does not exhaust the mutual gains from trade realizeable at the going exchange rate. As these gains from trade come nearer to being exhausted, however, the market situation will clarify: it emerges either (*a*) as one of excess supply of goods and excess demand for labor or (*b*) as one of excess supply of labor and excess demand for goods. In case (*a*), real wages

29. Not redundant for several reasons the most important of which is that establishing the GE price vector is a necessary, but *not sufficient,* condition for "full coordination" of activities. It does not guarantee that transactors will find a way actually to execute all desired trades. This observation has been made the starting point of important work on the pure theory of money by my UCLA colleague Joseph Ostroy. Cf. his (1973). Also Ostroy and R. M. Starr (1974).

30. For brevity, I fudge matters; the exchange ratio for any pair of goods is bound to vary depending upon what pair of traders are observed; inconsistent cross-rates and corresponding arbitrage opportunities are likely to abound in disequilibrium, etc.

31. Naturally, markets need not clear continuously in this regime. When shifts of the basic parameters occur, producers and workers will spend time searching the other side of the market for the best bargain, etc., etc.

will tend up, in case (*b*) down. *In either case,* the observed volume of transactions, output, and employment will rise.[32]

Next for the contrasting case: a regime characterized by Clower's postulate *"Money buys goods and goods buy money; but goods do not buy goods."*[33] Money and no other good is a *means of payment.* Obligatorily, money separates each sale from corresponding purchases. Suppose we find this system in the "same" type of disequilibrium as the one considered above. Offering to sell now means to ask for money in exchange; offers to buy are no longer "valid" if not backed by ready cash.[34] If the desired supply of labor exceeds employment, producers will be aware of the excess supply in labor markets but receive no valid signal indicating that the demand for wage-goods exceeds output. If desired supply of wage-goods exceeds current sales and output, workers are not informed that demand for labor exceeds employment. Even if the ratio of money wages to money prices comes out as the GE real wage, we may be caught in the vicious circle where the unemployed cannot make their consumption demand *effective* until they have sold their services for money, and producers with excess capacity cannot bid for labor until they have sold their goods—which the unemployed do not have the cash to purchase, and so on.[35] *This failure of the markets to transmit messages about desired transactions from one side to the other is what we mean by the phrase "effective demand failure."*

The non-clearing market states for both our barter and our money system may be described in virtually identical terms, stressing the simple logic of the equal-value-in-exchange requirement (Say's Principle): since transactors do not succeed in selling more than they do, they cannot be buying more than they do . . . etc. But such descriptions of the states are *analyti-*

32. At disequilibrium prices, the short side of markets is assumed to predominate in determining actual transactions.

33. R. W. Clower (1967) reprinted as "Foundations of Monetary Theory," in Clower, ed., (1969). Cf. pp. 207–08.

34. Suppliers who are sold out and face a queue of dissatisfied customers with cash in their pockets will increase their orders and raise prices; they will do neither when observing lines of starving, out-of-pocket unemployed. (Use of Say's Principle in the construction of the model precludes analytical consideration of acts of mercy.)

35. This is a Barro-Grossman "B-solution" again. The Barro and Grossman paper does not stress the distinction between constrained purchases and constrained demand-signals developed in this sub-section, however.

cally incomplete[36] or it would be clear what happens next, namely, the first ("barter") system homes in toward a coordinated state, the second (monetary exchange) system does not.

Since it carries a reminder of this analytical fact, I now prefer the term "cash-constrained" to the earlier usage of "income-constrained" (behavior, process, etc.). For similar reasons, one sometimes needs to distinguish between situation of "deficient aggregate demand" and those characterized by "effective demand failure," and not treat "effective demand" and "aggregate demand" simply as synonyms.

B. Theories of the Consumption Function

This section can be brief; the main ideas I have stated elsewhere,[37] and their underpinnings have just been discussed in some detail.

I referred above to Keynes' simple consumption-income relation as the nexus of all the "singularly Keynesian, obviously anti-Classical" properties of standard macro-models, including the Multiplier and the independence of consumption demand from labor supply. One reason for calling Keynes' consumption function "anti-Classical," we recall, is that it makes the consumption of households depend, not on utility maximization constrained by prices and endowments, but on "realized sales of factor services" (current income).

The so-called "postwar forecasting debacle" in the United States was attributed in large part to use of this function to predict the consumption component of aggregate demand.[38]

36. In the sense that, in mechanics, a description giving only, say, the mass and space-coordinates for a body at a given point of time would be incomplete in omitting information about its (directed) velocity. Cf. the earlier discussion above concerning analysis of non-clearing market states using standard steady-state tools.

37. Cf. Leijonhufvud (1969). pp. 42–45.

38. My own hypothesis to account for why the U.S. economy did not lapse back into "great depression" is simple, perhaps naive: it was put back into "the corridor" through the huge balances of liquid assets that war finance allowed the private sector to accumulate and then insured against a new departure from it by pre-Accord monetary policy which, to put it favorably, made certain that the well would not run dry again.

If this hypothesis be "true" (whatever that might mean with reference to a generalization so broad), the conclusions drawn from the forecasting debacle caught only part of the trouble. They were, in effect (1) that what is nowadays the standard Keynesian textbook model was all right, but (2) that its consumption function needed repair. The

Later work on the problem—some of the best work we have seen in macroeconomics—produced the "modern consumption functions" of Modigliani-Brumberg-Ando and Friedman. Theirs is the seminal work, but there have been many important contributions both before and since.

It is impossible to do this literature justice in short compass. Ignoring operational empirical issues altogether, the main theoretical theme is this: current consumption is to be predicted, not from current income, but from what I will call "perceived wealth."[39] If we treat wealth—defined as the present value of current and expected future income—as the main determinant of consumption, and define income as the rate of change of wealth, it is clear that no stable relationship between consumption and income can be predicted for short time periods. Even for consumption and income flows cumulated over, say, a calendar year, the influence of income on consumption should be relatively weak and unreliable. What then remains of the "Keynesian nexus"? A low marginal propensity to spend on consumption goods[40] means weak multiplier effects, ineffective fiscal policy, etc., etc.

The transmogrifications of "wealth," in this context, are

results of that diagnosis seem to have been a "very nearly" neoclassical consumption function stuck into a Keynesian model.

It just might be that that peculiar combination won't fit *any* state of the world, be it inside or outside "the corridor."

39. How large a step back towards pre-Keynesian theory this represents does not seem to have been generally appreciated. Although there are some fairly subtle conceptual problems, the wealth concept used here is not all that different from "the value of the endowment" concept that appears in intertemporal neoclassical constructions.

For reasons partially adumbrated in the preceding note, these theories do not go all the way back to neoclassicism, but occupy in effect a curious halfway house. Keynes' preoccupation with "involuntary unemployment" states of the system allowed him to split the traditional model of household behavior down the middle, separating the consumption decision from the labor supply decision. Income is not the result of household choice, but "involuntarily" determined. Traditional determinants of the labor supply decision, etc., may then be ignored and the consumption decision treated as determined by income. Modern consumption function theory has not put the theory of household behavior back together again. The generalization of Keynes' current income to (the present value of) current plus expected future income still treats future wage-income as parameteric to the household's consumption-accumulation decision.

40. Admittedly not the same thing as consumption—but we can't go into that. For an up-to-date assessment of empirical work in the Friedman branch of this literature, cf. M. R. Darby (1974). Darby shows that "the econometric procedures which have been utilized in the estimation of permanent income have biased upwards the estimates of the weight of current income. . . ."

about as numerous and difficult to deal with as were those of "realized sales" in our earlier discussion.[41] We note just two: (i) wealth represents a "subjective estimate of maintainable living standards," and (ii) wealth constitutes a (presumably objective) intertemporal constraint on expenditure.

Suppose for the moment that the effect of a change in the level of current income (over an undefined, but not indefinite "period") on "wealth" in *both* senses were of the second order of smalls. Consumption should then be unaffected, and secondary (multiplier) effects on aggregate demand should not be observed. Consequently, no effective demand failure would be observed in our archetypical case. But suppose next that a drop in income impinges on a household whose balances of cash and other highly liquid assets are zero; the household has no liquid "buffer stock" at the date of impact of the disturbance. Still its "wealth" is, by assumption, unimpaired. In what ways could it finance a maintained level of consumption? I suggest that the empirically relevant opportunities for so doing can be described as "distress" sales of non-human assets and "distress" borrowing against future income prospects.[42] Either avenue of action would, *if taken*, (*a*) reduce "wealth" in sense (ii), and (*b*) reduce "wealth" in sense (i) *by more than is avoidable* by simply cutting current consumption until income starts once more to flow at its "permanent" rate. It appears that situations may occur for which "wealth (ii)" is not the relevant constraint on expenditure.

In such situations, the system exhibits effective demand failures. Its self-regulating capabilities are drastically reduced. With cash constraints operative, at least on households, further disturbances will trigger deviation-amplifying multiplier processes—an opportunity for effective, pump-priming, fiscal action.[43]

When would we then expect to observe effective demand fail-

41. This is true quite apart from the fact that the human capital component consists largely of income from "not yet realized" sales of labor services. This helps account for the "imperfect" market in loans secured by human capital collateral which is of importance to our argument, but we cannot enlarge upon it here.

42. For (badly needed) amplification, see my (1969), pp. 43–44.

43. Cf. Leijonhufvud (1968b).

ures, sizeable multiplier coefficients and the rest? In brief, *when liquid buffer stocks have been squeezed out of the system.* This takes a "large displacement"—an *unanticipatedly* large displacement.

We "supposed for the moment" that it was legitimate to discuss whether multiplier effects can occur while holding permanent income constant. It is now clear that this simplifying assumption has to be given up at the same time (if not sooner) that cash/income constraints become binding. We are considering a hypothetical situation in which the transactor has been subjected to an income reduction of larger magnitude and longer duration than he anticipated in planning his liquid asset holdings. This *necessarily* means a drop in income of a magnitude and duration such that he must revise downwards the subjective estimate of his permanent income. He could not otherwise consistently (*a*) regard it as wholly "transitory," and (*b*) not have ensured himself of a buffer stock of liquid assets, credit lines, and unemployment compensation rights larger than our illustration supposes.

Outside the corridor, therefore, effective demand failures come to dominate the dynamic motion of the system due to two factors: (i) the exhaustion of liquid buffers, reinforced (ii) by dysfunctional[44] revisions of permanent income expectations.

A final note is in order under this heading. At this stage, it is clear that our theory implies a *variable width of the corridor.* Transactors who have once suffered through a displacement of

---

44. "Dysfunctional" in the sense of being self-fulfilling prophesies of future incomes below the incomes that would be earned could the system be returned to the "ideal path." For a turgid elaboration on this sort of thing, cf. my (1968a), Chapter IV, Section 5.

Note that the same sort of expectations-revision will apply to the earnings of corporations. When this happens, the present value of equity shares in them will—*even if evaluated at the "natural rate" of discount*—fall below the market price required to call forth the rate of investment needed for the system to return to the "full coordination time-path." Cf. my (1968b).

The point is worth enlarging upon. Within the corridor, transactors that either over- or under-estimate the present value of earnings from assets in prospect along the "fully coordinated" time-path will, in Knightian fashion, suffer losses or forego profits and tend to be weeded out. This means that transactors who persistently act on "socially dysfunctional" evaluations have a low (private) survival probability.

The opposite tends to be the case outside the corridor. This conclusion applies symmetrically to inflationary and deflationary "large displacements."

I am indebted to Professor Henry A. Latané for forcing my attention onto this issue.

unanticipated magnitude (on the order of the Great Depression, say) will be encouraged to maintain larger buffers thereafter—until the memory dims. . . .

C. Quantity Theories of Money Income Determination

On the topics treated so far, I have enjoyed the customary psychological comforts of an author: I know more than I have said. In this section, I will say more than I know—but there will be less of it. In any case, something needs to be set down under this heading to round out the picture this paper has tried to present.

Since Quantity Theories, ancient or modern, usually do not specify equations for the so-called "real sector," it is clear that they are essentially mute on the subject of effective demand failures. But such failures do not seem to fit in. The Quantity Theory approach to income determination and effective demand theory can be brought to confrontation by focusing on the multiplier implications of the latter.[45] Modern Quantity Theory, in its elemental form, predicts income from three equations: (1) a money demand function with income as the independent argument; (2) a money supply equation stating that the money stock is exogenously determined; and (3) a "demand equals supply" equilibrium condition. The Quantity Equation is nowadays invariably interpreted as the reduced form of this little system. To allow Keynesian disturbances to displace it from equilibrium, this closed system has to be opened up; we do so by putting the interest rate in as another unknown in the money demand function. The result is a "variable velocity" model.

Now, assume a "decline in the marginal efficiency of investment." The impact effects are an excess supply of commodities and an excess demand for securities. The latter is eliminated by a fall in the interest rate. This increases the amount of money demanded as of the initial income, thus producing an excess demand for money (equal to the "remainder" of the excess

45. . . . or by listening to my colleague, Earl Thompson, to whom I am indebted for bringing about the confrontation in my own mind.

commodity supply). Standard quantity theory reasoning now applies: income must fall until the excess demand for money is eliminated. Utterly Keynesian so far.[46]

But that is it. The adjustment process should stop right there. To restart it would take another shock to create a new excess demand for money. There is no suggestion here of an ensuing deviation-amplifying multiplier process or of the system's ability to recover being impeded by effective demand failures.

The Quantity Theory could be made to accommodate the *possibility* of "cumulative processes" in various ways, e.g., (i) by making the money supply endogenous in such fashion that the "first-round" decline in income does not remove the excess demand for money; (ii) by assuming money demand dependent not only on "steady-state" income but also on changes in income in such a way that short-run "rachet effects" are obtained. These alternatives I leave aside.

The revival of the Quantity Theory has been accompanied by much inconclusive debate about the proper operational definition of "money". Which assets and how many should be aggregated in measuring "M"? I have nothing conclusive to add to add to that debate; the following discussion leaves the choice to the reader. There has been virtually no discussion of the *other* aggregation problem. Granted that stable demand functions for money exist for individual transactors, how confident can we be of the existence of a stable aggregative money demand function.[47]

At this point, we must take a drastic short cut. I hate being mathematical about it, but consider the equation:

$$MV = PX, \tag{1}$$

where *PX* stands for aggregate expenditures on *final goods.* Instead of the modern interpretation of the equation as a reduced

46. The version of Keynesianism enshrined in the textbooks invariably assumes a stable aggregate demand function for money. That assumption is as crucial to that construction as it is to any quantity theory. Since it it, to say the very least, unclear that this was the original idea, it might be better to refer to IS-LM models as "variable velocity quantity theories."

47. The reason why the question has not been raised even by fervent anti-Monetarists is provided, I think, in the preceding note. Anyone who is tempted to grasp upon the (empirically unsubstantiated) argument that follows as a new weapon against Monetarism should be forewarned that it is double-edged. If there were to be sizeable ag-

form, we adopt an old-fashioned one: V is taken to represent the "average propensity to spend on final goods out of money balances." We will assume (a) that stable underlying money-expenditure relations exist for all transactors, and also (b) that, within the ranges relevant to our conceptual experiments, all these relations are linear with zero intercepts. For each transactor, the average and marginal propensities to spend out of money balances (APSM and MPSM) are equal and constant.[48]

We have k relations of the simple form

$$m_j v_j = P x_j, \text{ where } v_j = APSM_j = MPSM_j. \tag{2}$$

What assumptions would justify replacing these individual functions, k in number, with equation (1)? The usual first two lines of defense of such aggregations are: (1) that it is permissible to assume that all the v_j's are of equal magnitude so that there can be no distribution effects; (ii) that, although the v_j's differ, the proportional distribution of the m_j's can be justifiably assumed constant over the time-period and population of transactors studied. I will suppose that we can agree that (i) is "obviously untrue." I will then infer that the implicit justifying assumption for the aggregation over transactors, in Quantity Theories, generally is of type (ii).

We may now proceed directly to the analytical possibility that intrigues me. Note that what follows definitely is a *special case*— and it takes the conjunction of the following, separate assumptions to produce it. Following Gurley and Shaw,[49] we divide all transactors into two groups, referred to as "deficit" and "sur-

gregation errors in one of the functions of the standard model, there must *a fortiori* be corresponding "instabilities" elsewhere in it.

The converse double edge to Friedman's insistence on the instability of the multiplier is, cuttingly, pointed out by F. H. Hahn (1971).

48. Readers already uneasy with this shortcut may fortify themselves by interpreting these individual money-expenditure schedules as stock-flow equilibrium loci of the type constructed in G. C. Archibald and R. G. Lipsey (1958). This type of construction will not support our argument below, however, beyond the point where income account and capital account transactions are separated.

In my argument from this point on, I have been greatly fortified by the theoretical investigations of Peter Howitt and by numerous discussions with him during his 1971–72 stay at UCLA. Two of his papers are particularly relevant: (1974) and (unpub.). The finite-time dynamics of Howitt's model in the latter paper exhibit "the corridor"—for reasons that, while formally more formidable, are at bottom the same as those loosely sketched below.

49. E.g., their (1956).

plus" units, respectively. We assume (*a*) that, over the period that we focus on, migrations between groups do not occur; units are allowed to proceed, at most, to the boundary line of running a balanced income-account budget; and (*b*) that, on the average, the v_j's of the deficit group exceed those of the surplus group. This completes the setting of our special case. It implies the following: if we were to trace all income account transactions in the system, while ignoring those on capital account, we would observe a net cash flow from the deficit group to the surplus group. If that was all there was to it, we should—*vide* assumption (ii)—observe total expenditure on final goods declining in the system. Since the money stock is held constant, this means that observed average velocity declines. Consequently, I enlarge upon the earlier inference concerning the implicit aggregation-justifying assumptions of the Quantity Theory: it assumes that capital account transactions (sales and purchases of existing assets as well as credit transactions) occur so as to offset continuously the tendency of net flows on income account to "upset" the given proportional distribution of cash. For brevity, I refer to these offsetting capital account transactions as "cash reshuffling."

We come then to the point: when should we expect monetarist income predictions to "break down" (and do worse relative to simple Keynesian multiplier predictions than "normally").[50] Even omitting supporting argument, the answer is, I think, clear: during episodes when conditions in asset and credit markets are so "abnormal," that normal cash reshuffling processes are likely to be seriously impeded.[51] Again, we would look for "large displacements" removing the system from the corridor. The most obvious possibilities involve *the same* conditions as those that we previously suggested should be present when effective demand failures occur. Consider the household. The tight cash/income constraint becomes binding when its income earners have been unemployed long enough to exhaust savings deposits and rights to unemployment compensation—and, of course, the availability of credit on "reasonable terms."

50. Cf. M. Friedman and D. Meiselman (1963).
51. Here we can only hint at financial instability themes developed by Professor H. P. Minsky in numerous contributions.

In that situation, its *MPSM* should also be high relative to transactor units with healthier balance sheets.[52]

I suggest that those well known conditions of the 1930's that have been widely interpreted (by Keynesian writers) as attributable to a static "liquidity trap" property of a stable aggregative (excess) demand for money function are *at least* equally well accounted for by the hypothesis just outlined. If we can assume that open market operations are transactions between the central bank and units with below average MPSM, monetary policy will be atypically "ineffective" under the conditions assumed. In the same conditions, fiscal policy should be atypically "effective" even if unaccompanied by injections of money. It can be so because of the opportunity to borrow from low-MPSM units and to channel the funds through the budget discriminatively into the hands of high-MPSM units—in a situation where the normal endogenous reshuffling mechanisms are inoperative.

A final proposition regarding the corridor: Cantillon-effects will be strong and relatively long-lasting outside, weak and evanescent inside the corridor.[53]

III

Hopefully, the various themes of this paper will be seen to form an intellectually coherent *theory*. Rigorously consistent, it is not; solid empirical support, it does not have. As advertised in the

52. Interference with the cash reshuffling process could also occur in inflationary situations. Consider, for example, "disintermediation" phenomena consequent upon nominal interest rates piercing legal ceilings. The widely discussed disintermediation problems in the United States in the late 1960's apparently coincided with previously relatively reliable monetarist velocity equations producing predictions later found to be *over*-estimates. I am indebted to Sam Peltzman for this observation.

For those taking the fashionable literature on "Optimal Monetary Growth" seriously, there just might be a warning here. The policy suggestion has been made that the rate of return on money balances "ought to" be manipulated into equality with the rate of return on real capital. As pointed out to me by Earl Thompson some five or six years ago, this entails killing off all intermediary institutions, since no margin between borrowing and lending rates will remain for them to live on. More generally, it completely eliminates the incentive for surplus units to lend—just letting the cash pile up brings the same return. And so on and so forth. The social optimality of this sort of thing is not obvious.

53. I define "Cantillon-effects" as occurring whenever the effects on aggregate money income of increases in the money stock are found to depend upon the *route* by which the injection of money takes place.

beginning, it is more than anything else an *agenda* for—and invitation to—*needed* modelling and empirical work by those who find it plausible enough to be worth pursuing. I have little doubt but that the results of such work would sooner or later show the idea of the "corridor" to be too crude a generalization. Meanwhile, however, *some* image of how our contending interpretations of post-World War I experience may be reconciled seems needed. It will not have escaped the reader's attention that many an issue controverted these many years between various "schools" is rather defused if the theory outlined here is judged provisionally acceptable.

CHAPTER SEVEN

The Wicksell Connection:
Variations on a Theme*

I. INTRODUCTION

The theory of the interest rate mechanism is the center of the confusion in modern macroeconomics. Not all issues in contention originate here. But the *inconclusive* quarrels—the ill-focused, frustrating ones that drag on because the contending parties cannot agree what the issue is—largely do stem from this source.

This essay seeks to clarify the relationships between some of the major schools in modern macroeconomics by tracing the development of the theory of the (real) interest rate mechanism. It claims to get to the bottom of the Monetarist controversy and to the origin of the Two Cambridges controversy. My own position has differed from that of the Cambridge Keynesians as well as from that of the Neoclassical Keynesians and will be reasserted here as a third Keynesian (of sorts) alternative to Monetarism.[1] Some aspects of recent work on Rational Expectations will also be considered.

* An earlier version of this paper was given as a Faculty Lecture at the Institute of Advanced Studies in Vienna in June 1976. The version preceding this one was written at the Institute of Advanced Studies in Jerusalem, Summer 1978. I wish to thank my good friends in both places for their interest in my work and their hospitality during my stays. The number of people who are not responsible for the remaining errors of this paper is almost embarrassing: I am grateful to Yoram Ben-Porath, Clive Bull, Stephen Ferris, Lars Jonung, David Laidler, Dale Mortensen, Mack Ott, T. K. Rhymes, Robert Solow and Richard Sweeney. The advice of my wife, Earlene Craver-Leijonhufvud helped me through the last couple of revisions of the manuscript.

1. In this essay, "Monetarism" will refer to the pre-Rational Expectations position of Milton Friedman. Cf., e.g., Friedman (1968) and Gordon (1973). "Cambridge Keynesians" will refer to Joan Robinson and Richard Kahn. For reasons to be discussed later,

The following family tree of major twentieth-century macroeconomists helps outline the argument of the paper (Figure 7-1). It shows the theories using the saving-investment approach, starting with Wicksell, as an offshoot from the ancient and honorable Quantity Theory main stem.[2]

Until Friedman revived the Quantity Theory, the saving-investment approaches dominated the field in this century. All Keynesians, of whatever description, belong to this branch. The Stockholm School and the Austrians also descend from the Wicksell Connection.

In Wicksell's theory of the cumulative process, the maladjustment of the interest rate—the discrepancy between the market rate and the natural rate—is the central idea. It is also the idea that motivates the analysis of changes in the price-level (or in nominal income) in terms of saving and investment. It is a simple but fundamental point. Use of the saving-investment approach to income fluctuations is predicated on the hypothesis that the interest rate mechanism fails to coordinate saving and investment decisions appropriately. This is where *all* the Wicksell Connection theories differ from Monetarism. In Monetarist variants of the Quantity Theory, saving and investment have to do with the allocation of output but nothing to do with the determination of aggregate income or the price level. This is true because Monetarist theory assumes that the interest rate mechanism can be relied upon to coordinate the intertemporal decisions of households and of firms.

Some twenty years of IS-LM exercises and applied econometrics failed to isolate this point as fundamental to the Monetarist controversy.[3] Some twenty years of mathematical modelling similarly failed to spotlight incompatible ideas about the interest rate mechanism as being at the root of the Two Cambridges controversy. To clarify these matters—and, also, explain why they have not been more obvious all along—we will trace Wicksell's theme through a number of analytical variations.

I do not have a name or names to typify Neoclassical Keynesianism. The term should be taken to refer, somewhat loosely, to those Keynesians who, in contrast to the Cambridge Keynesians, accepted the so-called Neoclassical Synthesis.

2. Or, from one perspective, I suppose, as a bunch of suckers that should be pruned back to allow the main stem to bloom more abundantly.

3. None of the authors in Gordon (1973) or in Mayer (1978) have a clear statement of it, for example.

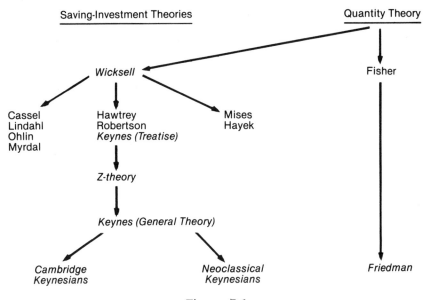

Figure 7-1.

The original idea is simple. In allocation theory, we learn that household saving decisions and entrepreneurial investment decisions are to be coordinated by the interest rate mechanism. In money and banking, we learn that "the" interest rate is governed by the supply and demand of securities (or of "credit"). Imagine a situation where the interest rate cannot do both jobs at once, i.e., in which that level of real interest that equates the supply and demand for securities does not serve to equate saving and investment. What could be the *causes* of such a maladjustment? What might be its *consequences?*

In the generation following Wicksell, we find suites on his theme composed by the Swedish, by the Austrian, and by the Cambridge schools. Before the *General Theory,* it was the dominant theme in monetary and business cycle theory as an imposing parade of names will testify: Cassel, Lindahl, Ohlin, and Myrdal; Mises and Hayek; Hawtrey, Robertson, and Keynes were among those who put the theme squarely in the center of major works of theirs. After the *General Theory,* however, the theme is no longer prominent. It was abandoned by monetary economists and left to antiquarians. So, what happened?

133

What happened, essentially, was that Keynes so obfuscated the interest rate mechanism that the later Keynesian literature almost entirely lost track of Wicksell's theme. The basic idea remains central in the *General Theory*. (Its middle name was "Interest," after all.) In Keynes' last variation, however, the theme comes in a guise that has proven the almost perfect disguise. The failure to recognize its presence and role has proved productive of much later misunderstanding and confusion.

To see what happened, we take the theme through four variations.[4] Numbers 1, 2, and 4 are, respectively, Wicksell, the *Treatise on Money*, and the *General Theory*. Number 3 is an analytical interpolation between the *Treatise* and the *General Theory*. It may be described either as "the *Treatise* plus quantity-adjustments" or as "the *General Theory* minus the Liquidity Preference theory of interest." (For a less cumbersome label, it is designated as "Z-theory" in Figure 7-1.)[5]

Although it is a doctrine-historical fiction, this Z-theory is (at the very least) useful in enabling us to judge how much of Keynes' "revolutionary" theory of unemployment is independent of the Liquidity Preference (LP) theory of interest and precisely what properties of Keynesian models derive from it. It is my own position that Z-theory incorporates all of Keynes' contribution that should be preserved and developed; that the LP hypothesis should have been rejected from the start; and that, failing this, propositions derivative from it ought system-

---

4. Telling this tale allows me to correct and clarify earlier work. My *On Keynesian Economics and the Economics of Keynes* (1968) stresses two clusters of ideas. One was the "multiplier" process, the analysis of which starts from assuming quantity-adjustments, rather than pure price adjustments, as the immediate response to deflationary pressure. The other cluster of ideas belong to Wicksell's theme.

The "multiplier" part of the book has received much more attention than the rest. For this, admittedly, the writing rather than the reading is to blame. Nonetheless, neither set of ideas is of much "revolutionary" significance without the other. It is the combination of the two that produces a challenge to the "Classics" (or Neoclassics or Monetarists).

In "Effective Demand Failures," [Leijonhufvud (1973)] I gave my second thoughts on multiplier matters. This paper is a belated companion piece. They belong together.

5. Z-theory is on the whole what I presented as the "Economics of Keynes" in 1968. In so doing, I was not taking the Liquidity Preference theory of interest quite seriously but opted to stick with what I still regard as the much superior interest theory of the *Treatise*. But the Liquidity Preference theory, whatever its theoretical deficiencies, has been historically important. Many of the weaknesses of "Keynesian economics" really stem from it. I failed to give it its historical due.

atically, if belatedly, to be rooted out of modern macroeconomics.

Keynes' obfuscation of interest theory inheres in his LP hypothesis but stems from his insistence on the saving-investment equality as an identity. If saving and investment are always equal, they cannot govern the rate of interest, nor can the interest rate possibly serve to coordinate saving and investment decisions. Hence, the LP theory: money demand and supply govern the interest rate.

The elimination of the Loanable Funds (LF) mechanism and the impossibility of saving and investment decisions being coordinated by the interest rate in a system from which it is totally absent are the original propositions from which later Cambridge Keynesian positions on growth theory and related matters logically develop.

The denial of the LF mechanism makes nonsense of the very notion of a "natural rate" of interest. The Wicksellian theme is lost. The affirmation of the LP theory contradicts the dynamic hypothesis that is fundamental to Quantity Theories, namely, that the excess demand for money governs the price level. The rationale for the saving-investment approach and the relationship to Quantity Theories are both confounded.

The Neoclassical Keynesians have never managed to clear up the resulting muddle. This murkiness on critical issues of what was for so long clearly the majority doctrine has befuddled friends and foes alike in the Monetarist controversy. Most obviously, perhaps, the failure to grasp the role of the Wicksellian maladjustment of interest rate in Keynes' theory of unemployment has caused the Keynesians more difficulty than necessary in marking out for themselves a theoretically justifiable answer to the Natural Rate of Unemployment doctrine. A "Keynesian" answer to this doctrine would be that unemployment will not converge to its natural level *unless* the interest rate goes to its natural level—and that the latter condition will not always be fulfilled. Instead, American non-Monetarists have tended to take up positions that were either largely irrelevant (the interest-elasticity of transactions demand for cash) or indefensible (the stable Phillips curve).

Another consequence of the muddle is the, at least, occasional failure of Keynesians to come to Monetarist conclusions under the appropriate conditions. Whenever the market rate of interest keeps to its natural level—and, surely, they do not always diverge?—the Keynesian model should reduce to a Monetarist one.[6] In failing to bring this out, Keynesians have allowed the simplest and most important lessons of monetary experience to come to be regarded as quintessentially Monetarist insights.

II. BENCHMARK

In the "long run" of price theory, all adjustments have taken place. Originally, the distinctive characteristic of the "short run" was that stocks need not be fully adjusted but that net investment or disinvestment may be going on. For the rest, all activities were "equilibrated." More recently, however, new short-run notions have begun to proliferate in the literature to fit various and sundry cases of incomplete adjustment being investigated.

In macroeconomics, a full adjustment benchmark different from the traditional long run is more appropriate and more useful. Call it *full information*. In full information macroeconomics, we study states of an economy in which agents have managed to *learn* all that can be (profitably) learned about their environment and about each others' behavior. Such states should be equilibria in the sense suggested by Hahn, i.e., market interaction will not teach agents anything that significantly alters their beliefs.[7]

To develop an entirely satisfactory concept of full information will not be a simple matter. The desired combination of precision and of realism (of a sort) is not easily achieved. The objective, however, will at least be clear. We want, on the one hand, to put a safe distance between full information macroeconomics and notions of costless information and perfect fore-

6. Although some of the Keynesian models dealt with here have Velocity "unstable," all treat Money as a definite, meaningful aggregate, just as do Quantity Theories. Keynesian models crossbred with the Hawtrey-Radcliffe strain (or the Gurley-Shaw strain) have been put arbitrarily beyond our purview. The consequences of so doing are a bit uncomfortable to the author here and there, but the issues involved would only encumber the paper to little purpose.
7. Cf. F. H. Hahn (1973).

sight. On the other hand, we strive to retain a role for equilibrium constructions. The objective itself is controversial. Certain authors—e.g., Kaldor, Lachmann, Robinson, Shackle—argue that a realistic appreciation of the role of ignorance in the human condition must preclude the use of equilibrium models. However that may be, this paper cannot do without. We postulate that a feasible equilibrium growth path will "exist." The main purpose of full information macroeconomics, however, is merely to define the adjustments that must take place if the system is to adapt fully following some disturbance. Use of such constructions does not commit us to the belief that the system will always or normally adapt smoothly and rapidly no matter what the disturbance; nor does it force us to preclude the very rapid convergence of the economy on full information equilibrium in certain cases—as in certain Rational Expectations models. The notion of a full-information state should not be invariably associated with either the short run or the long.

To justify, to define precisely, and to derive the analytical properties of a full information model cannot be attempted here. Instead, we simply propose a number of model properties that are to serve as the full adjustment benchmarks for the purposes of this paper:

1. labor supply and derived labor demand determine output, employment, and the real wage rate;
2. money supply and money demand determine the price level; and
3. saving and investment determine the rate of capital accumulation and the interest rate.

In full information comparative statics, moreover, it should be true that *monetary shocks have no real effects* and that *real shocks have no monetary consequences.*[8] The first of these generalizations

---

8. The only "real" shocks considered here are those that shift the investment or saving functions.

While they are not needed for the purposes of the paper, a few other properties will help suggest the flavor of full information constructions: (4) government resource absorption will crowd out private sector resource use; (5) future tax liabilities are fully discounted in calculations of private net worth; and (6) the Fisher equation for the relation between real and nominal interest rates holds.

When the term "real interest rate" is used in this paper, it means simply the Fisher-deflated money rate of interest, i.e., the money rate minus the expected rate of infla-

simply asserts the neutrality of money. The second is more controversial in that it denies significant interest-elasticity to the steady-state (non-speculative) excess demand for cash balances. So here we are out on that limb onto which Professor Friedman is always urged but that he has steadfastly refused! In textbook parlance: a vertical LM curve. Some comments on the matter are in order.

In standard theory, if the economy is required to traverse from one growth-path to another, it must also change its price-level. As an example, consider the case that Keynes thought to be the main economic problem facing the civilized world in his day, namely, a non-transitory decline in the marginal efficiency of capital. The rational response for the system transfers resources from capital goods producing to consumption industries and has the economy settling down at full employment on a lower growth-path with a lower rate of profit. At lower rates of profit and interest, however, transactors supposedly demand larger real cash balances per unit output. Consequently, the system's adjustment will require, *ceteris paribus,* a reduction in money prices and wages.

The notion that the interest-elasticity of the transactions demand for cash should prevent the economy from traversing without also deflating (or inflating) runs counter to my intuition. It does not seem right. So saying, however, will not get one around the models of Baumol, Tobin, and Patinkin[9] all of which imply that the interest-elasticity should be significant. Nor will intuition dispose of the empirical evidence.[10]

For a counterargument try the following. Consider Patinkin's model. His agents hold real balances to insure themselves against the personal consequences of default. The lower the rate of interest the more such insurance they invest in. Here the penalty cost consequent upon default is treated as a con-

---

tion. In particular, use of the term does not mean that we deny or "assume away" the multiplicity of commodity own rates. For the most part, we will deal with problems where the distinction between real and nominal rates is not required.

9. W. J. Baumol (1952), J. Tobin (1956), D. Patinkin (1956). Note however that Clower and Howitt do not find an unambiguous sign for the interest-elasticity of transactions demand in their more general inventory theoretic model. R. W. Clower and P. Howitt (1978).

10. E.g., H. Latané (1954). For a survey, c.f. D. E. W. Laidler (1969).

stant. But is not this arbitrary? Instead of bankruptcy as the typical consequence of not having cash when a bill is presented for payment, the representative agent may envisage incurring certain costs connected with a *delay* of payment. A delay of payment is not a default (yet). What should be the appropriate penalty for it? For concreteness, suppose the creditor is entitled to triple damages. That is three times the *interest* on the sum due over the period of the delay. If that is the structure of the choice, the interest-elasticity of transactions (and precautionary) demand should be zero—for *permanent* changes in the level of the interest rate.[11]

The point of all this is not to deny the relationship between velocity and interest rates over the business cycle but rather to shift the emphasis in the interpretation of the time-series evidence from theoretical steady-state to non-steady-state properties of money demand. In particular, cyclical variations in real cash balance demand per unit output will be attributed to speculative demand or to transitory changes in "flexibility preference."[12] The observations that account for the interest-elasticity, for example, of Latané's equation, may not belong on the steady-state transactions demand for money functions. Instead, we suggest, they are associated with departures from full information time-paths.

For the full information equilibria of the model suggested above, we assume that agents have consistent beliefs about current and future market determined magnitudes; that these beliefs are realizable in that they are consistent with resource and technology constraints; and that all individual and mutual adjustments of behavior to this knowledge have been completed. Relative to the benchmark time-paths provided by such a model, we may then distinguish two types of coordination failures. Each corresponds to a distinct approach or emphasis in modern macrotheory.

11. The option of not paying promptly is not incorporated in the decision-calculus of either Baumol's or Tobin's transactor. Putting it in, I conjecture, will not do the trick as long as the brokerage fee is not also proportional to the interest rate. One would have to rely on Clower and Howitt instead.

12. On flexibility preference, cf. A. G. Hart (1942). Sir John Hicks (1974) Lecture II, explains the distinction between flexibility and liquidity in the sense of Tobin-Markowitz portfolio theory and develops flexibility preference theory in exactly the context most germane to the concerns of this paper.

One is the "spanner-in-the-works" malfunction[13] for which we may imagine that agents actually do have full information (so that all the nuts and bolts of standard theory can be used) but are prevented from acting on what they know. The obstacle to appropriate adjustment may be coercion or past commitment to a (possibly implicit) contract or to a particular structure of physical capital. Coordination failures of this sort may well be characterized as equilibria. This approach to macrotheory will be altogether ignored in this paper.

The other main type of coordination failure, of course, comprises *incomplete information* states of the system. Since we are on a taxonomic course, we may again distinguish two kinds of such states. In the first kind, agents have mutually consistent but incorrect beliefs: they all believe the same thing and they are all wrong. Consistent beliefs should produce temporary equilibria.[14] In the second kind, agents are acting on *inconsistent beliefs*. Such states will be called disequilibria in what follows.[15]

As in my previous work, this second incomplete information approach is the one pursued here. We shall apply it to the interpretation of a number of inherited macrotheories. But, first, some anachronistic preliminaries.

III. DOUBLE CROSS

The macroeconomics we actually teach, of course, bears no clear relationship to full information macro (FIM). Instead of the static properties of the FIM model, the beginning student may be given one or the other of two crosses to bear. Call them "Model A" and "Model T." Model A uses the Keynesian saving-investment cross to determine nominal income; Model T employs a given money stock and a "Cambridge k" money demand to the same purpose.

In either case, the student has had a switch pulled on him before he even got started. In our FIM model, saving and in-

---

13. Cf. Leijonhufvud (1968), p. 395.

14. Cf. J. R. Hicks (1965), Chapter VI, and J. M. Grandmont (1975).

15. Use of "inconsistent beliefs" rather than the more fashionable "asymmetric information sets" is deliberate. The intention is to suggest transactors acting at cross-purposes. "Asymmetric information" is coming to be associated (I think) mostly with equilibria where the information advantage on one side of the market persists.

vestment have nothing to do with the level of income, whether real or nominal; and money supply and demand determine the price level and not real income or the product of the two. Full information macro admittedly has little direct bearing on the problems that motivate the study of macroeconomics. But why does "relevant" macroeconomics start off with this surreptitious[16] double switch of crosses? Since A and T differ from FIM, the answer should be that certain information failures are taken for granted—so much so, in fact, that they are built into elementary models as inescapable features of the real world.

The Monetarist controversy started off, in effect, with a confrontation between Models A and T. No economist alive will confess to a belief in either one. Nonetheless, all the Round I issues are produced by putting these simplistic constructions on collision course: the relative "stability" of the consumption-income and the money-income relations; the appropriate empirical components to be included in "autonomous expenditure" or in the "money supply," respectively; the "autonomy" of investment and the "exogeneity" of the money stock; the effectiveness of fiscal and monetary policy actions and the predictability of their consequences.

These direct statistical contests between A and T did not serve to focus attention on the question of how A and T, respectively, depart from a full information model. The information failures implicit in the debate were not brought to light. Yet, the discord largely stems from this level. To clarify the theoretical issues, we obviously need to define the information problems that are presumed to be ever-present—or ignored as implausible—by each side. For Model T, we have the diagnosis recently made familiar by Lucas, Barro, Sargent, and Wallace et. al.: anticipated changes in money affect prices, but unanticipated ones affect real income. In the case of Model A, as later sections will show, the corresponding diagnosis runs: whereas (in FIM) recognized changes in the realizable rate of profit affect only the interest rate and the growth path, unrecognized changes will affect money income and (in A) *all* such changes go completely unrecognized.

16. Most textbooks keep the student in the dark about these (presumably pedagogical) goings-on.

From A or T, our student graduates to IS-LM. On this loftier plane, it is no easier to see what is going on. In our FIM model, real and monetary phenomena were independent of one another. Then the switch again: In IS-LM, as usually taught, real disturbances have monetary consequences and vice versa— unless extreme assumptions are made about the elasticities of IS and LM. Is it plausible that this interdependence also stems from information failures of some sort?

Start back with A and T, with propositions fundamental to each. Money income, in Model A, will decline (say) *if and only if* intended saving exceeds intended investment (so that we have an excess supply of commodities). In Model T, money income will decline *if and only if* the prevailing state is one of excess demand for money. Thus so far the two are consistent. When money income is falling, we should have both an ES of commodities and an ED for money.

But we have two contrasting hypotheses about causation. In A, a decline in investment produces the ES of commodities. In T, a reduction in the money supply produces the ED for money. If we scrutinize the A story with the suspicious eyes of a T-believer and then let an A-believer have his turn with the T story, we obtain two questions about "transmission."

> *Question 1:* Why should real disturbances be expected to cause an excess demand for money and thus a change in the nominal income level (and, if money prices and/or wages are inflexible, a change in activity levels)? Empirically, do they? Always, sometimes, or never?

The Keynesian answer is that they *always* do. Monetarists think "never" is the more plausible conjecture.

> *Question 2:* Why should monetary disturbances be expected to cause saving and investment intentions to diverge (and thus to change nominal income, etc.)? Empirically, do they? Always, sometimes, or never?

In the schools stemming from Wicksell, it is presumed that they generally do.[17] In modern Monetarism, it is presumed that

---

17. The exception would be those Keynesians who at one time maintained that monetary policy was ineffective because of liquidity traps and/or interest inelasticity of saving and investment.

they generally do not. Poles apart on this spectrum of views, one finds the Austrians and the Chicago Monetarists. Among Wicksell's intellectual descendants, the Austrian business-cycle theorists were particularly insistent that monetary impulses must disrupt the coordination of saving and investment decisions and shove the system off its equilibrium growth-path.[18] Among the Monetarists, Friedman has most strongly argued the view that the banking system cannot, except very transitorily, affect the real rate of interest on which saving and investment depend.[19] The later Rational Expectations Monetarism need not invoke the interest rate as part of the transmission mechanism at all.

If we link Models A and T by "the" rate of interest, the resulting IS-LM construction will suggest what has by now for decades been the standard textbook answers to Questions 1 and 2. Consider the shocks that typically produce deflationary pressure.

Answer 1. A decline in investment demand shifts the IS-schedule left; the decline in investment is associated with a decline in loanable funds demand; this reduces the rate of interest; at the lower rate of interest, the amount of money supplied will fall short of the amount demanded at the initial income level.[20]

Answer 2. A reduction in the money supply shifts the LM-schedule left; the excess demand for money is associated with an excess demand for loanable funds[21]; this drives up the rate of interest, so that intended investment now falls short of planned saving at the initial income level.

Thus IS-LM gives us a handle of sorts on the interaction of real and monetary phenomena: the "real" disturbance leads to a "monetary disequilibrium"; and the "monetary" impulse changes the rate of real capital accumulation. The exercises suggest, moreover, that the elasticities of IS and LM are crucial

18. F. A. Hayek (1931) and (1933), and G. P. O'Driscoll (1977).

19. M. Friedman (1968) and R. J. Gordon, ed., (1973), pp. 35ff. and p. 54.

20. The process just described we will call the *Loanable Funds Sequence.* For the *Liquidity Preference Sequence,* cf. Section VIII below.

21. It may be pedagogically preferable to refer to the ED for loanable funds as an ES for "bonds" instead, since this makes it clear that Say's Principle is adhered to at each step.

to the strength of the interaction. Round II of the Monetarist controversy—in which the Round I issues were transplanted into the IS-LM frame and Crowding Out and Gibson's Paradox were added—pursued the notion that the issues could be narrowed down to the values of these elasticities.[22] The discussion tended to presume, moreover, that the elasticities were stable properties of the system, that the results of time-series regressions gave information on these steady-state elasticities, and that qualitative results from a priori static choice theory had a bearing on the issues in that they sufficed to exclude extreme values.

In this elasticities view of the controversy, there are two extremist possibilities. The "Fiscalist" extreme would postulate a vertical IS and a horizontal LM; the Monetarist extreme would postulate a horizontal IS and a vertical LM. Putting it this way tends to suggest that, surely, all moderate men of sound judgment will take a position somewhere in the middle—although leaning a bit toward one extreme or the other will be permitted without prejudice to one's reputation for reasonableness. The trouble is that this moderate position implies that real impulses *always* must affect income and that monetary impulses *always* must put a wedge between the plans of savers and investors—i.e., that the "rational" FIM adjustments can never happen. And going to the monetarist extreme is hardly more palatable for, in context, the resulting model answers "never" to the empirical part of Questions 1 and 2 above. In either case, "sometimes" is the empirical possibility that is being excluded by construction.

Note that *if* it were to be the case that these short-run interactions of real and monetary phenomena are due to incomplete information on the part of agents, then the elasticities view is

---

22. Cf., for instance, Tobin in Gordon, ed., (1973), p. 77, or Bronfenbrenner in Mayer (1978), p. 49, n. 5, or B. M. Friedman, *ibid.*, pp. 94–95.
    Milton Friedman has emphatically denied that the elasticity of LM is at issue. Cf. Gordon, *op. cit.*, p. 142. At the same time his use of what is basically an IS-LM structure in presenting his own theory, and his oft-repeated insistence that no theoretical issues but only questions of empirical magnitudes within this shared theoretical frame separate him from his opponents, have apparently fortified others in their belief that (whatever he says) this elasticity *must* be crucial. Furthermore, Friedman has himself played around with elasticities, for example, in advancing the notion of a horizontal IS curve. Cf. his Comments in J. L. Stein (1976), p. 311.

seen to be seriously misleading on several counts. What the response to a particular impulse will be then depends upon the state of information and not just on steady-state behavioral parameters. What counts is the extent to which the nature and extent of the shock is recognized or unrecognized, anticipated or unanticipated, perceived as permanent or as transitory. The same impulse should not call forth exactly the same responses over and over again.[23] In this setting, also, it makes little sense to ask whether fiscal or monetary policy is more "effective" or to measure their relative effectiveness by time-series regression. The effectiveness of a given set of policy measures depends on the nature and seriousness of the disequilibrium one is trying to correct.[24]

In Round III of the controversy, the Monetarists shifted the focus away from the elasticities and towards the "stability" of the system. IS-LM hardly lends itself to analysis of conflicting beliefs about the strength of equilibrating tendencies, speeds of convergence, and the like.[25] The framework does not even help to explain why macroeconomists should divide into opposing camps over the Phillips curve in the same way as they did over the issues of Rounds I and II. Why should belief in the autonomy of investment, the predominance of real disturbances, the stability of the consumption function, a significant interest-elasticity of money demand, and the effectiveness of fiscal policy prejudice you in favor of the notion of a stable (even if expectations-augmented) Phillips curve? What does the exogeneity of some "M," predominance of monetary shocks, stability of velocity, and effectiveness of monetary policy have to do with convergence to a natural rate of unemployment? There is, as we shall see,[26] a fairly straightforward answer to these queries. But IS-LM does not suggest what it is.

It is instructive to consider how our simple IS-LM analysis would have to be amended to accommodate a theory that allows the answer to Questions 1 and 2 to be "Sometimes." These amendments will suggest, in the first case, that the elasticities

23. Cf., e.g., R. E. Lucas, Jr. (1976).
24. Cf. Leijonhufvud (1968b) and (1973).
25. Cf. Leijonhufvud (1976), pp. 70–71.
26. Cf., below, Section VI.

may be variable rather than stable and, in the second, that the elasticities may on occasion be altogether irrelevant. Those observations pertain to the mere mechanics of so adjusting the model that it will accommodate a different theoretical conception. It is more to the point to note that, in both cases, these mutations of the simple model are forced by changes in the assumptions we make about the information possessed by transactors.

The first case is straightforward. The possibility of "sometimes" having the marginal efficiency of investment change, as in FIM, without significant change in the velocity of money and in money income can be incorporated, for example, by postulating a speculative money demand function that does not depend on the absolute level of the interest rate, $\underline{r}$, but only on the difference between $\underline{r}$ and the perceived "normal" rate, r^*:

$$M^d = f(Y, \underline{r} - r^*)$$

In the thus modified model, *if* the change in MEC is correctly perceived and seen to be permanent, the normal rate will be adjusted accordingly, and the adjustment of the whole structure of yields can take place without creating an excess demand (or supply) of money.

In the second case, the possibility of "sometimes" seeing the money supply and nominal income change without concomitant changes in the interest rate and rate of capital accumulation can be accommodated if we allow both the reduced forms to shift together and at the same time. The usual classroom practice of shifting one schedule while keeping the other constant rests on the strong assumption that a disturbance that shifts, for example, the IS-curve will have the ED (or ES) for commodities matched by an ES (or ED) for bonds with *zero* impact on the ED for money. Similarly, when LM shifts the implicit matching excess demand is in the bond market with no direct impact on commodities.[27] But it is, of course, entirely

27. Without this strong assumption, moreover, IS-LM does not make sense as a modelling strategy. Analyzing income determination in terms of these two particular reduced forms is illuminating and convenient only insofar as this assumption is approximately justified. It is not just that IS-LM happens to direct attention away from direct interactions of money and commodity excess demands. It is *meant* to do so, being predicated on the judgment that the direct link is seldom of appreciable significance.

possible to have disturbances that directly create an ED for commodities with a corresponding ES for money or vice versa. These cases have both IS and LM shifting.

This question of the excess demand distribution at impact of various shocks illustrates a more general problem. One of the stock complaints about IS-LM is that it is "too static." But it may well be that it causes us more problems because it is not as static as it seems. IS-LM contains a number of built-in assumptions about *the sequence in which things happen* even as its simultaneous equation form gives the impression that the temporal order of adjustments is irrelevant. As with any period-model, of course, there is first the distinction between the things that happen within the short run and those that will take place "later." With many Keynesian constructions of this genre, one should recognize the further category of the adjustments that "never" happen—such as a return to full employment. What is perhaps less obvious is that the sequence of events *within* the model's period is neither arbitrary nor irrelevant. Take the same example: When LM is shifted, holding IS fixed, so as to create an excess supply of money, it is implied that it takes a reduction in the rate of interest *before* we get our excess demand for commodities and the rise in nominal income.

The temporal order of events is analytically significant when (some) transactors have to act on incomplete information. Conversely, models with built-in sequences contain important, though often implicit, assumptions about "who knows what when."

A more detailed IS-LM story of the once-over money injection would run through the following course of events: (i) assume that the initial state is an FIM equilibrium; (ii) the banking system expands, creating an ES of money and an ED for securities; (iii) interest rates decline until the securities ED is zero; demand prices for assets rise relative to their rental values and relative to their initial supply prices; investment thus exceeds saving so that the state of the economy at this stage is one of money ES and commodity ED; (iv) nominal income rises;

The early Keynesian literature managed with some frequency almost to make a riddle of how money could affect aggregate demand . . . in a system where the circular flow of income, after all, shows money being spent for goods and factor-services (and not just for bonds).

some part of this rise takes the form of an increase in real output and employment; (v) any overshooting of output and employment is discovered and corrected and prices increase further—so that we end up in a new FIM state with the monetary impulse having affected only nominal magnitudes.[28]

Once the sequence is spelled out in this way, it is obvious that the analysis definitely assumes incomplete information.[29] It also becomes apparent that IS-LM is a cumbersome, inappropriate frame for representing theories that make different assumptions about the knowledge possessed by transactors and, consequently, about the time-phasing of events.

In the above sequence, incomplete information is implied at two points: first, where the real interest rate and the relative price of assets and their services change away from their FIM values; second, where activity levels and not just nominal values rise. In Friedman's Theory of Nominal Income, the first of these is minimized, but the second is admitted. In a Rational Expectations version of the once-over (anticipated) money injection, the entire sequence implicit in the IS-LM analysis is short-circuited—we jump directly to the endpoint where both schedules have shifted.

If agents were to have full information to begin with, an excess demand for commodities at the old prices and interest rate emerges as soon as the intentions of the Central Bank are known. The increased supply of credit by the banking system is offset by increased demand on the part of non-bank transactors anticipating a rise in prices. The rate of interest does not move and never plays any role in the "transmission" of the monetary

28. In the classroom, the story should be accompanied by visual aids. There are two ways of doing it. In one, we put real income on the horizontal axis, show LM shifting out at stage (i) and then have it shifting back at stage (v). In the other—used below—nominal income is on the axis, LM shifts out at (i) and IS follows suit in stages (iv) and (v). If the teacher passes too quickly from (i) to (v), however, the diagrammatics will tend to look strangely superfluous. To repay students for their investment in learning to construct the two reduced form schedules, etc., one might pause in the middle to single out a "short-run solution" for special attention—preferably at early stage (iv) where LM has shifted and IS is "only just about" to move. The elasticities of IS and LM might figure prominently in analyzing this intermediate position whereas, once we reach (v), they no longer have anything to do with the result.

29. . . . and that it is these ignorance assumptions and not the steady-state interest-elasticities of money demand or investment, etc., that count in explaining the positions of the system at stages intermediate between FIM states.

impulse.[30] In the standard exercise, by the same token, the lowering of the rate of interest serves to cajole *those who do not know what is going on* into nonetheless increasing their spending. When agents do know, there is no "transmission problem" and the notion of a "transmission mechanism" becomes somewhat meaningless. Fully informed agents have no need for a price mechanism to inform them about what is happening. Prices merely reflect what they already know.

Does this sort of thing apply also to the other standard IS-LM exercises? It does. Take the shift of the marginal efficiency of capital (MEC) once more. For this once, to be in accord with the usual textbook version, assume a non-speculative money demand function that nonetheless has significant interest-elasticity. In this instance, we draw the diagram with real income on the horizontal axis. Hence: (i) an initial FIM state; (ii) the MEC declines creating an ES of commodities and a corresponding ED for bonds; (iii) the interest rate declines until the ED for bonds is zero so that we have an ES of commodities and an ED for money; (iv) nominal income falls; some part of this decline takes the form of a decline in output and employment if wages are inflexible; (v) if the wage inflexibility is a temporary rather than permanent phenomenon, the ES of labor drives money wages down; prices fall, shifting LM rightwards until the real rate of interest is low enough for investment to equal saving at the full employment level of real income. Here, again, we have an initial FIM state disrupted by one of the reduced forms shifting; after several intervening stages, the second reduced form also shifts so as to complete the "rational" adjustment to a new FIM state. And again it is clear that, possessed with sufficient information, transactors would short-circuit the whole sequence.

In these two examples we have made certain that the initial as well as the terminal state of the process are full information equilibria. In actual IS-LM practice, of course, such sequences

30. Back in the days when the effectiveness of monetary policy was still in debate, Monetarists used to explain that it was more powerful in Monetarist theory than in Keynesian theory *because* "a change in the rate of interest" had a much broader interpretation in the former; correspondingly the transmission mechanism was conceived of as much more robust and effective than in Keynesian theory, etc. The latest generation of Monetarists have little use for the interest rate.

are often truncated both fore and aft. The process neither begins from nor ends in a FIM state. It may not end there, for example, because wage-rigidity is assumed so that the last stage of our processes "never" occurs. If full adjustment to a disturbance never comes about, it makes no sense to assume that the initial state is such an equilibrium either. Whether or not full adjustment will ever occur is not, at this juncture, the point at issue. The point, rather, is that without a full information equilibrium to refer to we cannot define precisely what the coordination failure is that is supposed to be present. The inability to do so, in turn, is bound to bedevil our attempts to explain precisely *why* the coordination failure exists and persists.

Discussing the most simple-minded rather than the most sophisticated version of a model is the cheap way to produce an unfavorable verdict. It should be admitted, therefore, that most of the shortcomings of the simple-minded IS-LM can be remedied.[31] But we shall not set out on the tack of trying to clarify recent controversies through bigger and better IS-LM's. That approach has been tried and it has a bad track record. IS-LM provided the ground rules for the Keynes and the Classics debate—and obedience to the rules produced the wrong conclusion.[32] It has not been an at all helpful vehicle for the Monetarist debate.

To recapitulate: We began with the question of why real disturbances should have monetary effects and vice versa when these interdependencies do not occur in FIM theory. Answers of a sort were obtained by linking the two primitive A and T constructs by the rate of interest, while noting that choice-theoretical arguments strongly suggest both that commodity ED in A and that money ED in T should depend on the rate of interest. The resulting IS-LM construction has interdependence both ways *because it will not allow the rate of interest to adjust appropriately* "in the short run." Monetary disturbances have real (allocative) effects because the interest rate changes—when in

31. Perhaps this accounts for the model's staying-power? Nothing is as successful in economics as a construct all shot through with remediable shortcomings.

32. The conclusion was that Keynes produced a revolution in economic theory by postulating wages too high for full employment and rigid downwards as the explanation of unemployment. That Keynes' contribution to economic theory can be thus summarized is disputed in Leijonhufvud (1968) and (1969).

FIM it should not. Real disturbances have monetary consequences because the rate of interest does not change far enough. In either instance, *it is the maladjustment of the interest rate that is supposed to provide the link.* These maladjustments, moreover, are to be ascribed to incomplete information. The IS-LM short-run "equilibria" are, in effect, transitional states in a sequential process that should eventually produce a new FIM state (unless, of course, there is a spanner in the works). If we go through the exercise of assuming full information, we find that these transitional states are skipped.

Hence, we can reassert our introductory contention that the maladjustment of the interest rate is a problem central to modern controversies. And we may now add that IS-LM is more a hindrance than a help in coming to grips with it. We will abandon IS-LM, then, in favor of a more explicit sequence analysis that will make it easier to keep track of how—and why—the economy is supposed to diverge from its full information timepath. For the next several sections, Monetarism is left to one side as we trace the development of Saving-Investment approaches, beginning at the beginning, with Knut Wicksell.

IV. WICKSELL

The point of departure is the Quantity Theory of Money. Wicksell regarded it as the only solid foundation for monetary theory and saw his own contribution as a development of the Quantity Theory.[33] With Quantity Theory, however, he understood simply the equilibrium proposition that prices will be proportional to the money stock in the long run and not the modern Monetarist proposition that exogenous changes in base money drive nominal income and prices. Comparative static propositions about the invariance of real magnitudes to proportional changes in nominal values are of limited use in applied monetary analysis, however. To make the Quantity Theory useful, Wicksell thought, one needs to understand both what sets in motion a movement of money and prices from one level to another and the dynamic interequilibrium process itself.[34] Hav-

33. Cf., e.g., Wicksell (1935), Vol. II, pp. 141 ff.
34. Wicksell (1935), Vol. II, pp. 159 ff.

ing conceived of his theoretical objective in those terms, Wicksell had to come up with a "disequilibrium" analysis of some sort to meet it. His Cumulative Process was it. It is worth keeping in mind that this is how the Saving-Investment approaches originally came to branch off from the Quantity Theory trunk.

How did saving and investment come to figure in a more "dynamic" Quantity Theory? The basic theoretical conception is simple enough. It combines our Models A and T in a particular manner. Model A is based on the "circular flow" notion. The Gestalt is of an economy consisting of two sectors: households (savers) and business firms (investors). The interaction of these two sets of agents determines income. Model T is a stock-flow model. Again, there is but one basic sectoral distinction—between suppliers (the banking system) and demanders of money. Their interaction determines money income.

In Wicksell's basic image, the bewildering complex of interactions in the economy is reduced to a readily intelligible pattern of three sectors. The banking system is placed between the household sector and the business sector in the "circular flow" (Figure 7-2). Household savings flow into, business investment finance flows out of banks.[35] Here, banks are perceived in the first instance as loan intermediaries between the household and business sectors, rather than as money suppliers. In the short run, this theory of nominal income determination will focus on changes in the flow of bank-intermediated credit rather than in the stock of money.[36] By lending more to the business sector than flows in as savings from the household sector, the banking system will cause the circular flow to expand. By lending less, they will make it contract. When nominal income is rising, investment exceeds saving by the net addition to loanable funds

35. It is instructive to note that, although more primitive, Model A is not earlier but later than Wicksell. The conception outlined in the text is the original one. The idea, pioneered by Wicksell, that the saving-investment approach is a useful way to analyze movements in nominal income stems from it. The Keynesian cross is a degenerate version resulting from letting the Banking system fade out of Wicksell's model.

36. Milton Friedman and Anna Schwartz (1963) have a very clear statement distinguishing sharply between their own "monetary" (i.e., money stock) theory and those older theories of business cycles that used to be called "monetary" but would more accurately, they note, be called "credit theories." The distinction is sharp for a purpose—Friedman and Schwartz disassociate their own theory from the entire class of "credit" theories. This class would include Wicksellian theories. Cf. also Friedman in Gordon, ed., *op. cit.*, pp. 146–48.

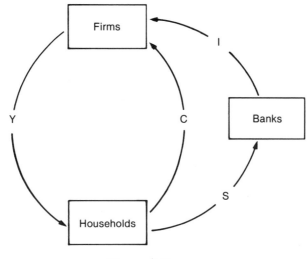

Figure 7-2.

injected by banks. When nominal income is falling, banks let loanable funds "leak out" so that savings exceed investment. In income equilibrium, saving should equal investment; this requires that banks do no more and no less than intermediate the desired savings of the household sector. When they behave themselves "neutrally," the excess demand for final goods at the prevailing level of money prices should be zero.

The road from theoretical conception to analytical model is strewn with restrictive assumptions. A couple of the more important ones are institutional and time-bound and deserve notice here. For example, bank-financed consumer credit is ignored as of no quantitative significance. Bank injections or leakages of purchasing power into or out of the circular flow augment or curtail the spending of firms, not that of households. This, one may assume, was appropriate enough for Wicksell's time. Similarly, the banking system is assumed to dominate the outside financing of business investment—the organized securities markets are ignored. For the economies that Wicksell had some familiarity with—mainly Sweden and Germany around the turn of the century—this was defensible as a "stylized fact." Again, the focus on bank credit rather than on the banking system's monetary liabilities should presumably be viewed against the contemporary institutional background. Currency was the predominant means of payment in Sweden in Wicksell's time; the volume of checking deposits was relatively insignificant; the central bank did not yet have a monopoly on the note issue; banks were not constrained by reserve requirements calculated on their monetary liabilities on the later American pattern. Consequently, Wicksell defined "money" as currency, and treated this stock of currency as determined, at least to a first approximation, by the demand of the non-bank public. Wicksell's "money" varies endogenously in his cumulative process; it does not play a significant causal role.

For the analysis of the cumulative process, it will be convenient to have our theoretical terms and the relations between them defined in such a way that the following propositions hold true:

i. the circular flow of money income and expenditures will expand if and only if there is an excess demand for commodities;
ii. "investment exceeds saving" implies "excess demand for commodities" and conversely;
iii. investment will exceed saving if and only if the banking system lengthens its balance sheet at a rate in excess of that which would just suffice to intermediate household saving;
iv. the economy will be on its real equilibrium growth-path (capital accumulation path) if and only if savings equals investment;
v. the value of the interest rate that equates saving and investment at full employment is termed the "natural" rate.

It would seem that all sorts of things could happen that would violate one or more of these propositions. The theory, presumably, says that these eventualities are either improbable or of little consequence. Nonetheless, what restrictive assumptions are we making to rule them out? The following may not be exhaustive but will illustrate what is required.

First, note that proposition (iii) requires that expansion or contraction of bank credit be associated with any increase or decrease of nominal income. Hence, we should rule out any changes in the money volume of the circular flow in which the banking system does not play a part. Thus, we assume that changes in the spending flow associated with hoarding or dishoarding of cash already in the non-bank sectors by either the household or the business sector may be ignored. Similarly, we ignore the possibility of changes in the aggregate money value of the demand for commodities associated with all-around expansion or contraction of non-bank trade-credit. Second, we want to ensure that any discrepancy between saving and investment be associated with a corresponding discrepancy between household sector supply of loanable funds and business sector demand for loanable funds. To that purpose we assume that business sector financial saving may be ignored and that firms do not finance investment out of retained earnings. Also, that households do not use any part of nonconsumed income for direct investment. Third, we define "saving" as the household sector's "desired non-consumption" of current output, and "investment" as the business sector's desired capital accumulation out of current output. Saving and investment, thus defined, have to be equal at full employment output for the system to be in intertemporal equilibrium.

This is quite a lot to build into the language! One had better not get *too* used to this brand of saving-investment analysis, obviously.

The central concepts of Wicksell's analytical apparatus are, of course, the *market rate* and the *natural rate* of interest. The terms are names for two values of the same variable.[37] The market rate denotes the actually observed value of the rate of interest, the natural rate the hypothetical value that the interest rate would take if and when the system is in equilibrium.

Equilibrium is used here in two senses at the same time. Their tight linkage is a result of the construction of Wicksell's model that we have outlined; in other analytical settings we might well want to keep them distinct. First, the equality of the market rate with the natural rate is a condition of "monetary

---

37. Not to be confused with Fisher's *nominal* and *real* rates of interest which are names for two distinct variables, related through his well-known equation.

Wicksell's analysis does not deal with expected rates of inflation. It can be generalized to incorporate the Fisher idea. But this paper will dodge the issues connected with expected inflations.

equilibrium" in the sense of the system remaining at a stable price level. Second, it is also a condition for maintaining "real equilibrium" in the sense of an allocation of current resources between consumption and investment such as to be consistent at the same time with the intertemporal consumption preferences of households and with the intertemporal production possibilities perceived by firms.[38] The two are tightly linked in the sense that a divergence of market from natural rate will upset both at once and neither can be upset except by such a divergence occurring.

It is worth being a bit pedantic about this. Decades of Keynesian hegemony have accustomed us so much to one saving-investment approach that we almost accept it as *the* natural language for analyzing changes in the income level. The equality of saving and investment is a condition for constancy of the aggregate price level in this model because of propositions (i) and (ii) above. But we *forced* these to be "true" (as properties of one saving-investment approach language) by making numerous restrictive assumptions. The result of making (i), (ii), and (iii) "true" is an analytical language[39] that would be highly artificial and inconvenient to use for anyone who believes that, empirically, hoarding and dishoarding by non-bank sectors (i.e., variable velocity) and changes in the money stock are the most frequent and significant "causes" of changes of nominal income, and that neither cause need necessarily distort the intertemporal allocation of resources.[40] The saving-investment approach language is really designed for someone who believes

38. Warning! This is anachronistically put in terms of the much later literature on neoclassical growth. Draining the Böhm-Bawerkian capital theory from Wicksell will no doubt seem offensively impious to some, but I do not want to burden this paper also with those complexities.

39. Note that Proposition (iv) is hardly self-evident either. From it and (v) we can obtain familiar-sounding phrases: "the interest rate will equate saving and investment in equilibrium," etc. But in a monetary model with futures markets only for money, the interest rate clears the bond market, the price for newly produced capital goods clears that market, and "saving" defined as "non-consumption" is inclusive of "hoarding." And in the context of a Fisherine non-monetary 2-period model, where the interest rate (or rather the discount factor) does clear the intertemporal consumption goods market, the concepts of "saving" and "investment" are pretty artificial. Cf. Hirshleifer (1970), pp. 36–37.

40. Note that in neoclassical models of balanced inflationary growth we have (with the help of the Fisher-equation) "real" equilibrium *without* "monetary equilibrium" in Wicksell's sense. In these models, the tight link has been loosened.

to begin with that "real" disturbances are responsible for observed income fluctuations.

For the description of the cumulative process itself it hardly matters, however, whether it is set off by "real" or by "monetary" disturbances. We start from some historically given equilibrium—saving equals investment at full employment and with stable prices. A Wicksellian "monetary" disturbance would have to be in accord with (iii) above, i.e., it is triggered by the banking system moving the market rate away from an unchanged natural rate—neither the preferences of savers, nor the investment prospects perceived by entrepreneurs have changed, so no reallocation of resources is called for. In the case of real disturbances, we start with a shift of either the investment or of the savings function. The allocation of resources between consumption and capital accumulation should change if the system is to adapt appropriately. Coordination of the intertemporal allocation of resources by consumers and by producers requires a change in the interest rate, i.e., the natural rate moves. If the market rate is prevented by the banking system from keeping up with the change in the hypothetical natural rate, the cumulative process starts. But the description of the process is the same whether the banking system plays the active or a permissive role in it.

From the taxonomy of possibilities, we take the one that Wicksell himself concentrated on. In Figure 7-3, we have saving and investment schedules represented in real terms. Initially, we are in equilibrium with the interest rate at r_0. Assume an upward shift in the investment schedule from I_0 to I'. The impact-effect of this disturbance is to create an excess demand for commodities measured by the investment-saving gap, $I'(r_0) - S(r_0)$. To this there corresponds an increase in the demand for loanable funds of the same magnitude.[41]

41. This already simplifies Wicksell by more simultaneity and less sequencing than the original tale. This simplified version will suit our further purposes better however.

For purposes of doctrine history, a more accurate rendition should go approximately as follows: (1) Producers borrow enough money to finance $I'(r_0)$ at last period's prices—which they expect to continue. (2) The banks now close (hence, the system will not "explode" today). (3) The labor market opens and producers use the proceeds of last period's sale of final goods plus the newly borrowed money to bid for labor. Money wages rise, falsifying the expectations mentioned in (1). (4) Production takes place and, finally, households bid for consumer goods, raising their prices.

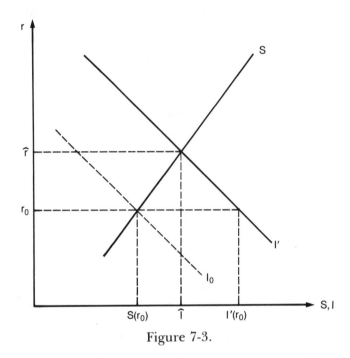

Figure 7-3.

To avoid inflation and, at the same time, obtain the proper allocation of resources, we require the interest rate to move to its new natural value, $\hat{r}$. A rise of the rate from r_0 to $\hat{r}$ would decrease the demand for consumption goods by $S(\hat{r}) - S(r_0)$ and that for capital goods by $I'(r_0) - I'(\hat{r})$; together these adjustments of the spending intentions of households and firms would just suffice to eliminate the excess demand for commodities, and consequently the associated inflationary pressure, opened up at impact by the postulated disturbance. At the saving-investment equilibrium corresponding to $\hat{r}$, we would also have the economy on the new and higher growth-path appropriate to the now more favorable collective judgment of firms about

The advantage of such a sequential tale is that it brings out very clearly that, precisely because all mutual adjustments are *not* assumed to have taken place simultaneously, some agents must find their plans defeated by events in the course of the dynamic process. The disadvantage, as the later literature in this vein abundantly demonstrates, is that too many such tales can be told, all equally reasonable or unreasonable, with slight variations in the sequencing.

the terms on which society as a whole can convert present into future goods.

The market rate of interest is governed, not by the investment-saving discrepancy, but by the excess demand for loanable funds. When this excess demand is zero, the rate will not move. Now, by the assumptions discussed previously, we have ensured that saving equals the supply of loanable funds by households and that investment equals the loanable funds demand by the business sector. If there were to be no other components to the excess demand for loanable funds than these two, therefore, the interest rate *would* be driven to its natural level at which saving and investment intentions are consistent and compatible with retained price stability. But, of course, the banking system is also in the loanable funds market—in Wicksell, in fact, it *makes* the market. We will get exactly the desired adjustment of the economy *if and only if* the banking system sticks to the "neutral" policy of just intermediating household saving without generating any net injection (or leakage) of loanable funds on its own.

In the cumulative process, of course, the banking system does not stay "neutral." To avoid complicating the diagram, we may assume the extreme case where the banks—usually with the connivance of the Central Bank, presumably—simply accommodate all of the loanable funds demand, lending on all "good paper" that comes their way, at the initial rate of interest. The credit market then "clears" at what is, from a general equilibrium standpoint, a disequilibrium level of interest rate, $r_0 < \hat{r}$. The excess demand for commodities, represented by the investment-saving gap at this market rate, will then drive the price-level up.

In this process the consolidated balance sheet of the banking system will be lengthening at a rate in excess of what would be the equilibrium real growth-rate of the economy. This, of course, can just as well be looked at from the standpoint of the liabilities side of that balance sheet. There we would find an acceleration in the growth-rate of "money"; it should show up independently of whether we have chosen to define "money" as currency, as M_1, or as M_2. The expansion of the money stock is endogenously determined in the process, yet the process is en-

159

tirely consistent with observed velocity being constant. The link of Wicksell's work to the pre-Monetarist Quantity Theory would, indeed, be more obvious if we added in an explicit "Cambridge-k" demand function for currency. Then, as nominal prices go up, non-bank agents will choose to hold a corresponding fraction of the growing liabilities of the banking system on hand as cash.

In the Wicksell process, two sets of agents are acting on incorrect or incomplete information. The banks fail to recognize (the full extent of) the rise in the realizable real rate of profit. Entrepreneurs (and other non-bank transactors) fail to foresee the rate of inflation that the policy of the banking system implies.[42] The process would go on cumulatively as long as the market rate is kept below natural rate. The only way to ensure that it will not proceed indefinitely is to see to it that a banking system acting in this way will necessarily find itself running out of reserves. As long as non-bank agents do not learn to anticipate the inflation, and as long as the real determinants of saving and investment behavior do not change, each successive period would start with an excess demand for commodities *in real terms* equal to $I'(r_0) = S(r_0)$. In nominal terms, of course, the gap keeps growing. If inflationary (rational) expectations take hold before the banks mend their ways, things get worse: the inflation accelerates[43] and a move of the (real) market rate into equality with the (real) natural rate would now merely stop the acceleration but would not suffice to end the inflation. The Fisherine complications of expected inflation will, however, be dodged here and in what follows.

V. KEYNES: TREATISE

From his early book on *Indian Currency* (1913) to the *Tract on Monetary Reform* (1923), Keynes remained a Quantity Theorist in the Marshallian Cambridge tradition mainly concerned with questions of how to regulate the supply of money, how to stabi-

---

42. Watching "M"—if statistics were available—would not be of much help in forming rational expectations. In a world like Wicksell's, the money stock would be a lagging indicator. The growth rate of M is not driving the cumulative process.
43. Wicksell (1936), pp. 96–97. David Laidler drew my attention to this passage.

lize the monetary liabilities of a fractional reserve banking system against inflows and outflows of international reserves, and how to structure the international monetary system so as to minimize such problems. Much of the *Treatise on Money* (1930) deals with these same problems.[44] In fact, the *Treatise* as a whole is very much a work still recognizably in the Quantity Theory tradition, despite its emphasis on problems of the short run. Here, however, these older themes are left aside to focus on the novel ideas of the work: the first Keynes variation on Wicksell's theme.

The problem now is deflation rather than inflation. As with Wicksell, we have to conceive of the system as initially in an equilibrium state with stable prices, etc. Here we must take particular note of the initially existing stock of money for in our analysis of the basic process we are just going "to leave it there"—taking the banking system out of the picture. In Keynes' version, the main character of Wicksell's morality play is written out of the plot!

To Keynes, familiar with the City of London, "the" interest rate is determined, not by the banking system, but on the Exchange. It is a good example of how monetary theory is adapted to changing institutional circumstances. In Wicksell, the market rate was governed by the excess *flow* demand for loanable funds. In the *Treatise,* analysis of interest determination is a *stock-flow* problem—a matter not just of the financing of new investment but also of trading in the outstanding stock of "old" securities.

We now consider the consequences of a decline in the marginal efficiency of capital (using Keynes' later terminology) from I_0 to I' in Figure 7-4. At impact, we get an excess supply of commodities at the old interest rate measured by $S(r_0) - I'(r_0)$. To this there corresponds an excess flow demand for "new" securities. Households intend to accumulate securities at the rate $S(r_0)$, while the business sector intends to float securities only at the rate $I'(r_0)$. This puts upward pressure on securities prices, and the market rate of interest starts to decline. The banks, we assume, stay put and do not intervene to

44. And so did the Bretton Woods negotiations.

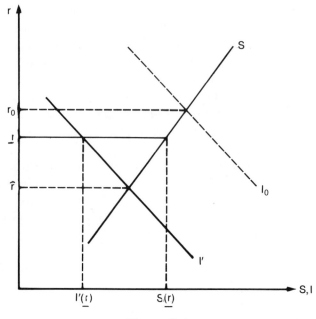

Figure 7-4.

confuse the communication about intertemporal tastes and opportunities between households and firms. But speculators on
the Exchange do. Having experienced for too long rates of
yield in the neighborhood of r_0, the market turns predominantly bearish as securities prices edge up. At $\underline{r}$, we suppose,
bears are selling off "old" securities to savers at a rate that ex-
actly makes up the gap $S(\underline{r}) - I'(\underline{r})$ and are absorbing "idle" cash
out of the "active circulation" at the corresponding flow rate.
The securities market now "clears"; from a general equilibrium
standpoint, the interest rate rests at a disequilibrium level with
no tendency to adjust further. The incomplete interest rate adjustment leaves an excess supply of commodities, matched by
an excess flow demand for cash, both measured by the gap at
$\underline{r}$—with a consequent deflationary pressure on nominal income.

Wicksellian business-cycle theorists of that time were apt to
acknowledge that when, with the market rate above natural
rate, nominal income declines, real output and employment re-

actions must be expected to occur. Keynes was no exception.[45] But in so doing, they were informally realistic rather than formally analytical. Output reactions could not be handled by Wicksellians—whether Swedish, British, or Austrian—as of 1930. If we want to draw clear-cut comparisons between the two variations on our theme, therefore, we had better take them literally and consider the process that is being explained in each case to be one of pure deflation at the historically given full employment position.

First, the obvious contrast. Wicksell's would be a deflation associated with a declining stock of money—it drains out of the non-bank sector. Possibly, observed velocity could be constant. Keynes' deflation shows declining velocity—cash is going into the "hoards" of bearish speculators. Possibly, the observed money stock could be constant. Actually, both men would presumably have been "reasonable" about it and would have acknowledged that both the money stock and its velocity should be expected to decline in a "real world" deflation. For our present purposes, however, allowing such informal realism will make us miss the point: that the behavior of the banking system is edging out of the focus of Keynes' developing analytical scheme. By the time we get to the *General Theory,* it is out of the picture altogether.

Second, the disequilibrium of both theories stems from the divergence of beliefs about economic prospects between two sets of agents. Keynes' bear-speculators disagree with the appraisal of entrepreneurs.[46] So, in effect, do Wicksell's banks. In either model, if all agents acted on consistent beliefs, there would be no problem—not even if they were all wrong.[47]

45. Wicksell *was* an exception. Wicksell never applied his Cumulative Process analysis to short-run business-cycle problems and was rather scornful of Cassel who did. Cf. Cassel (1928).

46. This is simplistically put, even too much so perhaps. But the point is obscured by a more circumspect statement, and it is important that the gist of it be grasped. We return to the matter in Section XI below.

47. I.e., there would be no problem within the short-run period, in the sense that, with everyone acting on consistent beliefs, there should be a temporary equilibrium that would coordinate their activities. If they are wrong about "productivity" (or some other aspect of the State of Nature), however, this should be revealed—at least to some people—by the outcome of the coordinated actions of the short run.

If it is only revealed to some people and not to all, then in the second period we are back in the situation discussed in the text.

Agents acting on inconsistent beliefs is what disequilibrium means. Who then is wrong and who, if anybody, is right? I think it is in the spirit of both Wicksell and Keynes to suppose that, in the early stages of a nominal income decline at least, the entrepreneurs are roughly right. One might argue this supposition à la Hayek. The individual entrepreneur will have more and better information about the particular circumstances relevant to the prospects of his firm and his branch of industry than will speculators in general.

Third, then, beliefs—even if qualified beliefs—in the "automaticity" of a private enterprise market system will rest, in part, on the presumption that the working of the price system will either teach agents acting on the wrong beliefs to mend their ways or else deprive them of the wherewithal to influence the course of events in the large.

This presumption is by and large still supported by the two disequilibrium theories thus far considered—although they suggest that it may take time. But as long as the system deflates while remaining at full employment, Wicksell's banks would have to continue period after period to let net deposit growth plus repayments of old loans run ahead of their new lending. It is an unprofitable policy, and the cumulative process would also cumulate the pressures on the banks to reduce their rates. Keynes' speculators would have to continue, period after period, to sell off income-earning assets from their portfolios and to replace them with cash.

In either case, then, the disequilibrium strain in the economy is brought home on those responsible—*and* in such a way as to induce them to revise that price which is "wrong" in the "right" direction. And the longer they persist in the behavior inimical to the coordination of activities in the system, the more expensive it gets.

VI. INTERPOLATION: Z-THEORY

The big difference, it is generally agreed,[48] between the *Treatise* and the *General Theory* is that, in the latter, the system responds

---

48. Cf. the proceedings of the symposium on the writing of the *General Theory*, edited by D. Patinkin and J. C. Leith (1977). The main paper by Patinkin sets "the systematic

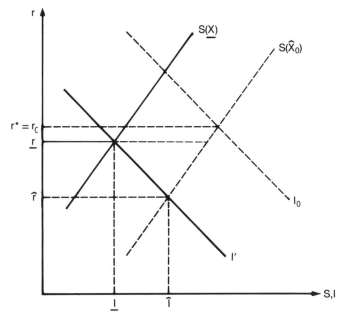

Figure 7-5.

to deflationary pressure with a contraction of output and employment. Let us proceed first *as if* that was the *only* difference. Suppose then that the deflationary pressure on nominal income comes about exactly as in the *Treatise*. Incorporation of the output and employment response into the analysis will change the story profoundly in two respects:

(1) Real income falls from the full employment level, $\hat{X}_o$, until saving equals investment at a real income of $\underline{X}$. In terms of the diagram, the saving schedule shifts over until it intersects I' at $\underline{r}$ (Figure 7-5). This market rate, *ex hypothesi*, exceeds the nat-

equilibrating role that changes in output—and consequent changes in saving—play in the *General Theory*" as the theme for the conference.

I find two things amiss with the discussion of this theme by Patinkin and the other participants. First, no answer emerges to the questions: Why does the switch from price-level to output adjustment amount to anything more than the *Treatise* with "frictions"? Wherein does the "Revolution" inhere? Second, the part of Keynes' new theory that explains why the rate of interest is *not* the variable that equilibrates saving and investment hardly gets mentioned. But, in explaining what went on (and what went wrong) between the *Treatise* and the *General Theory*, it is almost as important as the part that asserts that output is the variable that *does* equilibrate saving and investment.

ural rate, r̂, i.e., the interest rate that would prevail on the system's equilibrium growth-path. As in the *Treatise* and in Wicksell, although the price is "wrong," this market "clears." But *unlike* Wicksell and the *Treatise,* we no longer have an excess flow supply of loanable funds whose accumulating time-integral progressively distorts the balance-sheets of banks and/or bear-speculators. With saving and investment equal, Keynes' speculators need no longer sell off more securities every period to maintain the market rate above the natural level. In this variation on the theme, the system is *not* generating pressure towards the appropriate adjustment on the right point.

(2) In the labor market, we have instead unemployment at the going money wage rate. Note that, if the interest rate had gone to its natural rate level before any quantity-reactions set in, the labor market would have cleared at this money wage. The relationship between the money stock and the money rate is still the same as in the earlier full employment situation. The adjustment of the system to a decline of the marginal efficiency of capital does not per se require a general lowering of money wage rates.[49] In relation to the price vector that the system would have exhibited, had it managed to stick to its equilibrium path, money wages are not "too high" for full employment—they are (roughly) at the right level. Yet, in this market, there is heavy excess supply pressure on the price.

That is not the end of the trouble, of course: In this market, where the price is where we want it, excess supply persists and downward adjustment of the price *will not remove it.*[50]

---

49. It is perfectly reasonable for labor to hold out for the wages that would be earned in equilibrium. Their expectations are "rational"—and how are they to know that entrepreneurs and speculators are about to act on inconsistent beliefs? What information would workers have on which they could base their short-run reservation wage? They know (i) what they earned yesterday; (ii) that their physical productivity is unimpaired today; and possibly (iii) that the money stock has not decreased. It is true (iv) that their value productivity in terms of future goods has gone down—since we postulate a decline in MEC—but *if* the interest rate falls correspondingly (as it should) their discounted marginal value product should be (roughly) the same.

So, to repeat an old refrain: If this is the exercise, why complain about "less than perfect flexibility of wages." They *should be* sticky.

50. One should be careful to note what Keynes' theory maintains about "wage flexibility": *Perfect flexibility could prevent unemployment from developing to begin with—but it will not remove it once you have it.*

Wage "stickiness" in the first short-run "period" is obviously a *critical* assumption—since otherwise we stay in the realm of Wicksellian full-employment deflations (as in the

This diagnosis of the early recession phase of a developing depression, and the dynamic sequence postulated to lead up to it, are *central* to Keynes' case. His deep depression theory, which adds in the induced deterioration of entrepreneurial expectations about future demand, is the basis for his pessimism over the effectiveness of monetary policy and for his advocacy of fiscal policy measures; but the deep depression analysis is derivative in relation to this variation on the Wicksellian theme. *Keynes' fundamental contention* that a competitive, private enterprise market economy (with all its prices "flexible") may fail to home in automatically on its equilibrium time-path stems from the contemplation of states like the one just sketched: the interest rate is wrong, but that market "clears" (without "punishment," so to speak, of those responsible); the money wage is right, but large-scale unemployment prevails and persists and even the willingness of labor to reduce the money wage will not help. The system's "automatic" adjustment tendencies, presumed in pre-Keynesian analysis to be self-regulatory, are working to change prices that are right and leaving those we need to have changed alone; the response of price to excess supply of labor does not bring about a meshing of quantities in that market.

All of this was missed in the earlier Wicksellian literature. It is instructive to note why. In that literature—of which the *Treatise* is a good example—the task of explaining business cycles was approached in two stages. At the first stage, one concentrated on the causes of price level movements. The saving-investment theory presented at this first stage was relatively formal and, although in verbal dress, came pretty close to what today would be recognized as "modelling." At the second stage,

---

Treatise). If unemployment develops initially, and if the unemployed are income-constrained, then it will not help to have reservation wages give way to adverse experience and start an accelerating decline. . . . The reader will recognize where this leads: Keynes' *pari passu* argument, the Keynes-effect possibility and, of course, that false, frail reed: the Pigou-effect.

Within a stable monetary framework, a reduction in money wages should produce an increase in the perceived marginal efficiency of capital. Keynes recognized this as a possibility but did not treat it as a probability. He was, of course dealing with a process that took place to the accompaniment of a collapsing monetary order. That is the setting that has to be presumed, I think, for the *pari passu* argument to be entirely acceptable in its original formulation.

one then gave informal, *ad hoc* recognition to "frictions," i.e., to the stylized fact that an economy under deflationary (or inflationary) pressure will in the short run respond with output and employment adjustments and not only with pure price adjustments. This amounts to changing the interpretation of the Stage 1 saving-investment model, treating it as a theory of changes in nominal income, leaving it to Stage 2 to determine—as if it was a separable question—how much of the nominal income change is a real output change. This procedure presumes, in effect, that allowing real income to vary should not significantly affect the Stage 1 analysis. This overlooks the dependence of real savings (loanable funds supply) on real income.

It was precisely his discovery that this two-stage approach would not do that prompted Keynes to tear up the *Treatise* and spend the next six years rewriting it—with the quantity adjustments worked out explicitly *within* the short-run period. We get a measure of the extent to which we have lost track of what Keynes was about, therefore, when in the context of a controversy over what distinguishes Keynesian economics from other doctrines, today's macroeconomists revert to the two-stage approach that was in general use in the 1920's. After some forty years, the two-stage approach reappears in the Monetarist controversy and is used, without objection, by both sides: nominal income changes are predicted or analyzed first and then some Phillips-curve notion is brought in to decide their breakdown into price- and quantity-adjustments.[51]

The lesson that Z-theory adds to what can be learned from the pre-Keynesian business-cycle literature is that one should not analyze the characteristic Wicksellian interest maladjustment and its consequences as if it does not matter whether the system maintains itself at full employment or not. *At full employment, there will be unrelenting pressures towards correction of any "unnatural" rate of interest—but otherwise not.* Neither can one analyze unemployment and its persistence as if it does not matter

51. Cf., for example, Milton Friedman's "Theory of Nominal Income," reprinted in Gordon, ed., (1973). Friedman, however, is no more responsible for re-initiating the practice than any number of other writers. Note that none of his Keynesian critics in the Gordon volume—or elsewhere?—object to it.

whether the market rate equals the natural rate or not. *With the interest rate at the right level, market forces should make unemployment converge on its "natural" rate—but otherwise not.*[52]

In Section III, we asked why macroeconomists should split into Keynesians and Monetarists over the Phillips curve in the same way as they had previously done over the issues defined by Model A versus Model T and by IS-LM. The answer is now clear. Monetarists believe that interest maladjustments are unlikely to be of much consequence; hence, the coordination of saving and investment is not a serious problem; consequently, flexible wages should serve to coordinate labor supply and demand; the speed of convergence on the natural rate of unemployment is merely a matter of "frictions," the strength of which raises empirical but not theoretical questions. Keynesians believe that flexible wages would not always ensure convergence on full employment. They seem to have forgotten why, however.

VII. THE GENERAL THEORY: THE LIQUIDITY PREFERENCE THEORY OF INTEREST

Our Z-theory "interpolation" between the *Treatise* and the *General Theory* is still recognizable—indeed, unmistakeable—as a variation on Wicksell's theme. Without the maladjustment of the interest rate, there is no story to tell. But the *General Theory* is not just the *Treatise* with output variable.[53] There are other developments between the two works. And, for the Wicksellian theme, they add up to the nearly perfect cover-up. The main one, to which the others are subsidiary, is the Liquidity Preference theory of interest.

---

52. Flexible wages should restore full employment unless the wrong interest rate prevents equilibrium of investment with saving out of full employment income. Conversely falling money wages and money prices will not restore full employment if relative prices are wrong and the deflation is "balanced." For a detailed discussion, cf. Leijonhufvud (1968), Chapter V.

The statement in the text presumes a stage of the recession where entrepreneurial demand expectations underlying investment demand have not yet been undermined by the recession experience. Cf., e.g., Leijonhufvud (1968b), for a discussion of the deep depression case.

53. Even if that, on the whole, was what I presented as the "Economics of Keynes" in my 1968 book.

In Wicksell, the excess *flow* demand for loanable funds governs[54] the interest rate. The *Treatise* has a *stock-flow* treatment where the interest rate must clear a market that trades not only in new issues but also in outstanding securities. In the *General Theory,* Keynes goes to a pure stock-analysis of interest determination. This last step would be retrogressive in itself.[55] But, on top of that, it is the excess stock demand, not for securities, but for money that—he argues—governs the interest rate. Not an intuitively appealing doctrine! How did he get stuck with it?[56]

The trouble starts with "Savings equal Investment." Keynes used both terms, in Marshallian fashion, to denote observable quantities (rather than planned or desired magnitudes—as would be the Walrasian fashion). He went on to show that, adopting certain not unreasonable terminological conventions, *ex post* saving had to be *identically* equal to *ex post* investment. Having absorbed that point, take a "fresh look" at Wicksell's image of the circular flow: If household saving and business investment are necessarily and therefore continuously equal, then it would seem that the banking system cannot possibly be doing anything else but simply serving as an obedient go-between. So, we can just as well erase it and adopt the simplified picture of the circular flow that goes with the Keynesian cross.[57]

If saving and investment are continuously equal, the rate of interest cannot possibly be governed by any difference between them. The possibility of a corresponding excess flow demand for loanable funds has then also been defined away. The loan-

54. In general equilibrium statics, one is often reminded, "everything determines everything." Common usage dictates how "determine" is to be used. The price of peanuts is "determined" by the simultaneous solution of the entire set of excess demand equations. If the time derivative of the price of peanuts depends only on the excess demand for peanuts, this excess demand will be said to "govern" the price.

55. Various modern models of financial asset prices do the same thing, however, i.e., impose zero excess stock demands as the conditions determining the structure of asset-prices and yields without worrying about flow rates of accumulation and new issues in the "short run." A similar stock-flow muddle pops up in numerous places in the literature on investment functions where it is argued that the demand-price for capital goods is independent of—or even, cannot be dependent on—the rate of accumulation. So, we have not made much progress—especially since Keynes was not prone to the last-mentioned error.

56. The answer, or most of it, is in *General Theory,* chapters 6, 7, 13, and 14.

57. The 45°-degree identity Keynesian cross, of course—not Model A. Model A, it will be recalled, admitted statements of the type "When S > I, there is an excess supply of commodities, and income will fall." We can't have that here!

able funds interest mechanism is gutted. Hence, the flow part of the *Treatise*'s stock-flow analysis should be erased. The speculative element remaining from it now has to make do as a complete interest theory. Loanable Funds are out; Liquidity Preference is in.

This Liquidity Preference theory, moreover, can be nothing but a "bootstrap" theory, as D. H. Robertson termed it.[58] Beliefs about where the rate will be tomorrow determine where it will be today. But in deciding where it is likely to be tomorrow, speculators have no reason to contemplate "real forces" of Productivity and Thrift. In a system lacking the loanable funds mechanism, there can be no tendency, however weak or fitful in its operation, for the interest rate to converge on the natural rate consistent with the equilibrium growth path. It is an obvious but important property of our Z-theory that the market rate will track the natural rate *unless* banks or speculators intervene to "fix" it at some other level. The *General Theory* emphatically denies any such basic tendency—whether in the short or in the long run—for the interest rate to find its FIM value. And it makes no sense, in context, to ask what the rate would be unless speculators "fixed" it.[59]

Thus, we arrive at Keynes' short-hand characterization of how the *General Theory* corrects the "errors" of the Classics: *Saving and Investment determine Income, not the Rate of Interest.*[60] The

---

58. As far as I can understand, Robertson was consistently right on every aspect of the interest rate controversy between himself and Keynes and Keynes' Cambridge followers from "Mr. Keynes and the Rate of Interest" onward. Hicks has collected all the most relevant pieces in Robertson (1966).

59. Nor does it make sense, in context, to argue as follows: "The most stable, and the least easily shifted, element in our contemporary economy has been hitherto, and may prove to be in future, the minimum rate of interest acceptable to the generality of wealth owners." (*General Theory*, p. 309). Either this empirical belief, or the bootstrap theory—or both—should be false. In a *Treatise* world, the formation of strong beliefs about the "normal" level of long rate is plausible. In the bootstrap world, it is not plausible at all. Cf. Leijonhufvud (1968), p. 240n.

60. That saving and investment determine the rate of interest "is what I myself was brought up on and what I taught for many years to others" (*General Theory*, p. 175). Upbringing aside, what Keynes should have taught is that loanable funds supply and demand govern the rate of interest and that it takes numerous restrictive assumptions to make saving and investment correspond to LF supply and demand, respectively. He could then have proceeded, with justice, to argue that this "Classical" doctrine did need to be amended to take securities market speculation into account as organized exchange markets grew in importance.

Money Supply and Liquidity Preference determine the Interest Rate, not Income.

With these last two propositions, any intelligible connection to mainstream Quantity Theory abruptly disappears. In the earlier variations on the Wicksellian theme the relationship to the Quantity Theory was obvious. Wicksell used the saving-investment approach to explain how a real disturbance may trigger an expansion of the banking system and, hence, a rise in prices together with growth of the currency stock. Keynes, in the *Treatise,* used it to show how a real disturbance may reduce velocity and thus put an economy under deflationary pressure. A Quantity Theorist of non-Monetarist persuasion, used to organizing his analysis of price level changes in terms of factors affecting money supply and money demand, would have no trouble understanding the use of the saving-investment approach in these Wicksell variations. But in the *General Theory,* a decline in investment demand will reduce the rate at which money is being spent for goods without, apparently, having at all affected the excess demand for money (whether by decreasing the supply or increasing the demand). And, indeed, money supply and money demand are emphatically said to have nothing to do with expansions and contractions of the circular flow (of money), except insofar as they have an indirect influence via the rate of interest on the saving-investment balance.

The other idea lost sight of in the firecracker string of brilliant paradoxes, ignited by the "insight" that the equality of saving and investment is an identity, is that of the maladjustment of the interest rate as the root of the trouble. It is clear enough that the interest rate is "too high" in the simple sense that, were it only lower, investment and hence employment would be higher. But the same could be said of the solution values for all of the other endogenous variables as well—they would have to be different to be consistent with full employment. That the emergence of the gap between market and natural rate is a crucial link in the causal story of how the persistent unemployment state develops is almost totally obscured. The bootstrap theory of interest erases the natural rate notion and thus leaves no equilibrium reference mark by which to define the "divergence" of the market rate.

The trivial last touch to the cover-up is terminological:

I am no longer of the opinion that the concept of a "natural rate" of interest, which previously seemed to me a most promising idea, has anything very useful or significant to contribute to our analysis. It is merely the rate of interest which will preserve the *status quo;* and, in general, we have no predominant interest in the *status quo* as such.[61]

The reasons for getting rid of the Wicksellian terminology should be obvious in the context of this section. Keynes' wording of the disposal is of interest mainly because it reinforces the impression one gets from his controversy with Hayek, namely, that he had given very little thought to problems of capital and growth theory.[62] Wicksell's *status quo* was always a state on an equilibrium growth-path. There are then two options for someone who wants to free Wicksellian theorizing from its dependence on the assumption that "yesterday was equilibrium." One is to tie the notion of the natural rate to the preservation of yesterday's income and employment level. The other, of course, is to identify it as the (FIM) rate of interest consistent with equilibrium growth—and, therefore, with the allocation of resources between consumption and capital goods producing industries which, at full employment, will entail equilibrium growth. Keynes, we notice, took the conceptually trivial option.

So, in this fourth and last variation, Wicksell's rabbit has been stuffed back into Keynes' hat, not to be seen again. An astonishing sleight of mind!

VIII. CAMBRIDGE KEYNESIANS

Liquidity Preference *versus* Loanable Funds marks a critical fork in the road for professed followers of Keynes. D. H. Robertson turned back to a personal view very much like Z-

---

61. *General Theory,* p. 243. The "natural rate" is, indeed, of no use as a reference point in a Keynesian deep depression. Once the failure of sales-expectations to be realized during the recession has induced a further decline of the (subjective) marginal efficiency of capital, unemployment will persist even if we have *both* $\underline{w} = \hat{w}$ and $\underline{r} = \hat{r}$. Cf., e.g., Leijonhufvud (1968b). The general equilibrium values for prices are significant *only insofar as* they reflect full information.

62. Keynes' reaction to the overinvestment theory of Hayek's *Prices and Production* was, simply, that while overinvestment in the past might have been regrettable, he could not see that it should cause any problems in the present; the only result would be to leave us with more capital in the present—and so much the better off for it. But here Keynes is, so to speak, a dead duck in shallow water. His argument reveals, of course, an aggregative concept of capital on his part that would hardly be tolerated in Cambridge of later days.

theory. Joan Robinson and Richard Kahn, like the Master, took the Liquidity Preference turn, soon to go beyond where Keynes left off. The Neoclassical Keynesians—going flat out in their brand-new IS-LM machine—failed to see any fork and ended up in the bog between the roads.

Robinson and Kahn in their writings on the matter[63] make clear that the crucial aspect of the LP theory is not some assumed property of a comparative static model but is an hypothesis about a sequence in a dynamic-historical theory. A stock-flow dimensional argument[64] can, moreover, be utilized to free the hypothesis from too obvious a reliance on the *ex post* saving-investment identity.

The sequence (in my paraphrase) goes as follows. Assume an initial equilibrium. Suppose some event such as will reduce the marginal efficiency of capital. At impact, saving now exceeds *intended* investment at the initial levels of income and interest. This saving-investment gap, it is maintained, can have *no effect* on the rate of interest. In the very short run, stock supplies and stock demands determine asset prices and yields; the excess supply of loanable funds, being a flow, is of no consequence; Liquidity Preference and the stock of money determine the rate of interest; since neither was affected by the shock to MEC, the interest rate remains constant at this stage.[65] The interest rate, consequently, cannot play any part whatsoever in closing the saving-investment gap opened up by the postulated disturbance; it has to be closed altogether through income adjustment. Next, then, the required fall in income will "release" some stock of transactions balances;[66] these "excess balances" drive down the rate of interest to the level required for them to be voluntarily held given the prevailing state of Liquidity Preference.[67]

63. Cf., esp. J. Robinson (1951) and R. Kahn (1954).

64. H. G. Johnson (1951–2) surveys the discussion inside Cambridge.

65. An alternative argument stresses Keynes' so-called Finance Motive. As far as I can understand, it only introduces a lag in the adjustments of output and loanable funds flows without otherwise affecting the sequence discussed.

66. Agents discover that they have "too much cash" only *after* income has fallen; it is not the case, here, that requirements for transactions balances are scaled down already when spending-intentions (by entrepreneurs) are cut back. When people decrease their rate of spending of money on goods—so says the LP theory—the resulting increase in the ratio of their cash balances to their income is unintended and unanticipated.

67. As noted, Quantity Theorists will have a hard time. It is not that an excess demand

This Liquidity Preference *sequence* is crucial. Clearly, any theory that incorporates it will attach a *probability of zero* to a successful traverse from one growth-path to another. The economy cannot do it for the simple reason that the only price mechanism that might do it never gets into play to coordinate saving and investment decisions.

In this theory, furthermore, "Saving equals Investment" simply because investment must "cause" savings to a like amount. In the closed economy, investment is always self-financing.[68] Saving, on the other hand, is a "passive" variable of no causal significance.[69] Saving-behavior, consequently, has nothing to do with determining capital accumulation and growth—except insofar as *higher* saving propensities give you *lower* output and employment for any given volume of investment (basically, the "Paradox of Thrift").[70] The theory of capital accumulation, therefore, has to be tackled—à la Sraffa, Kalecki, Robinson, or Kaldor—without relying on intertemporal preferences as one of the determinant factors. The results are fables in which growth is determined by "animal spirits," perhaps themselves animated by the share of profits in income, and the technology for producing commodities by means of commodities. As a trivial corollary, various neoclassical fables, in which saving "causes" capital accumulation, rather than the other way around, are seen to be specious and not fit to conjure with.

for money causes nominal income to decline here—it is that falling income causes an excess supply of money. Cf. Leijonhufvud (1968), pp. 30–31, 182–83.

68. Go ahead and invest—the savings cannot help but be there. It is a notion that will make Economic Development seem almost too easy.

69. Part of the problem here, actually, is the conventional definition of saving. Keynes was happy to find general agreement on saving meaning non-consumed income and dispensed, therefore, with any detailed discussion of the concept. (*General Theory*, Chapters 6 and 7). But "non-consumed income" can be (at least) directly invested, placed in securities or intermediaries, or hoarded. It is one of the more common muddles of macroeconomics that we do not know what an "increase in non-consumption" means for the state of excess demands in these various markets.

70. Harrod also shared the LP theory of interest and thus the position that growth is *not* the result of the coordination of saving and investment decisions. He proposed instead the question: What rate of capital accumulation, if entrepreneurs happened to set out on it, would be sustained by the resulting aggregate demand? It will be recalled that the saving propensity enters into the formula answer. Saving, however, enters into the theory, not as a demand for securities and other stores of wealth, but as "non-spending," i.e., a leakage from the aggregate demand that alone can keep animal spirits up. The Paradox of Thrift mechanism is built into the model, and it is it that makes the warranted path a knife edge. The Hicks-Goodwin cycle models of the 1950's also had this property.

From this Cambridge perspective, Neoclassical Keynesians are seen to be prone to heresy because of their uncertain grasp of the fundamental dogma that "Investment causes saving but saving does not cause investment."[71] And the Monetarists, of course, are the very heathen, still in the grasp of the ancient superstition that the excess demand for money governs money income while saving and investment govern the interest rate rather than the other way around.

On the controverted issues of Keynesian theory, finally, the Cambridge Keynesians have always understood quite clearly that, however disguised, our Z-theory argument remains imbedded in the *General Theory*. Consequently, they reject all the main elements of the so-called Neoclassical Synthesis, i.e., the Liquidity Trap and/or rigid wages interpretation of Keynes' unemployment theory, and the notion that the Pigou-effect "saves the logic" of pre-Keynesian doctrines. Their adherence to the LP theory of interest, however, precludes them from reasserting Keynes' argument against the Synthesizers in the unabashedly Wicksellian terms used here.[72]

Adherence to the LP theory of interest also explains, one assumes, why Cambridge Keynesians since the death of Keynes have showed no further interest to speak of in monetary theory. The LP theory deprives the rate of interest of its role in coordinating saving and investment; without that role, the interest rate is a variable of little, if any, significance; and money supply and demand, in Cambridge Keynesian theory, have no other job but to govern this uninteresting variable.[73] Monetary theory is seen as a dead-end street.

There is some irony here. Keynes worked his way to a theory

71. Cf. J. Robinson (1937), Chapter II. This book is especially helpful in getting a picture of the original Cambridge Keynesian position. Note that the preface to the second edition (1969) leaves unmodified those aspects of the theory that concern us here.

72. Professor Robinson would, I think, reject the use of neoclassical growth theory even for the limited purpose of constructing "notional reference paths" with which actually postulated system motions might be compared in order to see what has gone wrong. (This is, of course, the method used throughout this article.) A statement of the type "The system has got stuck at a rate of interest higher than the rate consistent with coordinating saving and investment decisions on a full employment growth-path" would be judged meaningless by a Cambridge Keynesian, since the basis for the comparison is a state which we, if we adhere to the strict LP theory of interest, cannot imagine the real-world system to produce under any circumstances.

73. The price level, for example, is governed by wage-push.

of the malfunctions of a capitalist economy through a maze of monetary and financial complications. To the Cambridge school, his preoccupation with such questions has come to seem an embarrassing concession to pre-revolutionary ways of thinking. Kalecki, who never entertained the notion that the system might work and who saw little need to explain why financial markets might not coordinate saving and investment, becomes the more logical figurehead. This is especially true since Keynes, shorn of his contributions to monetary theory, would not amount to more than a minor pre-Kaleckian. As an economic scientist, Keynes was nothing much, if not a monetary theorist.

IX. NEOCLASSICAL KEYNESIANISM

Where are all the Keynesians now? Was there ever such a school? I for one would feel cheated if the answer were: No.[74] Who could doubt that there was an American Keynesian school back in the days of Heller, Ackley, and Okun at the Council? How could one write the history of economics over the last forty years without it?

Only a few years ago, it was said: "We are all Keynesians now." Today, one asks: Who were they? What did they believe?

There obviously was an American Keynesian school in the days of Alvin Hansen's famous Harvard seminar and for some time thereafter. One cannot off-hand date its demise. But it is doubtful that anyone who has gained prominence in the profession and is now under the age of 40[75] would accept the label "Keynesian" for himself. So we know the school is done for.

Over the intervening decades, most of the major names in economics and almost all the most admired technical innovators occupied a macroeconomic position in some sense in the center

---

74. When I wrote *On Keynesian Economics and the Economics of Keynes,* I did not identify who these "Keynesians" were. I could not come up with any major names to whom I felt one could with confidence attribute *belief* in the cluster of propositions I was dealing with. Having turned a quick reputation on making critical noises about the "Keynesians," I do not really want to press the case for their never having existed. In any case, my readers did not seem to share my vague unease about this—it is one of the things on which I cannot remember being challenged.

75. Forty-five? Do I hear a 50?

between the Cambridge Keynesians on the one side and the Monetarists on the other. This macroeconomic center has been routinely called "Keynesian" in the United States. But, on the issues of this paper, it is curiously difficult to say what the centrist position has become or what is "Keynesian" about it. The topnotch people in the center can only be described as "eclectic" in theory and "pragmatic" in policy. Those terms, however, are descriptive of judicious temperament rather than expressive of a shared and coherent system of beliefs. On occasion, Robert Solow or James Tobin will make it his business to explain where Joan Robinson or Milton Friedman go too far. But this is not enough—unless "anti-Monetarist" is to become the residual definition of "Keynesian." Would there be no Keynesianism any longer except for Milton Friedman?[76]

This American Keynesianism also exists at another level—that of teaching and textbooks. Here one can find the Paradox of Thrift surviving[77] and a continuing emphasis on the saving-investment problem.[78] The trouble with the textbook tradition is that one does not know whether anyone of consequence takes what it says seriously.

It is clear, I think, that Keynesianism has had no Champion in the United States for quite some time. There have been no leading figures concerned to maintain a semblance of intellectual coherence in Keynesian macroeconomics. Nor has there been a Keynesian "research programme" for perhaps twenty years. The best people in the center have been neo-Walrasian all along. Some of them have used the designation "Keynesian" as a flag of convenience when sailing in the muddy waters of short-run stabilization policy. As such, it is recognized as signalling belief in the usefulness of discretionary fiscal policy, etc. But its use entails approximately the commitment to the integ-

76. The latest serious attempt to give a positive definition to "Keynesianism" may indeed be that of Friedman in his *Monetary Framework*. It is as if he was seeing the imposing enemy that he has battled for twenty-odd years turning into a windmill before his very eyes—a process one must try to reverse!

77. Into the tenth edition of Samuelson's *Principles*, for instance. The Paradox is, of course, implicit—even when not asserted—everywhere that the Keynesian cross is employed.

78. Cf., e.g., Gardner Ackley (1961), Chapters VII to IX. One of the strong points of Ackley's book is that he is so clear on the Wicksellian antecedents of Keynes' saving-investment problem.

rity and development of Keynesian theory that the world's ship-owners harbor for the peace and prosperity of Panama.

Well, no one was obliged to keep the Hansen school running. Nor could one argue that our intellectual resources would have been better allocated if, say, Paul Samuelson or Lawrence Klein had taken time out for the purpose. The point is simply that we must recognize American Keynesianism for what it is: a tribe of no chiefs, all injuns.[79]

The trouble is that this makes Neoclassical Keynesianism difficult to get a grip on. Obviously, it has drifted far away from the Hansenian verities. But it is difficult to say where American Keynesianism has ended up. Critical changes in doctrine have come to pass virtually without controversy, or without a clear verdict on whatever controversy did take place. It is as if change were almost inadvertent—or as if nobody cared. The accumulated result is an intellectual mushiness that defies attempts at sharp definition.

Most astoundingly, Neoclassical Keynesianism has ended up in a position that has proven difficult to demarcate from Monetarism in any significant way. But, *how could that be?* When Warburton stated the essentials of the Monetarist position in the 1940's,[80] the Keynesians were too sure of themselves to take his challenge seriously. Nonetheless, it is perfectly obvious what kind of arguments they would have employed at that time, had they deigned to answer him: "saving and investment decisions are made by different people; the interest rate cannot coordinate them; saving and investment determine income and employment; flexible wages will not restore full employment, if saving exceeds investment at full employment income" . . . and so on. A later generation of Monetarists has proven more difficult than Warburton to ignore. But in the battle against their growing influence, *these saving-investment arguments have played virtually no role at all.*[81]

---

79. . . . and them skipping the old reservation in ever growing numbers!

80. E.g., Clark Warburton (1946).

81. And when Milton Friedman, in a paper specifically intended to define the issues between Keynesians and himself, is content simply to leave "the saving-investment sector as unfinished business," his critics do not object or find it worth discussing. Cf. Friedman in Gordon, ed., (1973), p. 40.

The theory held by the dwindling center is some sort of "Keynesian" theory *minus* the saving-investment problem! This is most readily apparent in employment theory. In the course of the interminable Phillips curve controversy, the supposedly Keynesian centrists have used almost every conceivable argument against the natural rate of unemployment theory *except* the original Keynesian one—namely, that the economy will *not* home in automatically on full employment *unless* the interest rate is such that saving will not exceed investment at full employment real income.

Keynes without the saving-investment problem is like Marshall without supply and demand or Adam Smith without the division of labor. But the Neoclassical Keynesians traded in Keynes' hypothesis of intertemporal coordination failure for the old pre-Keynesian hypothesis of rigid wages as the central idea of their unemployment theory. In the process, the Wicksell Connection was entirely lost from sight.

The elimination of the Wicksellian idea of the maladjustment of the interest rate with the consequent saving-investment problem and the adoption, instead, of the rigid wages explanation of unemployment were both enshrined in the so-called Neoclassical Synthesis, that fake Keynes and the Classics compromise which was preached for decades by practically everybody—and in the end not defended by anybody.[82] The analytical vehicle for the Synthesis was the Hicks-Hansen IS-LM model. The full story of how American Keynesianism ended up in this position would make a long and tangled tale. Here, we simply note some of the steps on the way.

The troubles with keeping track of the Wicksellian theme in its Keynesian guises and disguises go far back in time. The original "Saving-equals-Investment" debate did not reach a clear-cut collective verdict. As Lipsey has recently shown, confusion persists—and is tolerated—on aspects of this issue to the present day.[83] The IS-LM framework did not lend itself too well to a sharp characterization of the question whether the excess demand for bonds or the excess demand for money governs the interest rate. It was concluded that the distinction be-

82. . . . except, of all people, Milton Friedman (in Gordon, ed., *op. cit.*).
83. R. G. Lipsey (1972).

tween the Loanable Funds and Liquidity Preference hypotheses was probably either pointless or misleading and that, in either case, the issue could safely be left unresolved. Correspondingly, Hansen found, Keynes' insistence that saving and investment determine income while money stock and liquidity preference determine the rate of interest (rather than the other way around) makes no sense once you realize that, in IS-LM, everything simultaneously determines everything.[84]

But the Liquidity Preference versus Loanable Funds debate did concern an issue that is crucial, that should not have been left undecided, and that cannot be put to rest with murmured incantations about the simultaneity of everything in general equilibrium. A metaphor may help to make the point. Consider flying in an airplane that is on automatic pilot. This auto-pilot, we assume, consists of two servomechanisms—one to check and correct your course, one to do the same for the altitude. As long as both instruments report zero error, lean back and relax—you are in general equilibrium. Suppose now, however, you learn that a drunken mechanic has crosswired the servos so that the instrument that detects errors in the course will trigger changes in altitude and vice versa. The Cambridge Keynesians insist that the capitalist system is crosswired. The Neoclassical Keynesians do not think it matters which way the thing is wired. Neither would leave it on automatic in any case but would rather trust to the discretion of some intrepid aviator at the manual controls.

Hansen's failure to understand the issue became of great importance, for his influence was such that all the issues separat-

---

84. Cf., A. H. Hansen (1949), Chapter 5, and (1953), Chapter 7. In Hansen's reading Keynes' interest theory was "indeterminate"—money supply and demand could not *determine* the interest rate, as Keynes would have it, but only give you the LM curve, etc. This way of looking at it misses the issue of which excess demand *governs* the interest rate.

One is reminded of Hansen's indeterminacy charge by Friedman's more recent argument that Keynes' theory suffered from a "missing equation"—and should be completed by adding an exogenously determined price level. Keynes' theory, like the others discussed in Sections IV through VIII above, was of the dynamic-historical variety. In describing the state of the system at some point in the sequential process, such theories make use of information about the system's initial (historical) state. Static models do not use historical information, of course, but have to have equations for all endogenous variables. Reading a dynamic-historical theory on the presumption that it is static, therefore, is apt to lead to the mistaken impression that it lacks equations and is indeterminate.

ing Z-theory from Cambridge Keynesianism were left unresolved among his followers. A contributing factor in this malign
neglect was the doctrine of the interest-inelasticity of both saving and investment, which held sway among Keynesians for two
decades or so. It made the problems of interest theory into
trivia questions: What does it matter which excess demand governs the interest rate, if movements in the rate could not in any
event coordinate saving and investment?

The interest-inelasticity doctrine did not last but, in the
meantime, the Pigou-effect came eventually to draw attention
altogether away from intertemporal coordination failure as a
cause of unemployment.[85] Saving tending to exceed investment
at full employment income could not be the trouble in a system
with flexible prices; a sufficiently large increase in real cash balances could reduce saving to the extent required; one might
imagine a deflation of such magnitude as to bring this requisite
real balance effect about. This argument left rigid wages as the
remaining explanation of unemployment.[86]

To American Keynesians in the 1950's, this return to the
Classical explanation of unemployment cannot have seemed a
very important concession to pre-Keynesian (or anti-Keynesian)
thinking. But it stored up trouble for the future. To the next
generation of Keynesians it was to make a riddle of stagflation:
How explain it except by now postulating the rigidity of the
rate of change (and, perhaps, higher derivatives) of money
wages? And it paved the way for a more comprehensive return
to Classical doctrines than the pragmatic Centrists were, in fact,
prepared to accept.

Other developments in the 1950's were part of the general
drift towards Monetarism and, eventually, the New Classical

85. Patinkin (1956) also preferred working with a single aggregate demand function
with income and interest rate as its arguments rather than with separate saving and investment functions. This practice does not draw attention to the role of the rate of interest in coordinating intertemporal activities and will not put the spotlight on its possible failures to play that role.

The emphasis by so many Keynesian writers on the national income accounting definitions of saving and investment is not helpful either. The equality of saving and investment bears no necessary relation to the equilibrium growth-path and the natural rate of
interest when the variables are defined so as to include "unplanned" or "undesired"
components.

86. For an appraisal of the Pigou-effect argument in the context of Keynes' theory, cf.
Leijonhufvud (1968), pp. 315–53. From a somewhat different angle the matter is again
taken up in Section X of this paper.

Economics. The speculative demand for money, for example, tended to disappear from view once Baumol and Tobin had provided rationales for interest-elasticity of the transactions demand for cash. The idea that conflicting beliefs about the future were at the root of the economy's disequilibrium was buried deeper and deeper. The substitution of an interest-elastic transactions demand for speculative demand also left a stable and predictable velocity function which, given that the Keynesians usually treated the money stock as exogenously fixed, reduced Keynesian monetary theory to a Variable Velocity Quantity Theory. From that position, in turn, it became difficult to see that the controversy with the Monetarists could possibly be about anything else than the interest-elasticity of money demand—although why one should make that number the occasion for such a deeply felt schism is hard to fathom.

Neoclassical theory was also being put into the IS-LM framework in piecemeal fashion as production functions, new consumption and investment functions were deduced from neo-Walrasian microtheory and replaced the original constructions. Interest rates settling at the "wrong" level, in Wicksell-Keynes fashion, could have been a problem in the formulation of the intertemporal aspects of these new IS-LM elements but does not seem to have been widely discussed as such. More indicative still, the 1960's saw the Harrod-Domar and Hicks-Goodwin models go back into the library stacks as their place in Graduate Reserve was absorbed by the burgeoning literature on neoclassical growth.

How far this neoclassical conversion went was, perhaps, not always realized because, with rigid wages (and interest-elastic money demand), the IS-LM model will still produce unemployment and a rationale for fiscal policy, etc., even if otherwise all its pieces are Classical. What it takes, however, is a wage rate that is *exogenously fixed,* which is to say a model without operative supply-and-demand mechanisms in its labor markets.[87] Keynes did not have wages "rigid" in this sense. Rather, his

87. If, in the normal case, current sales were the immediately binding constraint on demand, temporary price-inflexibilities would suffice to produce effective demand failures as in the fix-price models, for example, of Barro and Grossman (1971) and Malinvaud (1977). Reasons for not treating this as the normal case are discussed in Leijonhufvud (1973). In the present paper, attention is confined to "within-corridor" problems.

model had the money wage rate historically given in the short run, but market determined over the longer run. These are the same labor-market assumptions as in Friedman's model in which temporary wage-inflexibility allows for temporary deviations from the natural rate of unemployment but longer run market forces make unemployment converge on the natural rate.

In the 1940's, a macrotheory with wage rates exogenously determined (by non-economic factors) and unresponsive to market conditions was acceptable to many economists and perhaps to most labor economists. As the Human Capital approach later encroached more and more on an area where institutional explanations had been the rule and made progress with explaining relative earnings as market determined, the denial of an operative labor market mechanism eventually became an untenable assumption. By the early 1960's, in addition, the stable Phillips curve had become, somehow, a characteristically "Keynesian" doctrine. The most plausible seeming rationale offered for its shape was that the rate of change of money wages was a function of the excess demand for labor, i.e., that the system does have an operative labor market-mechanism.[88] The resolution to this was to admit a labor market-mechanism, but one that works rather slowly.

Now, someone whose macrobeliefs consist of neoclassical growth, variable velocity Monetarism, and unemployment caused by lags in wage-adjustment should not fight Milton Friedman, but join him. But *that* conclusion, of course, the Neoclassical Keynesians have refused to draw. One may appreciate their steadfast resolve to rather fight than switch. But it is not at all clear that their version of Keynesianism gives them a leg to stand on.

This branch of Keynesianism managed, somehow, completely to evade the issue of the interest mechanism. Does it or does it not work to coordinate the intertemporal decisions of households and firms? The theory does not say.

88. This should have precluded treating the Phillips curve as a convenient appendage to the textbook IS-LM model, which explains unemployment as the consequence of the lack of an operative labor-market mechanism. It did not. This is an example of what I mean by saying that intellectual coherence was not maintained in mainstream macroeconomics.

There are two clear-cut answers: no and yes. The choice is between Mrs. Robinson and Friedman. Both occupy coherently formulated theoretical positions so that the implications of the choice is clear. Side with Mrs. Robinson and you give up predictable velocity and neoclassical growth-models (and the neo-Walrasian theory they belong to). Side with Friedman and you accept Monetarism and the vertical Phillips curve.[89] The Neoclassical Keynesians would like to avoid both Scylla and Charybdis. But since they have failed to see the interest rate issues as central and have not understood that Keynesian theory and Keynes' contention are rooted in Wicksell's theme, they have not managed to chart a safe course between them.

The remaining, unexplored possibility of steering clear of both Cambridge and Chicago is that the interest rate mechanism (*contra* Mrs. Robinson) is capable of coordinating saving and investment but (*contra* Friedman) cannot be depended upon to do so always. This means a Loanable Funds theory with either speculation and/or the Central Bank capable of preventing or holding up adjustments of the real interest rate that are required for the equilibration of the system. Add temporary wage-inflexibility with consequent short-run quantity-adjustments and we are back with Z-theory.

Unless the real rate of interest goes to its natural level, unemployment will not home in on its natural level. This is true also of a system with an operative labor market mechanism. If and when the system fails to coordinate intertemporal activities by adjustment of intertemporal prices, the "flexing" of money wage rates in response to excess supply of labor will not guarantee a return to full employment. This is ground on which the Keynesians could base their opposition to the Monetarist doctrines of strong stability of the system in its real variables, the "vertical" Phillips curve at the natural rate of unemployment and to the associated strictures against discretionary policy actions.[90]

89. Here, I exclude the option of (a) assuming that interest rate maladjustments do not arise but (b) that wages are exogenously "fixed," so that (c) the (in any case ill-founded) notion of a stable relation between the rate of change of money wages and unemployment must be rejected.

90. The policy-implications for states of the system of the type considered in Z-theory, and for states developing out of them owing to the induced deterioration of sales-expectations, as discussed in Leijonhufvud (1968), Chapter VI, and (1968b).

It should be realized, however, that Z-theory will not salvage all the positions that Keynesians have assumed in their attempts to halt the spreading influence of Monetarism. In particular, it will not serve as a basis for resurrecting the accursed notion of a stable, downward-sloping (even if expectations augmented) Phillips curve. It suggests, rather, why we should not run regression lines through a Phillips scatter diagram. Such a diagram should be read as composed of data points drawn from different samples. If we were to label the points according to the diagnosis of the historical state to which they correspond, we might have the following:

  i. *FF-points* (Fisher-Friedman) for states of the economy when there was no saving-investment problem. These should either be close to the natural rate of unemployment or else be moving towards it relatively rapidly. "Automatic" convergence on full employment will not be prevented by saving-investment "gaps." Monetarist theory and policy prescriptions apply to this sample.

 ii. *WK-points* (Wicksell-Keynes) for states of the labor market that reflect maladjustments of interest rates and consequent saving-investment problems. These points should be off the natural unemployment rate and found to be moving towards it only sluggishly, if at all.[91] This sample of historical states would qualify for aggregate demand management.

iii. A few *K-points* (Keynes) from the early 1930's reflecting general Effective Demand Failures (outside the corridor).

 iv. Perhaps some modern *WF-points* (Wicksell-Fisher) for certain stagflation situations.

Z-theory should recommend itself as a theoretical home base for Keynesians also in that, with a little help from Irving Fisher, it suggests a straightforward hypothesis to account for stagflation. *Such business fluctuations as do take place in a policy regime providing monetary stability will not be eliminated by expected inflation* (nor will they be ameliorated by erratic stop-go inflation). To the extent that changes in entrepreneurial expectations about the prospective real return to new investment produce fluctuations in activity levels, these can just as well take place around

91. Accelerator-effects might cause subsequent observations to diverge even farther.

an average inflation rate of 10 or 20 percent. The simultaneous occurrence of inflation and unemployment (or even rising inflation and growing unemployment) will not appear as a riddle once one is freed from a theory that can explain unemployment *only* by invoking downward rigidity of wages.

Whether Z-theory as a last ditch against Monetarism will hold much water, one should not prejudge. One thing is quite clear: if it does not, all of Keynesian economics will have to be judged a big mistake.

X. FRIEDMAN

Over the course of the Monetarist debate, Milton Friedman has consistently maintained that the differences between his position and that of the Keynesians are empirical and *not* theoretical. From the other side, Franco Modigliani, for one, concurs.[92] But the theoretical framework they both use has failed to point out the maladjustment of the interest rate as an idea that is central to all the various non-Monetarist theories. There *is* an important theoretical issue separating Keynesian and Monetarist theory.

Monetarism evolved in opposition to Keynesianism. Consequently, the aspects emphasized as distinctive to the Monetarist position have been determined by what has commonly been understood to be the Keynesian one. The Neoclassical Keynesians abandoned or lost track of the Wicksellian theme. Thus Friedman has not been pressed to argue his own views on interest theory. Nor has he seen a need to do so for his understanding of Keynes and Keynesian theory is largely the conventional one.

In this section, we shall first attempt to piece together a picture of Friedman's theory of the real interest rate. Second, we shall comment on his interpretation of Keynes.

Sir John Hicks has distinguished between a Thornton tradition and a Ricardo tradition in monetary theory.[93] Thornton adumbrated Wicksell and Keynes. Friedman is placed in line of

92. Cf. Modigliani (1977), p. 9.
93. J. R. Hicks (1967), Chapter 9.

descent from Ricardo. In marking his departures from the Classics, Keynes quoted Ricardo:

> The interest of money is not regulated by the rate at which the Bank will lend . . . but by the rate of profit which can be made by the employment of capital, and which is totally independent of the quantity or of the value of money. . . . The applications to the Bank for money, then, depend on the comparison between the rate of profits that may be made by the employment of it, and the rate at which they are willing to lend it. If they charge less than the market rate of interest, there will be no amount of money which they might not lend; . . . .[94]

Keynes criticized this Ricardo passage for its Classical full employment presumption—Ricardo had derived the proposition that the rate of profit uniquely determines the interest rate by assuming the system to be at full employment. My impression of Friedman's thought over the years is that he starts by assuming Ricardo's conclusion and from it deduces Ricardo's assumption, i.e., he assumes that the market real rate will equal the natural real rate and concludes that an operative labor-market mechanism will make employment converge on its natural rate.

Friedman's favorite fable of capital and growth, apparently, is that of Frank Knight.[95] In a Knightian world, there is no difficulty knowing what the real rate of interest is and must be: you just check the Crusonia-plant to see how fast it tends to grow. In a von Neumann world of multiple commodities, it takes some calculation. But in neither system can there be any mistaking what the real rate is. It is independent of employment and of saving-propensities. It makes no sense to assume that anyone would speculate against it being what it is. The real rate is ascertainable without engaging in monetary calculations. The banking system cannot by its policies depress the market

94. J. M. Keynes (1936), p. 190, quoted from Ricardo's *Principles of Political Economy*.
95. The reader should realize that my "impressions" here amount to rather loose speculation for which, ordinarily, I would have to be prepared to apologize. I am sure, however, that Milton Friedman will not object to my proceeding "as if" they were true as long as the implications check out.
In Friedman's provisional *Price Theory* (1962), the chapter on capital and interest was altogether Knightian. But the fully worked out version (1976) has a stock-flow analysis which, although the discussion retains some Knightian touches, implies that the IS curve should in general be downward sloping. But then, again, we have the mention of a possibly horizontal IS in Stein, ed., *op. cit.*, p. 311, and also, for instance, Friedman's nod to Knight and von Neumann in Gordon, ed., (1973), p. 37n.

real rate below its natural level for any appreciable length of time. The problem that entrepreneurs have is forecasting changes in the money price level. In the Fisher equation, the real rate is known; uncertainty and information problems attach to the prospective rate of inflation. In interpreting Tooke's stylized fact (i.e., Gibson's Paradox) one need not worry about the possibility that the time-series of nominal interest rates might reflect, in part, significant discrepancies between the market real and the natural real rate. Instead, movements of nominal interest rates can be taken to reflect changes in the expected rate of change of the price level against the background of a steady real rate. The real sector of the economy is strongly stable and can only be disrupted by serious mismanagement of money.

This all fits. Knight's Crusonia-fable need not be taken literally, however. Instead, we should imagine a world for which it would make a serviceable metaphor: An economy with stable saving propensities and technological progress proceeding at a more or less steady pace; one in which entrepreneurs collectively are not given to "waves" of pessimism and optimism about future demand, but where competition tends with time to weed out both the overly pessimistic and the optimistic, and so on.

Friedman, like so many others, filters Keynes and Keynesian theory through the IS-LM model and, consequently, ends up where everyone else ends up: bogged down in the Neoclassical Synthesis, which is to say, with the conclusion that exogenous fixity of money wages was Keynes' explanation of unemployment. His discussion is notable for a sophisticated treatment of Keynes' demand for money function and for its sweeping endorsement of the Pigou-effect.

Friedman correctly specifies Keynes' money demand function as $M/P = ky + f(r - r^*, r^*)$, where y is real income, r the market rate, and r^* the "rate of interest expected to prevail." The latter we may refer to as the "normal rate."[96] Friedman then distin-

96. The "normal rate" here will mean, then, the long rate of interest that speculators have come to regard as "normal." Unfortunately, Wicksell has in some contexts used "normal" for his "natural" rate, but the latter has become so much the accepted label for Wicksell's concept in English that reintroducing the "normal rate" for a different concept should not cause confusion.

guishes between long-run and short-run "absolute liquidity preference." In the long-run, we should have $r = r^*$, so that only the absolute level of the interest rate enters into the steady-state money demand function. If, then, this long-run function becomes infinitely elastic at some very low rate of interest, we have "long-run absolute liquidity preference." This is the old Liquidity Trap idea. Friedman's "short-run liquidity preference" is Keynes' speculative demand, the interest-elasticity of which Friedman exaggerates by calling it "absolute."[97] He proceeds to insist on the "key role" of absolute liquidity preference in Keynes' theory:

> Time and again when Keynes must face up to precisely what it is that prevents a full-employment equilibrium, his final line of defense is absolute liquidity preference. . . . I do not see how anyone could read through these quotations and come to any other conclusion than that his "special twist" was highly elastic liquidity preference. . . .[98]

97. Friedman in Gordon, ed., *op. cit.*, p. 24, notes correctly that the elasticity will be larger the more homogenous the expectations of different holders of money and the more firmly they are held. He then goes on to assume: "Let there be a substantial body of holders of money who have the same expectation and who hold that expectation firmly, and f will become perfectly elastic."

Compare Keynes (1936), p. 172: "It is interesting that the stability of the system and its sensitiveness to changes in the quantity of money should be so dependent on the existence of a *variety* of opinion about what is uncertain. Best of all that we should know the future. But if not, then, if we are to control the activity of the economic system by changing the quantity of money, it is important that opinions should differ. Thus this method of control is more precarious in the United States where everyone tends to hold the same opinion at the same time. . ."

In England where everyone thinks for himself (and most people, therefore, arrive at the wrong conclusion), the monetary authority—Keynes is saying—can count on fooling some of the people all of the time. In the United States, the possibility that the mob might catch rational expectations is a threat to the powers of the Central Bank. Given the success of the U.S. authorities over the last 15 years in fooling all of the people most of the time, however, why envy the Bank of England?

98. Friedman, *op. cit.*, p. 169. This is argued *contra* Patinkin. I find myself unwittingly caught in the middle and trampled into the footnotes underneath as these two giants of monetary economics clash over this issue. Patinkin (in Gordon, *op. cit.*, p. 129) chides Friedman for favorably citing my 1968 book and then not paying heed to my rejection of "interpretations of Keynes that are based on the liquidity trap." Friedman replies that he thinks my analysis "justifies a different conclusion about the role of absolute liquidity preference than the one Leijonhufvud reaches (that it plays no important role) . . ." (*op. cit.*, p. 177).

My actual position has been and remains the following. (i) By "Liquidity Trap" I mean precisely what Friedman terms "long-run absolute liquidity preference." I maintain that it plays no role in Keynes' theory. (ii) I also maintain that the speculative demand for money *does* play a key role in Keynes' theory. I do not think Friedman's "short-run absolute liquidity preference" is an improved label for it, in part because there is no reason for insisting on it being "absolute." I do not think that Patinkin agrees with the importance that I attach to the speculative demand in my interpretation of Keynes.

One notes that Friedman makes no use of the distinction previously drawn between long-run and short-run absolute liquidity preference in this passage. The distinction is in fact critical, although it may be more appropriately put as one between full information and incomplete information analysis.

1. *The Liquidity Trap Case.* The problem here is the one that Pigou termed "Keynes' Day of Judgment." It is a problem in long-run, full information comparative statics. A state of virtual capital saturation is postulated, so that no opportunities for net investment at a significantly positive rate of return exist; yet, we assume, the community wishes to accumulate more wealth. The "absoluteness" of liquidity preference is an essential part of the predicament: the interest rate cannot be depressed further so as to stimulate investment and close the saving-investment gap.[99]

The original Pigou-effect analysis is the *right* answer to *this* problem. The rational solution is for the community to accumulate non-productive wealth, and this can be done by allowing the real value of cash balances to grow through a declining price level. If, instead, unemployment results, rigidity of wages and/or prices should be blamed.

2. *The Case of Misinformed Speculation.* The speculative demand for money is not a problem in either the long run or the short run *if full information can be assumed.* In a full information state, speculators will regard the natural rate as normal, so that we have $\hat{r} = r^*$. In the Keynes case, however, speculators have failed to recognize the full extent of a shift in the natural rate and are assumed to take positions against the required adjustment of market rate. We then have, as in Figure 7-5 (Section VI above), $r^* > \underline{r} > \hat{r}$.

That speculative liquidity preference be "absolute" is not really to the point here. It would merely mean that $r^* = \underline{r}$. What counts, of course, is the Wicksellian theme: $\underline{r} > \hat{r}$.

In such a situation, savers, speculators, and entrepreneurs are acting on *inconsistent beliefs* about future prospects. This, moreover, is reflected in *"incorrect" relative prices.* When market rate, $\underline{r}$, differs from the natural rate, $\hat{r}$, intertemporal prices are

---

99. As noted by Patinkin (1965), Chapter XIV:3, however, it is misleading to treat this lower limit to the range of variation of the interest rate as if it was a property of the money demand function.

wrong; in general, we expect that, as a consequence, the ratio of durable goods demand prices to consumer goods prices will also be wrong.

The Pigou-effect is *not* a solution to this problem. A change in the absolute level of prices is not the rational response to disequilibrium relative prices. A large deflation would only *add* the problem of a large error in the money wage level to an already confused system state.

In stressing "absolute liquidity preference" as a key feature of Keynes' theory, Friedman, obviously, is within an inch of coming up with the Wicksellian theme as *the* difference between himself and his opponents. Yet he does not follow up with a discussion of interest rate maladjustments, saving-investment gaps, etc. As previously noted, he is content even to leave the saving-investment sector "as unfinished business" in the model he is using to discuss the relationship between Monetarist and Keynesian theories. There appear to be two reasons for this. One is that he does not take seriously the possibility of a significant divergence between the normal and the natural rate. It is not clear whether, in neglecting it, he lays more stress on the assumption that the natural rate is unlikely to change or on the assumption that it will be generally known when it does change. That he does regard $r^* \neq \hat{r}$ as implausible is most evident from the postulate that he incorporates in *his own* theory:

> A nominal market interest rate equal to the anticipated real rate plus the anticipated rate of change of prices, *kept at that level by speculators with firmly held anticipations.*[100]

This, indeed, *is* absolute liquidity preference (and, consequently, a *stronger* assumption than Keynes employed). These speculators will keep $\underline{r} = r^*$. This, then, is a model of a world that would come apart into the worst possible Wicksell-Keynes shambles if, unbeknownst to these speculators, the natural real rate of interest declined.

The other reason, I think, is that Friedman feels that the Pigou-effect conclusively demonstrated that "there is no fundamental 'flaw in the price system' that makes unemployment the natural outcome of a fully operative market mechanism." Keynes'

100. Friedman, *op. cit.,* p. 42, italics added.

contention, therefore, was a definite "error [which] consisted in neglecting the role of wealth in the consumption function—or, stated differently, in neglecting the existence of a desired stock of wealth as a goal motivating savings."[101] But Friedman's own analysis of the Pigou-effect deals only with the Trap case.[102] It does not, therefore, dispose of the type of saving-investment problem considered in this essay.

Indeed, as applied to a Wicksell-Keynes (Z-theory) saving-investment gap the usual Pigou-effect analysis is in error—and it is in error precisely because it treats real balances *as if* they were wealth.

For simplicity, let us presuppose that the system's equilibrium path is unique. (This surely is in a "Classical" spirit in any case.) Given a money stock of M, let the unique equilibrium values for the current period be $\hat{r}$, $\hat{p}$, $\hat{w}$, $\hat{I}$, . . . , etc. In Keynes' early recession unemployment state (Figure 5), saving out of a depressed level of real income, $S(\underline{X})$, equals investment, $\underline{I}'$, at a market rate that exceeds the natural rate, $\underline{r} > \hat{r}$. In this state, $w = \hat{w}$. To get back onto the equilibrium path, the system must move market rate back into conformity with the natural rate. The Pigou-effect, of course, does not do this.[103] The argument asserts, instead, that a horrendous, all-around deflation, "balanced" so as not to change relative prices, will increase real balances to such an extent that consumption increases, with the saving-income ratio declining, until saving out of full employment income just equals investment—*at an unchanged level of market rate still in excess of natural rate.* At the point $(\underline{r}, \underline{I})$ the economy is allocating more of its full employment output to consumption and less to capital accumulation than is, by hypothesis, consistent with being on its equilibrium growth-path. Savers, one may suggest, are fooling themselves. They are supposed to regard the increased real value of their cash-balances as added "wealth." But the system has not added to its productive capacity. Unless satisfied to retire in their old age on a diet

101. Friedman, *op. cit.,* p. 16.

102. It is found in Friedman (1976), pp. 313–21.

103. The Keynes-effect, of course, does do it. But that is still a very strange way, indeed, for the system to effect the necessary traverse. Cf. Leijonhufvud (1968), Chapter V:1–2.

of liquidity services, households will discover that this Pigou-addition to wealth cannot be cashed in for added future consumption.

It should matter, one would think, whether we have full employment at, say, a 4 percent rate of interest with the money wage index at 100 or full employment at 5 percent interest with the wage index at .01 (or whatever). The alternative is to maintain that the full employment state brought about via the Pigou-effect is also an equilibrium. In that case, the system has an infinity of "equilibria." For, with a given nominal money stock, to any value of the interest rate there will correspond a possible price level that makes the real value of the money stock exactly what is required to adjust full employment saving to the investment forthcoming at this interest rate.

So, here is our choice: *Either* the full employment state brought about by the Pigou-effect is *not* an equilibrium but is instead a state where, even though employment is temporarily full, the system is *more disorganized than ever. Or* the system has an infinity of equilibria—any growth-rate can be an equilibrium path.

The standard treatment of the matter by Patinkin and others fails to reveal the issue. Yet, there is no error in the way these authors handle their models. It may be, then, that this tells us that something may be wrong with these models. If so, what needs revision? I will end by putting it as a question: Does the problem, perhaps, go all the way back to Hicks' "Suggestion for Simplifying Monetary Theory?"[104] It is a bit frightening to think that it might, for that could imperil the whole vast tradition of monetary theory that has been built up from the Hicksian Suggestion. Yet, it is from that early paper that the later literature stems which treats real balances as household "wealth" and which, in postulating saving as wealth-adjustment behavior, fails to distinguish between household "wealth" to which there does and to which there does not correspond, on the production side of the economy, the physical capacity to produce future consumer goods.

104. J. R. Hicks (1935).

XI. A RESTATEMENT

I turn at last to the group known euphoniously as the Leijon-hufvudians. Since the views of this querulous faction have insinuated themselves all over this essay, they had better be made explicit. This group is all chief and no injuns, which makes it easier.

Like the Cambridge Keynesians, and in opposition to the Neoclassical Keynesians and Milton Friedman (in an alliance that ought not to be consecrated), I reject the Neoclassical Synthesis lock, stock, and barrel. I have spelled out my reasons more than once. *Pace* Friedman, they are still good.

Unlike the Cambridge Keynesians, I do *not* accept the Liquidity Preference theory of interest of Keynes' *General Theory* or any of the "lemmas" that flow from it. I believe it to be theoretically unsound, empirically false, and practically dangerous. My views on the interest mechanism consist of a basic D. H. Robertson Loanable Fund theory,[105] complicated, when needed, by Keynesian bear/bull speculation (as in the *Treatise*) and/or Fisherian inflation rate speculation. In the context of the preceding discussion, this means that Z-theory is as far as I will keep company with Keynes in the development of his thought. I accept only half of the Keynesian Revolution.

What are the purely theoretical consequences of taking this position?

Keynes believed that the contemporary problem that the economy was failing to solve was that of "traversing" from a higher to a lower growth path. His revolutionary theory develops in the analysis and re-analysis of this case. One should not fall into the mental habit of regarding this as the "typical" problem in macrotheory—I do *not* think it is—but it will be convenient to continue to focus on it here.

The immediate consequence of retaining a basic Loanable Funds position is clear from Section VI: the rate of interest *will* go to the new "natural" level, and thus equate full employment

105. Correspondingly, of course, I side with Robertson in the controversy with Keynes—and later with the Cambridge Keynesians—that began soon after the publication of the *Treatise*. Cf. my (1968), p. 24n., pp. 28–31.

saving and investment, *unless* bearish speculators (with or without the connivance of the Central Bank) intervene to prevent it.[106] Consequently, it is *possible* for the interest rate mechanism to coordinate saving and investment decisions. The least we can conclude from this is that the equilibrium path of a neoclassical growth-model can legitimately be used as a notional reference path, i.e., that it makes sense to compare disequilibrium states with the notional equilibrium path in trying to diagnose what has gone "wrong."[107] But the point goes farther: If the system will find its way to the "natural" rate of interest, unless there is strongly preponderant speculation against it, then it is no longer true that speculators are just playing Musical Chairs and forecasting Beauty Contest winners. There may be a lot of that going on, but there is now a Natural Beauty in the contest; the individual speculator has an interest in learning to recognize her—and should not bet against her unless he is pretty sure the game is rigged.[108] Speculation against the level of interest consistent with Productivity and Thrift should not be the normal case.

Hence, we regain a concept of saving as something more than an antisocial refusal to spend. It matters that it is also a supply of loanable funds. Higher saving propensities should normally entail more rapid growth of the Wealth of Nations, not higher unemployment. It makes sense for governments bent on growth to encourage saving. And so on. We can make a

106. I am ignoring, obviously, the interest-elasticity of the non-speculative demand for cash-balances. Compare Section II.

107. I am anxious to make this point since it is the "method" I have been using in everything I have written on Keynesian subjects.

108. Keynes may well have been right that the marginal efficiency of capital was falling in Britain through the 1920s. It is not an unreasonable supposition. Recall, however, that the beauty contest was rigged from 1926 on—the Bank of England was defending an overvalued pound with high Bank Rate. It seems doubtful that either aspect of that historical situation deserves being encapsulated into some IS-LM story of a "typical" recession.

It is important also to be clear that British unemployment after 1926 obviously could have been cured by wage and price deflation (by improving the trade balance and removing the need to defend the pound). Consequently, "rigid wages" are pertinent to that historical situation. Benjamin and Kochin have recently found that Britain between the years 1921 and 1926 had saddled itself with a very ill-designed unemployment insurance system that could not help but keep reservation wages up. Cf. Dan Benjamin and Levis Kochin (1979).

clean break with one of the most dangerous and harmful con-fusions ever taught as accepted economic doctrine.

Next, note carefully, the implications of the "normal case" are Monetarist. When the securities markets keep track of the natural real rate of interest we are in a Monetarist world. Veloc-ity should not be "unstable," monetary policy does not "push on strings," stable money stock growth is to be favored—and un-employment converges on its natural rate. I cannot see any reasons whatsoever why "Keynesians" should resist those con-clusions. The conditions assumed are precisely those under which Keynes the Revolutionary fades out and the Author of the *Tract* and the Architect of Bretton Woods come back in.

If the theory here proposed might be challenged by those who remember the Great Depression for implying that con-vergence onto an equilibrium growth-path is possible, the ques-tion nowadays—in the first flush of Rational Expectations—is apt to be different: Does the analysis leave any room for wrong-headed speculation? Is it likely that the Keynesian case will *ever* occur?

How plausible this Keynesian "disagreement" between entre-preneurs and speculators strikes one as being depends on what fables of capital and growth one deems most instructive. Like the Austrians, and more lately the Cambridge Keynesians, but unlike Knightians, I would emphasize the heterogeneity of capital goods and the subjectivity of entrepreneurial demand expectations. There can be no "uniform rate of profit" infera-ble from production sector relations alone that could be calcula-ted *ex ante* by speculators as a guide to the equilibrium rate of real interest. The notion of entrepreneurs collectively "dis-agreeing" with the securities market about prospects I have put in oversimplified (and perhaps somewhat misleading) terms. Entrepreneurial pessimism or optimism cannot be concep-tualized as fluctuations in some agreed-upon "number," such as "the" internal rate of return. Rather, whatever coherence in in-vestment activities is achieved comes about through each entre-preneur taking the interest rate established in the market as the appropriate opportunity cost of financial capital and adjusting his rate of investment so as to obtain a subjective efficiency rate at the margin equal to the market rate of interest. A world of this sort does, I think, give enough play to the "Dark Forces of Time and Ignorance" that one cannot easily dismiss the Keynes' case.

The story can be told in terms that modern readers may find more congenial. Whether more congenial or not, comparison of the two variants is instructive. I have throughout used the language of the older business-cycle literature in which the separate economic functions or activities are attached to separate actors in an anthropomorphological style of discourse that goes back, I suppose, at least to British Classical distribution theory. Older business-cycle theories were written like *Commedia dell'Arte* plays; the plot could be varied but the stock characters had to be the same: entrepreneurs, bankers, speculators, consumers, and laborers. I like this language for obvious reasons; I also prefer it for a heuristic reason—in analyzing a state of the system, in which activities are not smoothly coordinated, this language permits one to dramatize the inconsistencies of such a situation either as conflicting beliefs or else as conflicts between the stock characters.

But, naturally, the theory can be told in a different language. So, let each entrepreneur be a speculator and all speculation be done by entrepreneurs. Then assume some event that lowers the MEC "in general." Each entrepreneur perceives that profit prospects for his firm have deteriorated so that the marginal efficiency of investment schedule has declined for the kind of machine that he invests in. He knows that he is not alone in thinking "business is bad" but, given the heterogeneity of capital in the economy, he does not know how much of the decline that he perceives is truly general. Taking $\underline{r}$ (Figure 7-5) as the plausible opportunity cost of financial capital, he cuts back his rate of investment in new machinery to the point where MEI equals this rate. With others acting in the same way, retained earnings pile up in firms while $\underline{r}$ becomes the market rate of interest. This, the reader will recognize, has a claim to being fashionable: it is a search theory of the unemployment of financial capital. The general decline in the rate of profit that the system can earn at full employment is $r_0 - \hat{r}$. What the theory says (roughly) is that it is only the unanticipated or, better, *unrecog-*

nized part, $\underline{r} - \hat{r}$, of this *real disturbance* that has an effect on aggregate real income and employment. That is as it should be.[109]

But how could it last? And why would not falling wages and prices help? General deflation will not help unless or until the Keynes effect eliminates the discrepancy $\underline{r} - \hat{r}$. That is standard. But why should not $\underline{r}$ simply come down to $\hat{r}$ as entrepreneur-speculators learn that no better placements are opening up? It will; and this should put the system back into equilibrium *unless* the disappointment of short-term sales expectations induces a further decline in the subjective MEC schedule. An induced ("accelerator") decline in MEC will produce a state where the interest rate is now right but the MEC schedule is too low for this to restore full employment. This transition from one type of disequilibrium to another puts the system into a state where discretionary fiscal spending is the preferred policy.[110]

Does advocacy of discretionary fiscal policy in this setting rest on the implicit assumption that the government "knows best"— and, in particular, knows better than the entrepreneurs? No.

---

109. Thus far, virtually all the work done within the Rational Expectations methodology has been at the same time Monetarist. There is no reason why we should not see Keynesian Rational Expectations models developed—although, naturally, one does not expect to see them developed by economists that remain wedded to Keynesian models of the cross-wired, spanner-in-the-works variety.

The basic outlook that this paper (and the others in this volume) shares with Rational Expectations theory can be simply put: Unless there is an information failure of some sort, economic activities will be properly coordinated. But this common ground is wide enough to leave room for any number of differences.

One of them should be pointed out. My emphasis on inconsistent beliefs is foreign to Rational Expectations theory as developed, in particular, by Lucas. If all transactors know the model and receive the same signals at the same time, they must have the same beliefs. Consequently, when quantities diverge from their "natural" values, it must be because everyone is making the same mistake. No *Commedia* here. The (stochastic) unanimity of beliefs produces a sequence of temporary equilibria. Fluctuations in employment come out of this as intertemporal reallocations of leisure induced by unanticipated money creation. In contrast, Monetarist unemployment theory à la Friedman is of "my" variety. An acceleration of money growth, for example, will cause temporary overfull employment in Friedman's theory because firms learn about the rising inflation before workers do. Consequently, firms and workers have inconsistent beliefs about the real value of the money wage. When, simultaneously, firms think it "low" and workers think it "high," the volume of employment agreed upon will exceed the natural rate of employment.

110. All of this is done in more detail, albeit in the *Commedia dell'Arte* manner, in my (1968b) and also (1968) Chapter VI.

Each entrepreneur, if he is "rational," knows that were he alone to expand output he would suffer losses while most of the gains due to the increased employment at his plant would redound to others. He also understands that if all firms were to expand at the same time they could all be better off.[111] The problem is how to organize this collective action. The government is there, already organized to do it.

So much for a Revised Standard Version of the *General Theory* (with the Liquidity Preference theory of interest omitted as apocryphal).

We have in effect, two versions (or two stages) of this Keynesian case where the coordination problem is that of effecting a traverse. In the first, using the old-fashioned language, the entrepreneurs are right and the speculators wrong; in the next, the speculators are right and the entrepreneurs collectively wrong in acting on pessimistic sales forecasts. But the challenge of changing the growth-path should not come up all that often. Are all other income fluctuations to be ascribed to "monetary" causes?

There is one more possibility that is of interest. In this case, we will have the speculators being right all along, since nothing will have happened to require the system to settle for a lower growth-path; the entrepreneurs, however, are not "disagreeing" in this instance but are, rather, hesitant and uncertain. Consider a "pause" along the equilibrium growth-path. By a pause, I mean a situation where the representative firm chooses to *postpone* investment. This may occur for many reasons. Temporary uncertainty induced by political events is an example. But even in the closest approximation imaginable to a process of constant exponential and proportional growth of all activities, there should be more than enough untidy Schumpeterian economic development to make firms "pause" for reassurance now and then before they resume putting more eggs into the same old baskets. A recession of this type is due to a temporary increase in "flexibility preference" in the Hart-Hicks sense.[112] The postponement of new "fixed" commitments until the situation clarifies has its counterpart in a transitory increase in de-

111. The reader will recognize this as a Prisoner's Dilemma case for fiscal policy.
112. Cf. A. G. Hart, (1942), and J. R. Hicks (1976), Chapter 2.

mand for money and for "liquidity" in general. Long rates of interest stay up, but short rates and observed velocity decline.[113] I would expect this story to fit minor recessions rather better than the Keynes' story. It seems, moreover, to bear a reasonable family resemblance to Lucas' way of telling the story of a minor recession.[114]

Finally, an economy may get into discoordinated states much "worse" and much more difficult of correction than the ones discussed above. This essay has concentrated altogether on the economy's behavior "inside the corridor" (as I have termed it elsewhere), For a discussion of "outside of corridor" pathology, I must refer the reader to an earlier companion piece of this paper.[115]

XII. CODA

In the present era of interminable monetary mismanagement, one feels almost apologetic for taking a continued interest in the problems of Keynesian economics. All the Wicksell Connection theorists had one presumption in common, namely, the notion that the "Dark Forces of Time and Ignorance," as Keynes put it, will make intertemporal economic activities the most difficult to coordinate and that the saving-investment problem, therefore, was the likely place to start in looking for the key to macroeconomic instability. Over the last fifteen years or so, however, the Forces cloaked by Darkness are not the future wishes of customers or innovations of competitors, but primarily the erratic monetary policies that emerge from the confused and unprincipled interaction of the Administration, Congress, and Federal Reserve System. It is probable enough, however, that we would experience some investment fluctuations even in the unlikely event of a return to monetary stability. That a policy regime that eliminated purely monetary sources of disturbance would also eliminate the business cycle

---

113. Note that the low short-rate/low-velocity data points, that would be generated in this way, do not belong on the steady-state money demand function. Hence, my suspicion, indicated above, that the usual Latané-type time-series estimates get too high a value for the interest-elasticity of the transactions demand for cash.

114. R. E. Lucas, Jr., (1977).

115. Leijonhufvud (1973).

remains a less than convincing Monetarist conjecture. It remains worthwhile to try to understand the Wicksell Connection theories correctly. This is so, for that matter, even when as now monetary mismanagement is the obvious source of our problems for it is not likely that monetary instability has made the coordination of intertemporal activities any easier.

CHAPTER EIGHT

Monetary Theory in Hicksian Perspective*

In one field of economic theory after another, Professor Hicks is now providing us with his considered views of achievements, problems, and prospects. Anyone must be impressed by taking stock of his recent output: first the greatly expanded second edition of *The Theory of Wages* (1963), then *Capital and Growth* (1965)—Part I of which could well have deserved the prominence that publication as a separate volume on Methods of Dynamic Analysis would have given it—and now the *Critical Essays in Monetary Theory*. Professor Hicks' judgments on the State of the Arts automatically command attention: in all of these fields he has made landmark contributions that have been influential in shaping their development. For more than three decades he has followed theoretical developments closely—his willingness and ability to keep abreast of tools and techniques one can only admire—and the sense of balance and proportion which this perspective so often lends to his recent works is not the least benefit that the reader has to gain.

The state of monetary theory is at present quite unsettled and Hicks' commentary on it is particularly welcome because of the immense influence that he has had over the development of modern "pure" monetary theory. Although the monetary parts of *Value and Capital,* as well as the "monetary reservations" appended to the "real" model of his *Contributions to the Theory of*

* A Review of Sir John Hicks, *Critical Essays in Monetary Theory,* Oxford: Oxford University Press, 1967. I am indebted to Meyer Burstein, Harry G. Johnson, and Earl Thompson for their comments and to the Relm Foundation for the grant on which this article was written.

Trade Cycle, made much less of an impact than the other parts of these works, his two famous "Suggestions" from the thirties have emerged in retrospect as the twin roots from which much of postwar monetary theory has sprung. Both these seminal suggestions—"A Suggestion for Simplifying the Theory of Money" (1934), and "Mr. Keynes and the 'Classics'—A Suggested Interpretation" (1937)—are reprinted here (as Nos. 4 and 7). For the rest, however, this collection consists almost wholly of new material.

The essays are "Critical." The tone is low-keyed and the style almost conversational, but this should not mislead—it is not by accident that the title does not present them as just plain "Essays." What lends particular interest to this book is that Professor Hicks' critical attitude in such large measure is directed towards aspects of modern monetary theory that stem from his Two Suggestions of thirty years ago.[1] His dissatisfaction with the current state of "pure" monetary theory is plain. Yet, although the critical observations are numerous, an overall Hicksian diagnosis of what ails it is hard to distill. Correspondingly, on the constructive side, Hicks makes clear in the very first paragraph of his Preface that he is not trying for a grand analytical synthesis but rather to illuminate the "many-sided truth" from different angles. Consequently, we find numerous—which is not to say just minor—suggestions for "Re-complicating the Theory of Money."

For the reviewer this means that, although dealing with a single author, the old Festschrift-excuse is almost unavoidable: It is impossible to give adequate attention to all the topics that Hicks comments upon. There is much here to stimulate—and to provoke—any monetary economist. By the nature of the book, however, different readers are apt to be stimulated or provoked by quite different things in it. It will be no surprise if, when the reviews appear, they will be hard to recognize as dealing with the same work. The critical reflections that follow are one man's reaction to this "many-sided book."

One thing is very clear: Professor Hicks' dissatisfaction with

1. These bear rereading—with the 1934 paper in particular it is probably a rare reader who will not, like this reviewer, experience a bit of a shock at how selectively he has remembered the original argument.

current doctrines stems in very large part from the feeling that we still have not got the "Keynesian Revolution" in the right perspective—and that, until we do, a firm foundation for further progress has not been achieved. So, Keynes' name, "and his alone, appears in every essay in this book" (p. ix).[2] It would be pure self-indulgence on this reviewer's part to pursue this theme in detail however; it is such a major theme of Hicks' book that it cannot be suppressed, but the book contains a wealth of other matters that call for attention.

The book falls into two parts. The first contains "a revision . . . and completion of Keynes's theory of money . . . in a narrow sense," i.e., basically Keynes' Liquidity Preference Doctrine. This is the theoretically most ambitious part of the book. The main argument is set out in three lectures on the "two Triads" (Nos. 1–3), to which is appended a paper on "The Pure Theory of Portfolio Selection" (No. 6). The 1934 Suggestion also belongs in this part.

The second part starts with the 1937 Suggestion and then backtracks—the main effort is to help us get the Keynesian Revolution straight less by analytical clarification than by providing historical perspective. It is best that we begin with the essays in this part for one of them does present a grand and sweeping generalization, such as the purely theoretical essays do not attempt, and which may, therefore, provide more of a clue to Hicks' overall views than can be found in the first part.

I

It would appear that Professor Hicks' disaffection with postwar developments in monetary theory began to crystallize with the appearance of Patinkin's first edition.[3] In that work, Hicks was, so to speak, brought face-to-face with his own Two Suggestions, now fully realized: (a) Patinkin's handling of the demand for real balances by including them in the utility-function followed the 1934 Suggestion to forget the old conundrum that "money

2. To those who have followed Hicks' writings in recent years, this is no surprise. Cf., e.g., *The Theory of Wages*, 2nd ed., pp. 355–62, and *Capital and Growth*, Chapters VII, X, XXIII.

3. D. Patinkin (1956).

is not demanded for its own sake," to drop the various mechanical contrivances for analytically handling monetary phenomena associated with it, and to deal with money as a "good" to which the proven tools of value-theory should be applied as to any other; (b) and the structure of Patinkin's model as a whole, of course, stemmed from the 1937 Suggestion as nurtured in the interim by Modigliani, Metzler, and many others. But Hicks, upon encountering his two brain-children thus fully grown, was dismayed. Something had gone wrong. For Hicks also felt himself a Keynesian and Patinkin's book was, as he perceived, not written "to elucidate the 'Keynesian Revolution,' but to deny that it is a revolution at all."

The choice before Hicks (and before the profession at large) at this stage of the "Keynes and the Classics" debate was threefold: (i) one could accept the Neoclassical Synthesis and the attendant conception of Keynes as a Classical writer with a particularly strong attachment to certain special assumptions, such as the downward inflexibility of money wages. Alternatively, one could stick to the view that the revolution was genuine and that people who did not see a yawning gulf between Keynes and the Classics must either (ii) have missed something quite important in Keynes, or (iii) have conceded altogether too much to the Classics.

Now, Hicks felt in 1957, and still feels in 1967 (p. vii) that his 1937 Suggestion was "not a bad representation of Keynes."[4] In his first attempt to grapple with Patinkin's challenge, he con-

---

4. In the view of this reviewer [cf. Leijonhufvud (1968a)], the IS-LM model has not served as an adequate representation of Keynes. But the very real virtues of the 1937 Suggestion should be acknowledged: (a) the distinction between the production of investment goods and of consumption goods—vital to both the *Treatise* and the *General Theory*—is not here obliterated as it later on became; (b) the relationship that the *General Theory* retained to Wicksell is appropriately emphasized as it has only seldom been since; and (c) the limitations of a strictly comparative static use of the basic apparatus are transgressed in several passages. Thus, one finds here, for example, the suggestion that the analysis of certain processes (i.e., not states) will require postulating an upward-sloping IS-schedule—a suggestion but recently revived and then by three writers at once. Cf. H. G. Johnson (1967), p. 250.

Yet, in reading the present volume, it is hard to escape the suspicion that Hicks' (tempered) satisfaction with the 1937 interpretation is due, in part, to the fact that there are certain important things about Keynes' theory of money "in the narrow sense" of which he has been aware for a very long time and which he has tended to take for granted in the re-reading—although they are not actually spelled out in the 1937 paper in sufficient detail to be readily apprehended by others and are, in fact, only now worked out in the "Two Triads."

sequently chose—in essence—alternative (iii), as indicated by the skeptical query that gave the title to his 1957 *Economic Journal* response: "A Rehabilitation of 'Classical' Economics?" It appears here as "The 'Classics' again" (No. 8)—significantly not as "Keynes again"—abridged by the omission of passages directly referring to Patinkin's book. In trying to show that the two theories "do not overlap all the way," Hicks' intuition took him to the right starting-point, namely, Keynes' preoccupation with "conditions in which the interest-mechanism will not work" (p. 143). But, on the mutually agreed-upon ground-rules between him and Patinkin, this meant putting the static "Liquidity Trap" case on center stage.[5] In belaboring this case, Hicks completely overlooked Patinkin's demonstration of how the real balance effect, acting through the wealth-saving relation, would get the system out of the postulated predicament. What the outcome showed, therefore, was that, *on the given comparative static ground rules*, Patinkin simply could not be dislodged.[6] Still, students have something to learn from the 1957 paper, namely, the various ways in which the IS-LM apparatus can be adapted to different sets of short-run and long-run assumptions.

Four more essays in this collection are predicated on Hicks' conviction that the major part of his trouble with Keynes is that his 1937 effort did "not get his predecessors . . . at all right."[7]

5. Cf. Leijonhufvud (1969), First Lecture:III.

6. The *General Theory*, as Patinkin pointed out, lends no textual support for stressing the static "Liquidity Trap" idea. Hicks' 1957 version also introduced what appeared, as worded, as a misleading distinction between Wicksell and Keynes (p. 153): "[Keynes] is maintaining that the LL curve becomes horizontal [over certain ranges] not because the banking system is choosing to make it horizontal, but because it is unable to act in any other way." Keynes' discussions of the reasons for the inflexibility of market rate focus on the inflexibility of long rates caused by speculation on the Exchanges, and even in the *Treatise* it is hard to find direct textual support for the idea that the trouble lies in the banking system's *inability* to act otherwise than it is doing.

Hicks has, however, returned to explain the point fully in *Capital and Growth,* Chapter XXIII and, as there elaborated, his view of the situation in the short-term end of the maturity spectrum is, indeed, a needed complement to the picture that Keynes gave of the long-term end. The *Capital and Growth* analysis focuses on the "gap" between the rate of profit expected on real investments (the maximum rate in the system) and the rate, if any, paid on money (the minimum rate). Within this gap, the whole hierarchy of financial intermediaries "has got to be squeezed in" while allowing room for them to "cover bad debts . . . and administrative expenses." Thus, the gap (p. 289) "is compressible to some extent, but it is not indefinitely compressible."

7. Cf. also the Memoir of Sir Dennis Robertson in Hicks' selection of "the best of D. H. Robertson" [Robertson (1966)], and the 1968 paper on Hawtrey included in Hicks (1977).

Of the four, the one dealing with the predecessor most important to understand—the Keynes of the *Treatise* (No. 11)—is in the nature of a Reader's Guide (for "those who have learned their economics since, say, 1940") and, as such, very useful. The distinctions between the "Three Stages" of Keynes' type of process-analysis introduced on p. 191, and then utilized to good effect, are something that every reader of Keynes should have a clear grasp of. The essay provides an introduction to, but does not treat, "the strictly monetary chapters of the *Treatise*" which, as Hicks rightly stresses, are the best of that work.[8]

II

The two remaining historical essays are the important ones. "Thornton's *Paper Credit*" (No. 10) introduces the modern student to a writer "in the front rank of monetary economists; he is the peer of those that we have seen in our own time" (p. 186). One quite agrees—Thornton, in fact, can provide needed escape from the monetary economics of our own time. To admirers of Thornton, Hicks' preoccupation with Keynes obtrudes—inevitably (one feels, having come this far in the book), Thornton is presented merely as a precursor of Keynes. An economist, on whom Hicks has the word of D. H. Robertson: "Oh, Thornton, he knew everything," could well deserve to stand on his own.

The Thornton paper should be read together with "Monetary Theory and History—An Attempt at Perspective" (No. 9), a key piece in this collection. The sweep and style of the grand generalization attempted in this essay is at first exhilarating—but on repeated re-readings increasingly troubling. Hicks sketches the evolution of monetary theory in terms of two opposed traditions, the "metallic money" school and the "credit

8. "The Hayek Story" (No. 12) serves to put a nowadays much neglected name before modern students. But it does not give the whole Hayek story, or the most important part of it, or even Hayek's final word on the part it does consider. It starts out as the story of one book—*Prices and Production*—and its impact on the London School group of that time, documenting their fascination with Hayek's analysis—and their utter disbelief in his result. It develops into a strange and curious exercise: a search for a different question (and a different set of assumptions) to go with Hayek's answer. It ends up by converting Hayek's early effort into a piece of modern growth theory that implies a warning against mismanagement of planning in today's underdeveloped countries!

school." The main protagonists are, on the one hand, Ricardo and, on the other, Thornton (supported, before and aft, by Hume and Mill, portrayed in their disequilibrium moments). The sketch is set against the backdrop of the historical evolution from metallic money systems to highly developed credit systems with a complex structure of financial intermediaries—an evolution punctuated by crises as it ran ahead of the theory, or means, of control.

Hicks takes a categorical stand on the import of this historical development that is best conveyed by quoting him directly:

> Even if we say that metallic money has given place to credit money, we are still not getting to the bottom of what happened. For credit money is just a part of a whole credit structure that extends outside money; it is closely interwoven with a whole system of debts and credits, of claims and obligations, some of which are money, some of which are not, and some of which are on the edge of being money. . . . In a world of banks and insurance companies, money markets and stock exchanges, *money is quite a different thing* from what it was before these institutions came into being. . . .
>
> Metallic money is an expensive way of performing a simple function; . . . That is the reason why the credit system grows. . . . there is the penalty that *the credit system is an unstable system.* It rests upon confidence and trust; when trust is absent it can just shrivel up. It is unstable in the other direction too; when there is too much "confidence" or optimism it can explode in bursts of speculation.[9]

In Britain, the Radcliffe Report influence is still strong, and such flat assertions may, perhaps pass all but unnoticed. Most American monetary economists, whether or not they generally agree with Friedman and Schwartz, Cagan, Brunner and Meltzer, Meigs, Morrison, et al., will recognize that "them are fighting words."[10]

The trouble is that it is hard to assign meaning to the statement that "the credit system is unstable" in the absence of a specific historical and institutional frame of reference: *Which*

9. Pp. 157–58, italics added.

10. For a position opposed to the view that "money is quite a different thing" in the presence of near-moneys, etc., cf. Yeager (1968). For Friedman's position on the "inherent instability of credit," cf. his Henry Simons lecture [Friedman (1967)]. Note also how Simons, as portrayed by Friedman, cuts clear across Hicks' line between the two traditions—to which we come below—in being a believer *both* in the "instability of credit" *and* in "rules" as opposed to discretion.

system are we considering? What kind of exogenous disturbances are we assuming it to be exposed to? Any banking-*cum*-intermediary structure, built on fractional reserves, will prove a house of cards in the event that the source of ultimate liquidity is pulled out from under. But Hicks, one infers (see below), is thinking of the monetary consequences of real disturbances. To judge what *degree* of "instability" is to be expected from such causes (or, in the extreme, whether trust is likely to absent itself altogether), one must first decide which factors on the monetary supply side can reasonably be impounded in the *ceteris paribus*—at which point some historical/institutional frame of reference must be brought to bear. In terms of pure comparative statics, it is true, it is sufficient that the monetary authority control *some* nominal quantity (and some rate of return).[11] But for the problem at hand, the theorems that emerged out of the Neutrality-debate are of little help. In practice, we would be interested in knowing whether the monetary authority's effective control extends only to some "liquid" stock, which the evolution of credit has reduced to the "small change" of the system, or whether we can assume—as the American Neo-Quantity Theorists would do—that it has the power and will to control some broadly defined "M." The amplitude of the fluctuations to be expected, if the controlled stock is held steady, should be less in the latter case. What will particularly provoke many American readers about Hicks' historical use of the "inherent instability of credit," however, is that his discussion seems to suggest that the Great Artists of Central Banking of the past can be rated largely on the basis of how important this notion loomed in their thinking.

Ricardo and his contemporaries, says Hicks, perceived the instability associated with credit money and "it frightened them quite a bit" (p. 159). To Ricardo:

> . . . it was natural still to regard the metallic money as primary; the notes and bills (which already existed) as a tiresome, but secondary, qualification. If only the secondary money would behave like primary money, there would be no trouble! So let us try to make it behave like primary money. Then we can carry on in our thinking with a simple, easily understandable, primary money model.

11. Cf., esp., Patinkin's review of Gurley and Shaw [Patinkin (1961)].

The passage suggests the dual themes that Hicks proceeds to develop as characteristic of the Ricardian monetary tradition: (a) the use of a "metallic money model," and (b) the preference for reducing monetary policy "to procedure by a mechanical rule" (e.g., p. 164).

Hicks associates the characteristics of the metallic money model with Ricardo's *long-run approach*—it is a model in which saving and investment solely determine interest rates, the level of activity solely depends on real factors, and the quantity of money acts solely on the level of prices (cf. p. 159). In sum, a model in which *monetary causes have no real effects*. It is conceded to Ricardo that he sometimes "acted as if he believed" in transient real effects of significant magnitude. But "he was the great creator of the static equilibrium method . . . ; it was his method. . . . [and] he tended to rush from one equilibrium to another much too quick" (p. 162).

That seems a fair characterization of Ricardo. It is when Hicks firmly connects it with the second theme and proceeds to map out "Ricardo's followers" that one realizes that one must part company with him someplace along the way. Ricardo and his followers maintained "that all would be well if by some device credit money could be made to behave like metallic money"—from which we are brought in one dizzying leap to the "Ricardians still among us" and the names of Milton Friedman and Jacques Rueff (p. 167)! Hicks' Preface fills us in on intervening names, however: Lord Overstone and his Currency School friends, Mises, Hayek, and Pigou.[12]

The "Credit School"—with the lineage from Thornton going over Tooke and the Banking School, Mill and Bagehot, to Hawtrey, Robertson, and Keynes—gets much the best of it on the criteria that Hicks' discussion suggests. There are corresponding dual themes—one analytical, one of policy-orientation—on this side. On both counts, Thornton differs from Ricardo by paying far more attention to problems of the short run. "*Paper Credit* is not, in form, a theoretical book; it contains no model-building, such as we find in Ricardo" (pp. 174–75).

---

12. . . . and (p. viii n.) "all the progeny" of Pigou's famous "The Classical Stationary State," *Economic Journal* 1943—here, one must presume, Hicks sees a criterion by which at last to disassociate himself from Patinkin.

But Thornton does not only recognize the stickiness of wages and, therefore, that "in the short period monetary casues may have real effects"; his analysis also recognizes liquidity preference and, therefore, that *"real causes have monetary effects"* [p. 164, italics added].

From the last point, as Hicks tells the story, the policy-orientation of the Credit School all follows:

> Thornton accordingly held that a credit system must be *managed.* It must be managed by a Central Bank, whose operations must be determined by judgement, and cannot be reduced to procedure by a mechanical rule (p. 164).

> [To Thornton] . . . to fall back on rules, making the monetary system mechanical, is a confession of failure (p. 187).

> Mill is unable to follow Ricardo in looking for mechanical rules by which credit is to be controlled; it can only be controlled by quite subtle appreciation of the "feel" of the market, by monetary *policy* (p. 166).[13]

American Neo-Quantity Theorists, as forewarned, *will* be provoked!

Now, *any* attempt to cut one clear dividing line through nearly two hundred years of tangled monetary controversies must of necessity be pretty brutal to some past writers and thus offend the sensibilities of some of the living as well—particularly when executed within twenty pages, as it is here. If the attempt could serve today's students as a preliminary introduction to a literature well worth consulting, it would still be worth doing. The question is whether Hicks is more brutal than strictly necessary. This reviewer finds his sketch overdrawn. The monetary history part lacks sufficient concrete detail. Generalizations about attitudes on "rule versus discretion" make little sense without reference to the specific rule being considered, to the methods of monetary management to which it is to be added, to the kind of disturbances that monetary management is viewed as having to cope with and, finally, without reference to the policy-priorities that the participants in the various controversies argued from. A few notes must suffice to indicate in what respects Hicks' schema fits ill:

13. Cf. also p. viii, on the "wing of the Credit party" which not only "believes in monetary management, but also believes that it is necessary to be eclectic in the kind of management, and the means of management, that are to be used in each particular situation."

Hicks lays much stress on Thornton's belief "in the necessity of monetary management" (p. 165). But Tooke and other members of the Banking School, that succeed him in Hicks' schema, were not only opposed to the Currency School's narrow definition of "money"—they also originated the "real bills" doctrine. And this doctrine, of course, does not argue the "necessity" of monetary management, but the exact opposite. There is much in Tooke and Fullarton about the "judgment of bankers," to be sure, but the judgement they were primarily espousing was that of the commercial banker considering the "soundness" of bills and the "needs of trade." [14]

Hicks does note (p. 171) that "In the old days, when monetary control was exercised by Central Bankers, their primary concern was the stability of the currency in terms of foreign exchange." I believe that the trouble one has with Hicks' discussion of the early writers is due in very large part to his failure to accord this, their fundamental preconception, the place it deserves. At the back of their heads they all had some version of the Price-Specie Flow Mechanism as the ultimate "natural" regulator of the value of money. In stressing that Thornton recognized that "real causes have monetary effects," Hicks notes that Thornton's favorite exercise starts by assuming a harvest-failure. But Thornton's harvest-failure does not work its monetary effects via liquidity preference as in Keynes or Radcliffe: It causes a temporary adverse turn in the trade balance and, therefore, an "external drain" of the bank reserve medium forcing a multiple contraction of the money supply (and, by all means, bank credit). The development of fractional reserve banking since Hume's time had added a disturbingly powerful amplifer to the Price-Specie Flow Mechanism. Later on the Bank of England was to develop the use of Bank Rate to help bring about the appropriate short-term capital flows to offset such erratic shocks to the trade balance, but in the first part of the century this problem was a very major concern of all the most prominent writers on monetary questions. In that context, if you did not dare let the amplified Price-Specie Flow Mechanism run its course without intervention, while at the

---

14. Cf. F. W. Fetter (1965), pp. 190–92, and T. E. Gregory (1928), pp. 25ff.

same time you accepted without much question as your "primary concern . . . the stability of the currency in terms of foreign exchange," then it becomes pretty natural to stress the need for the discretionary exercise of "judgment" on the part of the lender of last resort. Similarly, opposition to the "mechanical rule" of fixed reserve ratios is, in the same light, readily understandable, since it would doom you to experience amplified movements in the domestic money supply—particularly if defined as the Banking School (correctly) wanted it.[15]

But that rule, seen in the context suggested, obviously has a quite different import from the latter-day rule of stabilizing the (rate of growth of) the money supply. I cannot see any basis at all why opposition to the one should be regarded as foreshadowing opposition to the other. If we could have sampled these early writers for their views on the Friedman rule (assuming, implausibly, that we could first get them to agree on a definition of "money supply"), they would probably have argued that stabilizing the domestic money supply in the face of an external drain would be to endanger convertibility and thus to invite an even more dangerous "internal drain." But if we asked them to toy with the idea under the assumption that they were provided with an Exchange Equalization Fund, well-developed open market operations techniques, and a populace long accustomed to a fiat standard, it is difficult to imagine what they would say—except for expressing bewilderment at our strangely reckless monetary policy-ambitions and policy-priorities. But surely one could depend on Torrens, the old Colonel of Marines, sternly to excommunicate Professor Friedman from the "metallic money school" to which Hicks has assigned him: "Once deviate from the golden rule of causing fluctuations of our mixed circulation to conform to what would be the fluctuations of a purely metallic currency and the flood-gates are opened, and the landmarks removed."[16]

15. Fetter, *op cit.*, pp. 188–89, 192ff.
16. Fetter, *op cit.*, p. 193. But to surmise that Torrens would have thrust Friedman into the outer darkness reserved for flexible exchange rate advocates (there to keep company with Keynes—but not with Rueff) is not to say that Torrens could not (in Fetter's paraphrase) sound like Friedman too: "The need for discretion would never arise if the Bank directors had not previously misguidedly used their discretion . . ." (Fetter, *op cit.*, p. 169). Lord Overstone, however, will not fit the Neo-Quantity theorists at all: "Fluctuations in the amount of currency are seldom, if ever, the original cause of fluctuations in prices and in the state of trade" (Gregory, *op cit.*, p. 20n).

The "Perspective," finally, has been developed in order to place Keynes in it, and Keynes, of course, comes out as revolting against the Ricardian tradition in monetary theory. But surely, this is much too narrow a definition of the "Classics" that Keynes attacked. Ricardo on Money is so self-evidently long run that it seems very doubtful that someone with Keynes' concentration on short-run problems would ever have regarded him as a figure from whom it was necessary to "struggle to escape." On the one issue—Say's Law—where the *General Theory* really tears into Ricardo, he is lumped together with Mill.[17] There is only one reflection on Ricardo's monetary theory "in the narrow sense." It is hidden in the "Notes on Mercantilism, Etc." (p. 340), where Keynes commends Ricardo's predecessors: "There was wisdom in their intense preoccupation with keeping down the rate of interest . . . *by maintaining the stock of money* . . ." etc. [italics added].

Despite all one's objections to the overall schema, many of Hicks' observations on the opposing viewpoints of monetary writers strike one as being so tantalizingly *right* that the reader must be tempted to try his own hand at sorting out the viewpoints into Two Traditions. For example:

We may define "Quantity Theories" in the widest possible sense as all those approaches to monetary theory which start out by defining some given collection of assets as "M" and go on to analyze changes in money income in terms of the factors determining the demand for and supply of the good, "M." (This may, or may not, be couched in terms of changes in the M-stock and in the correspondingly defined "velocity.") Thus defined, "the" Quantity Theory has been the predominant approach through the history of monetary theory.

But there have always been heretics claiming that the focus on the M-stock (as contemporaneously defined) can be seriously misleading. Not always misleading, nor misleading perhaps when the "Long View" is taken, but likely to be misleading in the short run on occasion—the occasions being "when it really counts." Coupled with this criticism has been their insistence that changes in the M-stock should be seen as just one aspect of

---

17. And since, as Hicks emphasizes, the multiplier was the one piece of Keynes that Thornton did not have, Keynes might presumably have turned on him as well. For a re-interpretation of Keynes' attack on Say's Law, cf. my (1968), Chapter III:3.

changes in overall "liquidity" or "credit." But theories of the heretical description—which we may call the "Liquidity School," perhaps—have proved less amenable to rigourous formulation and algebraic manipulation than the Quantity Theories.

There have been several periods in which the heretics have been in the ascendancy for some time—the Radcliffe/Gurley-Shaw movement only being the most recent instance. Usually, this ascendancy has been gained when the heretics have become quite specific in their criticism—arguing that some particular development in payments practices, or the increasing use of some particular credit instrument, has made the reigning Quantity analysis, based on some inherited definition of "M," too unreliable for short-term practical purposes. Rejecting Quantity orthodoxy, because "velocity" has become too unpredictable, has then often been coupled with a plea for the "feel" of Central Bankers as the best guide remaining.

The evolution of the credit system, that Hicks stresses, has of course several times caught up with the inherited Quantity Theory of the day. But whenever, in the past, the heretics have seemed near gaining the majority, victory has, so far, always been snatched away from them by an adept redefinition of "M." So, we have gone from M equals stock of coins, by way of M equals coins plus bank notes, to M equals currency plus demand deposits, and in recent years the old controversy has flared over M_1 versus M_2, with some advocating various M_3's—and the ever-present heretic "purists" insisting on "liquidity in general" in the background.[18] There is always hope for the Liquidity school: In a decade or two, the computerization of the payments mechanism may catch up with Professor Friedman and associates! And there is no theoretical principle to ensure that there will always be a workable re-definition of "M" possible on the basis of which the Quantity tradition can regain its feet.

The schema is crude, of course. With reference to Hicks' attempt, the specific trouble with the above suggestion is that it

18. Of the two, the Quantity theory presents by far the better framework for empirical and historical research, the Liquidity approach far more, and more intriguing, riddles for "purely" theoretical work. Scientific philosophy or temperament may have a good deal to do with the division of Great Names that one would find between the Two Traditions.

leaves Keynes hovering uneasily between my Two Traditions. Keynes, who favored the M_2 definition throughout, was a "variable velocity Quantity theorist" at least up through the *Treatise,* and one hesitates to put him categorically in the Liquidity school on the basis of the *General Theory.*

III

Another, even broader, division of doctrine-history into Two Traditions is suggested by one of Hicks' most striking observations:

> Monetary theory is less abstract than most economic theory; it cannot avoid a relation to reality, which in other economic theory is sometimes missing. It belongs to monetary history in a way that economic theory does not always belong to economic history. . . . . a large part of the best work on Money is topical. . . . monetary theories arise out of monetary disturbances (p. 156).

A non-economist reading this passage would presumably conclude that the monetary theorists of the past must, because of their preoccupation with the particular issues of their own day, appear more "dated" and less interesting to the modern reader than the "general" theorists of the same period. But, indubitably, the very opposite is true. A modern monetary theorist will have much more to learn from Thornton than the price theorist from Ricardo. The reason, of course, is that value theory has progressed "cumulatively" in a way that monetary theory has not. A brief comparison of value theory and the Art of Central Banking will show why this should be so. It will also serve to indicate the perspective from which this reviewer has read the "Two Triads" while trying to decide in what respects these three new essays depart significantly from, or retain continuity with, the monetary theory of the 1934 Suggestion and of *Value and Capital.*

Value theory has been the study of equilibrium states. It concerns the logic of collectively consistent individual decisions. The effects of specified disturbances are studied in terms of comparative statics, going directly—and, for some purposes, much too quickly—from the initial state to a terminal (long-run) state in which each and every individual decision-maker has adjusted fully (in all those aspects of his behavior that are admitted as variable for the problem at hand). The restriction to "collectively consistent" states allows the system to be studied piecemeal with full faith that the pieces will fit together. The building blocks are provided by the logic of individual (optimal) choice. Since it is foreordained that all activities will mesh, the decision-problems of representative transactors are described *as if* they planned on the basis of full information (at least, in a probabilistic sense) of what everybody else *will be* doing. All plans are realized—the equilibria are states in which all participants occupy positions *"voluntarily"* chosen, while constrained by the activities of others only to obey the simple collective rule of giving equal value in exchanges of private property rights. The patron saint of this tradition ought (again) to be Ricardo, and the line of descent most pertinent here would go: Walras— Hicks' *Value and Capital*—Samuelson's *Foundations*—Patinkin.

The traditional subject matter of the Art of Central Banking has been banking panics and other monetary disorders. The reality dealt with is a mess not in the least resemblant of the states described above, and the field itself is undisciplined when compared with the logic of Value theory. The value theorist can use his equilibrium conditions to check the consistency of his analysis; the student of monetary disequilibria cannot do so, and engages in "no model-building, such as we find in Ricardo."[19] Analysis involves the description of short-run *processes*. The chain of events is often outlined in a manner that is wholly alien to value theorists in its "mechanical" handling of individual decisions and in its emphasis on their "forced" or "involuntary" nature. For example: "Gold flows out of the country and the Bank of England is *forced to* contract. The country banks lose reserves and *have no choice* but to contract their credit. The manufacturers refused credit *have to* shut down," etc. The patron saint is Thornton. Various writers from both the Banking School and the Currency School belong here, as does Bagehot and, perhaps, Hawtrey and the Radcliffe Report. Keynes, once more, will not fit neatly. He (and Robertson) tried to marry the

19. As Hicks (p. 175) says about Thornton.

two traditions by casting the analysis of monetary disequilibria in the form of "short-run comparative statics"—a *mèsalliance* that proved productive of momentous confusions.

Hicks' 1934 Suggestion was received as a call for value theorists to take over the undisciplined banking theory enterprise. In the hands of Patinkin, in particular, the value-theoretical method proved useful in purging the field of invalid dichotomies and sundry other confusions. But, on the more constructive side, the use of pure comparative statics gave predictably meager results: a class of neutrality or invariance theorems showing that, in a Walrasian full information world, monetary causes have no real effects. About monetary disorders the value-theoretical reformation of monetary theory had nothing new to say—it is silent on the traditional subject matter of the Art. In the United States the Art died out in the Keynesian Revolution and was never resurrected. When interest in monetary theory revived after the war it was all concentrated on "Ricardian" model-building. And this reformation defused Keynes completely.

So we come back to Professor Hicks' dissatisfaction with this development. The "Two Triads" report his reconsideration of the foundations of Monetary theory.[20] It is a thoughtful re-examination, conservative rather than radical in approach. To this reviewer, reading these essays from the viewpoint sketched above, they have the peculiar fascination of a high-wire balancing act—a balancing act between the Two Traditions: If you lean too far towards the Art, you lose the support of the rigorous models of equilibrium theory; if too far in the other direction, you lose analytical contact with the subject matter of monetary disequilibria.

From this standpoint, it is the first essay dealing with the means of payment function and the transactions demand that is the most fascinating of the three. The essay starts out insisting "on the primacy of the Means of Payment function" (p. x), and

20. The usual distinctions between money's functions as a unit of account, as a means of payment, and as a store of value gives Hicks one of his "triads." The other refers to Keynes' three motives—transactions, precautionary, and speculative—for demanding money.

ends up, intriguingly, on the very last page by drawing back from the brink of assigning primacy also to a Fisherian transactions demand.

Hicks begins by seeking to isolate the means of payment function for study, i.e.,

> . . . by constructing a model to which, in other respects, the Walras theory ought to apply exactly. I shall then ask how that model is to be developed, in order that a money, *which is to be no more than a means of payment,* is to be fitted in (p. 3).

The approach to this problem takes a different turn from what we are used to in Walrasian general equilibrium theory. The reason for this is, at least, implicit in Hicks' discussion. I would put it as follows: If we construct our explanation of the Social Contrivance of Money from the usual building blocks of the theory of individual choice alone, some aspects of the social institution will escape us in a way that can, embarrassingly, only be covered up by resort to brute tautologies—"Money is accepted because it is accepted," and so forth.

Hicks decides, therefore, that

> [to follow Patinkin and add to Walras' barter-model] a "demand for real balances" on the same level as the demand for commodities for want-satisfaction, seems to me to do no more than cut the knot.[21]

His approach from there on is, in effect, that known in the other social sciences as "functionalism." It is interesting to see how, in taking a different approach, his *language* soon comes to echo that which I have above associated with the older Central Banking literature and characterized as "alien to value theory."

The analysis consists of a series of conceptual experiments[22] involving alternative institutional arrangements that a society could adopt to minimize transactions costs under multilateral trade. Exchange of goods and services continuously generates enormous numbers of individual debits and credits, recorded in terms of a unit of account. The essential "social accounting problem"—and I wish Hicks had put even heavier stress on this—is to ensure that no one "gets away with" systematically

21. Hicks, *op cit.,* p. 3. Patinkin, needless to say, was just following the 1934 Hicks.

22. For an excellent effort along identical lines which must be accorded priority, cf. R. E. Kuenne (1963), pp. 288–301.

appropriating resources from the rest of the collective of a greater value than he contributes. The concept of *default* thus emerges as fundamental to monetary theory: "some arrangement which provides a guarantee against uncleared debts. . . . some sanction against the abuse of debt facilities is required" (pp. 8–9). If debits and credits to individual accounts are not to be kept track of indefinitely, they must be systematically extinguished. Hicks presents commodity money and clearing as two "pure" alternative arrangements to provide for this function. The payments mechanism provided by demand deposit banking emerges as a mixed form.

In the early part of the essay, Hicks deals with a single, once-and-for-all trading period. If, with the banking arrangement, it is necessary to have credits previously recorded at the bank, "it is tempting to say that bank credit has now become *money*. . . . But there is not yet any demand to hold this money" (p. 11). In this model, designed to isolate the means of payment function, "money is not demanded for its own sake." So:

> At the beginning of the day, none of the traders is in debt or in credit with the Bank. At the end of the day, the same is true. The "volume" of bank credit builds up while sales are proceeding. . . ; but it still sinks back to zero at the end (p. 11).

We then go on to a more recognizable world with continuous trading—staggered trading-periods. In such a world,

> . . . there would always be money (for instance, bank money) outstanding, even if the closing of accounts, as each participant finished his business, was scrupulously maintained. *But it could not be said that there was a "demand for money for transactions purposes" in the sense of a voluntary demand,* like the demand for commodities which could be forced—even with an effort—into the mould of marginal utility theory.[23]

Clower (1967) has recently taken this institutional, "involuntary" conception of transactions balances and raised the question of how the Walrasian general barter-equilibrium model would have to be modified in order to accommodate the restrictive postulate that "Goods can *only* be bought with money." But having reached this point—and it is a far cry from his 1934

---

23. Hicks, *op cit.*, p. 14, italics added. Note that this is the exact point at which Kuenne decides (as is always an option) to turn back to the value-theoretical fold and puts money back into the individual utility-function (Kuenne, *op cit.*, p. 299).

Suggestion and from *Value and Capital,* as he points out—Hicks abruptly, and disappointingly, turns his back on the whole approach.

The proportion of the total money stock that is normally absorbed into such transactions balances, Hicks notes, is very large. But some part,

> . . . even if it is quantitatively a small part, must be attributed to voluntary holding; and this part, whatever its size, is tremendously important. For it is through the voluntary part that monetary disturbances operate, and it is on the voluntary part that monetary policy must have its effect (p. 15).

Similarly, Hicks argues, it is the voluntary demand for money that "is the live and exciting part of the monetary problem."[24]

What part of a problem excites whom is hardly amenable to discussion. But the proposition that the "voluntarily" held part of the money stock is the "important" part is, unfortunately, not much more objective in nature.[25] The ambiguities surrounding the proposition in its context are not easily dispelled. It *may* reflect an empirical judgement on Hicks' part, namely, that changes in Liquidity Preference rather than changes in money supply (or "Liquidity supply," if one so prefers) are the more "important" disturbances to which the real world system is exposed. If that reading were correct, we would again face the undercurrent of opposition to the Neo-Quantity school that runs through some of the essays in this book. But we will not take up that issue again.

The proposition may be considered from an entirely different angle. Suppose that we start from a Clower-type world where either you are able to pay cash or you exert no effective

24. Hicks' parting salvo towards the conventional conceptualization of transactions demand will, at least, excite his readers: "It is not a *demand for money,* in the way (the demand for store of value purposes) is. There is no 'Transactions Motive' behind it. . . . The old Fisher MV = PT gives a better *picture* of it than the over-voluntarized 'Cambridge Quantity Equation.' "

There is a bit of irony here: Oxford's Drummond Professor emeritus is now the heir to the Cambridge monetary tradition. Chicago's Russel Professor is the heir to the tradition founded by Fisher at Yale. Who would you think prefers M = kY and who MV = PT?

25. Many readers will react strongly against the "voluntary-involuntary" terminology. I must confess to a fondness for its deep resonances in some of the most fascinating parts of monetary doctrine history—which, unfortunately, do not signify that it is analytically helpful. Yeager's (1968) excellent treatment of the "primacy" of the Medium of Exchange function shows that it is not needed. Cf., esp., pp. 59–65.

demand at all—*all* purchases have to be financed out of money held at the outset of the trading period. Also suppose, in the first instance, that no precautionary balances are held. In that world, the effect of monetary policy would then be brutally direct, opening up a gap between the actual money stock and ("involuntary") transactions requirements.[26]

Is this picture really so fundamentally changed by introducing a "voluntarily" held part of the money stock? The "brutality" of policy will be somewhat "cushioned" in a model modified in this way, it is true. A lag—presumably a variable lag—is introduced, and effects become less accurately predictable, at least in the short run. For the immediate purposes of this discussion, moreover, admission of other forms of credit and intermediation than just bank demand deposit business, only makes for a "thicker cushion."[27] But the impact of monetary policy must still be felt through the cushion, or otherwise we will have next to no interest in its consequences. Once we have followed all the ripples of substitution-effects running their merry course through the portfolios of the system, we should find the "important" ultimate effects *on spending* at those points where some transactors find themselves with a cash-position that they would "not voluntarily" have chosen. In this sense, then, transactions *requirements* remain the fundamentally "important" part of money demand.

The point is that Hicks, after having spent the better part of the next two essays on the Precautionary and Speculative demand for money as a store of value,[28] comes to much the same conclusion. The third essay on the "Two Triads" develops a highly suggestive general classification of assets into three categories: *running assets* that are *required* in order to keep an

---

26. R. W. Clower (1967).

27. Cf. Yeager, *op cit.*, p. 61.

28. Both of these essays are material for one's reading lists. I slight them here only because most of what I have to say about them would concern Hicks' reading of Keynes on the topics involved, and I will not bore the reader by comparing notes with Professor Hicks on these matters. Suffice it to say that some of the discrepancies between himself and Keynes that Hicks is bothered by simply disappear on my reading of Keynes. Hicks' treatment, consequently, seems even closer to a "completion of Keynes' theory of money . . . in a narrow sense" from my standpoint than it does from that of the author. Hicks' treatment, moreover, is much more carefully worked out—despite being also much more compact—than anything we find in Keynes.

economic unit operating on a given scale; *reserve assets* held in order to be able to meet a variety of contingencies—i.e., the motive is *precautionary; investment assets* held for their long-term yield or for *speculative* purposes. Money held to meet transactions requirements falls into the category of running assets.

When, armed with this schema, Hicks then returns to the question of the *modus operandi* of monetary policy, he spends most of his discussion on the "live and exciting part" of the problem, i.e., on tracing the repercussions through the reserve asset positions of various types of transactors. The pressure on reserve asset positions created by a restrictive policy he terms the "liquidity pressure effect." But this effect turns out, in the end, to be merely the "compression of the cushion." The effect *on spending* still occurs when some economic units find that they "have *no alternative but* to draw money from their running assets," when "the *only way* in which the gap can be filled is by raiding the firm's running assets."[29] This means that they have no alternative but to reduce their scale of operation. At the crucial point we relapse into the "involuntary" language of the old Art! In this sense, then, the primacy of the Means of Payment function means that the "involuntary" part of cash-balances must be the ultimately "important" part.[30]

---

29. Hicks, *op cit.,* p. 51, italics added.

30. By concentrating throughout on contractionary processes, the above discussion must seem to the reader to indicate that I share Hicks' position on the "asymmetry" of monetary policy, i.e., that you can be sure of your ability to force contraction but not to induce expansion. And I do—to an extent. But I also believe it to be a position that it is all too easy to overstate. Firstly, "irreversibility" (of a process) is less misleading than "asymmetry" (of a state). Causing inflation has been no problem anywhere in the post-war years. Secondly, recognizing the compulsion that the threat of default imposes on transactors is a bit like recognizing the force of gravity when discussing aerodynamics—one had better be aware of it, but the subject does not end there. There are almost always other "forces" that the Central Bank can ally itself with—Greed, Avarice, and Covetousness, to name a few. One must not call forth a picture of transactors forever wallowing listlessly in the interior of their opportunity sets. Thirdly, the empirical evidence that adherents of the "asymmetry" idea have in mind may be of somewhat the same nature as that which would underlie the statement: "You can always be sure of getting an airplane down, but you cannot depend on always being able to get it up again." True enough, but the only "policy-implication" for fliers that follows is: "Don't crash, if you can help it." Specifically, experience following the crash of the entire U.S. financial machinery in the Depression of the thirties provides little evidence to guide monetary policy under anything like "normal" conditions.

Hicks believes (pp. vii, 52) that the "asymmetry" argument distinguishes his position from that of Patinkin. Once again, he underestimates the difficulty of shaking loose from the theorist who has done the most to demonstrate how the Hicksian Suggestions must render Keynes harmless! Cf. D. Patinkin, (1965), p. 337.

All this should not be taken as arguing for Quantity theories, whether they be old or new. On the contrary: this "ought" to be the position of *Keynesians*. For without something of this sort, Keynes' multiplier is, for all practical purposes, gone. Modern consumption-function theories tell us that the ideas of households as to "what they can afford" to spend on consumption should not be at all closely related to variations in current income. If permanent income, or some such conception of their wealth-positions over the longer run, is the relevant budget-constraint in the short run, not enough will remain of the multiplier to make it interesting. Something has to be added, if the idea at all deserves the place it has achieved in policy-discussions, Keynes' own conception of it was definitely tied to the idea that you *"have to have"* cash to exercise effective demand. What needs to be added to the permanent income conception to get to Keynes' multiplier is a *cash-constraint*—which in the "cushioned" model is seen, less rigidly, as initially a matter of "liquidity." In either version, it is implicit that the sources, human or non-human, of the household's permanent income are "illiquid." They cannot readily be turned into current purchasing power—except at prices (or interest rates) which the household, for one reason or another, is unwilling to accept. Only in this kind of situation would households feel constrained to tying their consumption purchases to current cash-receipts from sales of services—as they do when obeying Keynes' simple consumption-income relation rather than one of the modern consumption-functions.

So, Keynesians must perforce face up to the question put to them by Friedman and Schwartz: "Is it *conceivable* that the Great Deflation of the thirties would have taken the course it did, if the money supply had been kept constant?" Which is not to say that there is nothing left to tell, once the story of the sins of Central Banks has been told.

IV

Professor Hicks' latest effort contains some disappointments for his admirers. The main disappointment is his failure to interest himself seriously in, and to face up to, the work that has fueled the monetary theory debate in the United States over the last decade. The empirical work of the American Neo-Quantity theorists surely substantiates his claim that "a large part of the best work on Money is topical." In this respect, American readers will find his *Critical Essays* a critical examination of the state of monetary theory as of ten years ago.[31]

Reviewers harp on their disappointments. What a review— however long—cannot convey fairly is how densely packed this little volume is with sharp, to-the-point observations on theoretical problems and on the approaches taken to these problems by other authors. The reader's excitement is sustained, by finding bothersome nails hit squarely on the head several times on almost every page, in a way that some misses will not dispel. It is one measure of Sir John Hicks that, despite its disappointments, this is a book that every monetary economist will have to read.

31. This review article was written in the summer of 1968.

CHAPTER NINE

Costs and Consequences of Inflation*

I. INTRODUCTION

One approach to the problem of the microeconomic foundations of macro-economics takes the frame and the components of standard "neoclassical" theory as the given starting point. One asks what can be used and what needs modification for purposes of representing the movement of a macro-system through time and into a future that is in some respects unknowable. The aim is to define and, if possible, solve the analytical problems that emerge at the levels of individual conceptual experiments, market experiments, and general equilibrium experiments. I have pursued this approach in other recent papers[1] but am running into diminishing returns.

An alternative approach is to start from the other end with some "applied" problem, preferably one of such importance that no macroeconomist can really afford to dodge it, and consider the difficulties that arise in trying to handle it in a "reasonable" way with standard micro-theoretical tools. From this viewpoint we get a different critical angle on the problems requiring solution if micro- and macro-theory are to be made to mesh. This is the approach taken in this paper.

The "practical" macro-question to be considered here is that of the social costs and consequences of inflation. A new view of the welfare costs of inflation has emerged in the last ten or fif-

*I am thankful to Armen Alchian, Robert Clower, Ben Klein, John McCall and Sidney Afriat for comments and obliged to declare them free from responsibility. Financial support of the Liberty Fund is gratefully acknowledged.
1. Leijonhufvud (1974, 1974–5).

teen years. It trivialises the cost of inflation. This new view is undergirded by essentially "neoclassical" theoretical constructions and may, indeed, be regarded as a by-product of work primarily oriented toward seeking neoclassical foundations for macro-theory. In the analytical exercise that is central to this view, inflation is treated as a foreseen tax on money balances and its costs are seen to lie in the productive and transactional inefficiencies induced by such a tax. Even a quite high rate of inflation will not imply a very sizable tax as taxes go in modern mixed economies; the inefficiencies that it may induce will be correspondingly trivial.

Some economists will feel that this work has helped us put the undesirability of inflation into proper perspective by dispelling old and murky myths about its dangers. To those, my topic will not seem a promising avenue towards a fuller understanding of the trouble we are having with microeconomic foundations.

It should thus be obvious and shall in any case be openly admitted that my choice of topic is predicated on the prior conviction that in advocating or letting go unopposed this new view of inflation we have been guilty of profound and appalling naïveté. I fear that the spreading influence of the new view is dangerous in so far as it directly or indirectly influences policy.

The new view on inflation is not altogether unassailable on its own terms. But the questions about it that may be raised strictly within the neoclassical framework are probably not the important ones. Neoclassical theory—or, more precisely, its scope—is itself at issue. The social consequences of inflation most germane to "wise" conduct of economic policy may fall largely outside its purview. For this once, I do not think inside ("immanent") criticism is the tack to take. This paper wilfully refuses obedience to the neoclassical rules of the game. We begin by taking an "institutionalist" view of monetary exchange.

The institutional approach has, of course, its own limitations. One cannot be perfectly "general" (i.e., refer to all times and all places) and still retain content. The time-space reference coordinates that I have had in mind in writing this paper are (i) the last ten years or so, and (ii) the United States. Similarly, the term "inflation" in the title is not to be read as denoting a theoretically defined "pure" concept but as referring to inflationary processes "like" the one of recent years.

II. AN INSTITUTIONALIST SKETCH
OF MONETARY EXCHANGE

Whether the true idea of money, as such, is not altogether that of a ticket or counter?

—Bishop Berkeley, *The Querist*

Some of the questions on the present theoretical agenda are much older than the current movement to provide microeconomic foundations for macro-theory: Why do people hold money? Why is the set of goods serving as means of payment so small? Why are "indexed" contracts so uncommon? Etc.

One approach to these questions starts by interpreting the mathematical structure of a standard general equilibrium model as representing a multilateral "barter" system. One then seeks precise formulation of realistic assumptions about information imperfections and transactions costs that can be shown to lend a "monetary" transactions structure to the G.E. model. It is not part of my aim to criticise this research, much of which I find interesting and promising.

The point to be made here is simply that these conceptual experiments should not be given historical interpretations. The proposition that "barter is costly and inefficient" will no doubt be part of any explanation of the "use of money." That "the inefficiency of barter *leads* to the use of money," would, however, be false as an historical generalisation. Monetary exchange systems have not evolved out of non-monetary exchange ("barter") systems but out of non-exchange systems. Both intertemporal and cross-cultural comparisons show us that in the spheres of economic activity where monetary exchange does not prevail, neither do we find predominantly "private" property rights, commercial contracting, and organised markets. (These are however institutional features presumed by the "non-monetary" G.E. model.) We will still expect to find a fairly extensive division of labour but the institutional arrangements—the systems of rights and obligations governing

229

the activities of individuals—devised to ensure that the community can depend on the benefits from the division of labour will be different in kind. "Custom and Command," in the terms of Classical Economics, or "Reciprocity and Redistribution," in those of Anthropology—not barter exchange—are the alternatives to monetary exchange.[2] The development of monetary exchange is, consequently, part of a complex evolution of institutions. Perhaps the best short statement is Wesley Mitchell's famous passage:[3]

> When money is introduced into the dealings of men, it enlarges their freedom. . . . By virtue of its generalised purchasing power, money emancipates its users from numberless restrictions upon what they do and what they get. As a society learns to use money confidently, it gradually abandons restrictions upon the places people shall live, the occupations they shall follow, the circles they shall serve, the prices they shall charge, and the goods they can buy.

In largely non-monetary economies, important economic rights and obligations will be inseparable from particularised relationships of social status and political allegiance and will be in the same measure permanent, inalienable, and irrevocable.[4] Assurance of stability of the economic order is sought in tying economic functions to social roles that carry particular rights and duties vis-à-vis particular individuals or groups. In monetary exchange systems, in contrast, "the value to the owner of [his human capital or] a physical asset derives from rights, privileges, powers, and immunities against society generally rather than from the obligation of some particular person."[5] And, paraphrasing J. S. Mill, "competition is the governing principle of such contracts" as leave particular agents with a debt-claim relationship.

2. All I can do at this point is to provide a personally favoured select list of "further reading": J. S. Mill (1909) Book II, Chapter IV; F. H. Knight (1965) Chapter 1; Dalton (ed) (1968) esp. Dalton's Introduction); Hicks (1967, Chapter 9; 1969); Michael Polanyi (1969).

3. W. C. Mitchell (1944). For a summary of Mitchell's views and further references to his writings, cf. Friedman (1952).

4. Feudal land-rents, for example, cannot be "decomposed" into a rental price on land "plus" a tax on the cultivator of it; nor can the overlapping rights and interlocking obligations of a peasant, of other village members, of the manorial lord, and of the sovereign with regard to a particular piece of land be disentangled in terms of modern notions of "ownership."

5. Cf. Burstein (1963), p. 105.

Neoclassical theories rest on a set of abstractions that separate "economic" transactions from the totality of social and political interactions in the system.[6] For a very large set of important problems, this separation "works"—since we are usually dealing with monetary exchange systems. But it assumes that the events that we make the subject of conceptual experiments with the neoclassical model of the "economic system" do not affect the "socio-political system" so as to engender repercussions on the economy of such significance as to invalidate the institutional *ceteris paribus* clauses of that model.

It is not "in the nature of things" that this assumption necessarily holds. There can be no epistemological guarantee that interactions between the "economic," the "political," and the "social spheres" of the system we study will be negligible. Double-digit inflation *may* label a class of events for which the assumption is a bad one. The neoclassical conceptual experiment of a steady-state inflation, which in time becomes accurately foreseen, and to which "everything adjusts"—*except* property rights, contract forms, and the organisation of markets[7]—is at the very least a most instructive exercise. But that does not suffice to make it a good theory. It is a long-run theory. But its institutional *ceteris paribus* assumptions may not hold approximately true for that long.

We should at least keep an open mind to this disturbing possibility. We do not now have the empirical knowledge to rule it out. It may be the case that in the world we inhabit, before the "near-neutral" adjustments can all be smoothly achieved, "society *un*learns to use money confidently" and reacts by restrictions on "the circles people shall serve, the prices they shall charge, and the goods they can buy."[8] If such reactions are in

6. Exactly what all these abstractions are and what conditions will allow them validity, we are not very clear about. We are content to live with the correspondingly hazy definition of the boundaries between economics and other social sciences for, I think, the simple reason that most of the time our work is shaped by the "economic method" we use—and letting "the way economists think" establish the limits to our "territorial imperative" will almost always be good enough.

7. E.g., the line between legal and "black" markets.

8. Historical processes are not reversible. The paraphrase of Mitchell here is not intended to convey some silly suggestion of a return to feudalism or even mercantilism. It is intended to convey the judgment that an analysis of inflation that does not attempt to take political feedback on the economic process systematically into account is, in contemporary jargon, "irrelevant."

fact endogenous to the social system, we mis-identify the consequences of inflation to the extent that we regard them as fortuitous "political" events exogenously impinging on "the economy."

Mitchell uses the term "money" in a sense so broad as to cover not just all of money and banking but also the "Legal Foundations of Capitalism" (J. R. Commons) and even the psychological attitudes and calculating modes of decision-making that go with life in a society where the range of alternatives subject to the common measuring-rod of money is very wide. But something need be said also about how "money," in the narrow sense of "M," fits into such an institutionalist schema.

The stability of any social order requires (i) an exhaustive and consistent allocation of rights to economic resources, and (ii) rules for the transfer of these rights and means for keeping track of the legitimate succession to them. Disputes over the possession of rights, where the legal entitlement of the parties cannot be tracked down or otherwise "fairly" determined, must as far as possible be avoided—since the residual method of settling conflicts will be the use of force.

In monetary exchange systems, the problem of keeping track takes a particular form. The "typical" basic forms of wealth are defined in terms of rights and immunities vis-à-vis "society in general." Transactors have discretion in what they choose to sell and buy and whom they choose to sell to or buy from. The institutional problem is to ensure that no one takes more out of the system than he puts in, so that everyone is assured of being allowed to appropriate resources from the rest of society "equal" to what he has contributed to others.

Hawtrey's insistence that every transaction generates a claim and a matching debt is helpful here in leaving all questions of settlements temporarily open. The first problem is the measurement of debts and claims. We may assume them to be recorded at the prices in terms of unit of account agreed upon by the parties. In the simplest multilateral exercise, we would have only "real" transactions—involving the transfer of a physical asset, real good or service (or the forward contract for such a transfer)—to consider. Assuming "rules" allowing no financial transactions or the running of financial surplus and deficits, a purely "imaginary money,"[9] tied to no real *numéraire* good, could perfectly well serve as unit of account. The conceivable ways of "policing the rules" are legion.

As an illustration, suppose we find a short closed loop in this system where repeatedly real resources are transferred from A to B, from B to C, C to D, and from D to A, and all links in the chain happen to be quoted by the two parties at the same value in terms of "imaginary money":

1. We might decide to run a central social bookkeeping office charged with keeping the respective balance-sheets of A, B, C, and D continuously up-to-date by adding on the debts incurred and claims gained in each period. The object is simply to check that each balance sheet continues to balance. If accurate addition is cheap enough to come by, we could as well let the balance sheets go on lengthening indefinitely. Going through the motions of extinguishing debts would be superfluous.

2. We might feed all debits and credits arising from resource transfers into a computer programmed to hunt for "closed loops" and to wipe out all debts and claims (up to the largest common numerator) in all such loops found. Shrill bells should sound and red lights flash whenever the computer ends its daily exercise with a residue of net claims, etc. With this system, debts are systematically "extinguished," putting less of a burden on central archives, but they are not "paid." None of the goods in the system is identifiable as the "means of payment."

3. A social abacus might be cheaper than a central computer. We might issue little pellets, "tickets or counters" (called "Berkeleys"), pronounce them legal tender and instruct every transactor to keep "paying" them out until his debts are zero. We could leave A, B, C and D alone to agree on how many Berkeleys extinguish a debt of one "imaginary" unit or we could try to help them out. Record-keeping and computational requirements will be drastically simplified by the expedient of handling "counters" around; even people

9. Luigi Einaudi (1955).

who had trouble with arithmetic in primary school can participate.

4. We could allow any transactor able to acquire the trust of the others to issue I.O.U.'s (in "Berkeley's") and have them handed around (or transferred between agents on his books) instead.[10] If experience tells us that people sometimes misplace their trust, we might intervene to force the "bank" regularly to extinguish its I.O.U.'s or stand ready to do so in either "our B's" or real goods.

5. Some transactor might be designated as a "credit card company" which allows others that it trusts to register the debts and claims arising from resource transfers between them on this company rather than on one another. The method or methods for extinguishing these debts and claims, we might leave to the company unless it proves prone to misplace its trust.

In a system where some mix of these (and perhaps other) arrangements is in operation, it is quite possible that we might find an empirically stable demand function for a suitably defined "M."[11] Securing its micro-theoretical foundations does not appear an easy task, however. Putting "real M" in utility-functions, for example, leaves one with a residue of fearful doubts; and proposals to reduce the marginal utility of M to zero seem of uncertain import.

The above sketch has not provided conditions assuring the stability over time of the relationship between "Berkeley's" and the imaginary accounting unit (I.A.U.). Changes in the relation of B to I.A.U. would, however, be of relatively limited concern as long as we deal with systems where the accounts receivable and payable carried over through time are small or zero, as assumed above.[12]

10. Cf. Hicks (1967), Chapter 2.

11. At least as long as arrangements (1) and (2) or variants and permutations thereof do not come to dominate the others entirely.

12. Horrible penalties for those found feigning the bishop's graven image on the counters or otherwise manufacturing "money" have been historically helpful. Sovereigns and legislators usually end up exempt, however, leaving them with the capability of appropriating resources from the private sector by "money" issue. The consequences of such "inflation taxes" should not be very serious however—as long as they do not also succeed in enforcing a fixed relation between the unit of legal tender and the unit of account in general use.

Nor is a stable relation between the I.A.U. and some "composite basket" assured by the sketch as far as we have carried it. The "I.A.U.-value" of the basket could be any positive number. It is interesting, however, that between Charlemagne and the French Revolution the drift of the *libra* was rather slow[13] and, more to the point, without dramatic discontinuous jumps. Comparative static models, defined to exclude "money illusion,"[14] will provide no reasons to expect this. Yet, it is possible for an "imaginary money," without secure real anchorage, to drift slowly enough so as to preserve its usefulness for economic calculation of the advantages of alternative courses of action (and, apparently, retain some—ill-understood—superiority over "composite basket" contracting units). But this, it would seem, could only be the case if agents faced with the task of setting prices today seek help in the memory of yesterday's prices; i.e., find value in "precedent."[15]

A sketch of this sort will have to leave many loose ends. Here, they are beyond counting. But we resolutely turn our backs to all that, hanging on to but one strand—that our various social bookkeeping devices have not been shown capable of "keeping track" in systems that allow nominally denominated debts and claims to remain outstanding from one "period" to the next.

III. INFLATION AND THE LAW

Mankind presumably has put more intellectual effort and ethical reflection over the centuries into the creation of the law

13. Cf., Einaudi (1953) *passim.*

14. The term "money illusion" is used here with apologies. Recent changes in professional usage have made it virtually useless as a technical term. Originally, it referred to individuals with a tendency to be fooled by currency reforms shifting the decimal point on all nominally denominated contracts or misers with an irrational passion for nominal money. This concept is trivial but clear-cut and useful. Later, in the Keynesian debate, the term came to be used with reference to the behaviour of transactors lacking complete information on their alternatives of choice. (Cf. Leijonhufvud, 1968, especially pp. 384–5). More recently still, in the literature on neoclassical monetary equilibrium growth models, some writers have used it to refer to agents who fail accurately to *foresee* the rate of inflation. This last step should signal general abandonment of the term.

15. Cf. Hicks (1970), p. 19: "In imperfect markets prices have to be 'made'; they are not just 'determined' by demand and supply. It is much easier to make them, in a way that seems satisfactory (because it seems fair) to the parties concerned, if substantial use can be made of precedent; if one can start with the supposition that what was acceptable before will be acceptable again."

than has yet gone into social benefit-cost analysis. If, then, re-peated rounds of gradually improved social cost calculations for inflation keep repeating the answer that it is relatively trivial, it gives one pause to note that the law is helpless to assure justice in inflations.

Because of this impotence of the law, inflations tend to accel-erate the secular tendency of most Western countries to move away from the Rule of Law toward Rule by Men. Associated therewith, we expect to observe a tendency for the dominant popular conception of social justice in democratic societies to shift from Equality under the Law towards Income Equality. The first of these conceptions focuses on the evenhanded appli-cation of the rules governing social and economic activities irre-spective of the identities of individuals and of the social status they occupy, etc. The second focuses on the *ex post* real outcome of individual economic activity.[16]

The two linked tendencies are, of course, subject to divergent value judgments. Some would cheer them on, others wish that they could be braked, halted, or even reversed. Here we are concerned to argue only that the strength of these tendencies will be associated with inflation and, consequently, that this as-sociation should be considered in assessing the consequences of inflation. One note might be added to this: namely, that infla-tions, even as they speed up the process, are likely to make or-derly and coherent evolution in the directions indicated more difficult to achieve.

The law is helpless to assure that a just real outcome is re-stored to contracts concluded in nominal terms. That is so for rather simple reasons. The expectations about the rate of infla-tion in prospect[17] that the two parties originally held cannot be

16. In order to get on with the topic, this paragraph had better be left as is—patently inadequate. Two references to cover my escape: Hayek (1973) and Rawls (1971). The basic opposition between Hayek's emphasis on "spontaneous orders" and Rawls's equally evident "constructivism" need not, as far as I can see, produce a clash in the context of this section (Chapter 10 would be another matter—but there I will avoid the issue).

17. Here and elsewhere we make use of *"the* rate of inflation" *as if* both parties to a con-tract would define inflation, with regard to their own best economic interests, in terms of money-price changes of *strictly identical* composite baskets.

This fudge seems unavoidable if we are to go ahead with the argument. *But*—could this condition ever be exactly fulfilled (while leaving room for gains from trade between

objectively ascertained after the fact.[18] The only "evidence" for what they then were would be what the two contending parties now allege and it, of course, is useless to the courts.

No independently defined measuring rod suggests itself as a standard of justice. Measures of the inflation that has taken place over the term of a contract cannot be imposed as a standard *ex post*.[19] If both parties initially expected 5 percent inflation (in the price of some agreed-upon composite basket) and the actual rate was 10 percent, a court using the actual rate to recompute a contract would fix a debtor loss of 5 percent as the legally enforced outcome. By simply enforcing the contract in nominal terms as written, the result would be a creditor loss of 5 percent relative to the original intentions of the contract. If, on the other hand, both parties had expected a 15 percent inflation, a 10 percent actual rate means that the debtor loses 5 percent if the contract is settled without dispute; if a court were to adjust the contract by adding on the actual inflation the resulting debtor loss would be 15 percent.

The parties may have had discrepant expectations about the rate of inflation in prospect. In that case, it will be impossible in pure principle to find an adjustment coefficient such that, when applied to what the contract says, one succeeds in realising the expected real outcome for both parties.

Finally, there will be a class of contracts in existence of which it is true that the parties would never have been able to come to terms—i.e., would not have found any mutual gains from trade in prospect—had their expectations (correct or not) about the future inflation rate originally been in agreement.

the two)? Assume two agents with identical, homothetic consumption tastes. If they are to trade, there must be division of labour (or differential endowments) between the two. No price will be more significant to their respective economic interests than that of the good that is the object of their specialisation of labour. The prices of what they sell must be included in the respective welfare calculations . . . and we are in trouble.

18. Note that the economist studying the "distribution effects" of inflation on the basis of data on the net monetary creditor or debtor position of transactors or groups will be in the same boat. The work of Armen Alchian and Reuben Kessel (reported in numerous articles) of some fifteen years ago is subject to this uncertainty. The solidity of the inferences drawn depends on that of the assumption that both parties expected price stability at the time their contracts were negotiated.

19. Some such standard may, in effect, be imposed *via* legislated price controls or incomes policies—but the courts would and could never do it (which is a sidelight of sorts on what incomes policies imply).

Consequently, the law refuses to recognise inflations as a source of "unjust" outcomes. If suit were brought claiming that the legitimate expectations of one party to a contract (e.g., a United States Savings Bond) have been defeated by inflation, such a suit would be thrown out of court. The price-stability fiction—"a dollar is a dollar is a dollar"—is as ingrained in our laws as if it were a constitutional principle. Indeed, it may be that no "real" constitutional principle permeates the law as completely as does this manifest fiction. Inflations (or deflations) end up being ranged with those Acts of God for which parties are not held accountable. But this is not because jurists have mis-identified the potentate responsible. It is because the law cannot tangle with "him," whoever he is.

To see this in proper perspective, one should realise how very wide is the range of contingencies with regard to which the law will adjudicate. The outcomes of any individual's efforts are contingent upon the present and future behaviour of others. The law seeks to provide a stable framework of social interaction within which people can form expectations about the outcomes of their actions sufficiently firm, if not precise, to allow them to plan their conduct accordingly. It does so, in the first place, by making certain broad classes of behaviour permitted or forbidden, in the penal code, to everyone. For a socio-economic system dependent upon a very high degree of specialisation of labour this will not suffice. The "rules of the economic game" (in the game-theoretic sense) must be given a more detailed, consistent structure or else the "positive sum" capable of being realised will be very modest and less than reliable. One system of design to accomplish this is to constrain the "strategies" of individual players or groups by restrictions of the type referred to by Mitchell. Individuals whose economic effort depends for its result on the behaviour of "the shoemaker" are provided the assurance that he will *have to* "stick to his last" . . . and his son after him, etc. The other system of design, of course, is that which provides the legal frame of "monetary exchange systems." One of its principal features will be provision for "free" contracting between parties. If your welfare is significantly dependent upon the behaviour of shoemakers, you contract with *a* shoemaker—depending upon the potential competition of other shoemakers to prevent him from holding you over the barrel. To work reasonably well, therefore, this system of legal design requires competition as a "governing principle of contract." It also requires dependable "money" if people are to be "emancipated from restrictions on what they do and what they get" and be let loose to do as they please. The vast, overwhelming majority of contracts will specify receipt of "general purchasing power" as the main right of at least one of the parties.

One of the dominant concerns of the law in an exchange system must then be to ensure the dependability of contracts. How is this to be done? It is a tempting but most naive notion to envisage a system of law that *guarantees* (in some sense) to everybody the realisation of the expectations held when the contract was concluded.[20] This is impossible even as just a general model of approach (e.g., with "scaled-down" guarantees—"90 percent as a minimum," or whatever). Some of the reasons are obvious—in particular, the omnipresence of a class of contingencies outside the control of the community as a whole: "Acts of God" and the behaviour of people outside the law's jurisdiction (OPEC). And, of course, people may and will sometimes expect more than they can get in any case. But the problem with outcome-guarantees is more fundamental than that.

It would not work even in a "closed system"—i.e., a system "closed" off from the wars, pestilences, and natural disasters of a wrathful Deity and the greed of foreigners alike. For the expectations of parties can never be made either to mesh perfectly with one another or to match all conceivable contingencies—putting aside the inconceivable ones that none the less materialise.[21]

20. Proponents of guaranteed real income schemes for everybody had better give some thought to the underlying rationale of the structure of inherited law in this respect. In Britain, during the autumn of 1974, there was some public debate of universal real income guarantees (by "indexing") as a notional device for snapping out of the "cost-push" syndrome. Some commentators envisaged guaranteeing the present real living-standards of the population—at a time when the United Kingdom trade-deficit amounted to 10 per cent of national consumption. This might be the simplest recipe for hyperinflation and unreconcilable social strife ever invented.

21. I am, of course, denying any "jurisdiction" to Arrow-Debreu contingency market models in the present realm of discourse. Hopefully, it is superfluous to elaborate on this. My indebtedness to the works of Ronald Coase and Steven N. S. Cheung will, on the other hand, be evident in what immediately follows.

The recorded terms of a contract will *never* reveal the original expectations of the parties "in their entirety" (whatever that might be made to mean); nor will they ever anticipate all relevant contingencies and specify outcomes preagreed upon for each. In part, the expectations held will be left unstated for the simple reason that the parties will often wish not to reveal to each other how they intend to "profit from the deal." But, more fundamentally, their expectations will in general not be completely structured; innumerable contingencies will be unanticipated, and not in the sense of being assigned a low or zero probability, but in the sense of not envisaging the situation that would arise, if and when they materialise, in the specifics of its behavioral structure. Expectations with regard to such contingencies are left "unformed." Contracts fail to state them not because of their "unspeakable avarice" (though that might often be a decent reason) but for reasons of a more Wittgensteinian profundity: "Whereof one cannot speak, thereof one must be silent."

The contingencies capable of significantly affecting the outcome to contracting parties will never be exhaustively enumerated. Again, one may explain this by reference to the "cost" of letting the fine print run on indefinitely. And this would be a true statement——no contract will explicitly cover all those contingencies that can be envisaged, for it does not pay to do so. But, beyond that, the conditions of human understanding will not allow for the anticipation of every relevant contingency.[22]

Economists, I firmly believe, need to do a great deal of further work in this direction. If we are ever going to get a firm grasp of what isomorphisms we may claim to obtain between our models and the real system, we need to understand much better than most of us now do *how* the law seeks to reduce the

---

22. The actual economic "game" that people find themselves "playing" has vast arrays of the pay-off matrix" blank *ex ante*. Entire dimensions of the outcome space are left unspecified (also in the probabilistic sense). What the parties *will* know about most of the "blanks" of the matrix, however, is that, if that is where they find themselves ending up, the courts will adjudicate: i.e., will provide an *ex post* definition of what the rules should have been understood to have been. They will expect, moreover, that such a ruling will most often, though not invariably, "make sense" to them. More importantly, they know that they will not end up deadlocked in an irreconcilable conflict.

One of the dimensions of the matrix should be reserved for changes in the value of money. Along that dimension, the above observations do not hold.

uncertainties of the human condition to (literally speaking) "manageable proportions" and, more importantly, *why* its solutions to this are structured in a particular way. But here we must leave off without attempts to transcend the naïveté with which the problem has been sketched above.

The point for present purposes is this: The set of contractually unspecified contingencies where the law will step in to adjudicate the outcomes to parties is almost infinite. But it is not exhaustive. "Changes in the Value of Money" are left out.

In adjudicating disputes,[23] the courts will, in effect, make a determination of what expectations the parties could *legitimately* entertain. The case will be settled so as to satisfy everybody's legitimate expectations, in this sense. Most often, this will be done by reference to precedents. A court will not hesitate to invoke precedents of which each party is and was manifestly totally ignorant. And it will make new law where no precedents are to be found. In so doing, it may argue from consistency with existing law, advancing the particular decision, as it were, as a novel "lemma" to long-established laws. More significantly, for our purposes, it may adjudicate a case without precedent by reference to general communal conceptions of what is and is not "fair," and hold the parties responsible for understanding and sharing these social conceptions. The law will have the most difficulty with those unprecedented cases with regard to which the public does not hold certain "Truths to be self-evident."

Yet, inflations—apart from hardly being unprecedented—are not like that. They are "unfair"—"everyone knows that." No social convention could be stronger and more universally shared. But the law is impotent. The next section attempts a preliminary analysis of the behavioural implications of this fact.

One subject has been ignored: "indexation." It is potentially a large one. I have little to say on it, except that I do not believe it gives us a way out.

The law is utterly permissive with regard to indexed contracts, escalator clauses and the like.[24] It will recognise and en-

23. My indebtedness to Hayek (1973, *passim*) will be evident here.
24. Many countries do, however, prohibit index contracts. It may be that in most cases such prohibitions are of old standing, going back to an age when sovereigns were

241

force nominally defined debts and claims, it is true, but it will allow the parties very wide latitude indeed in specifying mutually agreeable formulae whereby this nominal sum is to be computed.

Having emphasised, first, the impotence of Justice in inflations and, now, the permissiveness of the Law with regard to stable purchasing power clauses, one can only go on to suggest that there are deeper problems to indexation than is revealed by recent discussion.

For "indexation" persists, of course, in failing the market test [25] long after the force of any initially prevalent social convention of "money illusion" type must have been dissolved. Even the most ardent proponents of indexing schemes are usually looking for government to take the lead and put it into effect. But why are not governments, saddled with the borrowing requirements common today and given their record of printing money to "redeem" debt, forced by the competition of the private sector to rely on index-bonds? We have seen some spread of escalator-clauses in labour contracts. That only makes the situation more odd, however, since these are of short term [26]—short enough, generally, for models of "foreseen inflation" to possess some measure of putative relevance.

The fact that the system does not spread by itself, one must suppose, probably contains a few lessons for macroeconomists habituated to index-deflated "real magnitudes" as variables of scientific analysis. If transactors found no problem in finding a mutually agreeable composite basket, and saw no novel and potentially serious risks from using it, is it at all plausible that the system should not spread rapidly in the present age?

The mutually agreeable basket is not necessarily a problem so

struggling to establish their own coinage as a dominant money. Lending the powers of the law to the enforcement of private agreements concluded in contracting units that do not correspond to the payment unit of government issued legal tender would entail a self-imposed constraint on the sovereign's ability to rely on inflationary finance in a pinch. But in Finland the prohibition is recent, having been imposed following the abandonment of the celebrated Finnish experiment with indexation.

25. Cf. B. Klein (1976).

26. Such short-term employment contracts will not be affected by the capital gains provisions of tax-law. It may be that it is chiefly the tax law that inhibits the development of longer term index contract markets. I doubt, however, that this could be the whole story.

trivial as to be swamped by perception of the uncertainty of inflation rates. Even in the simplest case of the "pure consumption-loan" between two parties of identical, homothetic, time-independent tastes, we might expect to find some wrangling over the virtues of Laspeyre versus Paasche and over "the" rate of interest which should go with one or the other. Where the specialisation in production of at least one of the parties is part of the *raison d'être* of contracts, things get murkier. Suppose, both "shoes" and "apples" are in the composite basket used in comprehensive indexation of contracts. If the apple harvest fails badly, the shoe-producer finds himself obliged to increase wages. The apple harvest would not normally be a business risk that much concerned him. If demand shifts from shoes to apples and apple prices promptly go up, the shoe-producer might have to raise his own price in face of falling demand.[27] And so on.

With regard to the use of indexation to provide not just predictable prices and wages but predictable incomes, the work of S. N. Afriat shows that use of one common index number to scale up nominal income proportionally will not leave the real income distribution among income classes unaffected. In general, a different "marginal price index" should—in fairness—be used for each income-class and even that will fail to take care of individuals with atypical tastes in a given income-class.[28]

When the law draws a line between legitimate and "illegitimate" expectations of contracting parties, the result is, as we have indicated, a line between contingencies for which a party can and cannot seek redress at court. Inherited law thus embodies a "choice" of the adverse contingencies that parties must accept without recourse as well as of profitable outcomes that they need not share. Since the system as a whole does not possess "certainty in the aggregate," the law must necessarily contain some set of rules allocating risks in this manner. The particular rules that we have inherited might have a functional basis. If so, it is one ill-understood by the economics profession at the present time. In any case, it is clear that private parties

27. The point is Klein's.
28. S. N. Afriat (1978).

contracting on an index basis will thereby (a) redefine the sets of adverse and favourable contingencies for themselves, and (b) within the former set give novel definition to the sub-set for which some measure of redress can be sought. And, to repeat, they are not doing it.

There remains the question: Suppose everybody did, what would be the systemic consequences? Until we gain a better understanding of the considerations sketched above, we cannot hope to get a full answer to this one. But the point forcefully made in a recent paper by Davidson and Kregel suffices, in my opinion, to settle the question of the desirability of trying to bring it about. It would, they argue, "institutionalise" and give legal force to unitary elasticity of price-expectations. A system where expectations generally had this property would, as Hicks pointed out long ago, be on a knife-edge at best. Any small disturbance increasing one price could set "the price level" going up without end. And monetary restriction, Davidson and Kregel add, could then only serve to break virtually every index-contract in existence.[29]

IV. THE SOCIAL AND POLITICAL CONSEQUENCES OF INFLATION

In 1919, Keynes began a short piece on inflation by paraphrasing Lenin as having declared that "the best way to destroy the Capitalist System was to debauch the currency." And Keynes agreed: "Lenin was certainly right. There is no subtler, no surer means of overturning the existing basis of Society. . . ."[30] So, we have two thinkers with some influence on our times concurring that inflation is not to be trifled with. This sweeping judgement that they shared obviously differs not just in degree but in kind from that of those latter-day students of the problem who seek the social cost of inflation in the effects of a predictable tax on money balances.

But appeal to "authority" does, of course, exactly nothing to elucidate the issues for us. Indeed, to the extent that these are scarecrow authorities to some people, it may confound the is-

29. Paul Davidson and Jan A. Kregel (1975).
30. Cf. Keynes, *Essays in Persuasion* (1972), pp. 57–58.

sues. Besides, neither man has a spotless record as a social scientist. We are obliged to ask whether they knew what they were talking about. And if at the time they did, does it still apply to the world of the twentieth century's last quarter? Keynes, for example, was much preoccupied with the effect of inflation on the saving habits of the Victorian middle and upper classes. The bourgeoisie of the nineteenth century is no longer with us. So it is not at all obvious that Keynes's and Lenin's *obiter dicta* have any bearing on how the social consequences of inflation in the "mixed economies" of our age are to be assessed.

Keynes, moreover, can be pretty discouraging: "The process [of inflation] engages all the hidden forces of economic law on the side of destruction, and does it in a manner which not one man in a million is able to diagnose."[31] Any individual is entitled to the claim of being one in a million—in some respect. But not in this one. This famous line is quoted here only to lodge the complaint that the United States is short of the 200-odd experts on the "Social Consequences of Changes in the Value of Money" that, on Keynes's reckoning, we are entitled to.

What may be attempted at this stage, given how the whole problem area has been neglected in recent decades, can be little more than to state some of the questions that need to be attacked.

The social cost calculations of the output-loss attributable to inflation have had the dominant share of economists' attention in this area in recent years. It seems natural to start from them, therefore. Two sets of questions suggest themselves. First, have they the "strictly economic" effects of inflation right? Second, are the redistributive consequences of inflation correctly derived and are they then appropriately weighed on an acceptable scale of redistributive justice?

From the given state of the debate, these are the "natural" questions to pursue. They are questions that certainly may not be avoided in any attempt to assess the social consequences of inflation. But natural or not, I submit that they do not now belong on top of our agenda. The assumption that, once the

---

31. *Ibid.*

output-loss (if any) attributable to inflation has been estimated and taken into account, the Social Consequences of Inflation end with its redistributive incidence may be the single most serious stupidity to which economists are prone when discussing inflation.

In trying to think analytically about the question, we would do well to concentrate, to begin with, on a thought experiment that puts all the problems of the *ex post* redistributive incidence of inflation to one side. There will be an incidental benefit in so doing for, once those problems are brought on to the agenda, emotive political and ideological considerations inescapably impinge on our thinking. It is important that we direct our attention away from such divertissements, for as long as this can legitimately be done, and on to questions of the behavioural implications that flow from the experience of inflation. Its redistributive consequences are *not* the "final outcomes" of inflation; there are the further questions of how people experience them, of how their perceptions of society are thereby affected, and of how they adapt their behaviour in society as a consequence. And these *may* be the most important questions of them all; whether that is so or not, they *are* the questions that can put us on the trail of what Lenin and Keynes were talking about.

In order to set aside the immediate redistributive consequences, therefore, let us proceed "as if" we were dealing only with a set of individuals that are "representative" in the limited (and somewhat peculiar) sense that their *ex post* redistributive gains and losses cancel each other out in approximately the same way as for the economy as a whole.[32] To illustrate: For all I know, I may be such a "representative" individual. I am being swindled on my life insurance and my pension but am getting a sizable stream of ill-gotten gains on my home mortgage. Suppose these things cancel.

Does that mean that for people in this "representative" position inflation does not matter? Of course not. How silly ever to think so. That *ex post* real net worth may happen to be unaf-

32. For reasons already given in the last section, it is very doubtful indeed that we would be able to ascertain who exactly belongs to this set and who does not. But—no matter. . . .

fected does not mean that such an individual is living in the "same world" as provided by a regime of price stability. His socio-political attitudes will not be unaffected, unless he is uncommonly obtuse; his behaviour will change and adapt, unless he is "irrational."

What are for such an individual the most salient facts about inflation sum up to the sadly trite cliché: *Two wrongs do not make a right.* You may happen to come out even, as the dice fall, but the game is not inherently fair. At no point in time do its rules make sense. Besides, "the House" will switch them on you without warning. (That in a society with progressive income taxes, the House also takes a cut we here ignore.)

We can see that substitutions among patterns of socio-economic activities in two broad directions are indicated:

IV A

Being efficient and competitive at the production and distribution of "real" goods and services becomes less important to the real outcome of socio-economic activity. Forecasting inflation and coping with its consequences become more important. People will reallocate their effort and ingenuity accordingly.

The relative significance of two types of capacity for adaptation to changing conditions has changed. The product designer who can come up with a marginally improved or more attractive product, the production manager who in a good year is capable of increasing the product per man hour by a per cent or two, the vice president of sales who might reduce the real cost of distribution by some similar amount, etc., have all become less important to the stable functioning and/or survival of the organisations to which they belong. Other functions requiring different talents have increased in importance: the vice president of finance with a talent for so adjusting the balance sheet as to minimise the real incidence of an unpredictable inflation rate is an example. But the "wise guy" who can do a good job at second-guessing the monetary authorities some moves ahead is the one who really counts. Smart assessment of the risks generated by the political game comes to outweigh sound judgement of "ordinary" business risks. Other roles will gain in importance also (for reasons that we will come to). Among them is the lawyer capable of finding ways to minimise the impact of sudden new governmental interventions and that of the "operator" who is quick to spot ways of making profit (or avoiding loss) from new subsidy, quota, or price control schemes.

In short, being good at "real" productive activities—being competitive in the ordinary sense—no longer has the same priority. Playing the inflation right is vital.

Perhaps, we had better consider these to be primarily "economic" rather than "social" consequences. One had better not presume that their social aspects are negligible. But philosophising on what effects on the "quality of life" in society may follow from changing the relative rewards of "hard work" and "huckstering" seems neither inviting nor promising. If we postpone these considerations until we come to the Economic Consequences of Inflation we will at least find the jargon in which to talk about them more comfortable.

One exception has to be made, however. The most important of the effects of this type will straddle the boundary between "economic" and "socio-political" consequences no matter how we choose to draw that line. It concerns the great majority of workers. They, too, are put in a situation where individual effort and performance at work have become a less effective way of augmenting or just maintaining family real income. The increases in wages that an individual could hope to gain in any given year through bonuses or upgrading of his job classification, etc., are of little consequence in a double-digit inflation. Collective action becomes correspondingly more important. He will have to put increasing reliance on his union.

Since the United States has a lower proportion of workers unionised than most Western countries, the "theory" that puts the "blame" for inflation on union "militancy" has gained less currency in the United States than elsewhere. This should be to the country's advantage in trying to address its problems rationally, since this "cost-push theory" basically misidentifies the forces at work, making *the* "cause" for inflation out of what is a predictable *consequence* of inflation; namely, observably increasing union activism.[33] In any case, we should note that the association between high inflation and union activism, out of which has been conjured the inflation theory most "popular" in some other countries, is observable also in the United States. Unions will not only bargain harder and more frequently, they will also lobby more energetically and continuously in Washington and in State capitals. This brings us to our second set of observations about the behavioural adaptations that we expect to find.

IV B

People will rely relatively less on private contracts and relatively more on political compacts in trying to ensure for themselves a reliable frame for their economic lives.

Inflation, and particularly a ragged inflation, renders private agreements less reliable in their outcome. Inflation also renders private agreements less "agreeable"—shall we call it?—in the simple sense that the fact that both parties initially entered into an agreement "voluntary" carries much less of a guarantee that it can be carried out amicably and without rancour than is the case in a regime of stable prices.[34]

The "economic interest" of individuals goes beyond consuming food, clothing, shelter, health care, entertainment, and so on. We all strive to control our fates, to shape our lives, and to gain some sphere of relative autonomy in the midst of a world which "in the large" is quite beyond our control. Most of us are conscious that the trouble with unemployment and with poverty lies less in the reduced size of the "consumption basket"— which at other times and in other places has allowed people to live contentedly and with dignity—than in the loss of control and autonomy in this sense that individuals experience. Were it otherwise, a programme of adequate hand-outs could eradicate the social problem—a barbarous presumption.

33. While this should be to our advantage in trying to understand the processes in which we are caught up, it is one that we squander by simply going witch-hunting among big business and food-chain middlemen, etc., instead. The natural sciences have got rid of "animism" all the way down through primary school but "social animism" still is a far, far way from falling into general disrepute.

34. Cf. Hicks (1970): . . . direct economic loss and (very often) loss of temper as well."

In a regime of unstable money, it is *not* rational for people to rely on private contracts and agreements to the same extent as in a stable money regime. The substitute instrumentality is political.[35] We expect people to use their votes and lobbies increasingly to help ensure for themselves a predictable real income. Such activity may take the form of demands on the government itself for adjustment of taxes, for transfer payments, for "free" or subsidised government-provided services. Less obviously perhaps—but more importantly, probably—we expect our "representative" individual to rely less on competition and contractual agreements and more on legislated or administered regulation to control and constrain the activities of those other groups and agents in society on whose present and future behaviour the outcome of his own efforts most significantly depends.

The following observations seem pertinent in relation to this substitution of public political for private economic ways of goal-seeking:

i. Consider the polity as a feedback regulated machinery. If our political institutions allow unemployment to grow, the feedback will be in unmistakable clear text: You'd better do something about unemployment or else. . . ! If they err on the side of inflation, there will be widespread and general complaining about rising prices to be sure, but that diffuse message is quite drowned in the rising babble of *specific* demands and *concrete* proposals from *identifiable* interest groups—to compensate *me*, to regulate *him*, to control X's prices, and to tax Y's "excess profits," etc., etc.

The political demands triggered by unemployment are to reduce unemployment; those triggered by inflation are for the most part not obviously identifiable as "instructions" to stop inflating. There is an informational bias to the process.

ii. Inflation-induced political activities are not likely to be "neutral" in their budgetary implications. The "representative"

---

35. In less developed countries, a slowing down or reversal of the movement out of the "subsistence sector" and into the "market economy" may be the more feasible adaptation. In highly developed industrial economies, to withdraw into economic activities the outcomes of which are largely not contingent upon what others do will not be a relevant option for any significant number of people. It is ignored here. The process of economic development is not reversible—which is not to say that a developed economy could not unravel and come apart at the seams.

individuals whose undeserved losses are balanced by ill-gotten gains might be expected to lobby rather earlier and rather harder for compensation for their losses than for taxation of their gains. There is then a bias towards deficits to the political game of trying to re-redistribute the redistributions *via* governmental budgets. Growing deficits will make it harder to brake the inflation down even as the realisation that it does after all have deleterious social consequences spreads. And the economy generating the taxes is not going to get better at it from the proliferation of regulations and controls—even if these were not often half-baked as such interventions go, but fully studied, carefully considered, and intelligently implemented.

iii. The efficiency of the polity as a "productive organisation" should also be considered, however. Is it, perhaps, subject to laws of diminishing marginal returns to input of "issues"? It seems more than likely that inflation-induced politicking is overloading our political institutions. There are limits to what they can handle intelligently and wisely in any given session. Inflations create more "wrongs" than legislatures can put "right."[36]

Much has been made in American media of the legacies of Vietnam and Watergate as explaining the obviously mounting ill-temper of public debate, and impatience with "the system." How big a part of the story these events make is impossible to tell. But it is simply foolish not to note that the same phenomena are prominent in other countries, such as Britain, who were not involved in the Vietnam War and have had no Watergate but who have also failed to control inflation.

iv. The overloading of political institutions is exacerbated by another factor. Inflation will unsettle a number of political compacts and compromises reached in the past.[37] Consider mini-

36. In early 1975, President Ford attempted to get action on his own proposals by portraying the present Congress as a "do-nothing" Congress. He was rebuked by a Congressional leader who pointed out that the 94th Congress had already at that time passed a far greater amount of "significant legislation" than was passed by any of the Congresses where Gerald Ford was Minority House Leader. The number of "significant changes" per year in the laws governing a country would be an odd index to choose for either "wise" government or "health" of the polity. That number in any case is rising. But is there any indication whatsoever that our political institutions are thereby catching up with the demands for "Justice, Now!"?

37. Again, cf. Hicks (1970).

mum wages, for example. Economists are apt to think of the erosion of minimum-wage barriers to the employment of the young and of minority groups as a reminder that "there are good things about inflation too." But our professional disapproval of minimum-wage laws is not really to the point as long as the basic distribution of economic-political interests and the ways in which we have constitutionally agreed to let them take expression are as they are. All it means is that the lobbying, log-rolling, and so on will have to be done over again. With minimum wages we expect this to happen regularly, predictably, and in short order. But presumably this is not always the case. Issues regarded as long settled may be irrelevant in elections; politicians make no promises relating to them, and groups with a significant interest in them decide how to vote on other grounds. When such compacts come unstuck, the political "equilibrium" of which they were part will not necessarily be quickly reformed. Rights and privileges won in constitutionally fair political contests become more impermanent. Thus, the polity too becomes less reliable in delivering the goods.

Private economic contracts, we know, will be concluded for shorter contract terms, and, even so, be more uncertain as to their real outcomes. Both statements can be made also for political agreements.

v. The law and the political agreements in force embody the rights and privileges, immunities, duties and obligations that constitute the framework of social order within which individuals live their social lives and pursue their economic goals. A totally inflexible framework prevents such necessary adaptations to the social order in a changing world and will ultimately break. A totally "flexible" one is not a social order at all. Some measure of basic continuity must be present, must be maintained. One cannot treat *all* the laws and political compacts as perpetually "fresh" issues, up for renegotiation or open to fundamental reform in every season. This is so not so much because "change" will thwart particular individuals or groups in achieving their goals (whatever they may be and whatever we may think of them). It is rather because some continuity is necessary for any individual to "make sense" of his social setting, to be able simply to *set* goals for himself and his family and to formulate plans to work towards them. The rights, immunities, and obligations with which one goes to bed at night must be there in the morning and not found unpredictably reshuffled or a meaningful social existence becomes impossible.

Any society must strike and maintain a balance between conservatism (in the literal sense) and reformism.

There is a third bias to the inflationary process viewed in terms of its socio-political rather than "purely" economic consequences that should be pointed out in this connection. Consider once again the hypothetical individual who is "representative" of society at large in that his gains and losses from inflation balance. As long as the economic machine continues to turn out the goods in roughly the same volume, his consumption standard, etc., will not be impaired. He is suffering undeserved losses and will identify certain institutional arrangements as the instrumentalities whereby this has occurred, certain groups or organisations as the "privileged" recipients of the corresponding gains, and certain immunities of the law as barring restitution. He will side with others seeking reform of one or more of these features of the inherited social order which he sees as having combined to produce a manifestly unjust outcome. In the nature of the case, the set of institutional arrangements that produce his ill-gotten gains will not be (completely) the same. Those members of society that directly or indirectly are paying for his inflationary gains will be out to reform a different set of laws and political compacts.

When inflation gets into double digits by a good margin, one thus has to expect that virtually all the institutions providing the framework of economic order will in this way come under attack. To some extent, of course, they always are—there will always be critics with some following among dissatisfied groups. But normally most such "movements" will be ineffective; at any rate, we expect only a very few of them to make significant headway at any one time. Great inflations, however, are capable of letting loose a social epidemic of effective but uncontrolled and incoherent pressures for institutional change.

For where could we expect the defenders of continuity to come from? Whence the reserves of "countervailing powers"? Ordinary, decent, honest people will not stand up for the laws and institutions producing the gains they know to be ill-gotten.[38] Conscience forbids it and conscience, despite impressions to the contrary, is a widespread attribute. Our "representative" individual, who has so far come out even, is not likely to defend his ill-gotten gains when they come under political attack by others; he is more likely to respond by redoubling his efforts to remove the sources of his own losses.

The "representative" citizen will, on balance, be on the attack against, not on the side of the defence of, the inherited order.

vi. All of the above concerns the "rational," relatively deliberate and unemotional adaptations that people are apt to make to the experience of a rapid, but ragged inflation. But to assume that the degree to which they maintain their deliberate rationality is itself unaffected by the process runs counter to the most casual observation. The process is ill-understood by everybody; it is controlled by nobody; relatively few people will know themselves to benefit systematically, predictably, and lastingly from it. But the notion that "somebody is behind it," somebody who is in control and who is doing it for profit will be almost inescapable to a great many people. The habit of confusing the allocation of "blame" with the description and explanation of historical processes is almost universal. Thus public opinion increasingly acquires paranoid overtones. Opinion-making entrepreneurs make careers from such suspicions. The legislative process itself cannot remain—does not remain—entirely uninfected by irrational expressions of social strife.

V. INFLATION AND RESOURCE ALLOCATION

Observations about the "purely economic" effects of inflation—or, more accurately perhaps, about the state of our knowledge regarding them—are collected in this section. They are collected under three sub-headings; it will be obvious that these are not exhaustive of the issues. In this section, we attempt to retreat in good order—hopeful of avoiding a rout—to within the boundaries of standard economic theory. Constructive dis-

38. Cf. Keynes (1972), especially pp. 68–69.

cussion requires that we now obey the neoclassical "rules of the game"—more or less.[39]

Some remarks on the relationships of neoclassical constructions to what has gone before may aid in transition:

1. The standard model treats the economy as a subsystem whose interactions with the rest of the socio-political system may be ignored for the purpose at hand. The definition of protected property rights, permitted and enforceable contract forms, the kinds and extent of political intervention, are treated as parametric. The good x_i is x_i and stays x_i and that is that.

2. The model leaves no room for the production manager, product designer, distribution expert, et al., to whom we made reference in the last section. It represents a world without need for people whose Sisyphean job it is to try to keep you on the minimum cost curve, judge where the demand-curve is at, keep things "running smoothly" when somebody falls sick or the coffee-machine breaks down. The "efficient loci" are there for anyone to see and you will not drift off them if nobody pays attention.

3. It is at least unclear whether money is needed as a means of payment on a regular basis. Transactors apparently hold it as a buffer-stock against unplanned, temporary deficits in their balances of payments on current account but the representation of the system leaves the possibility open that most debts incurred might be extinguished by the delivery of (arbitrary?) baskets of non-monetary goods.

4. "Money" is not needed as an aid to economic calculation. Convex production sets and convex preferences meet for a coolly tangential kiss—hygienically separated by the Cellophane of a hyperplane—without such mercantile intermediation. A huge steel corporation, say, can be just as efficiently

---

39. In my "Maximization and Marshall," Leijonhufvud (unpublished) I forswore the use of the term "neoclassical" arguing that the conceptual differences separating Walrasians, Marshallians, and Mengerians are of greater significance to the microfoundations of macroeconomics debate than are whatever common denominators "neoclassical" might refer to. So much for New Year's resolutions. Here I need a broad blanket to cover standard micro-constructions of all sorts and, soggy as it is, "neoclassical" will do.

run by calculating all values in terms of apples as the numéraire (and will, as we have seen, not be embarrassed by ending up a profitable fiscal year with a rather long position in apples).

5. Since transactors are good at solving n-dimensional decision-problems simultaneously under "uncertainty," they make no use of other devices for simplifying calculation either. In particular, they have no need for Hicksian "precedents." Of course not all the constructions of standard theory represent worlds in which memory is of no use and the global equilibrium is recomputed from freshly gathered information in a daily before-breakfast *tâtonnement*. Memory, even if limited to the somewhat non-vertebrate capacity of storing no more than some half-dozen lagged G.N.P. terms, may well be essential to the formation of transactor's "expectations" in such models. But *ex post* values of observed variables do not enter into the decision-rules that agents use to guide their actions *given* these perceptions of their opportunities.[40]

Fair enough. Now what is there left to say about inflations?

A. Price Adjustment Processes and Price Signals

The first thing to say, surely, is that we know very little about how inflations work their way through the economy. Our empirical knowledge is scant,[41] which becomes less surprising once one notes that the theoretical work needed to lend it analytical structure has been neglected, too. The neoclassical monetary general equilibrium growth model has inflation as "near-neutral" as makes no difference. The Austrian tradition has infla-

---

40. In "Maximization and Marshall," I interpret the role of the "constant marginal utility of money" assumption in Marshall's theory of consumer behaviour along the lines hinted at in the text. Last period's MU_M—an *ex post* magnitude and hence a "constant"—is used by the consumer to simplify his n-dimensional decision-problem and achieve what he hopes to be a good approximation of the optimal outcome. Assuming cardinal, additive utility, the reliance on MU_M makes possible sequential decisions on purchases following the thumbrule to buy if and as long as:

$$(MU_X/MU_M) = P_X^d > P_X$$

Inflation will obviously wreak havoc with this decision procedure.

41. So scant that one is more than usually indebted to Phillip Cagan for his recent pamphlet, Cagan (1974).

tion associated with systematic and serious distortions of the price system and hence of resource allocation. It is difficult to see that we have the empirical knowledge that would discriminate between the two. My own "hunch" with regard to present-day conditions would be that the price distortions are apt to be less systematic than in the Austrian view but none the less serious. There is no good evidence for this view either. The procedure of arriving at indirect measures of "real G.N.P." by index-deflation of money value data gives us little indication of how sizable the losses might be.[42] But we might entertain the hypothesis that, when "everybody" complains of being worse off in the face of reportedly unchanged real *per capita* G.N.P., they may be right. The more popular hypotheses adducing epidemics of "money illusion" or spontaneous outbreaks of mendacious greed are not necessarily true.

How does the price-rise process work through the system? It depends on what type of markets we are talking about.[43]

For securities and commodities traded on the organised exchanges the usual "auction" model is probably good enough. So these we pass over with the observation that, in the United States, the prices of (the not very oil-intensive) basic food-stuffs have in the last years severed a long, close association with the other components of C.P.I. and wandered off on their own, while individual markets—meat, sugar, etc.—show rather uncommonly severe "hog-cycling," patterns.[44] It is not the case that everything is well in our "flexprice" markets.

For most manufactured goods, we have "fixprice" markets. For such markets, "my story"—obviously both impressionistic and incomplete—would go as follows.[45] An original increase in

---

42. E.g., if we move people from "real productive activities" into "inflation huckstering" (or price control bureaucracies, etc.) at unchanged salaries, "real G.N.P." might show no significant change. Suppose, for example, that the new price-controller's best efforts are precisely stalemated by the corporate manager newly assigned to precisely this task. The work of both may, to a first approximation, end up counted as "real service output" measured by their G.N.P.-deflated salaries.

43. The following discussion owes obvious debts to Sir John Hicks, particularly his recent *The Crisis in Keynesian Economic* [Hicks (1974)]. In a fuller treatment, I would lean more than is here done on P. Davidson (1974).

44. I am indebted to my colleague Larry Kimbell for driving home this point to me—with striking statistical illustrations.

45. The basic "plot" is due to Armen A. Alchian and William R. Allen (1967, pp. 86ff). Cf. also P. Cagan (1974) especially pp. 2–7, and 21–26.

monetary demand, increases rates of sales and reduces inventories faster than anticipated. Prices, I assume, are most often not put up at this stage. Some producers may have "sticky" prices simply because they are wary of the competition; others will prefer to "stick" because they hope over the medium-run to cash in on hitherto unexploited increasing returns. Orders to restock are passed backwards through the chain of intermediate goods producers, leading to inventory reductions at these levels. At various places down the line we finally run into producers who find themselves unable to expand output at constant cost. Now, price-increases begin to be passed forward through the same maze of interlocking customer-supplier chains. The demand-impulse comes back on the rebound as "cost-push." Cost increases that a supplier can be confident he has in common with his competitors will be passed on in fairly short order—also, I assume, by sellers, who, if assured of a permanently higher turnover, would find their present prices very profitable. Reservation-wages of labour will react in the same way to cost-of-living increases. We observe "mark-up pricing" in operation.

We know little about the overall lag-time of this process. How much "inflation" is still in train at some date following the termination of the demand-impulse will be almost impossible to predict. This matter was probably rather badly misjudged around 1964–5 in the United States and reaction-patterns have undoubtedly adapted to the experience since that time.

Presumably, the process of inventory depletions running backward and price increases passing forward does not proceed at uniform speed between sectors and industries. In some lines of business, moreover, the practice will be to adjust prices in fairly small steps at fairly frequent intervals; in others, to use a larger step-size with longer intervals of posted "fixprice."

Consequently, even if the inflation were balanced, it works its way through jerkily. At double-digit rates (on some smoothed average), one may expect sizable price increases on some subset of goods to be announced every week. What are the implications? They can hardly be discussed without at least bending the "rules of the game" a bit.

First, of course, it becomes a bother to keep up with it all.

Scale-economies will affect who does and who does not try hard to do so. Traders expecting to transact large quantities will invest considerable resources in keeping track of prices. (Still, one would not expect a 10–20 percent inflation to be "enough" to call forth inflation-trading specialists in large numbers—*die Gulaschbaronen* are not yet prominent amongst us). Most households will not try to maintain their stock of price-information at the "quality" they normally desire—even as they spend more effort at it. If beef prices go up in every odd-numbered week and potatoes every even week, sensible beef-and-potato eaters will resign themselves to a constant proportions diet that is nonoptimal every week—and curse the statisticians who assert their real income is unaffected by it all.

Perhaps that sort of thing is not important. But another proposition, I feel, is: *Transactors will not be able to sort out the relevant "real" price signals from the relative price changes due to these inflationary leads and lags.* How could they? Messages of changes in "real scarcities" come in through a cacaphony of noises signifying nothing . . . and "sound" no different. To assume that agents generally possess the independent information required to filter the significant messages from the noise would, I think, amount to assuming knowledge so comprehensive that reliance on market prices for information should have been unnecessary in the first place. Some adjustments in resource allocation that are needed will not be made. Some will be made that should not have been. Between the omissions and commissions, the vector of effective excess demands is distorted and the "hunt" for the G.E. solution vector goes off on false trails.

Transactors will gradually lose all firm conception of where the equilibrium neighbourhood for relative prices lies. Setting prices and determining reservation wages becomes a more difficult problem—and also a problem that no longer "makes sense" in the way it used to. We may safely assume that, even in more stable times imposing less pressing short-run information requirements, agents have not been used to consider the problem in n dimensions. Rather, your own past price was used as the main "precedent" to be revised in the light of new information on changes in demand and on developments in a relative small set of markets—for the main inputs and substitute products. With prices "popping all around" and in irregular sequence, such a partial "Marshallian" method makes less and less sense—the pot in which all its *ceteris paribus* presumptions have been thrown together is boiling furiously and cannot be ignored.

Consider the task of somebody put in charge of price control. When is it safe to freeze relative prices? Not right now is always the answer. Could they be regulated by some "rule of proportion" relating them to prices obtaining in a less discoordinated state at some date in the past? What date? Obviously, there never is a particularly "good" one to pick. Yet, price-controllers *invariably* find themselves making decisions based on changes from some past date or dates—although the economic theory they learned at school probably never featured decision-making based on precedents. Economic agents "at large" will have more and better information than, but possess no secrets of efficient decision-making not accessible to, price controllers.

What "value"—in some "real" sense—is the rest of society willing to pay for one's marginal product? We lose track of what can be expected. In the process, conceptions of what is "fair" also dissolve.[46] In their original choice of specialisation, producers are guided by expectations of what real rewards society accords this role in the overall division of labour, what frequency of unemployment might be expected in it, how this is affected by seniority, and so on. The role is voluntarily chosen and most people are, actually, fairly well acculturated to the understanding that the real reward is not socially guaranteed if tastes change or someone comes up with a better way to make a mousetrap. The irregular change in the real purchasing power of nominal income that occur in a ragged inflation cannot be traced to such understandable changes in what the rest of society will accord you.

We will tend to end up, therefore, with symptomatic struggles over "fair shares." It is not necessary to postulate that people's envy is excited by inflations to explain this. It suffices to note that the normal basis for making (reservation) price-decisions and forming income expectations has badly eroded.

46. Cf., once again, Hicks (1970).

People are forced to look around for some reasonably simple, even though inferior, guideline. What one used to earn relative to others is it.

Beyond this point we cannot go without ending up back in Section IV. We have bent the neoclassical rules of the game here but to bring in the further complications to efficient adaptation by transactors that political feedback will cause would be to break them entirely.

B. The Fisher Equation

In the models, from which it is argued that the cost of inflation is relatively trivial, the Fisher equation plays a crucial role. A full discussion of the questions surrounding this relation would ramify into all corners of monetary theory.[47] Here, I want to take up only one question. Letting $\dot{p}^e$ stand for $(1/P)(dP^e/dt)$, the relation is normally written

$$i = r + \dot{p}^e, \tag{1}$$

where i is the observed, nominal market rate of interest and r, called "the real rate," is interpreted as the real return facing savers and the real opportunity cost of funds to investors.

It would be much preferable, I believe, if our convention were to write it instead as follows:

$$(r_i^e + \dot{p}_i^e) = i = (r_j^e + \dot{p}_j^e), \tag{2}$$

where i and j denote individual contracting parties. We are dodging the additional formalism required to distinguish risk-classes and time-structures of contracts. We should think of (2) as referring to the market for a particular type of contract.

The first requirement for efficient allocation of a good is always that a single price should rule in the market. It is such as analytically trivial proposition that we get in the habit of passing quickly to more intriguing exercises in welfare theory.

Here, we may assume that *competition* establishes a unique value of i. If all individuals (somehow) perceived the same real

47. Touching, for example, on several of the core issues that separate the modern monetarists from all the various macro-traditions (e.g., Mises-Hayek; Lindahl-Myrdal; Robertson-Keynes-Hicks) that accord Wicksellian themes a prominent role.

rate in prospect, then trading in this market would go on until, at the margin of the positions taken, inflation-expectations were uniform—to put it very roughly. If inflation-expectations were uniform to begin with, then competitive trading would go on until perceived marginal real rates of return were equal. If we find it difficult to justify one *or* the other of these two assumptions, we cannot conclude that competition will produce $r_i^e = r_j^e$ and $\dot{p}_i^e = \dot{p}_j^e$ as separately holding conditions. But, presumably, one would like to establish some such proposition as part of one's case for the "near-neutrality" of (foreseen) inflations.[48]

Consider, first, the assumption that a common perception of real rates of intertemporal transformation is autonomously given. For a Crusonia world—does the plant still flourish on the South Side of Chicago?—this makes sense. Only use of money and inflation do not. Perhaps, it might be stretched to Fisher's paradigmatic two-period case, where a homogenous present good is subject to diminishing marginal rate of transformation into a physically identical future good. Accepting the assumption in that context amounts, however, to assuming that the pricing-process works as if "dichotomised." A single input, single (but transformed) output case might still do, at least if it is also point-input, point-output. But multiple stream-inputs, multiple stream outputs makes computation of "real rates" virtually impossible to conceive of[49]—unless, of course, fixed relative prices at a constant rate of depreciation of money were (somehow) guaranteed. But that would be the second case.

I can see no "mechanism" that we could plausibly adduce which would tend to bring inflation rate expectations into conformity. If we assume a world which has already been experiencing an unvarying rate of x percent for a generation or two, one has to agree that it is plausible people will expect it to continue—unless they learn of developments that might threaten the institutional arrangements of this peculiar "monetary standard." The analysis of this possibility is useful for

48. We say "presumably" and "some such" here because, intuitively sensible as the notion seems, it appears almost impossible to give it precise analytical formulation for the general case. Some of the difficulties are hinted at below.

49. The economic historical literature on late medieval, early Renaissance developments in accounting and the "rationalization" of business methods and on the innovations in business organisation that such (*necessarily*) "monetary calculation" made feasible is very instructive in this context.

various theoretical benchmark purposes. But surely one might justifiably postpone taking it seriously as a theory of how the world behaves until such time as somebody actually brings the trick off? Here, at any rate, it is simply left aside. Without it, it is still plausible that there will be some substantial degree of conformity with respect to the inflation rate in prospect for the more immediate future—i.e., that people will share some general auto-correlation notion: "Things won't change much overnight." But beyond that, what can we say?

While acknowledging that more theoretical work is needed, my own tentative position is as follows. Future inflation rates are not to be drawn from one of Nature's Urns. Decision-makers can hardly assume that current observations are drawn from some "normal distribution." What the rate will be five or ten years down the road is "uncertain," but it is not uncertainty in that domain of their "natural" expertise where transactors have learned to make (implicit) probability judgements. Farmers cope with uncertain harvest outcomes. In speaking theoretically of "decision-making under uncertainty" as a general rather than specific skill we tend to blind ourselves to important aspects of behaviour. To have learned to manage rationally despite the vagaries of weather, however, will not leave much experience applicable to coping with the consequences compounded from the vagaries of voters in future elections, of legislatures and governments, and of Central Bank responses to the contingencies that the polity produces. Nor do "rational expectations" models provide assurance. They require an underlying, relatively swift and sure "survival of the fittest" process anchored in relatively stable conditions of "real scarcities" for their results to be plausible.[50] Do we have something of the same sort governing the price level?

Benjamin Klein has discussed this matter in terms of the theory of monetary standards.[51]

1. With the old gold standard, it was "rational" to expect (roughly speaking) reversion of the price level back to its old level following a rise or decline.

50. E.g., the type of process we adduce in explaining to students why refraining from "destabilising speculation" has survival-value in commodity markets.
51. Klein (1974).

2. From the mid 1930s through to the early 1960s or so, "rational expectations" (for Americans) might have been to count on the monetary authorities to revert to a zero rate of change "as soon as feasible."
3. Klein refers to the situation of recent years as one of a "purely fiduciary standard." This is a fair description—*but* how would one describe the operating "rules" that would govern the "probability distributions" of future price levels?

I would not even try.[52] My impression is that the international monetary "system" has for some time been in a period of unstructured experimentation and "innovation." Whether this will converge to a stable institutional arrangement and, if so, what it will be like seems obscure indeed—if for no other reasons than that those doing the innovating do not understand what they are tampering with or know what their criteria of design should be.

In the United States, a transactor might listen to those economists who argue that policy should not be employed to reduce inflation, but at most to stabilise it. If he believes they rule the world, he will get unity as the lower bound to the elasticity of his price-level expectations.[53] Another transactor, looking back over the past ten years, might be more impressed with the fact that the Fed will still, whenever unemployment is "tolerable," listen to Congressional complaints of "high" (nominal) interest

52. The type of "uncertainty" envisaged in most standard economic models of decision-making under uncertainty may be illustrated by a game of dice. We know the properties of the mechanism generating the probability distribution of outcomes. If the agent does not know it—the dice may be biased, say—a Bayesian learning model may still be used to model his adaptive behaviour. For most economic decisions, the game of chess may, however, be the better source of appropriate metaphors. Here we cannot exhaustively specify all the possible alternative future positions in a game. Consequently, the "actuarial calculus" cannot be applied to the decision-problems of the game (cf. also p. 240 and footnote 22 above).

Consider then major business decisions, the outcomes of which are crucially dependent upon the future rate of inflation, and which have to be made in a setting where no rules, ultimately constraining the rate of money creation, are accepted as "constitutionally binding" by the legislature and monetary authorities. Observed inflation rates are not "drawn" from a probability distribution generated by a law-abiding mechanism. The appropriate metaphor for this case, I suggest, is that of playing "chess" in the presence of an official who has and uses the power arbitrarily to change the rules—i.e., a man who may interrupt at move 14 with the announcement: "From now on bishops move like rooks and *vice versa* . . . and I'll be back with more later."

53. Cf. again, Davidson and Kregel (1975).

rates and take the chance to deflate. If we surveyed people's expectations about *"the* price level" in 1980—assuming that they are tolerant enough to answer such a "dam"-fool question—and found them bimodally distributed, who is "irrational"?

The most plausible conjecture, I submit, is that perceived "real rates" are not brought into line so that "capital" is being misallocated all over. Question: Would this be favourable to the employment of labour?

Integrating the analysis of "ragged" price-rise processes (spot and forward) from Sub-section A with that of intertemporal allocation under conditions of non-uniform inflation-expectations is left as "an exercise for the reader."

C. The Demand for Flexibility

With a tax on "money," we expect people to substitute into longer placements and to reduce non-interest earning accounts receivable. With nominal contracts more uncertain, we expect people to substitute into "real" assets. The first-mentioned tendency would operate endogenously to accelerate inflations. If this has been happening, increasing "velocity" has had less to do with it than expected. With regard to the secondary tendency, stock-markets have not been noticeably firmed up by inflation.

When the future becomes more "uncertain," but the risk that increases is not a simple "actuarial" one, we expect people to avoid long-term commitments in favour of more "flexible' positions.[54] You steam slow waiting for the fog to lift (and sound your bullhorn a lot). The demand for flexibility is expressed by going "short *and* nominal."[55] Thus, this tendency will tend to counteract the two mentioned earlier.

That resource allocation will be affected is obvious. We will not elaborate on it. Flexibility is brought up here because I

---

54. For the concept of "flexibility," cf. A. G. Hart (1951). Long neglected in macro-theory, the concept is brought to prominence and the necessity of its inclusion in our tool-box driven home in Hicks (1974) Chapter II.

   With a "simple actuarial risk," I mean in the text to refer to cases where Hart's "compounding of probabilities" is not needed.

55. This is what Janeway has been talking about in commercials for savings and loan institutions that have much upset American economists.

believe it ranks in significance with the two topics already discussed, not because I have anything new to say in general terms. Instead, two pieces of "casual empiricism" plus a comment:

a. In the United States, short rates have been plummeting since the summer of 1974. Long rates are staying up. We expect short rates to move with greater cyclical amplitude than long rates. Yet, this time there may be a bit more to it. First, the weakness of long markets is properly appreciated only when the uncommonly short average duration of the massive Federal debt is recognised. Secondly, the fall in the short rate is to some extent deceptive. Many corporations (and New York City) have had their credit-ratings written down (Aaa to Baa, etc.). Reports in the press indicate that underwriters are hardly to be found for floating Baa bonds. Some borrowing demands are being rationed out. These prospective borrowers are missing from the supply side of bond markets. Lenders are going for short *and* safe placements in this kind of market. The fall in interest rates gives an exaggerated impression of all-around "credit ease."

b. In Britain, during the autumn of 1974, the inflation rate was close to 20 percent. Yet, much of the banking system was at or beyond the "prudential limits" conventionally deemed safe. The corporate manufacturing sector and much of agriculture were in bad liquidity straits with serious immediate cash-flow problems. Banks were unable to render further help which would require additional long lending against short borrowing. Meanwhile, the government was running a deficit such as to give a borrowing requirement corresponding to 10 percent of G.N.P. while, at the same time, the "fiscal drag" from inflation was proving *negative* (and sizable). With a rate of investment lower than desirable, the country was running a balance of trade deficit equal to 10 percent of national consumption, mostly financed by "petro-money" inflows so short as to increase the strain on banks. Money and liquid assets were piling up in the "personal sector" and in the portfolios of such institutions as Oxbridge colleges and insurance companies—"earning" their holders *obviously* negative real rates. No positive *and* safe real rates were perceived. Alternative placements would include lending to transactors to whom banks would not lend or purchase of shares in corporations whose equity might be expropriated by government as a condition for assistance with ready cash.

A rather different picture from the Quantity Theory of balanced inflations where one expects to find "dollars burning holes in *every* pocket"! An economist, ignorant of the rate of inflation, taking a look at the "real" situation by sectors of the British economy would see it as in dire need of "*re*flation."

In an earlier article[56] I outlined what was there termed a "corridor hypothesis" of the adjustment capabilities of (monetary) market economies. In brief, I proposed that within some range around its "equilibrium" time-path, such systems will tend to exhibit predominantly self-stabilising properties of the basic type that neoclassical models presume. Outside the corridor, on the other hand, (Keynesian) "effective demand failures" would increasingly impair the ability of market homeostats to get the system back on course. Two subsidiary hypotheses, proposed in this paper, about system behaviour outside the corridor seem relevant here:

i. we should expect to observe the emergence of distribution effects loosening the normal empirical relationships among monetary aggregates and between them and aggregate demand; this would be associated with increasing spreads between interest rates on safe and risky claims and with increasingly prevalent rationing of borrowers with low or deteriorating credit ratings;
ii. in such situations, monetary policy action should be expected to be less effective than normally—and particularly if operated against the current of a contrary fiscal policy.

This 1973 paper was written, out of ivory-tower mental habit, with prolonged large-scale unemployment as the problem foremost in mind. I would now like to add to it the claim that the *Gestalt* of the theory sketched there is one that will accommo-

---

56. Leijonhufvud [1973].

date discussion of double-digit inflation—including that stage of it where unemployment still stays safely within the "single digits."

VI. CONCLUDING REMARKS

I have attempted to point out a number of issues that appear to me germane to the task of providing microeconomic foundations for macro-theory. Still other issues are implicit above. An attempt at systematic summary and assessment would seem to little purpose here. Readers who have actually survived to this point might, I hope, agree.

Some concluding remarks on the "attitude" of the writer may save time in discussion. It will have emerged that I am (again) critical of general equilibrium theory and "neoclassical" models more generally and on several counts. Among those others who share my critical view (and would add to them), some will ask why one should bother with these branches of theory at all.

When faced with methodologically profoundly difficult problems of "relating"—never mind "integrating"—branches of economics that for long periods have developed along separate and independent lines, the easiest posture to take is outright and wholesale rejection of one approach or the other. Almost always, I strongly believe, this will prove too easy a way out. Epistemologically sophisticated and convincing cases why this or that aspect of reality can, in pure principle, not be captured *via* some particular approach will not often be much to the point. Such philosophical "impossibility theorems" have a bad track record in the history of science. All too often, "some damn fool" will go ahead and do it anyway and clean up his methods, or have others do it for him, afterwards.

In any case, this writer has never come close to considering "junking" neo-Walrasian constructions. If I have been more harpingly critical of this branch of theory than of any other, it is because in its highly developed modern form it gives us something *precise* to refer to. Although my own "beliefs" about how real world economies behave cannot be adequately represented by current neo-Walrasian models, I find that—for my "personal use"—they provide, as it were, clear *benchmark* reference motions that I would not do without. I do not expect other critics to share this mental habit, nor is there any point in attempting to convince them that they should.

The result, of course, of trying to hang on to achievements gained by as yet methodologically incompatible approaches will be a bit of a muddle. It is easily productive of sundry analytical tangles that will be merely tiresome to others. There is no wonder at all that many economists will see the incentives to plump for one exclusive approach.

This paper is a good muddle. It will have been evident to the reader that it draws on Marshallian, Austrian, and Institutionalist as well as Neo-Walrasian sources. The predominantly critical tone towards the last mentioned branch of economics is due, in the author's mind, simply to disproportionate reliance—with attendant diminishing marginal returns symptoms—on this branch in recent discussion of the paper's topic.

The time for deciding what approach to economics should be it, I believe, is not yet. Probably pretty far off, in fact. Meanwhile, we need all the help that we can get. Drawing from disparate traditions for "insight" means that one still accords legitimacy to "intuitionism" in economics, even as some of its branches develop so as to increasingly resemble some sort of science.

Hence, there is still in my view an important element of "art" in economics. With regard to the very broad problems in particular, one is obliged to "play it by ear." Whether the "chord" of Marshallian, Austrian, Institutionalist, and Neo-Walrasian "notes" struck here makes acceptable "harmony" to others, I do not know. Yet, in trying to understand the consequences of inflation, one should, I believe, search for some such balance.

CHAPTER TEN

Inflation and the Economists: Critique

I

About ten years ago, our collective confidence in what economists could accomplish in the area of stabilisation policy crested and we were not reluctant to tell anybody who would listen what we could do. The policy record (in the United States) since that time has been thoroughly lamentable, featuring mounting inflation and a "stop-go" pattern of policy response of increasing severity.

II

Five times the American public has been promised a campaign to end inflation:

1. the "Art of Central Banking" credit crunch of 1966;
2. the "Keynesian" tax surcharge;
3. the "monetarist" crunch of 1969–70;
4. the price freeze of autumn 1971 plus the price control "stages";
5. the 1974 biggest crunch of them all.

Rounds (2) and (4), in one sense, should not count. They were interludes during which the monetary system was stoked up for a resumption of worse inflation. In another sense, they do count, namely, as parts of the pattern showing our policy-institutions consistently failing to deliver on ballyho'ed promises. The public has come increasingly to doubt that policy-

271

makers will persevere with their stated policy-intentions and that standard fiscal and monetary policy instruments can do the job. Quite apart from exogenous complications (OPEC, etc.) therefore, our situation has become steadily more difficult to manage:

i. anti-inflationary policy becomes more difficult and costly to conduct, and the lags in its effects more tricky to predict, when you are playing it "against" a public that does not believe its goals will be realised. Stabilisation policy is easier to conduct when the private sector regards the stated policy-intentions as good, strong predictors of the future state of affairs.

ii. The mistakes of past years have constantly buffeted the system every which way. The economy is today (spring 1975) in a more disorganized state than at any time since 1950 or so. We know a fair amount about how the economy behaves in the neighbourhood of "full" employment and with reasonably stable prices. We cannot have at all the same confidence in our knowledge about how it will behave and will respond to policy actions in the present situation. Our accumulated store of quantitative information is less reliable for purposes of extrapolative forecasting.

Round (5)—the harsh monetary restraint of last year (1974)—is now regarded by some media commentators as having "licked inflation" at last. They cite the sharply reduced rate of increase particularly of the wholesale price index in the last couple of months. Not many economists share the view, even as we look forward to more months of the same as efforts to reduce inventories and weak commodity markets continue. The last downward kick of the whip-saw has simply been the hardest kick so far—plunging us into serious recession. The policy machine has already been put into reverse and is picking up maximum steam in the opposite direction. We have yet to see how a $80-billion deficit will be financed. The second half of 1976 and 1977 should tell whether 1974–5 was when we snapped out of inflation or was "merely" another phase in a time-pattern of divergent oscillations. I think the odds are on the latter.

III

Economists have not controlled events, of course. One can tell this deplorable story as a sequence of hard-to-handle exogenous disturbances combining with abnormal obstacles to the formulation and execution of a consistent, coherent stabilisation policy—Peruvian sardines conspiring with Arabian sheikhs to make things difficult; first a President intent on "guns *and* butter," then one inattentive because of Watergate; a Congress too preoccupied with Vietnam or Watergate to produce the right fiscal policy with short enough lags; and, of course, the *always* accursed Fed. The "full" story of the last ten years would be a very complex tale indeed; obviously, having that tale told right would be useful. But the trouble with a complex tale is that one cannot draw a simple Moral from it.

Could it be that through this tangled web of events there runs a skein of systematic error in policy-response? If so, why—and why not earlier? And, if we systematically fail to do things right, does the economics profession have any part of the responsibility?

It may be that simple Morals follow only from outright Fables. Perhaps my impressions add up to no more than a Fable.

IV

It has become a widespread view among American professional economists that the economic costs and social dangers of inflation tend to be grossly overestimated by the general public and among policy-makers, particularly in relation to the social costs and dangers of unemployment.

I disagree with this "New View." Indeed, I am apprehensive that the undesirability of inflation is, if anything, underestimated by politicians, media commentators, and the public. Hence, as an economist, I am quite untypically fearful of inflation. In any scientific field, the untypical view is most likely to be quite wrong.

But the economics profession as a whole has not done its homework on inflation. We have little in the way of well validated knowledge about inflationary processes, such as the one of the last decade, and their economic, social, and political consequences. Theoretical analysis and empirical research alike have been neglected—presumably *because* of the attitude that inflation is not such a serious social problem. The New View just is *not* on solid ground. Where science is ignorant, one does not get at Truth by attitudinal surveys among scientists.

The general type of statement with which I want to take issue may be exemplified as follows:

a. "For the purpose of abating inflation it will almost never be worth incurring any non-trivial increase in aggregate unemployment."
b. "If the action required to reduce the inflation rate by 10 per cent will increase the unemployment rate by 1 per cent (for t quarters), it ought not to be done."
c. "It is always better policy to stabilise the ongoing inflation rate (whatever it happens to be) than to reduce it, since the latter alternative will always create some unemployment."

Some economists hold opinions adequately paraphrased in this manner. A probably far greater number see an obvious, serious, known social cost to unemployment while recognising that, in terms of present-day economics teaching, the costs and dangers of inflation appear uncertain, intangible and possibly trivial. The feeling that it would be irresponsible to countenance incurring known costs for benefits considered "speculative" in nature and unknown in extent makes the policy pronouncements of this latter group for all practical purposes of the same import as the advice of those who express opinions, such as those paraphrased, with conviction.

V

The policy-making institutions are endogenous to the system the behaviour with which we are concerned. A change in the perceived ratio of the costs associated with inflation relative to those associated with unemployment will change the response-pattern of the policy-making "sector" and thereby the dynamic behaviour of the system as a whole. A reduction in the perceived ratio of inflation to unemployment "damages" will imply a tendency for the historical "stop-go" pattern to change towards longer, harder "go"-phases and shorter, more hesitant "stop"-phases; it would make you more prone to use your major, proven policy instruments to keep employment high and to try doubtful, *ad hoc* measures to hold inflation down, "hoping for the best." It also brings with it a tendency toward more myopic, short-horizon decision-making on policy. The cost of unemployment that comes first to mind is that of the output irrevocably lost *right now*, whereas the benefits of price stability are those of a lasting regime. The politick "Short View" tends to take precedence over the statesmanlike "Long View." You go hard for the best feasible policy-outcome *this* year and cross next year's bridges when you come to them.

Changes of this sort in the pattern of policy response can, of course, suffice to change significantly the dynamic behaviour of the system. They could account for the emergence of gradually divergent policy-oscillations around an underlying trend of mounting inflation in a system previously showing much more "favourable" behaviour. Is this what has happened? To make a convincing case that it is would admittedly be very difficult.

A change of the ratio of perceived costs would in any case not be the whole story. Lack of policy co-ordination and an inappropriate allocation of responsibilities for "national goals" among Congress, the Executive and the Federal Reserve has also been part of it. There was no significant alteration in these institutional arrangements in the early 1960s, however. Yet, their weaknesses did not show up in such a serious way earlier. The new attitude towards the costs of inflation, on the other hand, was gaining ground in the economics profession from the early 1960s on.

VI

Now, I "feel" that the New View on inflation is "unsound" and would use the same word for the various statements about the "ratio of social costs" or the "social marginal rate of substitution" between the two ills of unemployment and inflation. I say "unsound" rather than "wrong" because it is unclear whether the categories "true" or "false" are pertinent to them. It is no less unclear, moreover, whether categories of ethical judgment or of political preference, etc., apply to their appraisal.

They are statements of a sort that is difficult to debate. What kind of propositions are they? What are their basis? Where do they come from? The last of these questions looks easiest.

VII

The notion of a stable Phillips Curve is gone. By now, everybody's Phillips Curve shifts and tilts and loops, now clockwise, now counterclockwise—and goes north by east when the Gods are against you. The original idea has evaporated. But it has left us a curious legacy—the empty space where it used to be. And we stay there, spinning perilous confusions in it.

The original problem was to explain the rate of change of money wages. Suppose, like other prices, they move in response to "excess demand." How measure it? Unemployment must surely reflect "excess supply" of labour. Suppose observed unemployment to be a stable proxy for the theorist's concept of "excess supply." A reasonable hypothesis that deserves a try. Phillips tried it and thought the results encouraging enough to warrant further pursuit of the general approach. But the hypothesis was falsified in the same paper where it was advanced. The "loops" in the data and the vertical scatter at low unemployment showed that the two variables were not related by a (single-valued) function.

In a famous paper, Samuelson and Solow[1] used a Phillips Curve regression as the basis for a discussion of the policy-maker's "Dilemma"—he cannot have price-stability and a tolerable level of unemployment at the same time. This Dilemma discussion set the context in which the Phillips Curve became popularised, quickly gaining entry to the textbooks and from there into the financial pages.

The change in the perception of the Phillips-curve construct that this came to entail was of considerable significance. The Dilemma discussion tentatively treated Phillips Curve regres-

1. Samuelson, P. A. and R. H. Solow (1960).

sion results, in effect, as information about an "opportunity set" facing policy-makers. Although this seems a natural enough extension of Phillips's attempt to predict the rate of wage-inflation from unemployment data, the opportunity set notion turned developments onto a completely new track. To non-economists the notion had tremendous appeal—the Phillips Curve in this version, promises to dispense with the need to learn a lot of "technicalities" of inflation and unemployment theory, wrapping up what you need to know about both subjects in one neat package. But economists too were influenced—much of subsequent research and discussion has been in pursuit of the opportunity set Phillips Curve rather than "merely" wage-inflation prediction.

The change in the perception of the Phillips Curve has had two effects:

a. It entirely changes the research question. Finding what variables will give a good proxy for the excess supply of labour and thus provide an equation predicting wage-inflation is one research task. Finding a stable reduced form relating inflation and unemployment is a completely different one. One task may be feasible and promising and the other a fool's quest. In any case, they are not the same. Much of the later Phillips Curve literature strikes one as confused in this regard.
b. It recast the theory of stabilisation policy as a "choice problem" exercise in the conceptual space given by the two axes of the Phillips Curve.

With (a), we will not concern ourselves. The entire tangle of problems referred to as the "Phillips Curve controversy" is irrelevant to what follows. We will be concerned with (b) only.

VIII

The inflation rate and the unemployment rate are considered as "outcomes" of policy. To alternative policy programmes under consideration there will correspond combinations of the two forecast ("for next year") with more or less accuracy. The locus of these combinations is thought of as an opportunity set boundary for policy-makers. It may shift, tilt, etc., but at any given date, there it is.

The habit of thinking of any consciously undertaken action as requiring, if it is to be intelligible, a preference ordering over the alternative "outcomes" now takes over. Where there is an "opportunity set" there must be "tastes." Otherwise, how could one decide at all? So a preference ordering with the "outcomes" of alternative policy actions as its arguments must exist. Except for being defined over "bads" rather than "goods," why should it not have all the same general properties that give stability, convexity, etc., to a consumer's utility-function (for, say, apples and oranges)? Except, of course, that this one ought, in a democratic society, to be a "social welfare function,"—i.e., a hypothetical preference ordering over alternative "states of society" that does not represent the policy-maker's own interests and sympathies but is derived, somehow, from similar preference orderings held by individual members of society.

Voilà. We have managed to squeeze a very complex question of what is a "wise" course of policy for a nation into a two-dimensional conceptual space (with, let us say, the unemployment percentage on one axis and the rate of CPI inflation on the other). And we have partitioned the problem "neatly" into questions of feasible "opportunities" and of appropriate "tastes."

What are the consequences of accepting this conception of the problem and of purveying it in public places?

The practical consequences we have experienced and are still experiencing. But leave that aside. What twist will acceptance of the conception give to the work and discussions of economists?

The partitioning of the problem complex into questions of "opportunities" and of "tastes" appears very nearly to be a partitioning between questions about which one makes, respectively, "positive" and "normative" statements. Suppose we take it that way.

Then the economist will tend to think of his strictly professional responsibilities as confined to the determination of the "policy options"; i.e., to the tasks of forecasting. On this side of the partition, where positive statements rule, the disciplined Popperian process of Conjectures and Refutations will operate.

Having defined the rest of the problem for himself as "a matter of preferences" he will tend to ignore the *factual consequences* of inflation and unemployment as subjects of research. Value judgements he knows to be statements irreducible within economics itself. Economic enquiry halts where it runs up against normative propositions and does not trespass on the ground beyond them.

Since the political process does not in fact grind out a social welfare function, no one knows what it is. For an economist who looks at this as "a matter of preferences," it is by that token also a matter on which "everyone is entitled to his say" including, of course, he himself. At the same time, however, to such statements about what "should be" done will apply that part of the professional credo which runs: *De gustibus non est disputandum.* Here, then, we do not necessarily expect to see a Popperian process in operation. So when economists earnestly lecture students, newspaper readers or members of Congress on what the public good dictates with regard to the inflation-unemployment trade-off to be made next, what they say may not have been through any crucible of Popperian criticism. But they are likely to get a serious and attentive hearing anyway. Many people will defer to some degree to our opinions on the rather natural assumption that, selectively filtered through personal value judgements as these normative recommendations may be, what has been thus filtered must still be a much more detailed, objective knowledge of what inflation and/or unemployment *"means"* than laymen would possess. But is not such deference quite misplaced?

"Values" and "knowledge" will be conflated in what they hear and read, all right. But how they are fused and how they might be disentangled is obscure. And when their expression takes the form of an indifference map in Phillips Curve space, who is to distinguish shoddy ethics and sketchy knowledge from their genuine, warranted counterparts?

IX

The unclear fusion of values and knowledge poses a nasty predicament for whoever thinks he sees "unsound" views gaining ground. To join debate means to get oneself entangled in the "rules of the game" associated with this entire conception. There seems to be no avenue by which the "real issues" can be reached that does not lead first through a quagmire of "ideology" and what not. Fastidious aversion to mud on your face will put you on the sidelines. So one wades in.

For example: In 1973 (say), someone who had retired on a private pension in 1966 or thereabouts had already been taken for one-third of his life's savings. Stabilising the inflation rate as it was going would mean that he could only look forward to more of the same. At the same time, the unemployment rate was high but the average duration of unemployment was not yet such as to cause a substantial fraction of the unemployed to exhaust their rights to unemployment compensation. "Cyclical" or "non-structural" unemployment is to the individual a temporary status; he is partially compensated for it through transfer payments; he may possibly have options for investing in human capital that are profitable during the period when forgone current earnings are reduced; he may by his own subsequent efforts "undo" some of the loss of his lifetime earnings, and so on. None of which—one is quick to add—makes his unemployment a matter of social indifference. The man on a private pension shrinking in real purchasing power will not see his current real income loss reversed; he is not compensated for it; he is beyond the age where learning additional skills or working harder will get him back "nearly" to his pre-inflation wealth-positions.

And so on. Hopeless, isn't it? These two hypothetical individuals are not the only ones affected. They are not "typical." Even if they were, such arguments could not lead to conclusions with which any decent person will be compelled to agree. They cannot settle what our social value judgements "ought to be."

Still, as matters stand, it is *not* pointless to pursue such discussion. On the contrary, reluctant as we will be to get into such a compromising, unscientific tangle, such debate cannot be dispensed with. For it will reveal to others (and remind us of) two things. First, it will reveal the immense, tangled complex of factual consideration—meaning the fates of individuals—relevant to any responsible judgement *and* how little we know about that. Second, it will make clear to everyone that there is *no* simple, coherent, widely acceptable ethic—or, indeed, party platform—such as to enable us, once the factual consequences are taken into account, to derive general (time-independent) guidelines of the type "one unemployment percentage point is as bad as *x* inflation points."

In an older tradition of scientific enquiry, that posed *Wertfreiheit* as an approachable even if unreachable ideal, the economist was obliged to keep his social values to himself and out of his work. This conception no longer rules even in the natural science fields from which it was at one time presumed to have been imported. The "right" to state and argue for one's social value judgements is now no longer challenged. But this "right" may be on the way to something more—to becoming a privilege with which to cloak sketchy analysis, casual empiricism, and shallow thinking on questions of gravity to the common weal— and with which to shield the basis for judgements from critical scrutiny.

X

Since disputing over tastes is so fruitless, one is tempted to try another tack. Professional training may "pervert" an economist's attitudes to social questions to some degree, but they are naturally shaped very largely by the same influences that operate on everybody else. If disputing these attitudes is pointless and/or illegitimate, those critical of them are tempted into sociological reflection to "explain" them instead. For example:

i. In some not too sharply defined sense most economists are egalitarian at heart. Do we think, implicitly, of the pensioner (again) as someone who, if he "really" has a lot to lose from inflation, must by that token be "pretty well-to-do"? And of the "working classes," who risk unemployment, as *prima facie* poor? Does the reluctance to put a brake on inflation stem-in-part from a vague feeling that anti-inflationary measures amount to "regressive" economic policy? If so, are the generalisations about the groups affected behind that presumption sound ones? Or, are we concerned, in this illustration, with groups that, since they differ in age, differ also in their respective ratios of inflation-taxed net worth to relatively inflation-proof human capital? And, if it were the case that letting inflation rip is indeed the "progressive" thing to do, is it also the constitutionally and politically sound way to go about the redistribution of wealth?

ii. The memory of the horrors of the Great Depression of the 1930s still runs deep in the American polity—which, until now, has not experienced serious inflation. But the economics profession is probably the particular repository of this tribal memory of large-scale unemployment—it is ingrained in assistant professors that were not born then in ways they are hardly aware of. (Meanwhile the intellectual immigrants from Continental Europe who so greatly contributed to the flowering of economics in the United States, and who *had* experienced serious inflations first-hand, have moved out of influence in Academia into retirement—promptly to be swindled out of their retirement income by inflation. Do their still active colleagues sometimes send them a grateful thought?) The view that unemployment is the worst of all social ills is the lesson American economists have drawn from the 1930s. Their advice on the unemployment-inflation trade-off is heavily influenced by it. And that advice is contributing to impoverishing the retirement years of that very generation which suffered through the unemployment years of the 1930s (and then went to war).

iii. We used to assume that equities and other real assets were inflation-proof. One lesson of the last several years is that human capital is virtually the only reasonably reliable store of value in periods like the present. Is it just coincidence that active academics (*not* the emeriti), media commentators and "intellectuals" in general think the rest of society makes too much fuss over inflation as a social problem? Or is it perchance the case that these groups—who conduct the public debate on social, economic, and political issues—are composed disproportionally of individuals on whose personal experience the consequences of inflation are not brought home with full force? The real value of top-grade "intellectual" human capital is insensitive to inflations and, for that matter, unless complemented by strong political convictions, to changes in political regime. Over the last century, the "intellectual classes" have a sorry record of toying with revolutionary notions. On occasion, the "man in the street" will show a ready appetite for them. Ordinary people who would, on such occasions, rather keep the hell out of the street will feel differently.

XI

The last ten years have brought a spreading realisation among economists that subjective value judgements on the relative social undesirability of inflation and unemployment are not good enough and that the presumed objective components of the policy recommendations made need be brought out in the open. One result of this has been a number of simple social benefit-cost (or, rather, comparative social cost) calculations on inflation and unemployment. The early examples of this brand of Political Arithmetick have produced numerical results that, on the face of it, strongly *support* the most complacent attitude about inflation: it takes an inflation rate well into double digits or even near triple digits to equal the social cost of 1 (additional) per cent of unemployment. Such "objectification" of the issue compels adoption of a common unit of social cost-measurement; this, of course, is unnecessary when the problem is left in "preference space." The results obtained depend overwhelmingly on the choice of measuring-rod for social cost that has been made. For unemployment, the choice has been the national product loss attributable to the market inactivity of the unemployed. At first sight, this may seem a "natural" measure for the social cost of unemployment. A second look is less reassuring. In any case, this choice necessitates measuring the cost of inflation also in terms of "output loss"—a less obvious notion. What is thus quantified as the cost of inflation is some estimate of the productive and transactional inefficiencies associated with attempts to economise on the holding of money balances that will be induced by the negative real rate on money during inflations. This, of course, turns out to be a modest number. To the extent that inflation does not affect the size of the "G.N.P. pie" annually turned out by the economy, it is considered to have zero social cost.

This social cost concept, then, is drawn from a social welfare function into which "distributive justice" arguments do not enter in the sketchy, implicit, and haphazard way in which they tend to be present in expressions of "social preferences." On the unemployment side, the "output-cost" is the same whether the unemployed receive compensation or not. It is similarly invariant to the time that individuals spend in an unemployment pool of given size. If one individual is "voluntarily" unemployed and full of hope that he can do better than the employment opportunities immediately open to him while another individual in despair and resentment sees no better alternative than criminal activity—the measure of "social cost" is the same. On the inflation side, the neglect of all other consequences than aggregate output-loss may be given a semblance of respectability by assuming (a) that redistributive losers *can* be compensated, or (b) that they *will* be compensated, or (c) that, as the inflation is or becomes foreseen, transactors will be able to safeguard themselves so as to make compensation irrelevant. None of these (including the first one) is sound on the face of it. What particular mix of the three is relied upon in these cost-calculations is not always clear. The questions left dangling are without end: How is the probability of receiving or the ability of obtaining compensation distributed among losers? What is the probability that compensation will be paid by gainers? What institutional mechanisms exist or can be conceived to carry out re-redistribution? By what methods are the gains and losses to be ascertained and accurately measured? How are the skills required to conduct one's affairs successfully in an inflationary regime distributed in society? And assuming all these things to be known and settled, can we evaluate the results as if they were "final outcomes"? Or do, perhaps, further social consequences flow and economic implications follow from these "given" results?

Economists who have tried their hand at this sort of Political Arithmetick have not claimed anything more than rough-and-ready first approximations. The suggestion is rather that this type of "objectification" of "social preferences" gives us a starting-point for a Popperian Growth of Knowledge process of successive rounds of improved conjectures and more sophisticated refutations. Some work along this line, starting from one or another specific criticism, has been attempted. It has led to no more than trivial adjustments in the "numbers." What it *has* demonstrated is that the earliest such calculations were rough-ready-*and-robust* with regard to model specifications and estimating methods—which is to say, it has demonstrated that the initial choice of "output-loss" as the commensurable unit completely dominates the results.

For societies in which "Man lives by G.N.P. alone," is motivated in his conduct only by the collective total of G.N.P., and where it does not matter who gets it, by what rules, or through what institutional mechanisms, we can take it as firmly established that inflation is a trivial social problem. Further efforts to refine and adjust these estimates are superfluous. One may accept the result mentioned as an "arithmetical certainty."

Given what we have thus learned, it strikes one as odd—funny, even—that historians have all but invariably been so very harsh in their judgement of those statesmen and potentates who have presided over major inflations through the ages and that they have given such "inflated grades" to currency reformers and restorers of monetary stability. One infers that, as usual, historians have not had the right model. Having now learned better, thanks to modern quantitive methods, one must earnestly hope that our leaders will not be afflicted with an old-fashioned concern for those posthumous reputations that historians administer but will let their conduct be soundly guided by nought else than their prospects in the next election.

XII

I know I have not lived up to customary standards of rational, objective discussion so far. I feel compelled to take up these "issues," but I *cannot make sense of them.* Not being able to make sense of what I am talking about cramps my style.

The benefit-cost arithmetic is not my basic problem. It is the more general, underlying Social Welfare Function conception—of which these "output-loss" calculations represent a class of crudely "objectified" special cases—that does not make sense.

Two axes metered in apples and oranges; their relative market price; the budget of an individual; his fruity tastes; a budget-line, a convex indifference curve, a tangency point—and on to a "rational" solution to an economic problem. These are the notions that we have, by some analogy, transferred lock, stock and barrel into the conceptual space of the Phillips diagram. Inflation and unemployment are "bads" rather than "goods" but, *mutatis mutandis,* one naturally expects a "rational" solution to stabilisation policy to pop out of this thing, if it is only handled right.

It is then disturbing that the policy-record does not strike one as more "rational" since this conception took hold than it was before. Perhaps the analogy needs checking? Consider:

i. The polity is not "like" an individual consumer. The Crusoe metaphor, always far-fetched, fails us totally, for example. Or should we write a New Chapter? Wherein Robinson takes a house-cure for idleness, gets that sinking numéraire feeling and imposes a ceiling price on apples in terms of oranges and follows it up with an excess profits tax on oranges?

ii. Inflation and unemployment are not "like" apples and oranges—unless, perhaps, we are thinking of Discordia's golden apple (which may have been an orange—a tomato?—also a matter of dispute).

iii. Are inflation and unemployment in the "social welfare function" (S.W.F.) as indices of social discord and political unrest, perhaps? At least, such a version reminds us of the uneven incidence of costs and benefits and hence of the presence of conflicting individual interests. If A and B have directly opposing interests on a given issue, we do not ordinarily proceed by supposing that sundry conditions for the aggregation of their "tastes" are fulfilled so that a collective utility function for the social group AB can be formed, which is then optimised to resolve the conflict.

Aggregation does not make sense. But, then, neither does the notion that individuals have preference functions that, in addition to the usual arguments, include the rate of change of some price index and the national average unemployment rate. There is nothing to aggregate in the first place. But what kind of S.W.F. is it that is not built up by some specified aggregation procedure from the valuations of individuals? How do we "legitimise" it?

iv. Leave legitimacy aside and consider whether this could be some dictator's utility-function. It had better be a dictator confident in his own caprice—for transitivity, convexity, etc., will not go very far towards putting together a guiding Principle of Justice. But no matter—the thought experiment allows us to ask whether there might exist an underlying general welfare theory, too complex and costly in its information requirements to be implemented but in the operational version of which unemployment and inflation serve as "proxies" for the "real arguments"—regrettably poor proxies, perhaps, but the best that can be done. Our dictator should be "knowledgeable," therefore, and able to keep track of every subject's fate.

We should start from detailed state-descriptions of the system. The dictator's utility-function is defined over such States. The elements of a state-description would reflect "how individual subjects are doing." Not in terms of their own utility, however, but in terms reflecting their unemployment and inflation experience *separately*. Otherwise, the notion of a S.W.F. defined over unemployment and inflation "proxies" is lost from the start.

Consider unemployment first. Imagine a vector of some millions of elements, one for each working-age, able-bodied, sound-of-mind subject. Put a "1" for employed and a "0" for unemployed. We might suppose our dictator to be ranking all such vectors and his ranking to be transitive and all that. We now notice, however, that he is neglecting the duration of unemployment, the probability of re-employment tomorrow, the distinction between "voluntary" and "involuntary" unemployment—and many other things. So we should proceed to remedy these errors and omissions. Unfortunately, every step we take in this direction will carry us further away from a state-description for which a count of the unemployed could be a "proxy." It becomes clear, in fact, that the unemployment rate is if anything worse as a proxy for the relevant welfare consequences than it is as a predictor of money wage changes. So let us drop it and turn to inflation.

Here we might, as a first step, imagine a matrix where each

column-vector gives the balance sheet of a subject household. Again, let the dictator know "how much he likes" any state thus described. Consider the matrix as our operand. Some certain inflation-rate—say, 10 per cent on C.P.I.—will be our operator. Applying operator to operand, we obtain a state transformation resulting in a new matrix. (Use of a price idex, rather than individual prices, fudges the transformation, of course.) The new state has a different value to the dictator. Note, however, that we do not and cannot assign "utility" to the operator—the inflation rate; it is associated with *changes* in the value of the S.W.F. Note also that this association is *not a stable one.* Apply the same operator repeatedly and the successive transformations obtained are *not* the same. Nor can we have any guarantee that the process will settle down, after a limited number of steps, to repeated identity-transformations in such a way that evaluation of such steady states will serve as an acceptable approximation to the "utility" of the entire process. It may not settle down ever.

v. In the single consumer example, the apples and oranges are "final" and "ultimate" consumer goods. He eats them and they are finished with. Bygone fruits are bygones and leave no lasting rot in the system. Tomorrow we start all over again with essentially the same decision-problem.

Inflation and unemployment are not "like" apples and oranges in this respect either. With them you do not "step into the same river twice". Troy was never the same after Discordia's apple had been "redistributed."

They have further consequences. The behaviour of our dictator's subjects adapts to the experience. He needs to keep track also of another matrix (of individual "behaviour coefficients") and to evaluate the transformations that it undergoes as well. As a particular historical process unfolds, he will find, moreover, that the original matrix of balance sheets needs to be supplemented with additional information—for the property rights and contract forms that underlie its definition are themselves being transformed.

But here we may as well cease and desist, for it is clear that wherever such a search for the ultimate arguments of a S.W.F. of "true generality" might end up, the observed inflation rate will be utterly and totally hopeless as an "intermediate variable" in any reasonable procedure for evaluating such irreversible historical processes.

XIII

"The social welfare function is a concept as broad and empty as language itself—and as necessary."[2] Perhaps. With any given language, though, we need some set of injunctions: "Whereof one cannot speak . . ." etc.

The concepts of the "New" welfare economics at one time did useful service in identifying the dangers lurking in the "Old." Yet, in contexts such as the present one, what makes the S.W.F. notion survive—except fascination with its inexhaustible short-comings, so many of which will look potentially remediable.?

The Samuelsonian "necessity" of imagining a S.W.F. follows only from prior acceptance of the "necessity" of conceptualising any problem of policy in choice-theoretical terms. Of the concepts of choice-theory we may also say that they are "as broad and empty as language itself . . ." etc. Again, misuse of the language needs to be guarded against. Naiveté about the definition of the "outcomes" of choice may, as we have seen, set this engine of analysis to producing the most appalling muddles. But there are more serious questions to consider beyond such abuses. Is a choice-theoretical formulation always the *sine qua non* for "rational" conduct of policy? The "choice" may be between irreversible historical processes that we ill understand and which we can control only to the extent that a rodeo rider controls the Brahma bull. Squeezed into the apples and oranges frame, the world is portrayed "as if" understood and subject to precalculated control. When the "as if" clause hides *more* in the way of unrecognized distortion than of probabilistic approximation of the situation, the "constructivist error" is afoot. And that way lies the "Collectivisation of *Hubris*."[3]

We should be on guard against the type of mentality we are cultivating, or we will end up with students trained to translate human drama into jargon: Assume a young man named Oedipus X; his utility-function is quadratic, his opportunities strictly convex, and so, naturally, he. . . .

2. Quoted from Samuelson (1952), p. 37.
3. Cf. Spengler (1972).

CHAPTER ELEVEN

Schools, "Revolutions," and Research Programmes in Economic Theory

I met Imre Lakatos only once. I will not soon forget him. I still do not know how much economics he knew, but he was not lacking for very definite ideas about the paper he wanted me to write. The script that he ordered was to retell my version of the Keynesian revolution story,[1] attempt to make the issues comprehensible to a largely non-economist audience, reassess my earlier work with the benefit of hindsight, and discuss whether the story can be told to advantage as one of a Kuhnian revolution or as a shift from one Lakatosian research programme to another. I did not want to rehash my views on Keynes again. But the "Growth of Knowledge" literature holds fascination also for economists—even as the lack of social science case studies as inputs into this philosophical debate leaves us unsure about what exactly we can learn from it. Lakatos felt the time was ripe for philosophers of science to move into the study of the evolution of the social sciences. Economists would have to help out with supplying the case studies. He made a good case. But, mainly, he was simply a hard man to refuse—as those fortunate enough to have known that remarkable man for a longer time will, I am sure, well recall.

So, this paper will attempt what I understood Imre Lakatos to want. Part I deals in general terms with some of the problems in the way of applying recent Growth of Knowledge theories to the history of economics.[2] Part II draws on the

1. Cf. Leijonhufvud [1968a], [1969].
2. Part I is obviously philosophically amateurish. It cannot be overlooked, but I trust it will be forgiven. It is, in any case, the price philosophers will have to pay for the cooperation of economists.

Keynesian revolution "case" for somewhat more concrete illustrations of these problems.

I

I. 1

The new Growth of Knowledge theories combine the philosopher's traditional preoccupation with epistemology and the historical study of the actual evolution of the sciences. Methodology of the old, sternly normative brand never did have much appeal to scientific practitioners.[3] The recent Growth of Knowledge literature has gained a wider audience. One may conjecture that it is chiefly the efforts to explain the actual evolution of knowledge, and less the modifications in methodological prescriptions that such inquiry is producing, that accounts for the renewed interest among scientists in the philosophy of science. This is so, at any rate, in my own case. Could these new theories be used to structure an account of the history of economics that would give it a more readily intelligible, more instructive pattern? That is the most interesting question. To the economist, it also appears to have logical primacy, for his appraisal of any methodological prescriptions that the theory advances will be heavily influenced by the answer.

The problem is that philosophers of science tend to combine epistemology and historical analysis so as to make it exceedingly difficult, at least for philosophical dilettantes, to disentangle the normative from the positive aspects of their Growth of Knowledge theories. One starts out reading an often spell-binding historical tale—for they tend to have the merit of writing well—that ends up by degrees as a morality play. The outsider is apt to be similarly captivated by the skillful cut, thrust and parry of

3. When I was a child, the itinerant knife-grinder was still a common figure in Sweden. He would show up at the kitchen door and ask: "Want to have any knives sharpened?" Most often he was told: "No, thank you, we're all right." They tended to be persistent characters. Another knock: "Bet your knives are in bad shape. I know they are. People shouldn't be allowed to use knives like that . . ." And you would say: "We are busy today. Please go away." But soon he knocks again and there he is, demonstrating: "Look, with my knives you can split hairs!" Some farmers, it was said, would set their dogs, on people like that. Some philosophers of science may, of course, feel that, without the grindstone always in evidence, charges of vagrancy without visible means of support are inescapable.

the critical debates and controversial exchanges among philosophers of science—but not apt to be helped in this regard. Economists, in particular, who have themselves always to be on guard against mixing normative and positive statements, will be bothered by the Growth of Knowledge discussion's apparent "drunkard's walk" along and across this sacred line.

Lakatos's methodology of scientific research programmes (MSRP) presents one with this problem in its most difficult form—albeit for reasons that economists (themselves addicted to "rational reconstructions" of observed behavior) can well appreciate. Science history, in Lakatos, is "rationally reconstructed"—i.e. explained with the use of the assumption that scientists make the methodologically correct decisions. To the practitioner this may be an on the whole welcome change from those chastizing accounts of how science ought to be done whose stringent criteria not even the "best" work done in one's field ever seemed to meet. But it would seem to put in prospect much the same predicaments as those produced for economists by their use of the "maximizing behavior" postulate.

Consider, for example, what attitude to take towards apparently disconfirming empirical evidence. Should the constitutive hypotheses of the rational reconstruction theory all be retained in the "hard core"? If so, the behavior of scientists in the apparently anomalous historical episode was "appropriate" to their epistemological situation and the account given of that situation should therefore be reconstructed so as to eliminate the anomaly.[4] Or else, Lakatos's theory—regarded as a positive theory of the evolution of scientific knowledge—should be taken as falsified for the case in question. If rational reconstruction is truly in the hard core, the normative preoccupations of philosophers become superfluous—for scientists act in accordance with methodological prescription "whether they know it or not." If, on the other hand, the theory is to be taken as falsifiable, the strictly "internalist" Lakatosian position is imperilled. The assumption that the history of science can be

4. Compare Latsis' discussion of "situational determinism" in economics, in Latsis [1972]. I discuss the status of the Maximizing Behavior postulate in economics at length—and using Lakatosian terminology—in *Maximization and Marshall* (unpublished).

rationally reconstructed serves the same function of keeping "externalist rubbish" beyond the pale as does the maximizing behavior postulate in defending the economist from the threat of having to admit psychologists and sociologists to share in his enterprise.[5]

I. 2

The philosophical layman reading Kuhn or Lakatos, Hanson or Toulmin finds analogies to, or illustrations from his own field coming to mind in rich profusion. The temptation is strong to rush ahead and dress up one's account of, say, the history of economics in the same terminology. The exercise can be both exciting and genuinely stimulating—but it prejudges the applicability to economics of Growth of Knowledge theories developed to "fit" physics and biology.

Economists could benefit from the perspectives provided by a theoretically structured account of the history of their field. Philosophers of science, one presumes, would like to draw on the history of the social sciences for independent "test"-cases for Growth of Knowledge theories originally developed with reference to the natural sciences. If philosophers and economists are to cooperate to mutual advantage, the economists' end of the bargain must include the obligation so to present our doctrine historical episodes that anomalous characteristics calling for further work on the part of philosophers are brought out—or so that "falsification" (if admitted) is a possibility. Use of the concepts of philosophy of science theories so loose and impressionistic that the history of economics will automatically be made to "fit" will then not do.

Traditionally, the history of economic doctrines has for the most part been written as a straight historical narrative—as a chronological story of "progress" by accumulating analytical improvements in a field of inquiry of more or less stable demarcation and with a largely fixed set of questions. Such narratives are not structured in accordance with any explicit Growth of Knowledge theory[6]—and one cannot presume, therefore, that

5. Cf. the papers by H. A. Simon and S. J. Latsis in Latsis, ed. (1976).
6. One might perhaps take such accounts of economic doctrine history as "progress" as reflecting a Growth of Knowledge theory akin to the "absolutist" epistemology for

the categories in terms of which it has been found convenient to organize them will serve the task that Imre Lakatos had in mind.

Consider, for example, the various "schools" in the history of economics: the French Physiocrats, the British classical, German historical and Austrian schools, the Lausanne, Stockholm, Cambridge, and Chicago schools and several others. Were these associated with distinct Kuhnian paradigms? Do the labels denote Lakatosian research programmes?[7] We also have labels of wider coverage: Marxian economics, Keynesian economics, neoclassical economics. Are these, perhaps, better candidates? The division and subdivision of economics into fields and areas of inquiry cuts across these classifications into "schools." Do the cells of the resulting matrix provide more appropriate objects of analysis?

Similarly, the term "revolution" has become attached to certain developments in economics: the "marginalist revolution," the "imperfect competition revolution," the "Keynesian revolution." But since these were coined well before T. S. Kuhn and since Kuhn has no such social science episodes in the "sample" he worked with, there are no strong reasons to presume that our revolutions are of the Kuhnian class. Nor do we have a *prima facie* case for taking them to be shifts from degenerating to progressive research programmes.[8]

The "doctrines" and "schools" of economics are not all animals of the same species as, say, Ptolemaic and Copernican astronomy or the Phlogiston and Oxygene theories of combus-

which Toulmin chooses Gottlieb Frege as representative. Frege was primarily concerned with mathematics and, as a latter-day Platonist, took it as a model for the sciences in general: "Often it is only after immense intellectual effort, which may have continued over centuries, that humanity at last succeeds in achieving *knowledge of a concept in its pure form*, by stripping off *the irrelevant accretions which veil it from the eye of the mind*." (Quoted by Toulmin [1972], p. 56.) Economic doctrine histories that concentrate heavily on the history of "pure" economic analysis (which is essentially mathematical in nature) will tend to read as variations on this theme.

7. Is the designation of "schools" by city or country of origin a practice that tends to disappear with the maturation of a science?

8. Latsis [1972] denies the Theory of Imperfect Competition the status of an independent research programme. He treats it as a branch, degenerating from the start, of the neoclassical Theory of the Firm. I think his judgment of Imperfect Competition theory entirely justified. Note, however, that what he has to say about "situational determinism" applies as well to the neoclassical theory of Consumer Behavior. It is this approach to the analysis of the behavior of agents in general, rather than just to firms, that may qualify as a research programme.

tion; nor, moreover, do they very often succeed each other in such clear-cut fashion. In short, the basic objects and events in economics to which we might seek to apply the Growth of Knowledge theories developed for the natural sciences are not defined for us by previous work in the history of economics.

Economists are, of course, quite capable of enumerating the characteristic features of economic models and used to distinguishing between various theories through point-by-point comparisons of such properties. Although a necessary preliminary to the definition of paradigms or research programmes, such lists of model properties do not by themselves accomplish the task. They do not necessarily convey the essential *pattern* of theories nor yield criteria for deciding whether "different" economic models belong to distinct research programmes or the same programme.

The newer Growth of Knowledge theories emphasize the gestalt of clusters of theories. It is indeed largely this emphasis that is earning them so much attention outside philosophical circles. They address problems of genuine concern to scientific practitioners about which the older, more normatively oriented philosophy of science had relatively little to say. Scientists will on occasion be forced to reflect on the arational gestalt of their more basic beliefs—on the, as it were, "Gödelian" pattern that is not to be rationalized within the theory itself. From it flows the stuff of which hard-to-settle controversies are made: views on what questions a theory is and is not obliged to answer and on what does and does not constitute evidence; persistent adherence to a theory in the face of falsification of some of its hypotheses; translation-difficulties between "paradigms"; and Kuhnian (or Frankian) losses.

With these sometimes disturbing aspects of scientific work economists may be more thoroughly acquainted than most. Economics is a controversial subject and our controversies drag on. But controversies may rage within as well as between research programmes. Persistent controversy does not necessarily indicate to us a struggle between contending gestalt-conceptions of what the economic world is like; even if it did, the record of the arguments used by participants may not instruct us in how accurately to characterize the essentials of the two contending programmes.

Learning to do so will have to be the first order of business if we are to make the history of economics one of the proving grounds for Growth of Knowledge theories. But that is not an easy task. There is no—can be no— "canned programme" for how it is to be performed. In the absence of fixed rules, attempts so to characterize economic theories will themselves be controversial. Professional agreement on the adequacy of such gestalt-characterizations is apt to emerge, if at all, only through successive rounds of "conjectures and refutations."[9]

I. 3

One of the virtues of MSRP is that Lakatos gives us somewhere to start. Given a "list" of the characteristic properties of an economic model (or of the features that distinguish it from some alternative model), we should ask whether they derive from "hard core" propositions or from propositions belonging in the "protective belt." If all the distinguishing features of two models are of the "belt"-variety, the models belong in the same family; if some are found lodged in the "hard cores," we have distinct research programmes to contend with. Now, having the Lakatosian distinction between "hard core" and "belt" in hand does not, of course, give us an automatized "routine" for identifying research programmes in economics. The relevant judgments will often be hard to make. But clear-cut cases should be common. There will be propositions such that, if they are negated, one finds it impossible to patch up the model at all, etc.

Unfortunately, the matter will not end there for examination of economic models will never yield a full description of the corresponding research programmes. The formal structure of the model does not tell us anything about the "positive heuristic" of the programme. It does not, for example, define the scope claimed for the theory. Statements belonging to the positive heuristic must be regarded, Lakatos tells us, as part of the programme's hard core. But we will not get them off a "list" of characteristic model properties.

9. We need to consider such questions as (i) whether two (or more) of the "schools" traditionally recognized in the history of economic doctrines may not have the same "hard core" and thus belong to the same research programme, and (ii) whether one and the same "school" may not over time have shifted some of its main tenets from the "protective belt" to the "hard core" (and *vice versa*) and thus in effect transformed itself into a new research programme.

Trying to identify the research programmes of economics from such "lists" will miss some boats also for another reason. Economists are in the habit of using "theory" and "model" as synonymous terms. For the remainder of this paper, I will use them in distinct senses. With "theory" I will mean a "patterned set of substantive beliefs" about how the economic system works. (In Lakatosian terms, we can take "theory" to be what remains of a research programme if we exclude the "positive heuristic.") A "model" is the formal representation of a "theory," or of a subset of it, or of some aspect of it. We will seldom, if ever, have a "model" that gives an exhaustive account of the hard core of the corresponding theory. We may miss quite essential characteristics of research programmes, therefore, if we approach the problem only by inference from "lists" of distinctive model properties.

An example may be more helpful than further disquisition in general terms at this point. The long-lived "monetarist" controversy is illustrative. Is it the case that "monetarist" macroeconomics and "Keynesian" macroeconomics belong to distinct research programmes or are they to be regarded as competing theories fighting it out in the "protective belt" of the same one? A comparison of models commonly employed to represent the two theories will show, *inter alia,* that the magnitudes hypothesized for certain functional "elasticities" differ. If that is all there is to it, we should plainly consider them as belonging to the same research programme. Conclusive empirical evidence for the range in which the values of these coefficients actually fall may be hard to come by, but in principle—or so it would seem—both models should attach the same "meaning" to that evidence when and if obtained. And that should settle the matter.[10] It is as if we had two contending Newtonian theories that

10. The most widely known "monetarist," Professor Milton Friedman, has for a long time consistently voiced the position that "monetarists" and "(neo)-Keynesians" share essentially the same theory and that their differences all derive from contrasting hypotheses concerning certain crucial empirical magnitudes. (He has also, however, persistently denied that the issues can be defined as a "simple" matter of the magnitude of the interest-elasticity of the excess demand for money—an otherwise oft-repeated contention in the debate.) In his recent attempts to provide an explicit representation for his theory, accordingly, Friedman chose to use the "Keynesian," so-called "IS-LM" framework as his language of formal discourse. Cf. Friedman [1970], [1971].

In my opinion, as indicated in the text, there are "hard core" differences between the

differ by the value assumed for the coefficient of gravitation. But, as it turns out, this is not all there is to it. Monetarist "theory" differs from Keynesian also in including the "belief" that the economic system will exhibit strong tendencies to converge relatively rapidly to the equilibrium values of its "real" variables and that the equilibrium values, most specifically of employment and "real" interest rates, are (to a first approximation, at least) independent of general monetary and fiscal stabilization policies. Now this qualifies, in my judgment, as a distinct gestalt—the entire "vision," to use Schumpeter's term, of how the economic system works is at variance from that underlying "Keynesian economics."[11] We should recognize the monetarist controversy as involving two distinct research programmes, therefore. But the standard models in terms of which much of the debate has been conducted are static and incorporate no statements about convergence tendencies, adjustment velocities and the like.

In dealing with economic theories, therefore, we have to recognize that, in addition to those hard-core propositions that appear in (or may be directly inferred from) the formal model structure, there are likely to be additional hard-core "beliefs" belonging to the theory. The former set of hard-core propositions have been through the purgatory of incorporation in (more or less) rigorous formal models; the language in which they are formulated has been honed to fulfil requirements of mathematical consistency with other propositions; they are precise. When an economic theorist uses them, we can know exactly what he is *saying*—although we may be uncertain what he is *talking about* (if ignorant of the hard-core beliefs of his theory

two theories and ones, moreover, that the "IS-LM" framework will not help us define. Not only are these differences at the "cosmological" level not accurately represented by the models used, but they will also lead to divergent interpretation of empirical results.

The September/October 1972 issue of the *Journal of Political Economy* was devoted largely to a debate on Friedman's "monetary framework" between Friedman and five distinguished critics. Professor Tobin opened his critical commentary by thanking Friedman for having ". . . facilitated communication by his willingness to express his argument in a language widely used in macroeconomics, the Hicksian IS-LM apparatus." Yet, this round of the debate did little to clarify old issues and settled none. It did provide still more evidence of mutual misunderstandings.

11. The alternative "visions" afoot with regard to the efficacy of the system's self-regulating mechanisms will be the main substantive theme pursued in Part II below. Cf. also Leijonhufvud [1973a].

that may not appear explicitly in his model). The latter set, however, will—if ever made explicit—be less precisely, more informally stated. The scientific collective may show considerable uncertainty about "how best to put it." They are "hard core" in the minimal sense that they cannot be given up in the face of anomalies while preserving the research programme, but not in the stricter sense that their statement simply cannot be tampered with. They may be apparently quite wooly "grand generalities," somewhat in the nature of cosmological beliefs.

It will be useful, here, to have a distinct term for these informal and, in modelling contexts, implicit propositions. I will use "presupposition"[12] and reserve Lakatos's "hard core statement" for propositions appearing in formal model structures.

I. 4

Arriving at a definition of the research programmes of economics by acceptable characterizations of their essential gestalt-conceptions may be the first order of business, but it is far from being the only conundrum in the way of extending the application of Growth of Knowledge theories to economics. Economics is less mature as a discipline—especially as an empirical discipline—than are the natural sciences. It has to cope with a different and in many respects more recalcitrant subject matter. It is only to be expected that the Growth of Knowledge process observed in economics, will exhibit features, some of them methodologically problematical, that are without close analogies in the history—or, at least, "modern" history—of the physical and biological sciences. Whether these "atypical" characteristics of the collective learning process pose basic, novel problems to philosophers of science coming to economics[13] from the natural sciences will be a debatable question and is not to be prejudged here.

Two of these problematical features of the Growth of Knowledge process observed in economics are put to the fore in Sir John Hicks's essay.[14] The first concerns the always controversial

---

12. This is Collingwood's term. Cf., again, Toulmin [1972], where Collingwood is made to serve as the "relativist" pendant to the portrait of Frege, the "absolutist."
13. Hesitant souls may perhaps want to consult my [1973b] before taking the plunge.
14. Cf., Hicks [1976].

question of what role must be accorded "external" factors in a theory of the development of science. The second relates to the difficulty discussed in Section I.3 above as well as to other problems of "substance versus form" in economic theory which will occupy the rest of Part I.

I. 5

The universe that is the object of economic inquiry, Hicks points out, is not unchanging, but evolves. The evolution of the economy and the development of economic knowledge occur, moreover, on the same time-scale. Hence, the oft-quoted Einsteinian reflection that "The Lord is subtle, but not mean" will carry little comfort to economists who have to recognize that, by the time the subtle "laws" governing the economic system at some particular date have been found out, the system is apt to have undergone institutional transformations that will dictate the renewal of the quest.[15] This, by itself, will suffice to give "external" factors a role in the history of economics that they lack in the natural sciences and, by that token, render suspect historical accounts structured according to severely "internalist" Growth of Knowledge theories.[16]

Further considerations might be brought in to buttress the argument, but its point appears indisputable as it stands. One may still question, however, whether conceding the point compels one to renounce "internalist" epistemological theory constructions altogether.

The incorporation of all "external" factors, that may be found relevant to the chronological reconstruction of the history of economic doctrines, into a systematic theory of the collective learning process in economics seems an objective beyond reach. The alternative to attempting it would be analogous to what economists routinely do in their own field, namely, to

15. This is only to say, of course, that the economist's theory tends to take much of the institutional setting as "given" and thus fails to comprise the "laws of change" for the institutional framework of economic activity. (I am not denying that some worthwhile exploration has begun into these problem areas.) The Good Lord may not be mean, but if he is too subtle for you, the result is pretty much the same. The problems arising from the (so far) unmanageable complexity of the economist's subject matter we postpone to the subsections to follow.

16. MSRP is, of course, "severely internalist" and in this respect, to my mind, in clear line of descent from the Vienna Circle via Popper.

search for some classification of all the relevant explanatory factors into "exogenous" and "endogenous" variables such that a useful theory of the "open" system comprising the relationships among the endogenous variables may be formulated. Models of this sort will be ahistorical in the straightforward sense that the values of the exogenous variables at different dates must be supplied in order to make explanations of observed historical processes feasible.

A well-known metaphor of Knut Wicksell's may be converted to our purposes here. Consider the task of "explaining" and/or "predicting" the motion of a rocking-horse. Suppose the strength, timing, etc., of the forces impinging on it obey no known "laws"—"you never know what those brats will do next." Predicting its motion becomes a fool's game. (Here the analogy to economics is a bit too close for comfort.) But from the curvature of its runners, the distribution of its weight, etc., it will be possible to construct a model explaining the response to any given shocks. That is about what macroeconomists could hope to accomplish in the way of a "general theory"—except for the added complication that their horse is "live" and grows and develops. One might set a similarly limited ambition for theories of the Growth of Knowledge. They would then be "internalist," in a sense,[17] and relevant "external" factors would have to be brought in *ad hoc* in explaining the particular timing, and so on, of historical episodes.

The pursuit of such a goal will be based on an "ultimate presupposition," the adoption of which is an act of faith, namely, that "there exists a horse," i.e., that there exists a potentially identifiable subsystem, with stable rules of interactions among its elements that may be studied separately from remaining relevant factors. What this requires in the present context is that "internalist" criteria are in fact the predominant determinants of the survival probability of concepts and ideas and of economists' allegiance to research programmes. If political expedience, ideological advocacy or other, more honorable,

17. "In a sense" because the defense of concentration on internal factors—at least as a temporary strategy—essayed here demands that the definition of the line between "internal" and "external" factors be determined, not on *a priori* grounds, but according to whatever division between "endogenous" and "exogenous" variables is found to be feasible in theory construction.

"external" considerations significantly bias the selection among intellectual mutations, it will not work. We need be alert, therefore, to the possibility that even if an "internalist" theory of the Growth of Economic Knowledge appears to do well in "reconstructing" developments of recent decades, it may be entirely inadequate in dealing with the evolution of doctrines in periods antecedent to the academic "professionalization" of the field.

In Part II, we deal only with recent decades. The remainder of this paper will be governed by the "internalist presupposition." Note that this does not entail the fusion of descriptive and normative theory discussed in Section I.1. I will assume that the collective selection of ideas, concepts, models, etc., for survival and development is governed by the "internal logic" of economic inquiry as perceived by a largely academic corps of professionals. But the question whether the internal criteria used by economists are also "epistemologically rational" in the sense of Lakatos (for example) is left open. A "rational" reconstruction is necessarily "internalist," but the converse must not be assumed to hold.

I. 6

Professor Hicks also stresses the necessarily simplified structure of useful economic theories, i.e., their selectivity with regard to the "facts" and relationships included. The economist's models are but schematic or "partial" representations of the system he studies; the complexity of the economy is of an order that makes "general" representation impossible.[18]

18. The ultimate ambition of economics is similarly limited—the basic notion of an "economic system" is that of a particular set of interactions abstracted (by procedures never clearly specified) from the totality of interactions among individuals in the more complex social system. There is a "high-level presupposition," adopted by act of faith, here too—to wit, that economic activities are governed by their own "internal logic" that allows their study to be usefully separated from that of teenage courtship patterns and other social interactions that, in principle, *might* complicate the economist's task beyond what he can manage.

The "Maximizing Behavior postulate" has already been mentioned as an important link in the boundary defenses of economics. Jevons' so-called "Law of Indifference" is another instructive example. It states that "sellers will sell to the highest bidder and buyers buy from the source with the lowest offer-price." Its standard use is as a "harmless," technical postulate supporting the hypothesis of convergence to uniqueness of transactions-prices in a given market—a hypothesis needed, in turn, for "supply-and-demand" analysis. But it also has a sociological interpretation, namely, that transactors

External events will from time to time cause the focus of professional attention to shift from one family of models, one type of representation, to another. But such shifts in the concentration of research do not signify the victory of one research programme over another. There will be problems and policy-issues—for a time less pressing but apt to recur—for which the models in decline provide a better engine of analysis than do the models in ascendancy.[19] The Kuhnian losses in prospect are seen to be prohibitive were one analytical tradition to be promoted to the exclusion of all others. Hence, in economics, we find several analytical traditions surviving side-by-side.

Economic models "illumine different things," as Hicks put it. They are "partial" in the sense of highlighting different aspects of the same real world process and not just in the straightforward sense that the theory of optics deals with only part of the physicist's universe. Nor are the different analytical traditions in economics—Hicks's plutology and catallactics make perfect examples—complementary in the sense that the wave and particle theories of light are. Each of the latter give precise representation for a well-defined class of phenomena. Although the economist has to make use of both plutology and catallactics and finds each tradition to have a comparative advantage for different classes of problems, neither one provides a precise description for any of the processes that are the subject of inquiry. Actual economic systems are of a higher order of *complexity* than are the models of economics.[20] Economics, so far, makes do with "surrogate" models.

interact in markets on the basis of "most favorable price" and, in so doing, ignore relationships of status, kinship, caste, and so on. Nepotism is not a significant determinant of transactions-prices in the resulting theory, for example. So: sociology is kept out. Clearly, here too, we have an "internalist" (as it were) theory that may work well for certain periods and societies but not for others.

One may suggest from this that a study of the boundary-maintaining mechanisms of a discipline should be capable of producing important clues to some of its high-level presuppositions (or hard-core propositions).

19. "Decline" and "ascendancy" here because "degenerating" and "progressive" (in the precise Lakatosian sense) would be inappropriate.

20. Beginning students of economics often have a tendency to rebel against the more obvious and typical abstractions and simplifications of economic theory. Our textbooks, therefore, tend to include standardized sermons on the theme "all useful theory is abstract," that are illustrated, for example, by reference to the unwieldiness of relief maps built to natural scale and in complete detail. The fully acculturated economic

In economics, the *substance* and the *form* of theories are less tightly linked than in the physical sciences. In physics (or so the outsider supposes), practitioners would relatively seldom find reason to distinguish between the substance of a hypothesis and the formal statement of it.[21] There may, indeed, be only "one way to put it" (accurately) and all other formulations are, at best, crude metaphors suitable only in expositions directed to a popular audience. To economists, however, the distinction is anything but a matter to be left to the rarified speculations of philosophers—it is a workaday problem. Our beliefs about the economic world are one thing; what we manage to "catch" of these beliefs in formally structured representation is not altogether the same thing.

As a consequence, economists are forever concerned with the limitation of the languages they use to express what they know—or think they know—about their subject-matter.[22] The so-called "index-number problem" will be the best-known example of a constantly used device that suppresses aspects of theoretical structure or loses empirical information that the

student will gain confidence from recalling that Newton ignored the color of falling objects and got away with it.

It might be preferable to illustrate the relation that most economic models bear to their subject-matter by considering the use of models drawn from sciences dealing with systems of a relatively low order of complexity in fields grappling with systems of a qualitatively higher order of complexity. The use of mechanical models in anatomy and physiology is one such example—and it allows two points to be convincingly made: (i) the anatomist must handle the model with the same precision and "rigor" as is done in mechanics, if it is to be of any use; (ii) even though that is not "all there is" to the subject, refusing to utilize relevant models drawn for "simpler" fields means ignorance, not "wisdom."

Even the anatomist's use of mechanics may be too flattering a comparison for general purpose dissemination. The more frequent use of models drawn from less complex systems is strictly analogical. Terminological vestiges in modern economics bear witness to the historical importance of the field's development of the practice—"equilibrium" (like the political scientist's "balance of power") is an example. Some early influential Keynesians favored hydraulic systems analogies in explaining the behavior of the simple "expenditure-flows" Keynesian system. And so on.

21. A philosophical issue still remains, of course. Cf., especially, N. R. Hanson [1958], chapter 5.

22. These mathematical languages will in some important cases have been historically developed to serve some empirical science dealing with less complex systems. The calculus and classical mechanics (again) make the best example. The mathematically amateurish economist—of which there are quite a few—may be aware that the use of this language forces him to adopt some assumptions he would rather do without (for example, continuity and second-degree differentiability), but may not be alert to more subtle incongruities of "form versus substance." On this, cf. Karl Menger [1973].

economists, in either case, will know to be "relevant"—but finds himself unable to handle. Another example has already been mentioned: the use of atemporal equilibrium constructions and the comparative static method for the analysis of questions pertaining to real-time "dynamic" processes. Both illustrate a general and recurring issue, namely, how best to "trade-off" analytical or empirical manageability against precision of conceptual representation or of empirical reference (to actually obtainable data). The two last-mentioned objectives, moreover, are seldom entirely compatible. The one only too often has to be compromised in pursuit of the other. The most rigorous axiomatic models are frequently incapable of direct confrontation with data. Econometric models will have the measurements specified that are to yield the data for the values of every variable; in achieving that necessary objective, however, liberties often have to be taken with the strict logic of economic theory.[23]

The imperfect congruence between substantive "theory" and formal "models" means that the latter require *interpretation,* and that this is not simply a task of defining variables and primitive terms. Two very noticeably different models may be found securely rooted in the same "hard core," for simplification in pursuit of tractability will proceed by different paths depending on what is the main problem that the analyst seeks to bring into focus. Spurious disagreement is a nuisance but apt to be dissolved sooner or later; spurious agreement creates no "collective dissonance" and is, therefore, a more serious matter. Two economic models may be similar, even identical,[24] in form, but be subject to substantively different interpretations. Interpretation of two very similar models in conformance with the intentions of their authors may, indeed, show them to derive from

23. The concerted drive for greater precision—"quantification" was the motto—in economics may be dated back to the founding of the Econometric Society some 40 years ago. Its highly influential founders presumably envisaged mathematical economic analysis and statistical empirical measurement to develop hand-in-glove as in the physical sciences. In fact, mathematical economic theory and applied econometrics have developed as separate and distinct subfields of economics.

24. The Walrasian and the Marshallian versions of the basic supply-and-demand model for an "isolated market" are indistinguishable in the static form in which they are usually presented. Their divergent interpretations are discussed in my [1974*b*], a revised version of which will be included in *Maximization and Marshall* (unpublished). A somewhat desperate attempt to squeeze the gist of the matter into a few pages can be found in Leijonhufvud [1974*a*].

mutually inconsistent "cosmological presuppositions" and, hence, to be products of different research programmes.

On the other hand, the imperfect correspondence between the models of pure theory and those that are the vehicles of quantitative empirical work means that decisive falsification or convincingly accumulating confirmation of economic theories are hard to come by. In economics, theoretical traditions survive side-by-side, as Hicks emphasized, because their methods of analysis provide complementary ways of structuring perceptions of complex economic reality. To this point one should add Joan Robinson's sobering counterpoint: "In a subject where there is no agreed procedure for knocking out error, doctrines have a long life."[25]

These problems of the substance of beliefs, the forms of their expression, and their confrontation with reality are, of course, not novel in kind. They have long been the stuff of epistemological inquiry. Nonetheless, the degree to which they force themselves on the average practitioner and shape the collective style of the pursuit of knowledge in economics will pose problems for the extension of natural science-based Growth of Knowledge theories to the field.

I. 7

Lakatos makes empirical success with novel predictions or old anomalies the mark of the "progressiveness" of a research programme. It may be fair to say that, in so doing, he is simply making explicit what most philosophical students of the natural sciences would take for granted. In economics, this pattern is much less prominent and certainly not exclusively predominant. Quantitative empirical work has a less direct bearing on the appraisal of theories. Genuinely novel predictions are, moreover, relatively rarely made; what the "progressive" economist is usually engaged in is trying to incorporate more "things that have been well-known for a long time" (or taken to be so) into a logically consistent structure. And ordinarily these "things" are not quantified phenomena but qualitative "patterns

25. Joan Robinson [1963], p. 79.

of behavior." In economic parlance, a "new theory" need not refer to a set of substantively novel hypotheses and conjectures; it is, in fact, more likely to refer to a "new" mathematical language applied to "old" subject matter. A very great proportion of what economists consider theoretical work—or work in so-called "pure theory"—concerns the exploration of the potentialities of formal languages for ordering perceived economic realities.

As noted in Section I.1, Lakatos's MSRP is at once both normative and positive. At least in a first pass at the social sciences, it appears advisable to keep these two aspects of the "progressivity" of research programmes distinct.

From the standpoint of positive Growth of Knowledge theory, aiming to explain the historical development of a discipline but not to appraise it, we might term a programme "progressive" when it gives people in the field "something new and worthwhile to do." In judging the progressiveness in this sense of a programme, one might then view it as a historical sociologist of science would. A progressive programme should, for example, attract an increasing proportion of the members of a profession and especially of the best talent (most especially, perhaps, of the best young talent). Here, then, it is a fact that, in economics, professional interest and allegiance is, to a large degree, commanded by work in "pure theory." Such work may demonstrate, for instance, that an already familiar formal language can, by extension of well-known models, cope with phenomena hitherto given recognition only in *ad hoc*, unsystematic fashion. Or it may show that a "new" language is similarly capable of consistently ordering a richer picture of perceived reality and, perhaps, infuse "meaning" into economic behavior patterns previously neglected (as "not making much sense") by economists.

From the standpoint of normative epistemology, the basic question is whether the actually observed behavior pattern of a disciplinary collective is "progressive" in the sense of producing Growth of *validated* Knowledge. Empirical confirmation of novel predictions, I have just suggested, plays less of a role in making economists change the direction of their work than it does in Lakatos's account of "progressiveness" in the natural sciences. Thus, we have what appears to be a clear-cut issue: Either we weaken Lakatos's conception of progressiveness so as to accommodate the actual behavior of economists or else we recognize that one (at least) of the social sciences will not lend itself to "rational reconstruction" along Lakatosian lines.

The reasons for insisting that the two aspects of "progressivity" be taken one at a time go beyond the point just made. The question of whether a strong epistemological rationale can be provided for the actual behavior-pattern of a disciplinary group is not necessarily best answered with a "yes" or a "no." The criteria to which the group is seen to accord prestige may enable it to realize Growth of Knowledge in some directions but to miss out in others. They may slow the collective learning process down without halting it or making it veer-off across the "demarcation" line into pretentious "gobbledygook." To an economist, at any rate, it seems natural to ask whether a scientific profession may not misallocate its endeavours without altogether wasting them in epistemically irrational pursuits.

Given the formal difficulties in the way of providing suitable representations for dynamic systems of a high order of complexity, the prestige and priority that economists accord work in "pure theory" can hardly be totally "irrational." But it might be overdone. While many of those inside and outside the economics profession who habitually criticize "mathematical game-playing," etc., may have little appreciation of the significance of the technical limitations of language that theorists seek to overcome, the chances are that the enterprise as a whole would nonetheless gain from a greater number of hardworking empirical positivists—or even "naive falsificationists."

I. 8

Another problem (to the amateur, at least) relates to the issue just outlined. "Hard cores" do not always spring fully armed from the brow of some venerated Thunderer. Surely, they usually take a considerable time to "harden." Yet, Lakatos tells us little about this "hardening process." We probably need a theoretical account of it and criteria for recognizing it (before it is completed), for the process whereby a hard core hardens is apt, I believe, to bear at least some superficial resemblances to the activities mentioned by Lakatos as characterizing a "degenerating" research programme.[26]

In Section I.3 above, a distinction between "presuppositions" and propositions of "strictly hard-core" nature was suggested. A Lakatosian hard-core proposition is logically irrefutable and empirically untestable within the research programme in question. To adherents of the programme it is—it has become—a "necessary condition for the intelligibility of the phenomena."[27] A presupposition must be treated as indubitable as long as a given research programme is to be pursued. Without it, the programme "would not make sense."[28] Belief in it, we may still suppose, could be of a more "reasonable" and "hypothetical" character. That is by the way, however. Here, we want to stress that presuppositions "underlie" the formal structure of theory, rather than being incorporated in it, and are in varying degrees "informally" phrased. Consequently, while they have to be treated as "indubitable," the strictly logical categories of "irrefutability" or "refutability" do not apply to them.[29]

26. Note, again, that if we are to "rationally reconstruct" the choices that scientists make between programmes we have to presuppose that they can recognize which is which.

27. Cf. N. R. Hanson's discussion ([1958], chapter 5) of Newton's Laws as "statements (that) are in some sense empirical, yet they seem often to resist the idea of disconfirmation: evidence against them is sometimes impossible to conceive." Compare, Toulmin [1972], p. 70: "For what would be the effect of abandoning the general axioms of Newton's dynamics entirely? To do so would not merely falsify a large number of statements about 'forces,' and their effects on the 'momenta' of bodies. . . . It would actually strip these terms of meaning, so that the statements in which they were employed would cease to arise, be operative, or even make sense."

In my *Maximization and Marshall,* I discuss the "Maximizing Behavior Postulate" as an example in economics of a proposition that has (fairly recently) become a "necessary condition for the intelligibility of the phenomena."

28. "The substitution effect is always negative" is an example of a hard-core proposition (although not a primitive, but a derived one) in the sense that it cannot be negated without making nonsense of the formal structure of neoclassical theory. As an example of a presupposition, consider "A market economy is a self-regulating (or 'equilibrating') system." *Some such phrase* would indicate a belief that one treats as indubitable for doing equilibrium analysis—an activity which otherwise would be merely an intellectual game. But its formulation could be varied; the terms appearing in the phrase do not have the "hardness" and carry none of the "inevitability" of statements taken from rigorous formal models.

29. A presupposition such as "the market economy is self-regulating" will tend to be "untestable" in the common-sense meaning of the term, namely, no one can formulate and execute a test that will be collectively agreed upon to be decisive. It is not "untestable" in the strictly "hard-core" sense that would apply to Newton's Laws in classical mechanics, namely, that any conceivable experiment must use the hard-core concepts of that very theory to structure the observations to be utilized.

Consider, then, the possibility that the maturation of a successful research programme may involve the gradual transformation of "presuppositions" into "hard-core propositions," as the term is (with some license) used here. One aspect of this process *may* be an unbroken string of empirical confirmations of hypotheses newly deduced with the help of the proposition in question. Another aspect, however, would *necessarily* be entailed—namely, considerable work on the "refinement" of the formal language of representation. Common-sense definition of terms and an informal syntax will not produce statements having the character of "mathematical necessity."

Work on formal languages for the representation of phenomena is basically mathematical in character. A lot of effort is expended to assure that the theorems proposed will be "necessarily true" once the language is only used "correctly." It is not surprising, then, that much of the work in pure economic theory is better described by Lakatos's "Proofs and Refutations"[30] than by his later MSRP. "Monster-barring" and the rest of the tactics that Lakatos named in such colorful fashion will be intriguingly familiar to those acquainted with the advanced economic theory literature.

The development of the language conventions, without which "strictly irrefutable" hard-core propositions are impossible, pose a problem in applying Lakatos's theory (to economics, at least) in that the process will resemble that of degeneration. It is fairly clear that it will so appear to someone unsympathetic to the emerging research programme. What will this someone witness? That his criticisms and objections are increasingly met with the assertion of "tautologies." That anomalies are being "accommodated" (through "verbal legerdemain") and that certain hypotheses are gradually hedged around so as to remove all possibility of falsification. And, in some instances, of course, the enterprise seen to exhibit these repugnant symptoms *is* going nowhere in particular.

II

The "Keynesian revolution" once again, then. It is a story that has been told in various ways to yield as many different mes-

---

30. Cf. Lakatos [1963].

sages. How the "true" story should be told is, after forty years, still a "live" question. If we could be certain of the answer to it, the agenda for research in macroeconomic theory would look much clearer than it now does. That is what gives the question its continuing importance. It is a matter of understanding our past trek, so as to know better the present position of the subject, and be able to chart a course for the future.[31] Versions of the story that do no more than tell a tale of brave, bygone days and a battle over issues now as "dead" as the hero we can reject as false. If the story does nothing to inform us about present-day problems in economic theory, it cannot be right.

The question of what the "true" story of the Keynesian revolution might be only remains "live," of course, because some of the original substantive issues have not been laid to rest. With our part of the woods full of sharp-shooters gunning for them these past forty years, they would have been killed off for sure, had we ever had them truly pinpointed in our sights. We may infer, therefore, that the natural habitat of these difficulties lies on that murky "presuppositional" level where a clean shot is never to be had. Could we but once truly trap them in a tight model, they would be done for. Sundry reports of successful captures notwithstanding, that has not been accomplished yet. "Incongruities of form and substance" let them slip the net.

What did Keynes achieve—what was his contribution to economic theory? This question has been the favorite Snark of the hunt. The standard method has been to try to box the issues in by systematic comparisons of "Keynesian" and "classical" models; in so far as the quarry has eluded this pursuit, the presumption has been that more "rigorous" and precise formulations of these models would do it.

> That's exactly the way I have always been told
> that the capture of Snarks should be tried!

The debate has coincided with the mathematization of pure economic theory. The bright ethos of that movement has cast a shadow of disreputability on the informalities of meta-language

31. In recent years, a rising chorus of voices, equally as dissatisfied as distinguished, has urged economists to find a way out of the "present position of the subject" with as much dispatch as can be mustered. For a sample of representative references, cf. the introduction to Clower [1975].

discourse. A certain abstemiousness from it has made real obstacles of "translation difficulties" between "paradigms" that might perhaps have been less debilitating. As a result, the purely theoretical aspect of the Keynesian debate became, in effect, a straight contest for hegemony between two theoretical languages.

> "The question is," said Alice, "whether you *can* make words mean so many different things."
> "The question is," said Humpty Dumpty, "which is to be master—that's all."

In this contest, the Keynesian language—starting with the handicaps of most "revolutionary" tongues, and with its development entrusted to people who would rather save the world by action than by words—lost and lost badly.

An informal and improvised meta-language makes an uncomfortably blunt instrument of inquiry. But, perchance, "presuppositional" Snarks must be bludgeoned by such means? The sketch that follows proceeds on that presumption.[32]

II. 1

The first order of business should be to identify the research programmes that have had a role in the story. In important respects, the plots of various versions of the story differ simply as a function of the size of the cast of "characters." This matter had better be considered first, before an attempt is made to explain what it all has been about.

The simplest version puts but two actors on the stage —"Keynesian economics" and an opposing programme, variously labelled "classical" (by Keynes), "neoclassical," or "orthodox" economic theory, etc. Both programmes change and evolve as the story unfolds—appearing, for example, in the postwar acts in the guises of "macrotheory" and "microtheory"—but are here regarded as maintaining identities throughout that are readily recognizable even though the defi-

---

32. Below, I will have to state in crudely categorical form a number of points argued at greater length—and somewhat more "reasonably"—elsewhere. Non-economist readers should be warned that this part of the paper does *not* represent a summary of "generally accepted views" on Keynesian economics.

nition of their respective "hard cores" might remain uncertain and in some dispute.

This "Keynes and the Classics" version of the tale will bear telling in Kuhnian terms—up to a point.[33]

i. By external, sociology of science criteria, it was without doubt a genuine Kuhnian revolution. It cannot be disputed: ask anyone who was there! The period had a high incidence of 'conversions', *Sturm und Drang* among the young, resistance from the old, etc.[34] Perhaps, it should be particularly emphasized that "translation difficulties" were very much in evidence, since this particular theme of Kuhn's has found so little favor with critics.

ii. Such "external" professional behavior will necessarily have some strictly "internal" counterpart. Economists do not migrate from their bases of assured competence unless the new pastures beckon with something worthwhile to do. A massive migration into "Keynesian economics" did take place and the work done by the migrants within its fences was different from what they would otherwise have done or did before. And it would be quite ridiculous to suppose that some genuine Growth of Knowledge did not take place—and in novel, worthwhile directions.[35]

33. I am indebted here to J. Ronnie Davis for whose paper "Was There a Keynesian Revolution?," delivered at the 1973 Midwestern Economic Association Meetings, I was (*in absentia*) a discussant. Davis put his question in a strictly Kuhnian sense and argued a flatly negative answer. While I disagreed with him on a number of important points, I benefited from the interesting and provocative way in which he made his case.

Kuhn has been the subject of a bit of a fad in economics (as in other fields). The profession at large has become rather tired of facile employments of Kuhnian terminology (I was one of the earlier sinners), while those few of its members who have been intrigued enough with Kuhn to sample the subsequent philosophical discussion have become rather disenchanted with the evolution of Kuhn's position.

I ought perhaps to confess, therefore, that I remain an admirer of Kuhn's first edition. At one time, I found Kuhn (the historian) a great help in getting logical positivism into a more useful perspective—which was and remains enough! *Pace* Kuhn (the philosopher), I still have little sympathy with the criticisms, for example, of Masterman [1965]. Kuhn's original version comes off best if read as a work of historical induction. Twenty-odd descriptive statements to delineate the "novel" class of empirical phenomena named "paradigms" is then not too much. Read as a piece of philosophical model-building, twenty-odd definitions of a central primitive term for the deductive structure seems a bit much—and the difficulties will not end there. Thus, my attempt at assessing Kuhn's work has to end on a plaintive note: may one not read the work in the way that gives the best value—even if the author, *ex post*, won't cooperate?

34. Cf. A. W. Coats [1969]; J. R. Davies [1973], and for an eloquent testimonial, P. A. Samuelson [1946].

35. Note, however, that the macroeconomic work from the 1940s and early 1950s that has had the most lasting impact drew strength from two "research programmes" that

iii. Next, we come to "Kuhnian (or Frankian) losses." The fact that they figure importantly in the story is a plus for Kuhn. But they play a largely latent role with consequences quite different from the typical Kuhnian scenario. The losses in prospect from an outright abandonment of "orthodox" theory in favor of the Keynesian were of such magnitude as could not seriously be contemplated. For the central orthodox theory of value and resource allocation with its innumerable applications to important guns-or-butter issues the "revolutionary" Keynesian doctrine provided no sufficiently coherent and well-developed substitute.

As a consequence, Keynesian economics could not decisively displace orthodox economics. Instead, both survived in what in retrospect—given the underlying "presuppositional" discord between them—seems rather implausible comfort. Mutual tolerance was helped in part by institutional fence-building. From the early 1950s on, most teaching curricula split general economic theory right down the middle into separate, largely unrelated "micro" and "macro" segments.[36]

iv. The next act of the drama will not fit the Kuhnian scenario at all. On the theoretical front, it deals largely with the "Counterrevolution" (Clower) and "Neoclassical Resurgence" (Eisner).[37] By the late fifties, Keynesianism had been defused by a revived "neoclassicism" and gradually stagnated.[38] Significant empirical work, regarded by the profession at large as within the Keynesian frame, continued but on the basis of theoretical ideas derived from postwar "neoclassicism." The work by Modigliani, Brumberg and Ando on the consumption function

had developed quite independently of Keynesian theory, namely the work of Simon Kuznets (especially) under National Bureau of Economic Research auspices and what might perhaps be called the "Econometric Society programme" (for which the leading center was the Cowles Commission, especially during Jacob Marschak's tenure as research director).

36. This "split" would have seemed odd to an earlier generation of economists—and to Keynes who had hoped that his *General Theory* would serve to heal the (rather differently defined) split between the theories of Money and of Value.

37. Cf. Clower [1965], Eisner [1958].

38. "Degenerated" would be inappropriate here for the process was not marked by those accommodations to the new findings of an alternative and progressive programme that Lakatos stresses as symptoms of degeneration. There was not much forthcoming to which such accommodations would be required, for postwar neoclassicism no more addressed the main problems within the sphere of Keynesian macroeconomics than the latter did the traditional problems of microeconomics.

and by Jorgensen on the investment function are examples. By the mid-sixties, moreover, macroeconomics was drawing most of its excitement from the challenge posed by another "resurgence" of pre-Keynesian ideas—the "monetarist" or "new quantity" theory of Friedman, Schwartz, Cagan, Brunner and Meltzer.

This, I take it, will not fit easily within the Kuhnian schema. Kuhn's revolutions displace the respective pre-existing orthodoxies permanently and definitively. In his natural science based sample, there are no stories of short-lived triumphs—of the Oxygene theory being stalemated, for example, by "resurgent phlogistonism." MSRP, on the other hand, does not present us with this problem. Lakatos emphatically admitted the possibility of reviving a programme temporarily eclipsed by the competition and the "rationality" of keeping degenerating programmes alive with this prospect in view.

But this tale of two programmes will not make a satisfactory version of the Keynesian revolution story even in Lakatosian terms. The so-called "neoclassical synthesis"—of which more below—whereby the supposedly older programme regained hegemony in theory from the Keynesians did not signify the hunting down and laying to rest of the presuppositional Snark. It was the adoption, rather, of a formula whereby one could—for a time—in decency forget about him and let him run loose. The version that ends here cannot be the whole story. For the Keynesian revolution is still unfinished. A more useful tale will have more than just two protagonists.

My 1968 book, *On Keynesian Economics and the Economics of Keynes,* was concerned with the problems and conundrums resulting from the collision of Keynesianism with the, by then stronger, "neoclassical" programme. The then commonly taught "image" of the Keynesian past failed to suggest directions out of the theoretical stagnation of the programme that by the mid-sixties was so clearly evident. My own search for clues in the history of the Keynesian debates led to the conclusion that this image was seriously over-simplified and in parts false. One theme of the book—dramatized by the title, perhaps, to a dysfunctional extent—became the distinction drawn between Keynes's theory and the subsequently developing, largely

American, school of Keynesian economics.[39] The distinction is an important one to make, I contended, because it was this later version of Keynesianism that succumbed so readily to the "neo-classical synthesis."[40]

Though somewhat short of eternal, the "triangle" of Keynes, "the Keynesians," and the "neoclassicists," entertained in my 1968 work, allowed for a richer and more realistic plot than can be made out of a see-saw context between Keynesianism and neoclassicism. But three protagonists are still not enough.

Elements of another needed distinction were pointed out in my book, but it may be that less than enough was made of the matter and that a more systematic appraisal is required. Pre-Keynesian economic theory must be clearly distinguished from the picture of it propagated by Keynes and some of the later Keynesians. The propagandistic distortions committed in the cause and course of the revolution were often severe. While the Keynesian version of "classical theory" is not, of course, a re-search programme in a historical sense, this strawman must be

39. The British Keynesians, centered at Keynes's old Cambridge headquarters, should properly be left out of this part of the story. While their rendering of Keynes may be more true to the original, the Cambridge school has for some considerable time figured more prominently as critics of the "neoclassical" programme than as active contributors to the ongoing work in macroeconomics. As a consequence, the influence of this school has, in the later stages of the Keynesian debates, been relatively minor.

40. This distinction I sought to drive home by exhausting, if not exhaustive, exegetical documentation referring to a "list" of propositions that, while they had become commonplace in the later "Keynesian" literature (and were with some frequency attributed to Keynes), were not in fact integral to the theory that Keynes advanced. (For a brief—and hard-drawn—version of this "list," cf. my [1969].) Much of the critical attention that the book has received has concentrated on these matters with a resultant tendency to end up in argument about "what Keynes really meant." For my purposes, it was and remains important to insist on what "Keynes did not say" (but which later Keynesians got in the habit of saying). In the case of a yet not fully "hardened" programme, it makes a difference. The *General Theory* most certainly was not fully "hardened"; it will not lend itself to a tightly formalized interpretation—any fully consistent axiomatic "model" of the theory of that work is bound to leave something out or bring something in that was not there.

In significant respects, the *General Theory* was open-ended. Its significance today (if any) will lie, therefore, in "what Keynes did *not* say. . . ." What must be insisted on, in other words, is that the *General Theory* did not dictate the subsequent step-by-step development of "Keynesian economics" into the particular stalemated stage in which, some 20 or 25 years later, it found itself. Either there are "alternative futures" to the one realized open to us in the *General Theory*—or the book is dead and of no possible help to anyone.

There will remain those who insist that textbook Keynesianism presents us with the "real" Keynes skilfully embalmed by the faithful. Perhaps so—but have not the guts been removed from the mummy?

allowed to play his role in the story. To refuse him recognition would be as playing Hamlet without the father's ghost. It remains influential to this day and will not be easily dislodged from the textbooks. When this historically distorted image of pre-Keynesian economics is used as the frame of reference for defining and explaining Keynes's contribution to theory—as has so often been done—one cannot hope for an understanding of the Keynesian revolution that would help us get a grasp on contemporary problems in theory.

The errors, omissions and misjudgments, that with the "benefit" of hindsight I now see as bound to undermine the value to modern students of the doctrine-historical parts of the book, almost all stem from the undifferentiated notion of "neoclassical economics" that pervades it.

Firstly, it is necessary clearly to distinguish pre-Keynesian "orthodox" economics from the "neoclassical" theory that has been predominant in the post-war period. The latter is more accurately referred to as "neo-Walrasian" economic theory. Of all the "schools" mentioned in this paper, the modern neo-Walrasian school may be the one with the best claim to being a research programme with a distinct hard core, protective belt and positive heuristic. It is this programme that pulled off the "counterrevolution." But it was *not* the "orthodoxy" against which the original revolution was directed. The pre-Keynesian "neoclassicism" from which Keynes sought to break away was not neo-Walrasian.

Secondly, this "neoclassical" economics of the 1930s was not a homogeneous doctrine.[41] A number of "schools," dating from "marginalist revolution" days, were still distinctly recognizable despite cross-breeding and hybridization. Marshall's school dominated in Britain, the Austrian on the continent, with the Walrasian or Lausanne school everywhere a distant third. Among the then productive hybrids, one should mention the Stockholm school and the LSE school, with Austrian and Walrasian bloodlines most prominent in the former and Marshallian and Austrian in the latter. In most economics departments of repute, one must imagine, "the" theory that students

41. As usage has developed, the term "neoclassical" has in fact been rendered all but totally useless for historical purposes.

were taught would contain strains from all of these albeit mixed to local tastes.[42]

The analytical criticism and theoretical polemics in Keynes's *General Theory* were directed against the Marshallian school in which he had been trained and which at Cambridge—not so incidentally—had developed into about as good an example of British intellectual "insularity" as one is likely to find. Keynes's particular target was in fact Marshall's successor at Cambridge, A. C. Pigou—although his "classical doctrine" was hardly a fair representation even of Pigou's views. The very fact that Keynes advanced his new theory in opposition to the older Cambridge school means that he still shared many presuppositions as well as analytical method with the Marshallian school. This is of significance to an accurate rendering of the Keynesian revolution story, because the Marshallian school had begun to degenerate and was to be easily (and without climactic confrontation) swept aside by the neo-Walrasian programme which differed from it in ways that we are gradually coming to realize are important.

II. 2

What then was it all about? What was—and remains—the substantive problem to which these controversies pertain?

My label for it is "The Coordination of Economic Activities"[43] It should be said at once, however, that this label refers to as nearly an "internalist" conception of the problem as seems at

---

42. It may be that we will eventually come in retrospect to regard two or more of these "schools" as competing and essentially incompatible research programmes. That, however, is not yet clear for, until recently, most economists have remained quite content to lump them all together under the heading of "neoclassical economics." It could not have been clear to many economists back then. Economics in the interwar period did not have the technical equipment to bring deep-lying issues between "schools" to sharp confrontation. The notion that the distinctive contributions of diverse schools would in time reach their confluence in one grand system would seem—and, one suspects, probably did seem—a most sensible attitude to adopt to most teachers.

Ever since the interwar period, the more purebred "Austrians" have insisted on the distinctiveness of their tradition. Since, however, this (rather small) school has for a very considerable time been neither theoretically nor empirically progressive—its characteristic heuristic tending more to the "prohibitive" than the "positive"—its repeated challenges to the notional homogeneity of "neoclassical doctrine" have gone unheeded by all but a few outsiders.

43. Cf. Leijonhufvud [1973a], R. W. Clower [1975], and Clower and Leijonhufvud [1975], for a fuller statement of the argument sketched here.

all feasible. Thus conceived, the problem is to explain how, in an economic system, the activities that its numerous agents engage in, come to, are made to, or fail to "mesh." The coordination problem is particularly interesting when the system under study is one in which decision-making with regard to what activities to engage in or refrain from is decentralized to a high degree, i.e., "market systems." With regard to such economies, then, the central substantive problem of general macroeconomic theory is to determine the nature and limitations of the self-regulatory and self-organizing capabilities of market systems. In the 1930s, the issue used to be put as one of the "automaticity" of the private sector.[44]

But in the case at hand, the alternative "externalist" definition cannot simply be bypassed. From that standpoint, the problem was to contemporaries of Keynes—and remains in large measure to present-day economists—the Great Depression. How was that terrible, unparalleled disaster—from which the United States, the most "capitalistic" of the systems affected, suffered the most severely—to be explained? What economic policies might be adequate to cope with it? The Depression started in 1929 with the extraordinarily violent contraction of the U.S. banking system which was not halted until three years later when the international monetary system had also collapsed. Unemployment rose to unprecedented heights and remained at exceedingly high levels until the outbreak of the war.

For present purposes, two points will suffice about this "external" reference of the theoretical work with which we are concerned. (i) The monetary contraction in the U.S.A. and the ensuing collapse of the international monetary system were historical events of the sort often referred to as "unique." They would not lend themselves readily to abstract, "general" theorizing. The sheer magnitude as well as the ("monetary") nature of the *shocks* to the economic system that ushered in the Great Depression tended in fact to be lost sight of as the theoretical "Keynes and the Classics" debate developed. The prob-

---

44. It will be obvious to the reader that the problem can hardly even be stated so as to avoid entanglement in sundry political-ideological "beliefs." On complications arising from "external" influences of this particular brand, this essay will have nothing to say, however.

320

lem for general economic theory was that of the system's behavior in response to shocks. (ii) The duration and severity of unemployment at the time made it natural—indeed almost inevitable—that this last-mentioned problem should be defined by and for theorists by the question: Why does the "modern, capitalist" system *fail* to absorb unemployment?

Is this the "right question" to ask? As will become evident, I think not. The matter may be worth a digression, even though I am not able to make it of direct relevance to Lakatos's or Kuhn's theory. A philosophical problem would seem to be involved but, if so, it is a problem on which the Growth of Knowledge literature (to my less than comprehensive knowledge) has had little to say.

In the problem-area of the coordination of economic activities, it has always seemed to me, we have had a puzzling difficulty in keeping the basic question "right." It is as if it always tends to depreciate on our hands. Perhaps it is simply hard to maintain a requisite sense of wonder at things that happen every day and form part of our ordinary life more tangibly than they are part of our scientific life. The consumer wants milk in the morning. It is there on his doorstep, having arrived from a hundred miles away. The farmer milks his cow and has a consumer for it that he has never met a hundred miles away. How is this brought about and so on? How come shoes do not pile up unsold in New Mexico while people queue barefooted for shoes in Maine? In some parts of the world, such an event would not be all that unlikely. Consider a week's household purchases. To that "basket," there will be "value added" by individuals living and working on the other side of the globe who never knew of your existence. Again, how does it work? And so on.

Part of the problem with maintaining a sense of wonder about such trivial, everyday events may be that the easy, rather sloppy answer to such questions carries so much conviction exactly because of this daily acquaintance with the matter—but carries conviction, then, for no very good scientific reason.

The economist who finds it wondrous will ask: "How is it possible—how is it even conceivable that decentralized economic activities can ever be reasonably coordinated when nobody, really, is trying to ensure that outcome?" That, I believe, is the "right question." If the economist does not find it curious, he is much more likely to ask a different question—one that sounds so much more promising from the standpoint of "policy relevance," namely: "How come the system sometimes fails to coordinate activities?" or "How can there be persistent unemployment on a large scale?"

On what grounds can one argue that the former question is "better" than the latter ones? My only answer comes by way of analogy. The philosophical problem adumbrated above is, in a sense, to decide whether the analogy is or is not apt in this case and whether for reasons of basic principle it does or does not have more general applicability.

In studying systems that have not been "constructed" according to human "rational design" (to use a Hayekian phrase) but are simply "found" operating in nature or in society, it is tempting, the record shows, to start from the presumption that the system "works" because Providence wills it so or it works for unstated reasons of "natural law." If the human body is the system under study, its "natural state," on this presumption, is to be healthy. That being so, what is in need of explanation is: "How can people ever fall ill?" The obvious "policy-relevance" of this way of putting the question will reinforce the line of inquiry. One proceeds by "listing" illnesses, and perhaps ranking them in order of the apparent desirability of finding a cure, and goes on to tackle them one by one. The trouble is, of course, that the various attempts to find cures for the illnesses on the list are most unlikely to form a coherent research programme (in the Lakatosian sense), that inquiry in certain directions may be halted when a cure deemed effective is found, and that the accumulation of treatments found capable of alleviating specific symptoms—"aspirin for A, vitamins for B, psychoanalysis for C," etc.—will not amount to a "general theory" of how the body functions.

The ulterior motive behind the selection of this particular analogy will be obvious. The microbiological revolution, that in recent years has begun to transform medicine, came about when the presumption that "health is only natural" was abandoned and the basic question changed: "How is it possible that such an improbable arrangement of molecules as a cell maintains itself?" "How is it even conceivable that it could?" The changed formulation of the question reflects an exchange of "presuppositions" at a very basic level. To find the system under study in an "organized" or "coordinated" state is seen as unexpected and, consequently, in need of explanation. The *a priori* probability of some breakdown in organization, of a "coordination failure," is on the other hand seen as so large as not to deserve priority in the search for explanations. Nonetheless—and this, of course, is the point—the pursuit of answers to the question of how life is, improbably, maintained has proved more productive of ideas, hypotheses and results relevant to the important "failure" or "illness" questions than did the old "direct" approach. As answers to the "new" and "indirect" question begin to come in, it becomes apparent how tenuous life is in the case of the cell—how many things must "go right" for it to be maintained—and, consequently, at how many points it is possible for the maintenance mechanisms to break down.

A modern economy is a highly improbable structure. Yet, by and large,[45] economists have not, apparently, regarded it as such and have not assigned a high priority to the coordination question. In particular, the Keynesian debate has not proceeded on such a "presuppositional" basis.

The already mentioned "external" factor of the persistent, large-scale unemployment of the depression decade explains this only in part. It is both true and trite, of course, to note the common-sensical sanity of the "direct" approach in the face of a disastrous emergency. In the 1930s, the economist's attention *had* to be focused on what could be done immediately on the basis of available knowledge extended by the "best" conjectures that might be mobilized. But an "internal" logic to the epistemic situation must also be recognized if we are not to get too simplistic and one-sided an understanding of the origins of the Keynesian debate. The *General Theory,* one must remember, was "chiefly addressed to my fellow economists"—which is to say, chiefly addressed to the "internal situation" as Keynes saw it.

---

45. One should except most of the "Austrians" from this generalization and in particular F. A. Hayek whose now more than 30-year-old essays on this problem (collected in Hayek [1948]) are at last receiving deserved attention.

The inherited theory of the time—including in particular the Marshallian theory that was "received doctrine" to Keynes—presupposed the "automaticity" of the market system. The predominance of equilibrium analysis reveals the strength of the presupposition. Formal economic theory consisted almost altogether of static and comparative static models with mathematical solutions *only* for "coordinated states" of the system, i.e., of models from which nothing specific could be deduced about uncoordinated states and what happens to them. On that problem, the pre-Keynesians had for the most part been satisfied to "go along with" a sketchy and very informal "story" as sufficient justification for their concentration on the equilibrium method.

One of the targets of Adam Smith's attack on the mercantilist doctrines of his day had been the "presupposition" that "unfettered" private enterprise was bound to be "chaotic." The mercantilist writers cannot be rated very favorably as contributors to the development of an economic science. Still, they posed, in effect, the "right" question for Smith: "How is it conceivable that the system will work coherently if you let economic agents do as they please?" To which Smith produced his "Invisible Hand" analysis as an answer. That answer, it appears, was so satisfactory to succeeding generations of economists that for a long time little further work was done on the question.

The trouble with answers is that they tend to take the life out of questions.[46] A question remains interesting only as long as more than one answer seems possible. The satisfactory answer kills the alternative answers that earlier seemed possible. The question "dies" with them. Repetition of the one answer becomes a matter of rote-learning—you do not really *understand* it any longer. Something of the sort happened with the coordination problem between Smith and Keynes, As a result, the "internal" intellectual challenge to Keynes was to show how the system could "fail."

To the "orthodox" presupposition that the economic system "naturally" and "automatically" works to coordinate activities, Keynes's theory thus came to be posed as a *denial*. To pre-Keynesian theories (of various "schools") in which the system is

46. I am here paraphrasing the sociologist Dennis H. Wrong, whose [1961] has rapidly and justly become a classic.

presupposed *always* to tend "smoothly" towards a restoration of a full coordination state, we get the alternative theory of a system that would *never* move near that state—except by pure chance or government intervention. The "external" fact of the Great Depression had so traumatically jolted the implicit faith in the "orthodox" presupposition, that a theory advancing its polar contradiction found a prepared and ready audience among economists. Quite obviously, the message of the revolutionary doctrine at this presuppositional level was fraught with retrogressive potentialities for reassertions of mercantilist notions. British political economy has largely gone in that direction, taking British economic policy and Britain with it.

The dead hand of the past lies on these opposing presuppositions. Only minds caught in the rigor mortis of last century's ideologies could harbor the conviction that since one negates the other, the issue is to decide which one is "true" and which "false." When two positions have become defined as diametrically opposed, an underlying basic agreement is implied, namely, a common "understanding" of what the fundamental issue between them is. But if that issue is misconceived, neither camp will be in possession of the "truth." Rather each camp will possess some stock of perfectly genuine confirming "evidence" and of incontrovertible arguments. A decision can never be reached.

If pre-Keynesian economic theories may be said to have lost an adequate appreciation of the question to which they carried forward a stock answer, the Keynesian negation of that answer did nothing to turn economic inquiry onto a more promising tack for the longer haul.

But the story cannot be ended with that assessment. Two loose ends are in evidence at this point.

First, economists have lived since the Keynesian revolution with two bodies of theory ("micro" and "macro") based on incompatible presuppositions about what the real system under study is like. How could we possibly have done so? The two theories could not possibly be "true" of the same external world. Yet, they have survived side-by-side for decades in reasonably peaceful co-existence and without a climactic confrontation. That a relationship of victor to vanquished, of progressive to degenerating programme has not developed is easily understandable.[47] As previously indicated, each of the two is singularly ill-adapted for coping with the phenomena that the other accords the first order of priority. But the actual "truce," that allowed these two incompatible views of the world to be simultaneously entertained without acute intellectual discomfort by a couple of generations of economists, is so implausible on the face of it as to require explanation.

Second, there must be more to Keynes's contribution to economic theory than this turning of the tables on a basic presupposition of pre-Keynesian theory—or else our interest in it could be only antiquarian at this date. And, in fact—or so I have industriously maintained—the theoretical reasons that he gave for why the market system would not work towards coordinating activities did introduce fundamental ideas of genuine novelty that belong (I believe) also in the structure of a general economic theory that abandons this ill-conceived battle of opposing presuppositions. These ideas—which I would lump together under the heading of "effective demand failures"[48]— were swept under the rug of the so-called "neoclassical synthesis" which embodies the terms of the aforementioned truce. They have, therefore, not been developed as yet to the point where the work of the originator becomes uninteresting and irrelevant to present-day researchers.

In addition to these two loose ends to the story, that will need to be followed up, the discussion of this section leaves us with the suggestion of a criterion for the appraisal of macroeconomic theories that, while it can be only broadly and informally stated, nonetheless will be of use. It is simply this. They should not be built around basic presuppositions that deny either of the following. (i) Market systems do possess self-regulating and self-organizing properties. If this mode of economic organization did not possess reasonably reliable mechanisms for the coordination of activities, they could never have evolved. Nor would we find, as we do, that certain broad features of market

47. "Peaceful co-existence," of course, need not imply "co-equal prosperity." The two incompatible programmes could not very well prosper equally, if for no other reason than that the one seen to yield the "best" crop of questions is bound to gain a near-monopoly on the recruitment of first-rate theoretical talent—as the neo-Walrasian programme has in fact had for a long period.
48. Cf. Leijonhufvud [1973a].

organization tend "spontaneously" to assert (or reassert) themselves, practically speaking, wherever they are not actively suppressed or the conditions relevant to the security of property and contract anarchic. (ii) These self-regulating and self-organizing mechanisms of market economies will sometimes fail—and fail badly—in maintaining a socially tolerable degree of coordination of activities. If this were not so, the chances are that we would never have become aware of the coordination problem as one demanding scientific explanation but would still take the perfect "health"—and, indeed, immortality—of the system as granted by Providence. (A benign or malign Providence, of course, depending upon your ideological standpoint.)

II. 3

We turn then to the historical problem of the "implausible truce." The explanation, as I perceive it, is largely a matter of the incongruities of form and substance in economic theory that were harped on at such length in Part I above.

In form—what there was of it—Keynes's theory fitted the substance of his main problem badly in two respects. First, in directing his revolt most specifically against the Marshallian economics reigning in Cambridge, he sought to vanquish it with its own analytical weaponry. Among the main "neoclassical schools" of the time, the Marshallian stands distinct from the rest by its conscientious guardianship of the "plutological" analytical tradition.[49] Keynesian aggregative economics bears this plutological heritage. For the formal statement of the coordination problem, however, a "catallactic" approach would have been more appropriate.[50] Both the Austrian and the Walrasian "schools" were in the catallactic tradition—but with them,

---

49. Cf., especially, Shove [1942]. The terminology is Hicks'. Cf. his [1976].

50. It is entirely vain, of course, to "wish" that Keynes would have chosen a catallactic formulation because of the superior analytical precision that this tradition affords in the statement of the "purely theoretical" problems. The plutological tradition has the immense advantage, quite generally, that its conceptual categories have a fairly clear correspondence to National Income Account data, etc. It is empirically implementable in a way that catallactic theory has never been and consequently promises a practical "engine of analysis" with which one can come to grips in rather direct manner with the economic policy issues of the day. Keynes, without doubt, would in any case have preferred the plutological approach on this basis.

Keynes was not much concerned. Second, Keynes "cast his theory in static, equilibrium form" whereas the coordination problem will ultimately require the development of methods of "dynamic," "disequilibrium" process analysis. One reason for casting the *General Theory* as an equilibrium "model"—and, indeed, for insisting on it—may derive from a prior decision on his part to dramatize the presuppositional battle with "orthodoxy" by presenting a model where large-scale unemployment is an equilibrium state of the system. (Many Keynesians insist to this day that therein lies the "essence" of the Keynesian revolution.) But it seems more to the point to note that, whereas the choice of a catallactic in preference to a plutological formulation was open to him, the technical limitations of inherited modes of formal economic analysis left him no choice in this matter. Static, equilibrium modeling was the only technical form that we can reasonably say was available to him.

Had Keynes begun from the question: "How is it conceivable that activities are ever reasonably coordinated?" these incongruities of form and substance would necessarily have presented rather immediate embarrassments. Setting out, instead, to answer the question: "How has the system failed?" these problems were not that apparent either to him or to later followers and commentators. A model of a system that "just does not work" can dispense with representation of sundry "homeostats" that could not be omitted from a model of a system that could and often does work.

The Keynesian "model" portrayed a system that could be in "equilibrium" at *any* level of unemployment. Pre-Keynesian economists were not wont to deny evident facts of economic life so, naturally, orthodox theory would allow for the occurrence of prolonged periods of serious unemployment. But formal "orthodox" models would not allow "involuntary" unemployment as an equilibrium state. The primary task of the "Keynes and the Classics" debate became that of analytically isolating the atypical assumption or assumptions of Keynes's theory that were responsible for its "unemployment equilibrium" implications. In hindsight, one concludes that this red herring caught too much of the attention.

The task of isolating the property of Keynes's theory that made the crucial difference was to be approached by systematic analytical comparison of a Keynesian model and a representative "classical" model. Some "hard" elements of a formal model could be clearly discerned in Keynes's exposition of his theory. But a complete, coherent, formal macromodel the *General Theory* did not "nail down." It had to be provided. Similarly, what was available in the way of inherited "classical" models— non-monetary general equilibrium models, quantity theory models with the "real" sector not represented, etc.—would not correspond sufficiently to Keynes's structure to make comparisons feasible. So a "classical model" also had to be, if not made up out of whole cloth, then stitched together from inherited patches and pieces.

Things went askew over the course of the long discussion on three fronts. (i) Keynes's theory (I have maintained) was "dynamic in substance, but static in form." The constant feature of the debate was that it was conducted in terms of comparisons of static equilibrium models. Elements of Keynes's theoretical statement that were not to be captured by such representation drifted out of view. (ii) As the progressive neo-Walrasian programme gathered steam, and since the Marshallian tradition had stagnated already by the early 1930s, the model used to represent "classical" economics eventually came to be a monetary neo-Walrasian one. This substitution was aided by the widespread notion that all neo-classical theories were "basically the same" though the neo-Walrasian was better than the rest.[51] It meant that Keynes's model came to be reinterpreted as an "aggregative, catallactic" structure rather than being seen as a late product of Marshallian plutology. (iii) The completion of Keynes's open-ended model could be done in various ways. As the debate proceeded, various writers took sundry liberties with Keynes's own statement. In most instances, there may have been or seemed to have been good reasons for the individual amendments to Keynes's theory stemming from better empirical data or from improved analysis. But in the event the accumulation of such substitutions of "what Keynes ought to have said" for what he did say came to falsify the original gestalt conception.[52]

---

51. This notion also permeates my own earlier work on the subject—to its detriment.
52. Cf. Leijonhufvud [1968a].

In a cruel job of reviewing, Keynes said of one of Hayek's early works that it was "an extraordinary example of how, starting with a mistake, a remorseless logician can end up in Bedlam." The "Keynes and the Classics" debate ended up in the bedlam of the so-called "neoclassical synthesis." The last several steps to that conclusion were taken under the compulsion of virtual mathematical necessity. One has to trace back to the early slips between form and substance to find an escape from it.

Keynes was to play little part in the debate that ended in bedlam. But, ironically, he did "set it up" so that, once the matter was turned over to remorseless logicians, that is where his legacy to economics was bound to end up. Keynes sought to *"revolutionize"* the gestalt of the theory that he saw his "fellow economists" as entertaining. He attempted no "revolution" in inherited routines and methods of analysis. On the contrary, he went to great lengths to erect his novel structure of ideas using only the Marshallian tool-box (and a good dose of aggregation). But it may well be that no such feat is possible as *definitively* changing the "pattern of beliefs" without also changing the routines people use for checking the logical consistency of simultaneously entertained beliefs. Keynes left the price-theoretical equilibrium analysis machinery in place. Released from his control, the old, proven logical machine—almost by itself, as it were—set about to clean up and restore order—*the Old* Established Order. The process leading up to the neoclassical synthesis featured the standard equilibrium constructions mindlessly eating away at the main Keynesian ideas until nothing was left but the trite and trivial propositions that if wages are (i) "too high" for equilibrium, and (ii) "rigid downwards," then unemployment will exist and persist. That end-product is the neoclassical synthesis in a nutshell.[53]

This "synthesis," which concludes that Keynes's theory is that special case of "classical" theory in which wages are constrained to be "rigid," is patent nonsense any way you look at it. (i) From the "external" standpoint, the Great Depression in the United States had the worst, most dramatic wage-deflation on the his-

---

53. . . . . and such an appropriate container too!

torical record. How could a theory whose "critical feature" was the assumption that wages will not fall, no matter what, have any relevance to these external conditions? (ii) The first hypothesis that would come to *any* pre-Keynesian economist's mind, if asked to explain why the desired supply of labor (or any other good) was not being sold and why the situation persisted, would inevitably be that the ruling price must be in excess of the equilibrium price and that, for some reason, it would not come down. How could the use of that old standby in this instance constitute a "revolutionary break" with inherited theory? (iii) To top it off, of course, Keynes definitely did *not* assume wages to be rigid and did not argue that the depression stemmed from insufficient flexibility of wages. On the contrary, he went to great lengths to bolster his insistent contention that a higher degree of wage-flexibility would not help get the system out of the large-scale unemployment state but, instead, make the situation worse.

The "synthesis" gave an understandable answer to only one question, namely Humpty-Dumpty's: "Who is to be master?" The neo-Walrasian programme came out the master with the Keynesian subordinated to the role of one of its "special cases."

The inherited conception of how markets function to coordinate activities, which provided the underlying informal support for all pre-Keynesian equilibrium theories, was based on the twin presuppositions:[54]

i. that price-incentives effectively control the behavior of individual transactors; that transactors will respond to changes in relative prices by changing the quantities they desire to produce and consume in a qualitatively predictable manner;
ii. that prices tend to move—and are "free" to do so—in response to market excess demands or supplies and in such a manner as to induce transactors to alter their behavior in the directions required for all activities to "mesh."

These are necessary for the system envisaged by pre-Keynesian theory to work. Negate one or the other and the result is a theory of a system that cannot work. The "synthesis" concluded

54. Cf. Leijonhufvud [1968a], pp. 26ff.

that Keynes had thrown a spanner in the works of the "classical" system by, as it were, "fixing wages" so that they could not adjust to remove an excess supply of labor.

The novel theoretical idea in Keynes's work that was lost sight of in all of this was different. To appreciate it—and to appreciate how difficult it is to do it justice within the framework of equilibrium models—one has to envisage the possibility of coordination of "desired" transactor activities in the system failing because communication between them fails to convey the needed information.

It is one of the great achievements of general equilibrium theory to have shown that the vector of equilibrium prices conveys, in principle, all the information that each transactor needs to know in order to be able to coordinate his activities with those of everybody else in the system. When starting from a disequilibrium state with prices diverging from their equilibrium values, transactor plans will be inconsistent and the necessity of adjusting will be forced on them. How can we be confident that the ensuing adjustment process converges on that equilibrium price vector which provides the requisite information? As it turns out, this should be possible (given certain subsidiary conditions) if the adjustments of market prices were effectively governed by the discrepancies, in the respective markets, between the sales and purchases that transactors would "desire" to execute could they only be confident that they would be able to do so. But at disequilibrium prices not everyone will be able to sell or buy all that he might "desire."

The "classical" conception of the market as a feedback-regulated servo-mechanism assumed that the "error" in feedback that the mechanism sought to reduce to zero by iterative adjustments of prices would be the aggregative difference between these "desired" demands and supplies. Keynes's "Effective Demand Failure" theory challenged this assumption. The system will register, he argued, only those demand-signals that can be backed by ready purchasing-power. But transactors who in a disequilibrium state find themselves unable to realize their desired sales will not acquire the money with which to "back" what would otherwise be their "desired" demands. Consequently, the market excess demands that *effectively* govern price-adjustments are not the "appropriate" ones in such a situation.

II. 4

The "neoclassical synthesis" proposed a reconciliation of "Keynesianism" and "orthodoxy" on a purely formalistic plane. Substantively, each of the two world-views that were thus wrenched into the logical appearance of consistency was basically uncompromised by the adopted formula. Behind the formal screen, they stood poles apart. It is inconceivable that this deceptive "papering-over" of the stark inconsistency of substantive beliefs could be indefinitely sustained. Yet, surprise at the extent that this modelling formula gained widespread acceptance, *despite* the incompatibility on a basic theoretical level, is possibly misplaced. It may be that it "worked" in its time, rather, *because* it allowed the postponement of a confrontation that could not have been decided but that had tremendous latent potential for diverting energies away from the pursuit of "normal science" within each "paradigm."

Any attempt to distil from the literature a really adequate characterization of the two "cosmologies," noting (in fairness) the reservations appended to each by prominent and representative writers, etc., would cause the already distended frame of this paper to burst. Yet, it is necessary that some notion of the two be conveyed at this point. The crudity of the following metaphor may be objectionable but its use will have the advantage (in addition to brevity) that it is unlikely to be taken too seriously.

The simplest example of a self-regulating system is that of the hull of a ship. Let the "even-keel" state of the hull correspond, metaphorically, to a "fully coordinated" or general equilibrium state of the economic system.[55] Assume an external force impinging on the ship so as to displace it from the even-keel position. The stronger this "disturbance" the larger the deviation from "equilibrium" that it would, by itself, tend to

---

55. The ship may be on an even keel but on its way to an undesirable location. One must *not* entertain any presumption that the coordinated state of the economy would, if attained, be in any sense 'welfare optimal'.

bring about. Consider the strength (and direction) of the force exerted by the hull itself in the displaced position and how this force would vary as a function of the "degree of list."

Then, the "ship" of classical or orthodox economic cosmology has the following properties. It always tends to move back towards an even keel from any displaced position. The force acting to bring it back, moreover, is proportional—or, perhaps, even better than that—to the magnitude of the displacement. This ship cannot conceivably capsize—when turned upside down in the water its inherent "self-righteousness" would assert itself with maximum strength.

This caricatures the "basic" orthodox presupposition. Less "super-classical," more sensible variations are available. Time-lagged adjustment behavior is accommodated, for example, by allowing momentum to enter into the account of the physical system metaphor—following a "shock," the orthodox ship would go through a series of oscillations converging on the even-keel state. And so on. The basic presupposition is simply that the system will tend back to an even keel from any position, not that it will do so with maximum conceivable efficiency.

Thus, in broad economic terms, large-scale unemployment, for example, will not persist by itself. Unless the system is repeatedly exposed to adverse shocks "involuntary unemployment" should tend to shrink and disappear. In terms of general equilibrium theory, the homeostatic force back towards an "even keel" should be stronger the larger the displacement because, generally speaking, excess demands and supplies will be larger the farther prices in the respective markets diverge from their values in the general equilibrium "solution" price vector; the adjustment velocities of prices depend on the magnitude of excess demands (supplies) with the adjustment of activity levels depending, in turn, on the behavior of prices.

The "ship" of Keynesian cosmology is rather different—in fact, a tub "unsafe in any weather." Suppose we consider an external "shock" (a decline in government expenditure, say) that by itself would suffice to give it a list of x degrees. Then one problem—distressing to those who have mankind travelling on this boat—is that (for reasons not to be clearly understood) it never sails with its cargo properly secured. When the ship is exposed to an external disturbance, therefore, the cargo shifts in the hold, and the ship goes to a list, not just of x degrees, but of mx degrees ($m > 1$). This self-amplifying mechanism, that tends to increase the movement initiated by any given shock, is referred to as the "multiplier." (In clear contrast, all the feedback loops of our "classical ship" operate always in a strictly deviation-counteracting manner.)

Furthermore, this ship will simply stick in any position of list that the above process would bring about, showing no "inherent" tendency to right itself. Getting it into the reasonable neighborhood of an even keel will always—unless you are content to wait for the vagaries of wind and water to bring it about by chance—be a matter of "doing something about it." Having Central Bankers on the bridge "lean against the wind" and such will accomplish nothing, moreover. What it takes is having your trusty Treasury stevedores down in the hold doing the honest, sweaty work of shifting the cargo from larboard to starboard and back again as conditions demand.

That will do. There is little point in trying by further elaboration to make what can be no more than a crude metaphor more palatable to the initiated. For some considerable time, economics has managed to accommodate the cohabitation of two such "images" of the economic world. It is not a matter easily to be dismissed from mind by reassuring reflections on "complementary" perceptual structurings of complex phenomena. For certain important problems, economists use models which presuppose that the economy is "like a classical boat." Other, equally important problems, are approached with the aid of constructions based on the presupposition that we sail in a Keynesian contraption. But the two classes of problems occur simultaneously in reality—and the actual external world could not be "like" both ships at one and the same time.

It is not a trivial matter as two simple examples will suffice to show. (i) *Theoretical implications:* theories of the "orthodox" variety will predict that an increase in the "propensity to save" will raise the growth-rates of national income and wealth. It is something that governments might reasonably seek to encourage therefore. In the Keynesian view, on the other hand, an increase in the propensity to save will reduce the level of income, increase unemployment, and is also likely to have the "paradoxical" result that the actually realized growth-rate of the wealth of nations falls. It seems, in fact, "safer" for governments to discourage the private accumulation of wealth. Clearly, one or the other party must be capable of enormous mischief if put in a position, say, of guiding the policies of a developing nation bent on growth. (ii) *Empirical interpretations:* in comparison with the interwar period, Western economies have enjoyed high and relatively stable employment in the twenty-five years following World War II. In the Keynesian view, this improved employment performance is to be attributed to the much larger size of government sectors. More guns—more butter. In the absence of this expansion of state activity, Keynesians would infer, the postwar period would have had an employment record as dismal as that of the 1930s. In the more "classical" view, in contrast, the interwar period now stands out as an "abnormal" era sandwiched between the pre-World War I and post-World War II high employment periods. The high employment levels of recent decades reflects a return of the system to "normal" functioning. In this view, the expansion of the state has come at the expense of correspondingly slower growth of the private sector. More guns—less butter. Thus, the same data have entirely different meanings depending on what type of "ship" one believes one is observing.

A reconciliation on a substantive level is (naturally) feasible. What it eventually will be like cannot be forecast in very specific terms. Among the considerations that should play a role in shaping a "substantive synthesis," the following two should, I think, belong. (i) As noted in Section II.2, the general theory debates focusing on the "unemployment equilibrium" notion tended gradually to lose sight of the "historical" matter of the magnitude and nature of the disturbances to which the system had been exposed. This matter should be brought back in. (ii) From all other fields in which self-regulating "natural" systems and/or man-made mechanisms are studied, we know it to be the general case that the homeostatic capabilities of such systems are bounded. It is more than just likely that this is true also of economic systems.

In an earlier paper,[56] I proposed a "cosmological working-hypothesis" (as it were) which in terms of the previous metaphor would come out somewhat as follows. Consider a hull-type such as might have evolved and survived over the centuries. Displacing this boat from the even-keel position further and further, we would first find the force acting at a displaced position to bring it back toward "equilibrium" increasing in strength; at some point, however, it would reach its maximum and be found weakening for greater deviations from the even-keel state. Still further "out" we could locate a critical state where the ship's deviation-counteracting tendency is zero and beyond which it would capsize. (Whether this last part of the metaphor can be given any sensible social system interpretation is perhaps questionable.)

In economic terms, what is being suggested may be summarily stated as follows. For the "even-keel" state, substitute the economic system's general equilibrium motion defined as a path in gT-dimensional goods-time space. This is the motion the system would have to follow for all of its homeostats to "report" zero error in feedback throughout; hence, it should be regarded as a purely notional reference-motion and not as a description of any actual motion. Given this theoretical reference-motion, we are able to speak of actual states of the system as "displaced" from it to a greater or lesser extent. As before, we are concerned with the strength of the system's tendency to "home in" towards the general equilibrium path from various such "displaced" positions.

For states in the near neighborhood of the equilibrium path, basically the only tendencies at work will be those of the classical supply-and-demand mechanism (which will be deviation-counteracting). As the displacement being considered is gradually increased, these equilibrating forces would by themselves tend to grow in strength, but another element also starts to enter in as Keynesian "effective demand failures" begin to affect the operation of various markets. At some point, the resulting net equilibrating tendencies reach a maximum and, beyond

56. Leijonhufvud [1973a].

it, decline in strength as effective demand failures increasingly impair the system's capacity to adjust appropriately. For very sizeable displacements, the simple two-dimensional metaphor is a very halting one at best—as the system becomes increasingly *disorganized* its motion cannot be appraised in as simple a manner as that suggested by the notion of "directed momentum" in relation to an equilibrium reference path. Some prices and activity levels may be moving in the direction of their notional general equilibrium values; others, however, will be moving further away. Some prices and activity levels that are "wrong" may be unchanging, while those that are "right" move, and so on. In a "great depression" or "great inflation," the system could wallow sluggishly through a succession of such states without, unaided, taking a decisive turn for the better for a long time. The consequences of prolonged, serious discoordination will show up in transformations of the social, legal and political framework of economic activity—at which point the economist's pretenses to "tracking" the system through time with his theoretical constructions ought in all decency to be shed.

In simpler terms, consider a system that within certain bounds around the equilibrium path will "home in" in the way presumed in pre-Keynesian economics. Outside this "corridor" its behavior is more sluggish and well outside the forces emphasized in Keynesian theory predominate entirely.

The reasons for sketching a possible theoretical reconciliation having these broad features—naturally others might be contemplated—are (the reader will be glad to know) actually economic rather than nautical.

At a relatively simple level, where analytical manageability would seem within our present reach, the theory stresses the presence and functions of "buffer-stocks" in the system. Transactors maintain both physical and financial "buffers"—input and output inventories, spare capacity, liquid assets and less than fully utilized credit-lines, etc.—and do so exactly to prevent stochastically occurring disturbances from interrupting or disrupting the desired, "orderly" flows of their production and consumption activities. Although the timing, specific nature and concrete causes of such disturbances cannot be foreseen, as long as they are not larger in magnitude and/or longer in duration than was anticipated in planning for the prudent provision of buffer-stocks, the system will absorb the shocks and adjust smoothly. When they are larger and more sustained than transactors had found it reasonable to guard against, buffer-stocks run out, and the Keynesian effective demand failures (exacerbated, probably, by contractions of credit, bankruptcies, etc.) then disrupt the "normal" homeostatic adjustment mechanisms.

At a rather "deeper" level, the basic conception relates less readily to accustomed modes of economic modelling. The day-to-day coordination of economic activities relies on the utilization of knowledge that overwhelmingly derives from the past experience of transactors. The information required for the task could not be created (or in the wake of an amnesia epidemic, recreated) overnight. New learning takes place gradually and at the margin of accumulated experience. As long as the system evolves gradually, what was "normal" according to past experience continues to be a good guide to the present and transactors are able to update their conceptions of their economic environment in pace with its changes. An abrupt shock to the system of such magnitude as to require adaptation to a significantly different environment, wherein past experience is a bad guide to present behavior, is a different matter. Anyone who has moved to a foreign country and had to adapt to a very different structure of relative prices from the one he had been accustomed to will recall the time and effort required to create a new, "rational" and relatively stable consumption pattern in a new milieu. That however is the rather simple task of one individual adapting to the pattern in which activities are already coordinated, as reflected in the prevailing (near-equilibrium) price structure, in a smoothly running system. The situation we are envisaging is one in which all transactors are simultaneously thrown into an analogous situation and where no one can have a very confident notion of what equilibrium prices will eventually emerge.

Collective adaptation to a drastically altered situation is likely to be slow for much of the new information that any given transactor acquires will pertain to the actions taken by others on the basis of no longer applicable precedents. And so on.

To sketch a theory that seems to offer the prospect of a substantive reconciliation is easy—only too easy, perhaps. But if the trouble with the previous formal "synthesis" was that it did not make substantive sense, the trouble with proposals for a substantive "synthesis" like this one is that we do not know very much at all about how to provide a reasonably disciplined formal representation for systems behaving this way.

Mathematical general equilibrium theorists have at their command an impressive array of proven techniques for modelling systems that "always work well." Keynesian economists have experience with modelling systems that "never work." But, as yet, no one has the recipe for modelling systems that function pretty well most of the time but sometimes work very badly to coordinate economic activities. And the analytical devices and routines of neo-Walrasian general equilibrium theory and Keynesian theory will not "mix."

II. 5

The last several years have seen a growing interest on the part of economic theorists in the problems of finding a more viable formal synthesis of neo-Walrasian and Keynesian economics. Work directed towards this task has come to be commonly labeled as concerned with "the microfoundations of macroeconomic theory." In the last couple of years, a few of the most widely respected senior theorists in the profession as well as many of its sharpest young mathematical economists have begun to take a hand. Despite a considerable number of interesting contributions, however, progress has been disappointingly slow.

The recent admirable survey of general equilibrium economics by Arrow and Hahn leads up to a concluding delineation of the remaining "gap" between the two theories.[57] It is hard to know whether one should draw more encouragement or discouragement from this authoritative assessment of the state of the art. On the one hand, it is evident how much more clearly we are now able to define many of the obstacles in the

57. Arrow and Hahn [1971], chapters 13 and 14.

way of reunification of economic theory than was possible ten or fifteen years ago. On the other hand, the "gap" is thereby also seen to yawn wider and the remaining tasks to loom more formidable than they looked—to relatively innocent eyes in any case—in the early sixties.[58] The most helpful contributions in the recent literature have, on balance, been more critical than constructive in nature. Critical assessments, conceptual clarifications, sharper definitions of problem aspects will, of course, mark a natural and required first stage of inquiry, preliminary to constructive solutions of problems of this type. But, in this instance, one may by now begin to wonder whether this "first stage" is not threatening to become permanent—or as permanent as the patience of economists will allow before they walk away from the issues in disgust.

Are we yet again on the wrong track? It is almost always foolish to prejudge what may or may not be achieved by the dogged pursuit of a particular approach in a science. Still, it seems time to consider the possibility that we have withdrawn from the simple cul-de-sac of the "neoclassical synthesis" only to enter a more intricate maze (in which more fun is to be had) that offers no through street either.

The "microfoundations of macro" label attached to recent work on disequilibrium and monetary models in the neo-Walrasian vein is indicative of some presumptions (if not quite "presuppositions") that may bear examination. First, it conflates the distinction between micro- and macro-theory with that between neo-Walrasian and "Keynesian" theory.[59] Second, the phrase reflects a diagnosis of the state of the art and a view of the task at hand, namely, that the formally rigorous and so far progressive neo-Walrasian programme is in good intellectual health while the analytically mushy "Keynesian" models need to be cleaned up in order to get that stagnant programme restarted on a more promising track. The notion of what is to be done is thus one of shoving the firm axiomatic neo-Walrasian microfoundations in under the ramshackle "Keynesian" macro-

58. The reader might be wise to read this as simply an autobiographical statement. My innocence on some of these matters will shine through much of my [1968a] and [1969].

59. Construing, here, "Keynesian" as broadly as possible, for example, to include that brand of "monetarism" which, according to Friedman, may be fitted into some version of the so-called "IS-LM" modelling frame.

superstructure which, once safely propped up on that basis, might then be reconstructed without risk to the life, limb and good repute (for formal competence) of those engaged in the task.

The actual work done in recent years has perhaps taught us a few things about those weaknesses of "Keynesian" models that account for the lack of theoretical discipline imposed on their users and the ability of political economists to argue, with their help, for virtually any bundle of policies in almost any situation.[60] But, mainly, the results of this work have been of a character that should be rather unexpected to anyone who naively embraced the presumptions just outlined. For, in the main, the lessons learned have been about the *limitations* of inherited neo-Walrasian theory—about what cannot be done with it as it now stands. And "what cannot be done with it" includes, most specifically, of course, analysis of "Keynesian" macro-processes.

Rather than identifying microtheory with neo-Walrasian models and macrotheory with "Keynesian" ones, it might be better, I suggest, to emphasize a Lakatosian distinction between the two research programmes as the primary one and then to distinguish, secondarily, the micro- and macro-theoretical components of each. The result of putting it thus is to land us with two distinct questions in place of the previous one—"What microfoundations for 'Keynesian' macrotheory?" and "What macro-superstructure on neo-Walrasian micro?" These questions force recognition of the following observations:

i. There *were* some, albeit rudimentary, micro-underpinnings to Keynes's theory.[61] The elements of price theory utilized in the *General Theory* were not Walrasian, however, but Marshallian. Keynes's "freehand sketch" of these price-theoretical aspects was not developed to the point of providing coherent microfoundations for macrotheory. With the abandonment of the already then degenerating Marshallian programme, very little work on their development has taken place since. Inadequate as these rudiments will appear when compared to the

---

60. Compare Clower and Leijonhufvud [1975], p. 182.

61. The at one time fairly widespread view that price-theoretical *elementa* were absent from—and sometimes violated in—the *General Theory* was criticized as part of my attack on the "neoclassical synthesis" in my [1968a], [1969].

neo-Walrasian models that in the interim have seen 40 years of systematic development, they still do have the significant advantage to recommend them of being "all of a piece" with Keynesian macrotheory. That one cannot claim for the results of the piecemeal substitutions of neo-Walrasian for Marshallian price-theoretical constructions that has since occurred.

This suggests that, in trying to assure *sui generis* microfoundations for Keynesian macro, the possibility might be explored of assembling them from building-blocks left lying about the abandoned intellectual site of the once so imposing Marshallian "school."[62] Whether this is worth pursuing or not is, perhaps, anyone's guess. It is quite clear from the start that the attempt would be a major undertaking with a most uncertain pay-off. For the Marshallian school presumably did not degenerate from sheer inattention "without reason." We do not have a very clear idea of what the reasons were. They would have to be dug out and diagnosed in order to judge whether the decline of Marshallian economics was avoidable.

ii. There *are* some, not at all rudimentary, macro-superstructures erected on neo-Walrasian microfoundations. We find their prototype in Patinkin's classic achievement.[63] More recently, we have the products of the voluminous literature on "neoclassical growth" models.

If, in the recent discussion, there has been a tendency to overlook Keynes's Marshallian micro-elements, the tendency with regard to this neo-Walrasian macro-literature—which, looming imposingly in plain view, cannot be overlooked—has been to disregard it. Since it does not address unemployment or other discoordination problems and gives no prescriptions for stabilization policy, the attitude towards it tends to be that "it doesn't count." Yet, there is nothing "sketchy" or "half-baked" about it. There is no need to issue plaintive calls for the development of neo-Walrasian macro-structures. We already have a full-fledged macrotheory within this programme.

---

62. The reasons for insisting (above, Section II:1) that pre-Keynesian "neoclassical economics" was not a homogenous doctrine and that realization of the differences between the "schools" of 40 years ago will be of relevance to present concerns finally come to light here.

63. Cf. Patinkin [1956].

Instead, the question here is whether "this is all we are ever going to get" in the way of macrotheory out of the neo-Walrasian programme. May it be that Patinkin et al. have virtually exhausted the programme's potential in this important area and left only footnotes to be added?

My colleague, R. W. Clower, poses the matter this way.[64]

> . . . the logical and empirical implications—and so also the conceptual limitations—of Neo-Walrasian theory were simply not clear to anyone until after the Neo-Walrasian Revolution had pretty well run its course. In the interim, it was only natural for economists generally to proceed on the presumption that general equilibrium theory had no inherent limitations. After all, even quite specialized economic models generally admit of a variety of alternative interpretations; that is to say, it is usually possible to add new variables and behavior relations without having completely to reconstruct the logical foundations of the original model. In mathematics, axiom systems that possess analogous properties are said to be *noncategorical*. That any even moderately "general" economic model should be anything but *noncategorical*, therefore, would hardly occur naturally to any but a very perverse mind. That the elaborate Neo-Walrasian model set out in Hicks' *Value and Capital* might fail to satisfy this condition would have seemed correspondingly incredible to any sensible person at the outset of the Neo-Walrasian Revolution.[65]

The question Clower raises we may rephrase in Lakatosian terms: May it be that part of the neo-Walrasian programme's hard core must be relinquished in order to put Keynesian macrotheory on a consistent microbasis?

If the answer to this one is "yes"—and even now it seems premature to assert that it must be "yes"—the next question, and the crucial one, becomes: Which specific hard-core propositions of neo-Walrasian models are responsible for setting the limits to their extension in the "Keynesian" direction?[66]

64. Cf. Clower [1975], p. 134.

65. Clower's judgment that the neo-Walrasian revolution pretty well had to run its course before sensible persons could become aware of the programme's possible limitations may be compared with the—possibly overly "defensive"—discussion of the preoccupation of theoretical economists with the exploration of formal languages, above Sections I:6 through I:8.

66. To avoid misunderstandings, some observations are in order. First, these questions are likely to seem of little consequence to most of those that have contributed to and/or are presently working within the neo-Walrasian programme. That programme has been one of "pure formal exploration" to a degree that, in a natural science, would have made it a most curious anomaly in the history of science. Mathematical economists would be little discomfitted by a change in the basic ground-rules for further such ex-

SCHOOLS, "REVOLUTIONS," AND RESEARCH PROGRAMMES

On the first question, I tend, like Clower, to the belief that the neo-Walrasian hard core is limiting. With regard to the second, my suspicions focus (so far) on the Maximizing Behavior postulate in the particularly rigid form that it has come to take in neo-Walrasian economics, i.e. as a "necessary condition for the intelligibility of behavior."[67]

But, at the point where these questions are raised, this one-man's-view of the Keynesian revolution story has been brought up to date. It is a yet unfinished story. But the tale beyond the point just reached cannot be told without prejudging the answers to some questions that are still in the making.

plorations. To give up one or more of the formal "hard-core" postulates of this programme need, generally speaking, occasion no traumatic revisions of cosmological beliefs. It has in fact long been apparent that some of the most accomplished and admired contributors to neo-Walrasian economics do not attach to its models the substantive belief that "the world is like that." In particular—and quite contrary to the allegations of the "new Cambridge" economists (whom one must nonetheless credit with being out far ahead of the pack in arguing the fundamental irrelevance of neo-Walrasian general equilibrium theory to Keynesian economics)—the major contributors to this programme obviously have no ideologically based attachment to it whatsoever. Indeed, the "typical" neo-Walrasian (loosely speaking) tends to be an "interventionist" in matters of socio-economic policy; the "Chicago school" (equally loosely speaking) known for its "anti-interventionism" is notable also for its critical opposition to the neo-Walrasian mode of theorizing.

Second, much of what we have learned from neo-Walrasian literature—and it is a great deal—will carry over through a programme switch. These lessons of lasting value will not, in my view, be confined just to matters of techniques, "tricks" of modelling and the like, important as these legacies of the period of neo-Walrasian hegemony are.

Third, genuine progress on an integrated micro–macro "Keynesian" theory is undoubtedly much more likely to originate with mathematical economists known for masterful command of neo-Walrasian theory than to come from anywhere else.

67. Neo-Walrasian closed system models have so far been inadequate—or, at best, grotesquely cumbersome—vehicles for representing the role of ignorance and the passage of time in human affairs. This has so far stood in the way of satisfactory modelling of the "disequilibrium" motion of ongoing systems. Both problems are, it would appear, rooted in the hard-core heuristic routine of modelling the behavior of each individual agent so as to portray his every action as part of a comprehensively planned "optimal" time-path.

Marshall's theory did not insist on representing all acts as part of an optimal plan. The behavior of individuals in his models is to be characterized rather as "satisficing converging on maximizing." A theory cast in such form provides escape from most of the embarrassing riddles of time and ignorance met with in current "neoclassical" (growth) models.

These matters, however, can hardly be discussed adequately within brief compass. My *Maximization and Marshall* harps upon them at length.

CHAPTER TWELVE

Life among the Econ*

The Econ tribe occupies a vast territory in the far North. Their land appears bleak and dismal to the outsider, and travelling through it makes for rough sledding; but the Econ, through a long period of adaptation, have learned to wrest a living of sorts from it. They are not without some genuine and sometimes even fierce attachment to their ancestral grounds, and their young are brought up to feel contempt for the softer living in the warmer lands of their neighbours, such as the Polscis and the Sociogs. Despite a common genetical heritage, relations with these tribes are strained—the distrust and contempt that the average Econ feels for these neighbours being heartily reciprocated by the latter—and social intercourse with them is inhibited by numerous taboos. The extreme clannishness, not to say xenophobia, of the Econ makes life among them difficult and perhaps even somewhat dangerous for the outsider. This probably accounts for the fact that the Econ have so far not been systematically studied. Information about their social structure and ways of life is fragmentary and not well validated. More research on this interesting tribe is badly needed.

*Editor's Note: Since many of our younger readers are, with the idealism so characteristic of contemporary youth, planning to launch themselves on a career of good deeds by going to live and work among the Econ, the editor felt that it would be desirable to invite an Econologist of some experience to write an account of this little known tribe. Diligent inquiry eventually turned up the author of the present paper. Dr. Leijonhufvud was deemed an almost perfect candidate for the assignment, for he was exiled nearly a decade ago to one of the outlying Econ villages (Ucla) and since then has not only been continuously resident there but has even managed to get himself named an elder (under what pretenses—other than the growth of a grey beard—the editor has been unable to determine).

CASTE AND STATUS

The information that we do have indicates that, for such a primitive people, the social structure is quite complex. The two main dimensions of their social structure are those of caste and status. The basic division of the tribe is seemingly into castes; within each caste, one finds an elaborate network of status relationships.

An extremely interesting aspect of status among the Econ, if it can be verified, is that status relationships do not seem to form a simple hierarchical "pecking-order," as one is used to expect. Thus, for example, one may find that A pecks B, B pecks C, and *then C pecks A*! This non-transitivity of status may account for the continual strife among the Econ which makes their social life seem so singularly insufferable to the visitor. Almost all of the travellers' reports that we have comment on the Econ as a "quarrelsome race" who "talk ill of their fellow behind his back," and so forth. Social cohesion is apparently maintained chiefly through shared distrust of outsiders. In societies with a transitive pecking-order, on the other hand, we find as a rule that an equilibrium develops in which little actual pecking ever takes place. The uncivilized anomaly that we find among the Econ poses a riddle the resolution of which must be given high priority in Econological research at this time.

What seems at first to be a further complication obstructing our understanding of the situation in the Econ tribe may, in the last analysis, contain the vital clue to this theoretical problem. Pecking between castes is traditionally not supposed to take place, but this rule is not without exceptions either. Members of high castes are not infrequently found to peck those of lower castes. While such behavior is regarded as in questionable taste, it carries no formal sanctions. A member of a low caste who attempts to peck someone in a higher caste runs more concrete risks—at the extreme, he may be ostracized and lose the privilege of being heard at the tribal midwinter councils.

In order to bring out the relevance of this observation, a few more things need to be said about caste and status in the tribe. The Econ word for caste is "field." Caste is extremely important to the self-image and sense of identity of the Econ, and the adult male meeting a stranger will always introduce himself with the phrase "Such-and-such is my field." The English root of this term is interesting because of the aversion that the Econ normally have to the use of plain English. The English words that have crept into their language are often used in senses that we would not recognize. Thus, in this case, the territorial connotation of "field" is entirely misleading for the castes do not live apart. The basic social unit is the village, or "dept." The depts of the Econ always comprise members of several "fields." In some cases, nearly every caste may be represented in a single dept.

A comparison of status relationships in the different "fields" shows a definite common pattern. The dominant feature, which makes status relations among the Econ of unique interest to the serious student, is the way that status is tied to the manufacture of certain types of implements, called "modls." The status of the adult male is determined by his skill at making the "modl" of his "field." The facts (a) that the Econ are highly status-motivated, (b) that status is only to be achieved by making "modls," and (c) that most of these "modls" seem to be of little or no practical use, probably accounts for the backwardness and abject cultural poverty of the tribe. Both the tight linkage between status in the tribe and modl-making and the trend toward making modls more for ceremonial than for practical purposes appear, moreover, to be fairly recent developments, something which had led many observers to express pessimism for the viability of the Econ culture.

Whatever may have been the case in earlier times, the "fields" of the Econ apparently do not now form a strong rank-ordering. This may be the clue to the problem of the non-transitivity of individual status. First, the ordering of two castes will sometimes be indeterminate. Thus, while the Micro assert their superiority over the Macro, so do the Macro theirs over the Micro, and third parties are found to have no very determined, or at least no unanimous, opinion on the matter. Thus the perceived prestige of one caste relative to another is a non-reflexive relation. In other instances, however, the ranking is quite clear. The priestly caste (the Math-Econ) for example, is a higher "field" than either Micro or Macro, while the Devlops just as definitely rank lower. Second, we know that these caste-rankings (where they can be made) are not permanent but may change over time. There is evidence, for example, that both the high rank assigned to the Math-Econ and the low rank of the Devlops are, historically speaking, rather recent phenomena. The rise of the Math-Econ seems to be associated with the previously noted trend among all the Econ towards more ornate, ceremonial modls, while the low rank of the Devlops is due to the fact that this caste, in recent times, has not strictly enforced the taboos against association with the Polscis, Sociogs, and other tribes. Other Econ look upon this with considerable apprehension as endangering the moral fiber of the tribe and suspect the Devlops even of relinquishing modl-making.

If the non-transitivity of Econ status seems at first anomalous, here at least we have a phenomenon with known parallels.[1] It may be that what we are observing among the Econ is simply the decay of a once orderly social structure that possessed a strong ranking of castes and, within each caste, a perfectly unambiguous transitive status ordering.

GRADS, ADULTS, AND ELDERS

The young Econ, or "grad," is not admitted to adulthood until he has made a "modl" exhibiting a degree of workmanship acceptable to the elders of the "dept" in which he serves his apprenticeship. Adulthood is conferred in an intricate ceremony the particulars of which vary from village to village. In the more important villages, furthermore, (the practice in some outlying villages is unclear) the young adult must continue to demonstrate his ability at manufacturing these artifacts. If he fails to do so, he is turned out of the "dept" to perish in the wilderness.

This practice may seem heartless, but the Econ regard it as a manhood rite sanctioned by tradition and defend it as vital to

1. Cf. e.g., the observations concerning the Indian *jajmani*-system in Manning Nash, *Primitive and Peasant Economic Systems*, [1966], pp. 93ff, esp. p. 94: "For example, goldsmiths give polluting services to potters, and the potters receive pollution from herders, who in turn give polluting services to goldsmiths. In this exchange of ritually crucial interaction the goldsmiths are themselves above the potters and below the herders, but the herders are below the potters and above the goldsmith caste." Precisely.

the strength and welfare of the dept. If life is hard on the young, the Econ show their compassion in the way that they take care of the elderly. Once elected an elder, the member need do nothing and will still be well taken care of.

TOTEMS AND SOCIAL STRUCTURE

While in origin the word "modl" is simply a term for a concrete implement, looking at it only in these terms will blind the student to key aspects of Econ social structure. "Modl" has evolved into an abstract concept which dominates the Econ's perception of virtually all social relationships—whether these be relations to other tribes, to other castes, or status relations within his caste. Thus, in explaining to a stranger, for example, why he holds the Sociogs or the Polscis in such low regard, the Econ will say that "they do not make modls" and leave it at that.

The dominant role of "modl" is perhaps best illustrated by the (unfortunately very incomplete) accounts we have of relationships between the two largest of the Econ castes, the "Micro" and the "Macro." Each caste has a basic modl of simple pattern and the modls made by individual members will be variations on the theme set by the basic modl of the caste. Again, one finds that the Econ define the social relationship, in this instance between two castes, in terms of the respective modl. Thus if a Micro-Econ is asked why the Micro do not intermarry with the Macro, he will answer: "They make a different modl," or "They do not know the Micro modl." (In this, moreover, he would be perfectly correct, but then neither, of course, would he know the Macro modl.)

Several observers have commented on the seeming impossibility of eliciting from the member of a "field" a coherent and intelligible account of what distinguishes his caste from another caste which does not, in the final analysis, reduce to the mere assertion that the modls are different. Although more research on this question is certainly needed, this would seem to lend considerable support to those who refer to the basic modl as the *totem* of the caste. It should be noted that the difficulty of settling this controversial question does not arise from any taboo against discussing caste with strangers. Far from being reticent, the Econ will as a rule be quite voluble on the subject. The problem is that what they have to say consists almost entirely of expressions of caste-prejudices of the most elemental sort.[2]

To the untrained eye, the totems of major castes will often look well-nigh identical. It is the great social significance attached to these minor differences by the Econ themselves that have made Econography (the study of Econ arts and handicrafts) the central field of modern Econology. As an illustration, consider the totems of the Micro and the Macro. Both could be roughly described as formed by two carved sticks joined together in the middle somewhat in the form of a pair of scissors (cf. Figure 12-1).

Certain ceremonies connected with these totems are of great interest to us because of the indications that they give about the origin of modl-making among the Econ. Unfortunately, we have only fragmentary accounts by various travellers of these ceremonies and the interpretations of what they have seen that these untrained observers essay are often in conflict. Here, a systematic study is very much needed.

The following sketchy account of the "prospecting" ceremony among the Macro brings out several of the riddles that currently perplex Econologists working in this area:

> The elder grasps the LM with his left hand and the IS with his right and, holding the totem out in front of himself with elbows slightly bent, proceeds in a straight line—"gazing neither left nor right" in the words of their ritual[3]—out over the chosen terrain. The grads of the village skip gaily around him at first, falling silent as the trek grows longer and more wearisome. On this occasion, it was long indeed and the terrain difficult . . . the grads were strung out in a long, morose and bedraggled chain behind their leader who, sweat pearling his brow, face cast in grim determination, stumbled onward over the obstacles in his path . . . At long last, the totem vibrates, then oscillates more and more; finally, it points, quivering, straight down. The elder waits for the grads to gather round

2. This observation is far from new. One finds it recorded, for example, in Machluyp's *Voyages* in the account of "The Voyage of H.M.S. Semantick to the Coast of Econland."

3. The same wording appears in the corresponding Micro-ritual. It is reported that the Macro belittle the prospecting of the Micro among themselves saying that the Micro "can't keep from gazing right." The Micro, on their side, claim the Macro "gaze left." No one has offered a sensible hypothesis to account for this particular piece of liturgical controversy. Chances are that far-fetched explanations are out of place and that this should simply be accepted as just another humdrum example of the continual bickering among the Econ.

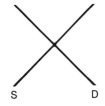

(A) Totem of the Micro.   (B) Totem of the Macro.

Figure 12-1

and then pronounces, with great solemnity: "Behold, the Truth and Power of the Macro."

It is surely evident from an account such as this why such a major controversy has sprung up around the main thesis of the "Implementarist" School. This influential Econographic School argues that the art of modl-carving has its historical origin in the making of tools and useful "implements," and that ceremonies such as the one described above reflect, in ritual form, the actual uses to which these implements were at one time put.

Fanciful as the "Implementarist" hypothesis may seem, it would be injudicious to dismiss it out of hand. Whether the Macro-modl can be regarded as originally a "useful implement" would seem to hinge in the first place on whether the type of "prospecting" ritualized in the described ceremony produces actual results. The Macro themselves maintain that they strike gold this way. Some travellers and investigators support the contention, others dismiss it as mere folklore. The issues are much the same as those connected with attempts to appraise the divining-rod method of finding water. Numerous people argue that it works—but no scientific explanation of why it would has ever been advanced.

We do have some, apparently reliable, eyewitness' reports of gold actually being struck by the Macro. While not disputing the veracity of all such reports, skeptical critics argue that they must be heavily discounted. It is said, for example, that the Econ word for "gold" refers to any yellowish mineral however worthless. Some Econologists maintain, moreover, that the prospecting ceremony is seldom, if ever, conducted over un-known ground and that what the eyewitnesses have reported, therefore, is only the "discovery" of veins that have been known to the Macro for generations.

One might ask how the practice manages to survive if there is nothing to it. The answer is simple and will not be unexpected to those acquainted with earlier studies of the belief-systems of primitive peoples. Instances are known when the ceremony has not produced any concrete results. When this happens, the Macro will take either of two positions. Either he will accuse the member performing the ceremony of having failed to follow ritual in some detail or other, or else defend the man's claim that the gold is there by arguing that the digging for it has not gone deep enough.[4]

It is clear enough that, whichever position is taken, the "phe-nomena are saved" in the sense that the role of the totem in the belief-system of the caste remains unassailed.

MYTHS AND MODLS

In recent years, interest in controversies about whether certain Econ modls "work" or not (or in what sense they may be said to "work") has dwindled. This is certainly not because the issue has been settled—it is fair to say that we are today less certain than ever of what the answers to the questions raised by the Implementarists would be. It is rather that our methodological perspective has changed so that the Implementarist issue is no longer seen as productive of "good" questions. The "New Econ-ology," as it is known, stresses *Verstehen* and, correspondingly,

---

4. The latter rationalization is the more palatable since it puts the blame on a different caste, namely the O'Maitres or O'Metrs (transcriptions vary) who do the digging work of both the Macro and the Micro.

The "diggers" caste is of special interest to those concerned with the underde-velopment of the Econ. Traditionally the lowest Econ caste, the O'Metrs, were allowed to perform only the dirtiest manual tasks and—more significant in Econ eyes—lacked a totem of their own. In more recent times, however, it is through this caste that indus-trialization has begun to make some inroads among the Econ. Free from the prejudices instilled through an education concentrating on modlcarving and the associated totemic beliefs, the O'Metrs take willingly to modern machinery and have become quite profi-cient for example, at handling power shovels and power mills. The attitude of the rest of the tribe towards these erstwhile untouchables taking the lead in industrialization is, as one would expect, one of mingled scorn and envy.

rejects attempts to appraise Econ belief-systems according to rationalistic criteria purloined from modern natural science.[5]

It has become increasingly clear that the Econ associate certain, to them significant, beliefs with every modl, whether or not they also claim that modl to be a "useful tool." That taking "usefulness" as the point of departure in seeking to understand the totemic culture of this people leads us into a blind alley is particularly clear when we consider the Math-Econ caste.

The Math-Econ are in many ways the most fascinating, and certainly the most colorful, of Econ castes. There is today considerable uncertainty whether the "priest" label is really appropriate for this caste, but it is at least easy to understand why the early travellers came to regard them in this way. In addition to the deeply respectful attitude evidenced by the average Econ towards them, the Math-Econ themselves show many cultural patterns that we are wont to associate with religious orders or sects among other peoples. Thus they affect a poverty that is abject even by Econ standards, and it seems clear that this is by choice rather than necessity. It is told that, to harden themselves, they periodically venture stark naked out into the chill winds of abstraction that prevail in those parts. Among the rest of the Econ, who ordinarily perambulate thickly bundled in wooly clothing, they are much admired for this practice. Furthermore, glossolalia—the ability to say the same thing in several different tongues[6]—is a highly esteemed talent among them.

The Math-Econ make exquisite modls finely carved from bones of walras. Specimens made by their best masters[7] are judged unequalled in both workmanship and raw material by a unanimous Econographic opinion. If some of these are "useful"—and even Econ testimony is divided on this point—it is

---

5. C. Levi-Strauss, *The Savage Mind* should be mentioned here as essential reading for anyone with a serious interest in the belief-systems of the Econ.

6. I.e., in several Math tongues—the Indo-European languages, for example, do not count.

7. The budding collector of Econographica should know that most of the work found on the market today is imitative and done by apprentices. Much of it is nonetheless aesthetically superior to, say, the crudely carved totems of the Macro and certainly to the outsized, machine-made modls nowadays exported by the "O'Metrs" who have no artistic tradition to fall back on.

clear that this is purely coincidental in the motivation for their manufacture.

There has been a great deal of debate in recent years over whether certain Econ modls and the associated belief-systems are best to be regarded as religion, folklore and mythology, philosophy and science, or as sports and games. Each category has its vocal proponents among Econologists of repute but very little headway has been made in the debate. The ceremonial use of modls (see above) and the richness of the general Econ culture in rituals has long been taken as evidence for the religious interpretation. But, as one commentator puts it, "If these beliefs are religious, it is a religion seemingly without faith." This interpretation seems to have stranded on this contradiction in terms and presently is not much in favor. More interesting are the arguments of those who have come to view certain Econ belief-systems as a form of quasi-scientific cosmological speculation. As an illustration, Mrs. Robinson's description of what she terms the "Doctrine of K," which is found prevalent among the members of the powerful Charles River villages, inevitably brings to mind the debates of the ancient Ionian philosophers over whether water, air, or fire was the "basic stuff" of the universe. The Doctrine of K bears, in fact, striking resemblances to the teachings of Anaximander.[8] It is known, moreover, that in some other depts a "Doctrine of M" is taught but we do not as yet have an understandable account of it and know, in fact, little about it except that it is spurned (as heresy?) by the Charles River Econ. Spokesmen for the cosmology view buttress their arguments by pointing out the similarities between the Math-Econ and the Pythagorean brotherhood. Whether the Math-Econ know it or not, they point out, they do obey the ancient Pythagorean principle that "philosophy must be pursued in such a way that its inner secrets are reserved for learned men, trained in Math."

8. Arthur Koestler, *The Sleepwalkers*, New York 1968, pp. 22–23, aptly summarizes Anaximander's teachings: "The raw material (of the universe) is none of the familiar forms of matter, but a substance without definite properties except for being indestructible and everlasting. Out of this stuff all things are developed, and into it they return; before this our world, infinite multitudes of other universes have already existed, and been dissolved again into the amorphous mass."

If one were to dignify this primitive doctrine with modern terminology, one would have to put Anaximander in the "putty-putty, bang-bang" category.

The sports and games interpretation has gained a certain currency due to accounts of the modl-ceremonies of the Intern caste.[9] But even here it is found that, though the ceremony has all the outward manifestations of a game, it has to the participants something of the character of a morality play which in essential respects shapes their basic perception of the world.

THE ECON AND THE FUTURE

It would be to fail in one's responsibility to the Econ people to end this brief sketch of life in their society without a few words about their future. The prospect for the Econ is bleak. Their social structure and culture should be studied now before it is gone forever. Even a superficial account of their immediate and most pressing problems reads like a veritable catalogue of the woes of primitive peoples in the present day and age.

They are poor—except for a tiny minority, miserably poor. Their population growth rate is among the highest in the world. Their land is fairly rich, but much of the natural resources that are their birth-right has been sold off to foreign interests for little more than a mess of pottage. Many of their young are turning to pot and message. In their poverty, they are not even saved from the problems of richer nations— travellers tell of villages half-buried in the refuse of unchecked modl-making and of the eye-sores left on the once pastoral landscape by the random strip-mining of the O'Metrs. It is said that even their famous Well Springs of Inspiration are now polluted.

In the midst of their troubles, the Econ remain as of old a proud and warlike race. But they seem entirely incapable of "creative response'" to their problems. It is plain to see what is in store for them if they do not receive outside aid.

One may feel some optimism that the poverty problems *can* be solved. While population growth may slow down in time, one can have little hope that the ongoing disintegration of Econ

9. One observer casts his account of this ceremony explicitly in parlour-game terms: "Each player gets 2 countries, 2 goods, 2 factors, and a so-called Bowley Box . . ." etc., etc., and also compares the Intern game, in terms of intellectual difficulty, with checkers.

culture will be halted or could be reversed. Here the sad and familiar story of a primitive people's encounter with "modern times" is repeating itself once again. The list of symptoms is long and we will touch only on a few.

Econ political organization is weakening. The basic political unit remains the dept and the political power in the dept is lodged in the council of elders. The foundations of this power of the elders has been eroding for some time, however. Respect for one's elders is no more the fashion among the young Econ than among young people anywhere else. Authority based on age and experience has weakened as recognized status has come increasingly to be tied to cleverness in modl-making. (As noted before, many elders will be inactive as modl-makers.) Although dept establishments have responded to these developments by cooptation of often very young modl-makers as "elders," the legitimacy of the political structure in the eyes of the Econ people is obviously threatened—and the chances of a constructive political response to the tribe's problems correspondingly lessened.

The Econ adult used to regard himself as a life-long member of his dept. This is no longer true—migration between depts is nowadays exceedingly common and not even elders of a village necessarily regard themselves as permanent members. While this mobility may help them to cope with the poverty problem, it obviously tends further to weaken political organization. Urbanization should be noted as a related problem—many villages are today three or four times as large as only a generation or two ago. Big conurbations, with large transient populations, and weak and ineffective political machinery—we are all familiar with the social ills that this combination breeds.

Under circumstances such as these, we expect alienation, disorientation, and a general loss of spiritual values. And this is what we find. A typical phenomenon indicative of the break-up of a culture is the loss of a sense of history and growing disrespect for tradition. Contrary to the normal case in primitive societies, the Econ priesthood does not maintain and teach the history of the tribe. In some Econ villages, one can still find the occasional elder who takes care of the modls made by some long-gone hero of the tribe and is eager to tell the legends associated with each. But few of the adults or grads, noting what they regard as the crude workmanship of these dusty old relics, care to listen to such rambling fairytales. Among the younger generations, it is now rare to find an individual with any conception of the history of the Econ. Having lost their past, the Econ are without confidence in the present and without purpose and direction for the future.

References

Ackley, Gardner [1961]: *Macroeconomic Theory*, Macmillan, New York.

Afriat, S. N. [1978]: *The Price Index*, Cambridge University Press, Cambridge.

Alchian, Armen A. and William R. Allen [1964]: *University Economics*, Wadsworth Publishing Co. Inc., Belmont, Calif.

Alchian, Armen A. [1970]: "Information Costs, Pricing, and Resource Unemployment," in E. Phelps, et al., *Microeconomic Foundations of Employment and Inflation Theory*, Norton, New York, 1970.

Ando, Albert and Franco Modigliani [1963]: "The Life Cycle Hypothesis of Saving," *American Economic Review*, March.

Archibald, George C. and Richard G. Lipsey, [1958]: "Monetary and Value Theory: A Critique of Lange and Patinkin," *Review of Economic Studies*, January.

Arrow, Kenneth J. [1959]: "Towards a Theory of Price Adjustment," in M. Abramovitz, et. al., *The Allocation of Economic Resources*, Stanford University Press, Stanford, Calif.

Arrow, Kenneth and Frank H. Hahn [1971]: *General Competitive Analysis*, Holden-Day, San Francisco.

Bailey, Martin J. [1962]: *National Income and the Price Level*, McGraw-Hill, New York.

Barro, Robert J. and Herschel I. Grossman [1971]: "A General Disequilibrium Model of Income and Employment," *American Economic Review*, March.

Baumol, William J. [1952]: "The Transactions Demand for Cash: An Inventory Theoretic Approach," *Quarterly Journal of Economics*.

Becker, Gary S. [1962]: "Irrational Behavior and Economic Theory," *Journal of Political Economy*, February.

Benjamin, Daniel K. and Levis A. Kochin [1979]: "Searching for an Explanation of Unemployment in Interwar Britain," *Journal of Political Economy*, June.

REFERENCES

Brunner, Karl and Allan Meltzer [1968]: "What Did We Learn from the Monetary Experience of the United States in the Great Depression?," *Canadian Journal of Economics*, May.

Burns, Arthur F. [1954]: *The Frontiers of Economic Knowledge*, Princeton University Press, Princeton, N. J.

Burstein, Meyer L. [1963]: *Money*, Schenkman Publishing Co., Cambridge, Mass.

Cagan, Phillip [1974]: "The Hydra-headed Monster: The Problem of Inflation in the United States," American Enterprise Institute, Washington, D.C.

Cassel, Gustav [1953]: *The Nature and Necessity of Interest*. Macmillan, New York.

—— [1928]: "The Rate of Interest, The Bank Rate, and the Stabilization of Prices," *Quarterly Journal of Economics*.

Clower, Robert W. [1965]: "The Keynesian Counterrevolution: A Theoretical Appriasal," in F. H. Hahn and F. P. R. Brechling, eds. *The Theory of Interest Rates*, Macmillan, London.

—— [1967]: "A Reconsideration of the Microfoundations of Monetary Theory," *Western Economic Journal*, December.

—— ed., [1969]: *Monetary Theory: Selected Readings*, Penguin, London.

—— and John F. Due [1972]: *Microeconomics*, Irwin, Homewood, Ill.

—— [1975]: "Reflections on the Keynesian Perplex," *Zeitschrift für Nationalökonomie*.

—— and Axel Leijonhufvud [1975]: "The Coordination of Economic Activities: A Keynesian Perspective," *American Economic Review*, May.

—— and Peter Howitt [1978]: "The Transactions Theory of the Demand for Money: A Reconsideration," *Journal of Political Economy*.

Coats, Alfred W. [1969]: "Is There a Structure of Scientific Revolutions in Economics?," *Kyklos*, Fasc. 2.

Dalton, George, ed., [1968]: *Primitive, Archaic and Modern Economies: Essays by Karl Polanyi*, Doubleday, Garden City, N. Y.

Darby, Michael R. [1974]: "The Permanent Income Theory of Consumption—A Restatement," *Quarterly Journal of Economics*, May.

Davidson, Paul [1974]: "Disequilibrium Market Adjustment: Marshall Revisited," *Economic Inquiry*, June.

Davidson, Paul and J. A. Kregel [1975]: "Keynes's Paradigm: A Theoretical Framework for Monetary Analysis," Rutgers University, mimeograph.

Davis, J. Ronnie [1968]: "Chicago Economists, Deficit Budgets, and the Early 1930s," *American Economic Review*, June.

—— [1973]: "Was There a Keynesian Revolution?" delivered at the 1973 Midwestern Economic Association Meeting.

Einaudi, Luigi [1936]: "The Theory of Imaginary Money from Charlemagne to the French Revolution," (translated from 1936 original by G. Taglia-

REFERENCES

cozzo) in F. C. Lane and J. C. Riemersma, eds., *Enterprise and Secular Change*, Allen & Unwin, London, 1953.

Eisner, Robert [1958]: "On Growth Models and the Neoclassical Resurgence," *Economic Journal*, December.

Fellner, William [1946]: *Monetary Policies and Full Employment*, University of California Press, Berkeley and Los Angeles.

Fetter, Frank W. [1965]: *Development of British Monetary Orthodoxy, 1797–1875*, Harvard University Press, Cambridge, Mass.

Friedman, Milton [1952]: "The Economic Theorist," in A. F. Burns, ed., *Wesley Clair Mitchell: The Economic Scientist*, National Bureau of Economic Research, General Series No. 53.

——— [1957]: *A Theory of the Consumption Function*, National Bureau of Economic Research, Princeton, N. J.

——— [1962]: *Price Theory: A Provisional Text*, Aldine Publishing Co., Chicago.

——— [1967]: "The Monetary Theory and Policy of Henry Simons," *Journal of Law and Economics*, October.

——— [1968]: "The Role of Monetary Policy," *American Economic Review*.

——— [1970]: "A Theoretical Framework for Monetary Analysis," *Journal of Political Economy*, March/April.

——— [1971] *Price Theory*, Aldine Publishing Co., Chicago.

——— and David Meiselman [1963]: "The Relative Stability of Monetary Velocity and the Investment Multiplier in the United States, 1897–1958" in *Stabilization Policies* (Commission on Money and Credit), Prentice-Hall Englewood Cliffs, N. J.

——— and Anna Schwartz [1963]: "Money and Business Cycles," *Review of Economics and Statistics*, supplement.

——— and Anna J. Schwartz [1963b]: *A Monetary History of the United States, 1807–1960*, Princeton University Press, Princeton, N. J.

Goodwin, Richard M. [1951]: "Iteration, Automatic Computers, and Economic Dynamics," *Metroeconomica*, April.

Gordon, Robert J., ed. [1973]: *Milton Friedman's Monetary Framework: A Debate with His Critics*, University of Chicago Press, Chicago.

Grandmont, Jean Michel [1975]: "Temporary General Equilibrium Theory," *Econometrica*.

Gregory, Theodore E. G. [1962]: *An Introduction to Tooke and Newmarch's A History of Prices*, London School of Economics and Political Science, London.

Grossman, Herschel I. [1971]: "Money, Interest, and Prices in Market Disequilibrium," *Journal of Political Economy*, September/October.

Gurley, John and Edward Shaw [1956]: "Financial Intermediaries and the Saving-Investment Process," *Journal of Finance*, May.

Haavelmo, Trygve [1960]: *A Study in the Theory of Investment*, University of Chicago Press, Chicago.

Hahn, Frank H. [1971]: "Professor Friedman's Views on Money," *Economica,* February.

—— [1973]: *On the Notion of Equilibrium in Economics,* Cambridge University Press, Cambridge.

Hanson, Norwood R. [1958]: *Patterns of Discovery,* Cambridge University Press, Cambridge.

Harrod. Roy F. [1951]: *The Life of John Maynard Keynes.* Macmillan, London.

—— [1964]: "Are We Really All Keynesians Now?," *Encounter,* January.

Hart, Albert G. [1942]: "Risk, Uncertainty, and the Unprofitability of Compounding Probabilities," in Oscar Lange, et al., *Studies in Mathematical Economics and Econometrics,* Chicago. Reprinted in W. Fellner and B. F. Haley, eds, *Readings in the Theory of Income Distribution,* Blakeston, Philadelphia, 1951.

Hayek, Friedrich A. [1931]: *Prices and Production,* Routledge & Kegan Paul, London.

—— [1931b]: "Reflections on the Pure Theory of Money of Mr. J. M. Keynes, Part I," *Economica,* August.

—— [1932]: "Reflections on the Pure Theory of Money of Mr. J. M. Keynes, Part II," *Economica,* February.

—— [1933]: *Monetary Theory and the Trade Cycle,* London.

—— [1948]: *Individualism and Economic Order,* University of Chicago Press, Chicago.

—— [1973]: *Law, Legislation and Liberty,* Vol. I., Routledge & Kegan Paul, London.

Hazlitt, Henry [1960]: *The Critics of Keynesian Economics,* Van Nostrand, Princeton, N. J.

Hicks, Sir John [1935]: "A Suggestion for Simplifying the Theory of Money," *Economica,* February.

—— [1937]: "Mr. Keynes and the Classics: A Suggested Interpretation," *Econometrica,* April.

—— [1946]: *Value and Capital,* 2nd ed. Clarendon Press, Oxford.

—— [1957]: "A Rehabilitation of 'Classical' Economics?," *Economic Journal,* June.

—— [1963]: *Theory of Wages,* 2nd ed., Macmillan, London.

—— [1965]: *Capital and Growth,* Clarendon Press, Oxford.

—— [1967]: *Critical Essays in Monetary Theory.* Clarendon Press, Oxford.

—— [1969]: *A Theory of Economic History,* Clarendon Press, Oxford.

—— [1970]: "Expected Inflation," Three Banks Review, September.

—— [1974]: *The Crisis in Keynesian Economics,* Blackwell, Oxford.

—— [1976]: " 'Revolutions' in Economics," in Spiro J. Latsis, ed., *Method and Appraisal in Economics,* Cambridge University Press, Cambridge.

—— [1977]: *Economic Perspectives: Further Essays on Money and Growth,* Clarendon Press, Oxford.

REFERENCES

Hirshleifer, Jack [1970]: *Investment, Interest and Capital,* Prentice-Hall, Englewood Cliffs, N. J.

Horwich, George [1964]: *Money, Capital, and Prices,* Irwin, Homewood, Ill.

Howitt, Peter [1974]: "Stability and the Quantity Theory," *Journal of Political Economy,* January/February.

―――― [unpublished]: "The Short-Run Dynamics of Monetary Exchange."

Hutchison, Terence W. [1968]: *Economics and Economic Policy in Britain, 1946–1966: Some Aspects of Their Interrelations,* Allen & Unwin, London.

Hutt, William H. [1939]: *The Theory of Idle Resources,* Jonathan Cape, London.

―――― [1963]: *Keynesianism: Retrospect and Prospect,* Henry Regner, Chicago.

Hymans, S. H. [1965]: "The Cyclical Behavior of Consumers' Income and Spending, 1921–1961," *Southern Economic Journal,* July.

Johnson, Harry G. [1951–52]: "Some Cambridge Controversies on Monetary Theory," *Review of Economic Studies.*

―――― [1961]: "The General Theory After Twenty-Five Years," *American Economic Review,* May.

―――― [1962]: "Monetary Theory and Policy," *American Economic Review,* June.

―――― [1967]: *Essays in Monetary Economics,* Harvard University Press, Cambridge, Mass.

―――― [1970], "Keynes and the Keynesians," *Encounter,* January.

Kahn, Richard F. [1954]: "Some Notes on Liquidity Preferences," *Manchester School of Economics and Social Studies,* September.

Keynes, John M. [1924]: *A Tract on Monetary Reform,* Macmillan, London.

―――― [1930]: *A Treatise on Money,* Vol. I, "The Pure Theory of Money"; Vol II, "The Applied Theory of Money," Macmillan, London.

―――― [1936]: *The General Theory of Employment, Interest and Money,* Harcourt, Brace and Co., New York.

―――― [1972]: *Essays in Persuasion* (Collected Writings, Vol. IX), Macmillan, London.

Klein, Benjamin [1976]: "The Social Costs of the Recent Inflation: The Mirage of Steady Anticipated Inflation," in *Carnegie-Rochester Conference Series,* Vol. III, North-Holland Publishing Co., Amsterdam.

Klein, Lawrence R. [1947]: *The Keynesian Revolution,* Macmillan, New York.

Klein, P. A. [1965]: *Financial Adjustments to Unemployment,* National Bureau of Economic Research, New York.

Knight, Frank H. [1965]: *The Economic Organization,* A. M. Kelley, New York.

Kuenne, Robert E. [1963]: *The Theory of General Economic Equilibrium,* Princeton University Press, Princeton, N. J.

Laidler, David E. W. [1969]: *The Demand for Money: Theories and Evidence,* International Textbook Co., Scranton, Pa.

Lakatos, Imre [1963]: "Proofs and Refutations," *The British Journal for the Philosophy of Science.*

REFERENCES

Lange, Oscar [1942]: "Say's Law: A Restatement and Criticism," in O. Lange, et al., *Studies in Mathematical Economics and Econometrics*, The University of Chicago Press, Chicago.

Latané, Henry A. [1954]: "Cash Balances and the Interest Rate—A Pragmatic Approach," *Review of Economics and Statistics*, November.

Latsis, Spiro J. [1972]: "Situational Determinism in Economics," *The British Journal for the Philosophy of Science*, August.

———, ed., [1976]: *Method and Appraisal in Economics*, Cambridge University Press, Cambridge.

Leijonhufvud, Axel [1967]: "Keynes and the Keynesians: A Suggested Interpretation," *American Economic Review*, May.

——— [1968a]: *On Keynesian Economics and the Economics of Keynes*, Oxford University Press, New York.

——— [1968b]: "Keynes and the Effectiveness of Monetary Policy," *Western Economic Journal*, March.

——— [1969]: *Keynes and the Classics*, The Institute of Economic Affairs, London.

——— [1970]: "Notes on the Theory of Markets," *Intermountain Economic Review*, Fall.

——— [1973a]: "Effective Demand Failures," *Swedish Journal of Economics*, March.

——— [1973b]: "Life among the Econ," *Western Economic Journal*, September.

——— [1974a]: "Keynes' Employment Function: Comment," *History of Political Economy*, Summer.

——— [1974b]: "The Varieties of Price Theory: What Microfoundations for Macrotheory," U.C.L.A. Discussion Paper, No. 44, January.

——— [1976]: "Schools, 'Revolutions' and Research Programmes in Economic Theory," in Spiro J. Latsis, ed., *Method and Appraisal in Economics*, Cambridge University Press, Cambridge.

——— [unpublished]: "Maximization and Marshall," 1974–5 Marshall Lectures.

Lekachman, Robert, ed., [1964]: *Keynes' General Theory: Reports of Three Decades*, Macmillan, London.

——— [1967]: *The Age of Keynes*, Random House, New York.

Lipsey, Richard G. [1972]: "The Foundations of the Theory of National Income: An Analysis of Some Fundamental Errors," in M. Peston and B. Corry, eds., *Essays in Honor of Lord Robbins*, Weidenfeldt & Nicolson, London.

Lucas, Robert E. [1976]: "Econometric Policy Evaluations: A Critique," in K. Brunner and A. Meltzer, eds., *The Phillips Curve and Labor Markets*, North-Holland Publishing Co., Amsterdam.

——— [1977]: "Understanding Business Cycles," *Journal of Monetary Economics*, supplement.

REFERENCES

Lwoff, André [1965]: *Biological Order*, M.I.T. Press, Cambridge, Mass.

Malinvaud, Edmond [1977]: *The Theory of Unemployment Reconsidered*, Blackwell, Oxford.

Masterman, Margaret [1965]: "The Nature of a Paradigm," in I. Lakatos and A. Musgrave, eds., *Criticism and the Growth of Knowledge*, Cambridge University Press, Cambridge, 1970.

Matthews, Robert C. O. [1968]: "Why has Britain had Full Employment Since the War?," *Economic Journal*, September.

Mayer, Thomas, et al. [1978]: *The Structure of Monetarism*, W. W. Norton, New York.

McConnell, Campbell R. [1972]: *Economics*, McGraw-Hill, New York.

Meade, James E. [1937]: "A Simplified Model of Mr. Keynes' System," *Review of Economic Studies*, February.

Meiselman, David [1962]: *The Term Structure of Interest Rate*, Prentice-Hall, Englewood Cliffs, N. J.

Menger, Karl [1973]: "Austrian Marginalism and Mathematical Economics," in J. R. Hicks and W. Weber, eds. *Carl Menger and the Austrian School of Economics*.

Mill, John S. [1909]: *Principles of Political Economy*, (Ashley edition) Longman, London.

Mitchell, Wesley C. [1944]: "The Role of Money in Economic History," *Journal of Economic History*, December reprinted in F. C. Lane and J. C. Riemersma, eds., *Enterprise and Secular Change*, Allen & Unwin, London, 1953.

Modigliani, Franco [1944]: "Liquidity Preference and the Theory of Interest and Money," *Econometrica*, January. Reprinted in F. A. Lutz and L. W. Mints, eds., *Readings in Monetary Theory*, Blakeston, Philadelphia, 1951.

———— [1977]: "The Monetarist Controversy," Federal Reserve Bank of San Francisco, *Economic Review*, supplement.

O'Driscoll, Gerald P. [1977]: *Economics as a Coordination Problem: The Contributions of Friedrich A. Hayek*, Sheed, Andrews and McMeel, Inc., Kansas City, Mo.

Ostroy, Joseph M. [1973]: "The Informational Efficiency of Monetary Exchange," *American Economic Review*, September.

———— and Ross M. Starr [1974]: "Money and the Decentralization of Exchange," *Econometrica*, November.

Patinkin, Don [1948]: "Price Flexibility and Full Employment," *American Economic Review*, September. Reprinted in F. A. Lutz and L. M. Mints, eds, *Readings in Monetary Theory*, Blakeston, Philadelphia,

———— [1956]: *Money Interest, and Prices*, Row, Peterson & Co., Evanston, Ill.

———— [1959]: "Keynesian Economics Rehabilitated: A Rejoinder to Professor Hicks," *Economic Journal*, September.

———— [1961]: "Financial Intermediaries and Monetary Theory," *American Economic Review*, March.

REFERENCES

———— [1965]: *Money, Interest and Prices*, 2nd ed., Harper & Row, New York.

Patinkin, Don and J. C. Leith, eds., [1977]: *Keynes, Cambridge and the General Theory*, London.

Phelps, Edmund S. [1968]: "Money Wage Dynamics and Labor Market Equilibrium," *Journal of Political Economy*, August. Reprinted in E. Phelps, et al., *Microeconomic Foundations of Employment and Inflation Theory*, W. W. Norton, New York, 1970.

Polanyi, Michael [1969]: "The Determinants of Social Action," in E. Streissler, ed., *Roads to Freedom: Essays in Honour of F. A. von Hayek*, Routledge & Kegan Paul, London.

Rawls, John [1971]: *A Theory of Justice*, Belknap Press, Cambridge, Mass.

Reddaway, William B. [1936]: "The General Theory of Employment, Interest, and Money," *Economic Review*, June.

Robertson, Sir Dennis [1966]: *Essays in Money and Interest. Selected with a Memoir by Sir John Hicks*, Collins, Manchester.

Robinson, Joan [1937]: *Introduction to the Theory of Employment*, 2nd ed., Macmillan, London, 1969.

———— [1951]: "The Rate of Interest," *Econometrica*, April.

———— [1963]: *Economic Philosophy*, Aldine Publishing Co., Chicago.

Roll, Eric [1958]: *The World After Keynes: An Examination of the Economic Order*, Praeger, New York.

Samuelson, Paul A. [1946]: "The General Theory," reprinted in J. E. Stiglitz, ed., *The Collected Scientific Papers of Paul A. Samuelson*, Vol. 2, The M.I.T. Press, Cambridge, Mass., 1966.

———— [1952]: "Comment" in B. F. Haley, ed., *A Survey of Contemporary Economics*, Vol. II, Irwin, Homewood, Ill.

———— [1963a]: *Economics*, 6th ed., McGraw-Hill, New York.

———— [1963b]: "A Brief Survey of Post-Keynesian Development," in R. Lekachman, ed., *Keynes' General Theory: Reports of Three Decades*, Macmillan, New York and London, 1969.

Samuelson, Paul A. and Robert M. Solow [1960]: "Analytical Aspects of Anti-inflation Policy," *American Economic Review*, May.

Schlesinger, James R. [1956]: "After Twenty Years: The General Theory," *Quarterly Journal of Economics*, November.

Schumpeter, Joseph [1954]: *History of Economic Analysis*, Oxford University Press, New York.

Shackle, George L. S. [1967]: *The Years of High Theory: Invention and Tradition in Economic Thought, 1926–1939*, Cambridge University Press, Cambridge.

Shove, Gerald F. [1942]: "The Place of Marshall's 'Principles' in the Development of Economic Theory," *Economic Journal*, December.

Sowell, Thomas [1972]: *Say's Law*, Princeton University Press, Princeton, N. J.

Spengler, Joseph J. [1972]: "Social Science and the Collectivisation of Hubris," *Political Science Quarterly*, March.

Stein, Jerome L. [1976]: *Monetarism,* North-Holland Publishing Co., Amsterdam.

Stewart, Michael [1967]: *Keynes and After,* Penguin, Harmondsworth.

Tobin, James [1956]: "The Interest Elasticity of Transactions Demand for Cash," *Review of Economics and Statistics,* August.

—— [1958]: "Liquidity Preference as Behavior Towards Risk," *Review of Economic Studies,* February.

—— [1968]: "Consumption Function," *International Encyclopedia of the Social Sciences,* Macmillan, New York.

Toulmin, Stephen E. [1972]: *Human Understanding,* Princeton University Press, Princeton, N. J. Vol. 1. [The Collective Use and Evolution of Concepts.]

Veendorp, E. C. H. [1970]: "General Equilibrium Theory for a Barter Economy," *Western Economic Journal,* March.

Walters, Alan A. [1969]: *Money in Boom and Slump,* Hobart Paper 44, Institute of Economic Affairs, London.

Warburton, Clark [1946]: "The Misplaced Emphasis in Contemporary Business-Fluctuation Theory," *The Journal of Business,* October.

Wicksell, Knut [1935]: *Lectures on Political Economy,* 2 vols., Routledge & Kegan Paul, London.

—— [1936]: *Interest and Prices,* Macmillan and Co., London.

Wiener, Norbert [1954]: *The Human Use of Human Beings,* 2nd ed., Doubleday, New York.

Wright, David McCord [1961]: "Comment," *American Economic Review,* May.

Wrong, Dennis H. [1961]: "The Oversocialized Conception of Man in Modern Sociology," *American Sociological Review,* April.

Yeager, Leland B. [1968]: "Essential Properties of the Medium of Exchange," *Kyklos,* No. 1.

Name Index

Subject Index